ACADEMIC ENTREPRENEURSHIP

THE ART AND SCIENCE OF CREATING THE RIGHT ACADEMIC PROGRAMS

MELISSA MORRISS-OLSON

ACADEMIC IMPRESSIONS | 2020
DENVER, CO

Published by Academic Impressions.

CR Mrig Company. 4601 DTC Blvd., Suite 800, Denver, CO 80237.

Copyright © 2019 Melissa Morriss-Olson.

Cover design by Brady Stanton.

All rights reserved.

No part of this book may be reproduced, or stored in a retrieval system, or transmitted in any form or by any means, electronic, mechanical, photocopying, recording, or otherwise, without express written permission of the publisher.

For reproduction, distribution, or copy permissions, or to order additional copies, please contact the Academic Impressions office at 720.488.6800 or visit:

http://bit.ly/2qbHuLr

Academic Impressions

ISBN: 978-1-948658-15-7

Printed in the United States of America.

ANOTHER BOOK YOU MAY ENJOY

Effective communication will make or break a department chair. Get a primer on the essential communication and conflict management skills that every department chair needs.

Explore the book at:
https://www.academicimpressions.com/product/communication-conflict-management-handbook-new-department-chair/

MELISSA MORRISS-OLSON

CONTENTS

FOREWORD	**1**
For New and Seasoned Academic Leaders	3
Navigating This Book	4
SECTION I—BECOMING AN ACADEMIC ENTREPRENEUR	**9**
OVERVIEW	11
CHAPTER 1 DISRUPTION, TRANSFORMATION, AND THE NEW NORMAL	12
Critical Disruptive Forces	15
The Impact of Demographics	17
The Impact of Strained Economics	23
The Impact of Technological Innovation	27
The Impact of Regulatory and Societal Shifts	28
The Impact of Changing Educational Paradigms	32
What's Next	41
CHAPTER 2 THE ENTREPRENEURIAL ACADEMIC LEADER—DO YOU HAVE WHAT IT TAKES?	43
The Entrepreneurial Mindset and Skillset	45
Assessment: Entrepreneurial IQ	59
What's Next	69
CHAPTER 3 FINDING THE ENTREPRENEURIAL SPIRIT WITHIN	71
7 Destructive Myths about Innovation	72
10 Ways to Cultivate Creativity	80
What's Next	95
CHAPTER 4 SETTING THE STAGE FOR INNOVATION ON YOUR CAMPUS	98
10 Common Barriers to Change in Higher Education	99

Identifying Your Key Barriers	107
Building the Capacity for Entrepreneurship and Creativity Across Your Campus	111
Checklist: Assess Your Institution's Organizational Readiness for Innovation	120
Innovative Project Evaluation Guide	125
What's Next	134
Helpful Resources	135

SECTION II—THE ART AND SCIENCE OF LAUNCHING NEW ACADEMIC PROGRAMS — 143

OVERVIEW	145
CHAPTER 5 IS IT TIME TO LAUNCH THAT NEW ACADEMIC PROGRAM?	146
What's Next	167
CHAPTER 6 THE SCIENCE OF BRINGING NEW PROGRAMS TO LIFE— THE FEASIBILITY CHECKLIST	169
Overview of the Process	170
The 10 Elements of the Feasibility Checklist	175
What's Next	220
Appendix A: Template for a New Program Feasibility Study	222
Appendix B	234
Appendix C	236
CHAPTER 7 FINANCIAL MODELING AND BUDGETING FOR NEW PROGRAMS	238
1. Enrollment and Pricing Assumptions	240
2. Revenue Projections and Assumptions	251
3. Expense Assumptions	252
4. Bottom-Line Projections	255
What's Next	268

Appendix A	270
Appendix B	271
Appendix C	272

CHAPTER 8 OPERATIONALIZING AND SUSTAINING NEW ACADEMIC PROGRAMS — 277

1. Think Long-Term with Up-Front Investments	278
2. Leverage Untapped Potential	279
3. Start Small, Invest Conservatively, and Build as You Go	281
4. Maintain a Spirit of Adaptability	282
5. Integrate Kaizen Principles and Practices	285
What's Next	289
Helpful Resources	291

SECTION III—OPERATIONALIZING ACADEMIC PROGRAMS — 297

OVERVIEW — 299

CHAPTER 9 POSITIONING YOUR NEW PROGRAM FOR SUCCESS — 300

1. Defining Marketing and its Value	302
2. Target Market Research Tools and Approaches	306
3. New Program Marketing Plan: Components and Essentials	321
4. High Impact Marketing Practices	340
5. Brand, Branding and Positioning	350
6. Social Media, Digital Marketing, Website, and Mobile Device Optimization	361
7. Best Adult Student Recruitment Practices	365
8. Metrics and Return on Investment	369
9. The Marketing Playbook	378
What's Next	379
Appendix A	383

| Appendix B | 413 |

CHAPTER 10 ACCREDITATION—WHAT DO I REALLY NEED TO KNOW? 435

The Role and Value of Accreditation	436
Types of Accreditors	438
Accrediting Process and Organization	440
Important Accreditor Expectations and Issues	443
Federal Requirements and State Authorization for Academic Programs	448
Best Practices for Accreditation Approvals	452
What's Next	457
Appendix A	459
Appendix B	463

CHAPTER 11 INFRASTRUCTURE AND RESOURCE PLANNING 465

1. Staffing	467
2. Instructional and Student Support Resources	470
3. External Board Support	473
4. Space and Facility Utilization	479
5. Technology and Equipment Requirements	488
6. Parking and Facility Maintenance	493
7. Integration with Key Institutional Planning Processes	494
What's Next	497
Appendix A	500
Appendix B	502
Appendix C	504
Appendix D	506
Appendix E	508
Helpful Resources	513

CASE STUDY	**519**
CASE STUDY ACADEMIC PROGRAM INVENTION AS A DRIVER FOR INSTITUTIONAL TRANSFORMATION: BAY PATH UNIVERSITY	521
Institutional Overview	521
Lessons Learned	542
FINAL THOUGHTS AND NEXT STEPS	**553**
ACKNOWLEDGMENTS	559
ABOUT THE AUTHOR	561
ENDNOTES	565

MELISSA MORRISS-OLSON

FOREWORD

The challenges facing higher education in recent times are well documented. The management responses that have served institutions and their leaders well for the past many years are no longer sufficient in this current highly fluid environment. Frankly, I doubt that the traditional higher education management strategies and responses to challenges have ever been optimal for creating long-term institutional resiliency. This was the focus of my doctoral dissertation in the mid-1990s. I studied the management practices and financial conditions of more than 100 small colleges and found that those colleges best equipped to survive and thrive in turbulent times exhibited something that I termed an "entrepreneurial mindset." At the end of the day, this mindset was more important in accounting for an institution's viability (or lack thereof) than any particular management skill set.

What is an entrepreneurial mindset? In my study, successful institutions developed and sustained an outward-looking orientation while also cultivating a discipline around driving entrepreneurial growth in strategic ways that leveraged and strengthened their mission.

Never before has it been so critical for colleges and universities, and their leaders, to adopt an entrepreneurial mindset. Especially for resource-constrained institutions (which is most of us), traditional financial management approaches (such as, resource prioritization, cutting one's way to sustainability, and/or trying to recruit one's way out of enrollment difficulties) are no longer sufficient long-term solutions. In this current context, successful institutions have a keen understanding about the forces that are most likely to disrupt or impact their institution.

They are highly strategic and savvy about leveraging their resources—particularly their academic program portfolio—in agile and responsive ways. This is what having an entrepreneurial mindset is all about—nurturing such a mindset at the institutional level requires art and science.

From my experience, both the art and the science are critical for ensuring financially sound, entrepreneurial growth in the current higher education context. Having a rigorous discipline that considers both elements allows you to avoid the twin dangers of either getting caught in "analysis paralysis" or making avoidable errors by flying by the seat of your pants. Such a discipline helps you move from "dream it → build it" to calculating what it will take to be successful. At the end of the day, these do not need to be mutually exclusive pursuits. I believe that true entrepreneurial thinking when applied in an academic context can help institutions fully tap their mission-centric innate potential. When art and science are applied in tandem, an entrepreneurial mindset can contribute to a deepened commitment to the educational mission of the institution.

I have spent my nearly 40-year career in higher education working in mission-centric, resource-constrained contexts, a wonderful environment for developing the ability to think and act creatively to meet the challenges that are always present. Indeed, I credit this experience for my personal formation as an academic entrepreneur. Throughout my career in higher education, I have been focused on looking outward and asking key questions, such as: "How can we do this differently," "What do we do really well that might be leveraged in new and unique ways," and "What market opportunities exist that we are uniquely equipped to meet?"

Across the span of my career, I have had the opportunity to lead the development of many new academic programs and initiatives and I have learned a great deal about what works. I have also experienced first-hand the difficulty of instituting change in an academic environment. There are many barriers to change at play at any given time in any college or university and the launch of a new academic program can sometimes serve as a lightning rod for surfacing resistance that might otherwise lay dormant.

Through teaching and mentoring other professionals in the "art and science" of new academic program development, I know that virtually anyone can become an academic entrepreneur. While someone may be innately creative or innovative, the attributes that comprise an entrepreneurial mindset can be taught and developed. That is what this book is all about.

For New and Seasoned Academic Leaders

This is the book I wish I'd had when I started out in higher education many years ago. Most academic leaders come to their roles without experience in entrepreneurial leadership or thinking or in how to strategically manage and leverage the institution's academic resources. This was certainly my experience. For those who are new to academic leadership, whether it be in a department or division chair, dean, or provost role, this book will provide you with a roadmap for setting the stage for innovation on your campus and developing and executing a strategic approach to managing your academic program portfolio.

This book will also be a valuable resource for seasoned academic leaders who want to become stronger entrepreneurial thinkers and hone their skills in identifying, evaluating, and operationalizing new academic program ideas. This book includes many examples from other institutions and templates that can be easily adapted to meet the needs of your particular campus.

Doing well in this current environment requires that academic leaders think and act differently than their predecessors did even a few years ago. In many ways, today's academic leader needs to think like an investment portfolio manager. Individual academic programs do not exist in isolation within the institution. Instead, each program resides in a complex web of inputs and outcomes, and every resource decision you make about an individual program has a bearing on the broader institution, its infrastructure, and its resource capacity. In considering new programs to add to the mix, provosts and deans need to evaluate how the entire academic portfolio will be impacted by this addition and what this might mean for the broader institution in turn. Indeed, the overall reputation, quality, and financial viability of the institution are determined in large part according to the particular mix of programs that you offer. Wise and savvy academic leaders are highly intentional in shaping and managing this mix to achieve the desired balance. This begins with having a clear-eyed understanding about each program's individual net financial contribution as well as the specific ways that each program promotes or detracts from the institution's reputation and brand.

Navigating This Book

This book is designed as a guide through the process of identifying and operationalizing new academic program ideas. It's organized in three sections, each of which focuses on an important aspect of academic entrepreneurship.

Section I is all about the art side of academic entrepreneurship starting with those important trends and key disruptive forces that are shaping the current wave of higher education transformation. Understanding the forces that are at work in your own particular campus context is a helpful starting point for identifying new initiatives including new program possibilities. Given the challenges facing higher education, entrepreneurial leadership skills are essential, yet most academic leaders come to their roles lacking the experience which can hone such skills. Chapters 2-4 provide tips and techniques that any academic leader can adopt to create a sense of urgency on his or her own campus as well to develop one's own personal entrepreneurial leadership IQ.

There is an abundance of resources that any academic leader can utilize to develop one's entrepreneurial mindset. Plus, there is a growing body of resources available to help provosts and deans nurture innovative thinking on an institutional level. What is critical is this: Academic leaders who are serious about driving entrepreneurial growth on their campuses need to adopt a management approach that balances the art with a rigorous and well supported process for identifying, evaluating, and operationalizing program ideas. This is the science part of academic entrepreneurship. An entrepreneurial mindset requires that academic leaders maintain a yin and yang kind of orientation to their work making sure to balance both the art and science in planning and decision making.

In **Section II** we turn our attention to the science side of academic entrepreneurship beginning with Chapter 5 where we consider strategies for fostering new program ideas on demand. While I believe that good ideas can come from virtually anywhere—anytime, I have learned that there are specific things that you can do to generate fresh thinking and specific ideas. It is also important to have a process for testing the viability of new program ideas before committing resources to a formal program development process. I typically have anywhere from five to seven new program ideas on my short list at any point in time and use the new program testing strategies reviewed in Chapter 5 as a filter for deciding which idea to move forward.

In Chapters 6-8 we will take a deeper dive into the science by providing a step-by-step process for bringing new academic programs to life. This is where things sometimes break down in academic organizations—as the best ideas in the world can easily get swallowed up when the pressure to retain the status quo is fierce. Having a well-articulated and transparent process that is followed consistently will go a long way towards building trust with faculty and heading off potential resistance to change. In Chapter 6, we review the important elements that should be considered as part of your feasibility study to support a new program. At my institution, these elements comprise the feasibility checklist, which all new programs must address as part of the review process. In Chapter 7, we review one additional and very important feasibility study component: the proforma. Most new programs succeed or fail based on their capacity to attract sufficient numbers of students and to generate sufficient financial resources. Section II concludes by considering those things that are important to your new program's long-term success and viability. Understanding that it's impossible to capture all variables on the front end, the potential viability of a program is difficult to fully assess until that program is up and running. While having a discipline around new program development ensures that you will anticipate most of the important potential impact issues, maintaining a culture of flexibility and responsiveness once the program is launched is equally critical for the program's success. Chapter 8 provides guidance for academic leaders in how to do just this.

In **Section III**, we will return to an important principle that runs as a theme throughout this book, namely, that academic program development is a process that exists within an ecosystem. This ecosystem is comprised of all of the elements, people, and resources that make up your institution not to mention the broader community and world in which your institution resides. Nowhere is it more critical to consider your program's impact and the impact it will have than in the area of new program infrastructure and resource planning. No matter how small your program is or how it's structured or delivered, it will make demands on your institution's infrastructure. To whatever extent you can understand and make these demands transparent and take steps to ensure that your program's needs can be met and are integrated into your broader institutional planning and resource decision-making processes, your program's potential for success will be enhanced.

Consequently, we will delve more deeply in Chapters 9-11 into three areas that can impact your new program's viability—short-term and over time--if not considered early in the program development process. These include program marketing and promotion, the regulatory context, and infrastructure and resource planning. With each of these areas we will review important issues that can hinder your success as well as best practices.

The traditional assumptions that framed resource planning even five years ago are no longer valid in this context, where resources are constrained and the notion of what constitutes "campus space and place" in the 21st century is evolving. While it's a challenge to plan for new programs in this context, to be sure, those institutions that harness and leverage the inherent opportunities found in this context will be at great advantage to create unique, responsive, and sustainable programs to meet the needs of the generations to come.

Each chapter concludes with key strategic questions for academic leaders to consider in applying the concepts and strategies reviewed. These questions are intended to help you think broadly and deeply about both the art and science of new academic program development while attending to the unique issues that are particular to your specific campus context and culture. Each section concludes with suggestions for additional resources pertaining to the topics covered. While not conclusive, these suggestions include resources that I have utilized personally and found helpful.

The book concludes with a case study that illustrates many of the principles and strategies reviewed herein. Over the course of the past twenty years, Bay Path University has undergone a significant transformation. Central to this transformation is the execution of a highly intentional, strategic, and well executed academic portfolio management plan that has leveraged the institution's mission in powerful and effective ways. In the concluding section, this case study will be used to summarize and highlight important learnings.

SECTION I—BECOMING AN ACADEMIC ENTREPRENEUR

OVERVIEW

Successful entrepreneurial academic leaders possess a key understanding about the environmental context in which their institution resides. Rather than feeling overwhelmed by the challenges at hand, the campus context often provides inspiration for these leaders. Section I provides guidance for academic leaders of all types and experience levels in how to leverage their unique context to identify and exploit new possibilities This is what having an entrepreneurial mindset is all about.

Given the challenges facing higher education, entrepreneurial leadership skills are essential, yet most academic leaders do not have the experiences or backgrounds through which this mindset and these skills are developed. In this section, I will provide tips and techniques that any academic leader can adopt to create a sense of urgency on his or her own campus, as well to assess and enhance one's own personal entrepreneurial leadership capabilities.

CHAPTER 1
DISRUPTION, TRANSFORMATION, AND THE NEW NORMAL

Higher education is experiencing significant disruption. Nearly every part of the system is undergoing upheaval. From increased competition and financial strain to heightened public skepticism about the value of a college degree, virtually no institution is untouched by the forces sweeping the American higher education landscape. Many prominent higher education observers have issued rather gloomy projections about the fate of the higher education industry.[1]

Often forgotten in these pessimistic observations about the state of America's colleges and universities is the fact that disruption and change are not new to higher education. A look back at the American higher education system since the founding of the first colonial college in 1636 finds several waves of disruption and transformation. Perhaps the most significant period of transformation dates between the Civil War and the early 20th Century. During this forty-year stretch, modern-day conventions of the higher education system were invented. The faculty role became professionalized as the concepts of tenure, academic freedom, and shared governance gained prominence. Also, we have the industrial revolution to thank for the invention and popularization of such characteristics as departments, majors, electives, letter grades, and the credit hour.

While the current wave of disruption is happening on many levels and at a lightning-speed pace, I prefer to view this current period as continuity of a system that has demonstrated remarkable resiliency and adaptation over the past nearly 400 years. In fact, adaptation and transformation are defining features of our American higher education system and might best be viewed as necessary triggers for keeping our system healthy and responsive to the broader and most critical emerging needs of our society. Throughout history, individual institutions and academic leaders who are adept at accurately reading the tea leaves and responding adaptively have proven able to withstand the forces and shift in response to the new reality.

However, what does this take? Disciplined foresight, agile responsiveness, and optimistic resiliency are essential leadership attributes for academic leaders in this new ear of uncertainty. Disciplined foresight means developing the practice of being outward looking along with a keen understanding of the forces that are most likely to disrupt or impact your institution. All paths of responsiveness are not equal; nor are all paths appropriate for each and every college or university. As illustrated in the *Many Paths Forward* vignettes that you will find distributed throughout this chapter, one institution's pathway may involve altering its mission (e.g., expanding to online education) while another may involve leveraging a missional strength through new and innovative programming. What is critical here is that leaders must take the time to understand the market context in which their institutions reside, including the forces that may be particularly relevant for their future.

There are often times unique, hidden opportunities that can be found in even the most threatening disruptive force if leaders look deeply to consider their institution's unique position and context.

MANY PATHS FORWARD

High Point University

When Dr. Nido R. Qubein became the seventh president of High Point University in 2005, the institution enrolled fewer than 1,500 undergraduate students at its landlocked North Carolina campus; students came mostly from the region. Flash forward to 2018: the traditional undergraduate enrollment grew to more than 5,200 students (the majority of whom were residential undergraduates), academic schools were established to highlight institutional strength in the fields of communication, health sciences, art and design, and pharmacy, and new programs in entrepreneurship, interactive gaming, and commerce were added along with new initiatives in physician assistant, pharmacy, and physical therapy. At present, students come from more than 50 states and more than 37 countries with 80% percent of students coming from out of state. During this transformative era, the school moved to a doctoral degree-granting institution and added masters and doctoral programs; they also invested heavily in state-of-the-art technology and resourced academic programs with personnel, facilities, equipment, and budgets. High Point reached the rank of #1 Most Innovative Regional College in the South for making the most innovative improvements in terms of curriculum, faculty, students, campus life, technology or facilities.

When I completed my doctoral dissertation research in the early to mid-1990s, the American higher education system was coming out of a similarly challenged era marked by college closures, mergers, and dire warnings about the decline of the system. Reagan administration cutbacks in higher education aid programs placed particular pressure on families as a result of steep declines in federal financial aid. Colleges and universities were stretched to make up the difference and some smaller colleges failed in the process. While the economic forces were painfully disruptive for a portion of higher education during this time, the current era is marked by the convergence of several disruptive forces unfolding at the same time. Given a college's mission, location, program mix, and resource base among other things, some of these forces will be more threatening than others. Likewise, some forces may present unique transformational opportunities assuming the institution has the courage and agility to respond.

Critical Disruptive Forces

One need not look very far to see the impact of disruption on what many considered to be a secure and recession-proof industry. Like higher education, print media is a 400-year-old institution. From modest beginnings, the newspaper industry experienced 200+ years of extraordinary growth, and expansion and from an industry perspective, enjoyed a stable environment. Then along came radio, and print media made some modifications which allowed it to survive. Then came the Internet. To appreciate the speed and power of technological change, consider the astonishing decline in print advertising revenue after the introduction of the Internet.

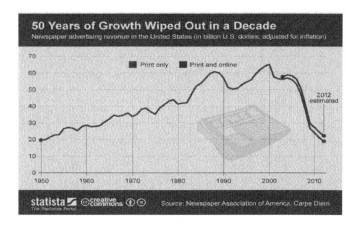

Some have argued that the conditions facing higher education today are very similar to those experienced by the print media industry just a decade ago. Clearly, digital disruption is one of the key game changing forces sweeping across nearly every industry including higher education. As the newspaper industry has transformed itself digitally in response to this new reality, every industry, including higher education, will need to consider the opportunities that are available through digital and emerging technology. While the transformation has not been easy, newspapers are now using data and digital means to better understand and serve customer needs, to deliver value in new ways utilizing technological breakthroughs, and to create consistent and relevant customer experiences. These are all things that are essential for colleges and universities to consider as well in order to remain relevant. When asked for his advice for newspaper business leaders, Flint McGlaughlin, Managing Director and CEO of MECLABS Institute, offered this: "Is news going away? News is proliferating. But, brand will still matter, and quality will still matter. And people will always pay for the things they believe are worth it."[2] This advice is certainly apropos for today's academic leader as well.

The Impact of Demographics

In recent years, demographics have shifted in several subtle and not-so-subtle ways that are having a profound impact across nearly all of higher education—especially for some regions of the country such as the northeast and Midwest where the declining birth rate and shrinking traditional college-going aged populations are outpacing the national average.

Three megatrends are worth noting here:

1. Total enrollment in the American higher education system is in a multi-year decline;

2. Critical demographic shifts are causing particular pain for certain segments of American higher education;

3. Online learning continues to increase at a rapid pace.

As shown in the chart below, enrollment has declined significantly only three times in the modern era. The most recent period of decline began in 2010 and is projected to be a long and protracted period extending well into the next decade and beyond.

Source: U.S. Department of Education. Institute of Education Sciences, NCES. 2017 Digest of Educational Statistics.

In numerical headcount terms, total enrollment in degree-granting institutions has declined by more than one million students in six years:

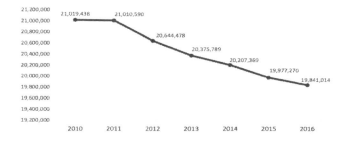

Source: Digest of Education Statistics

Most recently, the two-year and for-profit sectors have been especially hard hit; the two-year sector has lost 1.37 million students and the for-profit sector has lost nearly 850,000 students. The private nonprofit sector has remained relatively flat overall while the public four-year sector has experienced modest growth during this same timeframe.

The impact of this enrollment decline is obvious when considering the average growth rate of the higher education system over the past half century. Following a robust period of growth during the 1960s to the early 1980s, things have slowed to a snail's pace more recently. The growth rate is projected to remain virtually flat well into the next decade.

As academic leaders consider future options for their institutions, several implications of this slower growth pace should be kept in mind. Most importantly, colleges that have relied on traditional means of enrollment growth to

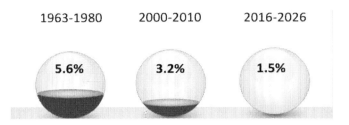

Source: U.S. Department of Education. Institute of Education Sciences, NCES. 2017 Digest of Educational Statistics

fund expansion will have to adapt to a slower pace and think creatively about the student markets their institutions are best equipped to serve. The traditional 18 to 22-year-old market will continue to shrink and the competition for these students will become increasingly fierce. Some, if not many, institutions that predominantly rely on this market for their sustainability will need to expand their horizons or face extinction. Leaders would be wise to level-set their growth expectations in light of their own unique market data and devote resources to tracking and managing market share with an eye towards new markets. Understanding the segments that make-up student enrollments across all markets will be a critical priority for the future.

These critical demographic shifts have implications in three other important ways: regional enrollment variations, ability-to-pay, and student academic preparation issues.

As shown below, the projections for the size of the traditional college-going-aged population (total U.S. public and private high school graduates) are dynamic.

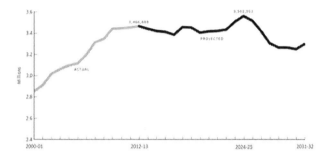

Source: Knocking at the College Door. Western Interstate Commission for Higher Education, 2016.

According to the demographers who prepare the annual Knocking at the College Door report by the Western Interstate Commission for Higher Education,[3] the drop in the number of public and non-public high school graduates over the next several years will be most profound in the middle and northeastern regions of the country. This shift will be compounded by a concurrent shift in ethnicity as the traditional going-to-college-aged population becomes increasingly more diverse. For those institutions that have historically drawn their enrollments from less diverse markets and have not yet readied their institutions for a more diverse student body, the impact will be significant.

Many colleges and universities will also need to consider how to meet the needs of students who will be increasingly underprepared for the academic demands of the college classroom. According to a recent report issued by ACT, *The Condition of College and Career Readiness*, on average, students of color are entering college today with significant gaps in academic preparation and readiness, especially in contrast to their White, Non-Hispanic classmates. The findings suggest that African American and Hispanic students are entering college today with significantly less academic preparation on average in English, Reading, Math, and Science than their White classmates.

A third critical impact resulting from these demographic shifts is the student's ability-to-pay for a college education. As reported by The College Board in its *Trends in College Pricing* report, Hispanic and African American families have median incomes that are approximately 61% of White families. Compared to Asian, non-Hispanic and White Non-Hispanic families who report average family incomes of $93,500 and $82,070 respectively, the average Hispanic family income is $51,110 and the average Black family income is $49,370.

With a shrinking pool of available 18 to 22-year-old students that is demographically stunningly different than the pool of students historically recruited, most institutions will not be able to maintain the status quo. Many will need to radically reimagine who they serve through a combination of **_new_** market penetration, market development, and program development strategies just to keep pace—not to mention stimulating demand in this low/slow growth and rapidly shifting context.

A third megatrend that needs to be on the radar of every academic leader is the growth in online learning. According to the most recent report issued by the Babson Survey Research Group (2018), online student enrollments at both the undergraduate and graduate levels have increased every single year since 2002. "The growth of distance enrollments has been relentless," said study co-author Julia E. Seaman, research director of the Babson Survey Research Group. "They have gone up when the economy was expanding, when the economy was shrinking, when overall enrollments were growing, and now when overall enrollments are shrinking." At the same time, the number of students studying on a campus has dropped by over one million (1,173,805, or 6.4%) between 2012 and 2016. More than 30% of all enrolled students report taking at least one distance education course with enrollments remaining local: 52.8% of all students who took at least one distance course also took a course on-campus, and 56.1% of those who took only distance courses reside in the same state as the institution at which they are enrolled.

> ## MANY PAThs FORWARD
>
> **Saint Leo University**
>
> When Dr. Arthur Kirk assumed the presidency of Saint Leo University in 1997, he inherited a tenuously balanced budget, significant deferred maintenance, including: leaking roofs across the campus, depressed salaries, and no funding with which to innovate. Even still, he led a bold reallocation process, abandoning some programs and activities, and cutting others to free up $600,000 to develop online infrastructure, content, and services to launch online programs. Kirk's boldness and foresight set the stage for the eventual transformation of the institution—from a small campus of 780 students, 91% of whom were enrolled on military bases, to a thriving campus of nearly 20,000 students, 2,300 of whom study on the main campus and the remainder taking classes at over 40 locations in several states and online. Under Kirk's leadership, Saint Leo University built one of the largest and most respected online education programs among private, nonprofit colleges in the nation and became one of the largest catholic universities in the country.

A related key shift that is important to consider is the fact that distance education enrollments are increasingly concentrated among a very small number of institutions. The Babson report suggests that approximately 5% of all higher education institutions enroll nearly 50% of all distance education students. The term mega university has been coined to describe these fast-growing institutions; institutions like Southern New Hampshire University (SNHU), a private institution that has grown from 8,600 degree-seeking students in 2008 to more than 122,000 in 2018 with a goal of tripling its enrollment by 2023 and Western Governors University, a nonprofit entirely online institution that currently enrolls 100,000 students with plans to serve more than one million learners in the not-so-distant future.[4]

The Impact of Strained Economics

Increasingly, higher education observers, politicians, economists, the general public, and even those within higher education are suggesting that the higher education business model is broken. For example, in a recent *Inside Higher Education* survey, 13% of presidents reported that they could see their own institutions closing or merging within the next five years. [5] A basis for these concerns can be found in the online tracking report for college and university closings and consolidations maintained by EducationDive. According to this source, between 2016 and 2018, more than 100 for-profit colleges and 20 nonprofit colleges have ceased operations, merged, or been acquired by other entities.[6] Even the larger university systems are experiencing strain as evidenced by recent high-profile consolidations, such as the set of mergers underway within the University of Wisconsin System, which will consolidate 13 two-year colleges into seven four-year colleges and the ongoing consolidation of the many campuses which make up the University of Georgia system. It is telling that the higher education industry was downgraded by Moody's from stable to negative in December 2017. Standard and Poor's followed suit in January 2018 with a negative outlook due to increased credit pressures.

The shifting enrollment demographics discussed earlier are certainly a critical contributing factor to the strained financial condition of higher education. However, this is not the whole story. The increasingly tuition-dependent financial model is not stainable—except perhaps for the top 100 institutions that can rely on multi-billion-dollar endowments. Independent institutions have historically balanced their budgets through annual tuition sticker price hikes and increased enrollments, two strategies that are difficult to make work in this new era. Evidence abounds that families can no longer keep pace with the cost of tuition and institutions need to dig ever deeper to fund the gap between sticker price, student financial resources, and family willingness to pay. The chart below shows how since 1978 college tuition has increased faster than virtually any other component of the U.S. Consumer Price Index.[7]

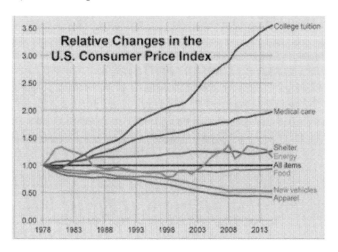

Increasingly, colleges and universities are stepping up to close the funding gap for students resulting in increased tuition discounting and decreased net student tuition revenue. According to a 2018 report by Moody's Investors Service, nearly a fifth of all private colleges report a first-year student tuition discount rate of 60%. [8] The annual NACUBO Tuition Discounting Study confirms the growing practice by many schools, a practice that if left unchecked could potentially risk the financial health of an institution.

Average Tuition Discount Rate for Private Institutions

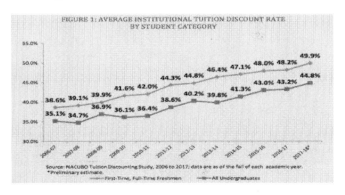

Tuition revenues rarely cover the full cost of delivering the education experience on most campuses, and endowment is an increasingly important part of the funding mix. Yet, the median endowment among all ranked institutions at the end of fiscal year 2017 was a modest $57.5 million with a handful of schools reporting endowments of less than $1 million.[9] Hundreds of institutions on this same list reported endowments of less than $100 million.

Institutions are also dealing with aging facilities that are in need of modernization to keep pace with the demands of

Many Paths Forward

Plymouth State University

Plymouth State University needed to change. A 16% drop in undergraduate enrollment over three years spooked administrators at the tuition-dependent regional public university. They also wanted to better prepare students for an increasingly interdisciplinary world, whether they went on to industry or to graduate school, according to Donald L. Birx, who became president in 2015. When Birx was still new to his role, he set his sights on overhauling the general-education curriculum, which was a distribution model in which students picked courses from a menu of options. In the years that followed, the New Hampshire college, surrounded by mountains and lakes, settled on a vision: Undergraduates would move purposefully from one of a revamped set of first-year seminars to interdisciplinary general-education courses and would connect their experiences with a senior capstone project.

While not everyone is on board with all of the changes, Plymouth State has started to unveil parts of its new curriculum. The college's experience, like that of other institutions, illustrates how fraught big general-education changes can be. "You have to work with faculty and convince them about the need for major change," Birx says. "At the same time, we also are overhauling the administrative side. It's got to be done together synchronously, because it's a system change." Universities change their core curricula for many reasons. At Plymouth State, the new president wanted to increase retention and enrollment by creating excitement around a new model.

today's student—not to mention a high fixed cost structure. Additionally, with anticipated budget cuts to both financial aid and grant funding, there will be continued pressure for institutions to make up the difference through alternative revenue sources and cost containment measures. For public institutions, the combination of declining state funding and mandated limits on tuition increases creates a structural deficit of a different kind. Public institutions have become increasingly privatized but often lack the flexibility to pursue options for alternative revenue funding that are more easily available to private institutions.

A recent report from Ernst & Young affiliate the Parthenon Group found 800 colleges vulnerable to "critical strategic challenges" due to their small size, compared to a much smaller share of colleges with enrollments over 1,000. The report lists several risk-factors for small colleges in particular, including: enrolling fewer than 1,000 students, the absence of online education programs, tuition increases greater than 8% and discounts higher than 35%, and depending on tuition for more than 85% of revenue.[10]

The Impact of Technological Innovation

With the introduction of the Internet, we began a slow creep toward the convergence between our physical and digital worlds. Today's traditional-aged college-going population was weaned on technology and they think and process information fundamentally different than their predecessors. In his groundbreaking article, "Digital Immigrants and Natives," Marc Prensky outlined the implications of this trend for how we teach this new generation.[11] He differentiates between digital immigrants (those born prior to 1974) and digital natives (those born after 1974) and suggests that by the time the average digital native graduates from high school they will have spent considerably more time engaged in digital activities than reading.

This translates into digital natives having very different expectations for their learning experience than the digital immigrants who are still primarily delivering the experience. This results in challenges as well as opportunities for educators who are willing to embrace these differences and adapt their approach to meet digital natives where they are. A few years ago, we instituted an iPad initiative on my campus. When I heard one of our professors talk about how he had started using the iPad to teach cell biology, the potential for students became obvious. This educator described an experience unconstrained by the physical classroom; instead, his classroom experience was boundaryless. He was connected to his students and his students to one another 24/7 regardless of where they were located physically. Essentially, what he described was an educational experience that places students in control of their learning with access to a rich array of resources accessible at their fingertips.

The Impact of Regulatory and Societal Shifts

With each new U.S. presidential agenda comes a host of political and regulatory changes that have the potential to impact higher education. In the current era, the deregulatory agenda coupled with selective increased restrictions is reaching every corner of the federal government, including policies and procedures that relate to higher education. For example, a recent slowdown in international student enrollment in American colleges and universities has led some educators to surmise that international students are being deterred by more restrictive policies on visas coupled with the Trump administration's rhetoric on immigration. It's important for leaders to be aware of these shifts and their potential impact on an individual institutional level.

At the same time, some changes are having an apparently lasting impact, such as the multi-year agenda to make college cost and value more transparent to the general public. Through the establishment of the College Scorecard, now freely available on the U.S. Department of Education website,[12] anyone can go online and immediately assess and compare an institution's cost and value. This is a wonderful benefit for the higher education consumer who can easily compare and contrast many institutions at the same time on such features as average annual cost, graduation rates, salary earnings post-graduation, financial aid, and typical student debt after graduation. This increased focus on transparency means that colleges need to be especially diligent about their public institutional data and the stories that the data tell to the external world. Institutions that are focused on providing the best value to their students and are smart about how they use and mine data as evidence for return on investment will be in a strong position in this new era of accountability.

Societal change is a second important concept for academic leaders to be aware of and is something most of us take for granted. Change is ongoing, always happening, and not something we typically take the time to understand, especially when we are in the midst of it. Yet, the profound social changes that are happening within our country and world right now are having a significant impact on how we relate to each other, how we work together, our workforce structures and needs, and opportunities for the future. Institutions that become adept at understanding and forecasting these social changes with a particular focus on what these changes might mean for workforce needs and demands will find many educational opportunities to exploit. A wonderful example of this can be found in the approach that Southern New Hampshire University recently took in developing its 2018-2023 strategic plan. As described on its website: "We pulled together our best thinking about the current context in which our students live and study (p. 13) and engaged The Institute For The Future to help us think through how the world would be different for our students in 2030 (p. 29, the SNHU 2030 section).[13] A review of SNHU's plan finds many new strategies that directly respond to this imagined reality and position the institution well for this future state.

As a case in point, a recent Pew Research Center survey[14] found that 87% of workers believe it will be essential for them to get training and develop new job skills throughout their work life in order to keep up with changes in the workplace. This survey noted that employment is much higher among jobs that require an average or above-average level of preparation (including education, experience and job training); average or above-average interpersonal, management, and communication skills; and higher levels of analytical skills, such as critical thinking and computer skills. As the U.S. economy moves deeper into the knowledge age, the need for lifelong learning and ongoing career skill upgrading will provide opportunities for institutions to present themselves and their program offerings in more relevant ways. The good news here is that the total amount of education needed for workforce relearning is significant and growing. The student of today and tomorrow will need more education—not less. Colleges and universities that are able to shift their educational mission from one that is entirely front loaded to one that meets the needs of learners of all ages and stages will find themselves at an advantage going forward.

As noted earlier, the shifting social and political climate has impacted the number of international students enrolled in U.S. colleges and universities. Since the 1950s, the U.S. has seen a surge in the number of international students, hitting a record high of 1.1 million in 2016/2017. As a percentage of all U.S. higher education enrollment, the percentage of international students has seen routine increases over the past several years with the biggest share coming from China, India, and South Korea. Even with the recent slowdown in international student enrollments, the potential market remains significant.

Increasing enrollment of international students is just one opportunity available to colleges and universities in this new global era. Technology has provided the means for all institutions to redefine their market positions and find a distinctive niche by weaving internationalization into curriculum in new and innovative ways. Even for a small liberal arts college in rural Iowa, with the Internet and the right program mix, their market context could be the world.

> **MANY PATHS FORWARD**
>
> **Indiana University**
>
> When Michael A. McRobbie became president of Indiana University in 2007, things were tough. The state's tax revenue was in a freefall resulting in a steep budget cut for the University—about six percent of its top line. McRobbie and the trustees pursued several of the typical austerity tactics including a salary freeze, cutbacks on travel, and limiting non-essential hiring. McRobbie also went much further, viewing the economic downturn as an opportunity for renovating and upgrading the campus at a relatively cheap price point. Instead of pushing the pause button and hunkering down to weather the retrenchment, McRobbie moved aggressively to add new buildings and programs, to borrow for construction at a cheaper rate, and to scale up fundraising efforts to pay for new construction. In overhauling and adding new programs, McRobbie repurposing and reorganizing under-enrolled majors to make them more market appealing and also highlighted signature areas such as informatics and global studies. Other new programs, such as engineering and architecture, were added to fill important regional market niches while taking advantage of the university's strengths.

The Impact of Changing Educational Paradigms

Perhaps the most seismic shift in recent times is the recognition that learning content and delivery is becoming ever more widely available and increasingly inexpensive.

We are already beginning to see a shift in the delivery of the learning experience from classroom-based to learning anywhere, from instructor-centric to learner-centric, from teacher as instructor to teacher as a facilitator of the learning experience, from mainly oral instruction to technology supported instruction, from fixed seat and place time to any time as learning time, from "you learn what we offer" to "we offer what you want to learn," and from education as a one-time activity to education as lifelong activity. In addition, the economic issues discussed earlier have resulted in a growing number of free tuition pilot programs at both two-year and four-year institutions and innovative educational models which are intended to bring down the cost of a college education, such as the Paul Quinn College model that combines academic focus, financial aid, and work to keep cost and debt to a minimum. More colleges and universities are also experimenting with open educational resources as a way to bring down the ancillary cost of a college education by replacing expensive textbooks with free or mostly free course resources.

While many institutions still rely predominately on face-to-face delivery mode, the range of delivery options now available to colleges and their students includes hybrid and online, to name just two, with many variations on each. Add to this mix the increased, less costly options available for credentialing (including badges, micro-credentials, nanodegrees, and other alternative models) and the options can seem limitless. Consider, for example, Georgia Institute of Technology's one-of-a-kind "MOOC-inspired" online Master of Science in Computer Science, built and launched in 2014 in partnership with for-profit providers Udacity and AT&T. Costing only a fraction of the cost of traditional, residential graduate programs, this collaboration brought together leaders in education, MOOCs, and industry to apply the disruptive power of technology to widen the pipeline of high-quality, educated talent needed in computer science fields. In just two years, the program has received nearly 8,000 applications and enrolled nearly 4,000 students, all working their way toward the same Georgia Tech M.S. in Computer Science as their on-campus counterparts.

Or what about the much talked about "Blockchain Revolution" which some suggest will be the most important technological innovation yet to transform higher education? Described as the second generation of the Internet, the blockchain provides a rich, secure, and transparent platform for creating a higher learning global network. According to tech experts Don Tapscott and Alex Tapscott, the blockchain will provide an unparalleled and boundaryless opportunity to transform the educational experience. They envision a network and ecosystem that brings together the world's best learning materials online and a worldwide network of instructors and educational facilitators with students who will be able to customize their learning paths from anywhere around the globe.[15]

Given that the preponderance of learners now entering the higher education system are digital natives, colleges and universities must clearly understand the potential and limitations of their current educational delivery mix. Understanding one's core competency or niche in the learning delivery space is perhaps the most essential strategic question today for most colleges and universities. It's important to be aware of the range of available options when considering new programs. While a bit dated, the Delta Initiative [16] worksheet shown here is a useful tool for academic leaders to use in assessing their current delivery models and mix.

You can carve out a niche and attract a new market (just in terms of delivery) if you understand what and how similar

Academic Entrepreneurship

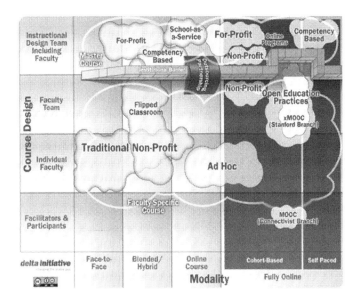

programs are being offered. For example, when Bay Path University launched its MFA for Creative Nonfiction, the feasibility study research found that nearly all similar programs required a residency experience which added considerable student cost. Armed with this market data, Bay Path launched one of the first fully online MFA programs with this particular program niche.

When innovating and developing new programs, it's not always necessary to do something entirely new or from scratch. Sometimes, you can capture a new market for a program just by changing the modality by which a program is delivered or by restructuring the course design. Georgia Tech had a long-standing graduate program in computer science when it launched its innovative new program using a different modality.

I want to end this chapter by summarizing the key issues which frame the current higher education landscape.

> ### Many Paths Forward
>
> **Trinity Washington University**
>
> President of Trinity Washington University since the late 1980s, Pat McGuire is widely credited as the woman who saved the dying Catholic women's college. One of the longest serving presidents in the nation, McGuire has doubled enrollment, expanded academic programs, completed successful capital campaigns, and led the transformation from college to university. While courageously and deliberately embracing a shift away from a traditional role of educating wealthy white women—a market it was losing—and toward a mission of educating low-income Washington women, including many Black, Latino, and immigrant students, McGuire ensured that the school remain faithful to its rich tradition. Founded by the Sisters of Notre Dame de Namur, TWU's mission remains focused on supporting the success of women through professional programs that are grounded in the liberal arts and that reflect the Catholic intellectual, moral, and social justice tradition. From revising the curriculum to expanding services and programs that support academic achievement and establishing signature initiatives—such as the $21 million Trinity Center for Women and Girls in Sports—McGuire bucked the traditional norms of higher education by carving out a mission centric niche and aligning the institution's resources to fully leverage and support this niche.

There are five that I believe are most essential for understanding the context and which provide both challenge and opportunity as you think about new programs and other possibilities for the future. The first has to do with *accessibility*. Several key questions are important for academic leaders to address: In the future, who will have access to my institution, and what kind of experience will they have? Who does my institution currently serve, and how might that need to change going forward? Will my institution be a place of destiny for the privileged or a place of opportunity for the growing majority who are not as privileged? Such questions require that we understand who we are enrolling in terms of demographics, family economics, and market position. This also means that we need to have a keen and accurate understanding about the student market we are best equipped to serve. For many institutions, the market opportunities for the future may look very different than what the institution has historically relied upon. There may even be new program opportunities that exist within these new markets. A few years ago, Bay Path expanded its long-standing Saturday One-Day campus-based program by adding a fully online degree completion option at a lower tuition price for adult women through The American Women's College (TAWC), a change that allowed us to provide a less costly educational access to women who do not have a college degree. Likewise, Pat McGuire's paradigm shift at Trinity Washington University embraces a mission of providing access for the underserved in TWU's backyard. Given the shifting demographics discussed earlier, most of us will need to adapt to both the changing size and characteristics of the new market. Considering the issue of access is a good place to start.

Affordability is a second key issue. It's perhaps best understood by asking these key questions: How will students and their families pay for a college education? Who can afford my institution, and whom can my institution afford to enroll and educate? Without a doubt, the cost of college has become a critical challenge facing institutions everywhere today. Over the last decade, many institutions have focused on using pricing and the financial aid strategy—primarily through discounting—to maximize access and revenue at the same time. But today, fewer students can pay the posted price of attendance, and many schools are maxed out in terms of their capacity to absorb the tuition discount. The essential dual question that most must face today is: Who can afford us, and whom can we afford? Not to mention, what implications might this have for the program mix? When Sweet Briar College began its long climb back from near closure. its strategy included an overhaul of the curriculum, a new and more flexible calendar, and a pricing reset. Their new strategy is designed to shift the focus from what had been a genteel women's college with horses and lakes into a 21st-century liberal-arts institution that provides an education that is both relevant and affordable. The institution now costs about the same as Virginia's flagship public universities. The long-term sustainability of most colleges and universities will require finding a similar balance that they can live with—something that is increasingly difficult.

The third issue—*accountability*—is reflected in these important questions: What kinds of outcomes should students, parents, and society expect of higher education? What promises do we make to our students about their educational experience on our campuses, and how well do we deliver on these promises? From the public's view of what we do, demands for accountability are closely tied to issues of affordability. The question being asked by an increasing number of students and their families as they consider enrollment is this: Is this an investment worth making? As you consider new program possibilities, you will want to think about programs that might increase your value to your community or key stakeholders in some way. As reported by Laurence Biemiller in the *Chronicle of Higher Education*, colleges and universities would be wise to redefine and re-imagine their role in terms of who they serve.[17] Shifting from a focus on serving individual students, Biemiller suggests that colleges consider themselves as a kind of community asset, a learning community for the region. For example, for institutions located within close proximity to retirement communities, the opportuneities for partnership are numerous. Consider The Forest at Duke that partners with the Osher Lifelong Learning Institute at Duke University to provide adult continuing education courses held on both the Duke campus and the retirement center. Another example is Antioch College's partnership with its local community in Ohio, offering memberships at its Wellness Center. At Bay Path, our decision to launch a graduate degree in Physician Assistant Studies was informed in large part by the growing shortage of medical doctors in western Mass-achusetts and our belief that we could help address this issue by preparing physician assistants who would stay in the region. The addition of this program has done more than just about anything else we could have done to enhance our reputation in the region and position us as a valuable partner in addressing pressing workforce needs.

The fourth issue—*sustainability*—is all about the institution's capacity to generate sufficient resources. For academic leaders, the key question is: Can my institution generate the resources it requires to continuously improve our academic and developmental quality and still remain accessible to students of all means? These twin objectives (resource generation and access) often compete with each other, especially at less wealthy institutions—and one typically loses. It is essential that colleges assess both their *real* revenue opportunity and their *real* expense value in the context of their *real* market position. This is a difficult thing for many colleges; their aspirations may not line up neatly with their operational capacity. Program mix can play a critically helpful role here if your program portfolio is intentionally developed and managed to include a balance of high demand and high revenue producing programs. To whatever extent that academic leaders can begin to view their program mix similarly to an investment portfolio with an eye on making the right programmatic decisions to maintain the right balance of resources and access, their institutions will be well served.

The fifth and final issue has to do with *differentiation*, which, according to marketer Marty Neumeier, is all about passing the "onlyness test."[18] More than ever, colleges and universities need to distinguish their programs and experience from the other 4,000+ options available. In this era of increased competition, the institutions that stand out have a much better shot at winning their share of students. Neumeier suggests that you cannot advertise your way to "onlyness"—it needs to permeate everything that you do. Your one and only strategic position comes from your organization's core and can be clarified by thinking deeply and clearly about the following statement:

Our _____ *(offering)*
is the ONLY _____ *(category)*
that _____ *(benefit)*.

Nearly all colleges like to cite similar things about their institutions: great faculty, personalized environment, quality programs, etc. Yet, this does not go far enough in defining your "only.'" I believe that every college and university has something in its DNA that can serve as a foundation for a truly "only" strategic position. This is where creative and smart academic program development and planning can be a powerfully helpful strategy. Nurturing a program mix that pulls out and leverages the unique DNA of your institution is one of the best things you can do to ensure success and security in our new economy. Consider the case of North Park University, a church-related liberal arts institution located on the northwest side of Chicago in one of the most diverse zip codes in the country. For many years, North Park took its urban location for granted, going so far as to play it down in admissions marketing out of fear that the urban setting would discourage enrollment. Under the leadership of a new provost, the institution considered this question of onlyness and created the following statement: "Our University is the ONLY faith-based institution that resides in the heart of a world class city." With this position in mind, the faculty created a new required signature experience that leverages the vast benefits of attending a college that exists on the rim of a world class city like Chicago. Called *Catalyst 666,* the program uses Chicago as an extended classroom with students given first-hand experiences that allow them to identify vocational interests, get inspired by leaders in their field, and establish relationships with invaluable professional contacts. Since the program's inception, North Park has seen a steady increase in its traditional undergraduate enrollment with many new students citing the existence of this program as a primary reason for enrollment.

What's Next

In this chapter, we reviewed a variety of forces that are causing disruption for countless colleges and universities across the country. It is essential that academic leaders understand the particular and unique context in which their institutions reside and respond accordingly. Adopting an entrepreneurial and adaptive management style is especially helpful during these dynamic times. The next chapter provides a guide by which academic leaders can assess and strengthen their personal entrepreneurial leadership IQ.

> **KEY STRATEGIC QUESTIONS FOR ACADEMIC LEADERS**
>
> These questions are designed to help you think about the disruptive forces that are particularly and uniquely impactful for your institutional context. While each force represents risk and challenge for sure, there are also opportunities to be found. Consider what opportunities might exist for your institution as you work through these questions:
>
> 1. In considering your institution's current context, which forces are potentially most disruptive?
>
> 2. How is your institution currently weathering these forces?
>
> 3. Do any of these forces suggest an opportunity for your institution?
>
> 4. How do you assess your institution's current capacity for responding to and/or leveraging these critical issues facing higher education: Accessibility? Affordability? Accountability? Sustainability? Differentiation?
>
> 5. To what extent does your institution occupy a one-and-only market position?

CHAPTER 2
THE ENTREPRENEURIAL ACADEMIC LEADER—DO YOU HAVE WHAT IT TAKES?

In an era of heightened disruption and revolutionary challenges, academic organizations require a new style of leadership and decision making. Academic leaders who possess the skills to initiate and execute innovations, and serve as catalysts for leading their institutions in complex and disruptive times, are increasingly in demand. This view was echoed by a recent AGB Trusteeship article which envisioned that, "in an environment of unprecedented disruption, rapid change, and nontraditional challenges, a new mode of leadership and decision making may be required." [19] The article identified several essential attributes required for college and university leaders today, including: courage, entrepreneurial aptitude, and experience in successfully leading change. Similarly, the respondents to a survey of Council of Independent Colleges (CIC) presidents identified leadership attributes they believe to be critical in hiring their senior staff: initiative taker being the most important, followed by relationship builder, problem solver, and emotionally intelligent. [20]

However, most academic leaders come to their roles through the traditional academic pipeline, lacking the experience needed to cultivate a more entrepreneurial mindset and skillset. A study compared the competencies, values, and traits of corporate executives with those of successful higher education leaders. In the resulting report, "Leadership Traits and Success in Higher Education," the authors concluded that the most significant difference between successful higher education leaders and corporate leaders related to entrepreneurial skills; higher education leaders demonstrated a lower proclivity overall to initiative taking, risk-taking, and creativity; whereas, commerce leaders were more likely to prioritize finance and business issues over other matters. [21]

PROFILE OF AN ENTREPRENEURIAL LEADER

Maria Klawe—Harvey Mudd College

When Klawe assumed the presidency of Harvey Mudd in 2006, virtually no women were studying computer science. Today, approximately 40% of graduating CS majors are women. How did she do it? Klawe aggressively hired female faculty, heavily recruited female students, and made them both feel welcome in the department. With a personal passion for bridging the gender gap in STEM fields, Klawe is the first to admit that her strategy was not rocket science. Instead, she drew on best practices in the field and aligned the execution of strategies with her ambitious goal.

See Aghajanian, Liana. "Maria Klawe: The Forward-Thinking President of Harvey Mudd College." LA Weekly. 14 May 2014. www.laweekly.com/news/maria-klawe-the-forward-thinking-president-of-harvey-mudd-college-4640479

I have been fortunate to work with two successful presidents, each of whom possessed an abundance of the "commerce gene" and from whom I learned a great deal about entrepreneurial leadership. My doctoral dissertation research confirmed the importance of an institutional innovative mindset, something that originates and must be modeled at the senior level of the organization. A recent profile of successful college and university leaders[22] suggested that a leader's entrepreneurial mindset drives the success of the institution while providing a roadmap for other institutions to follow.

The Entrepreneurial Mindset and Skillset

What are the skills and attributes that comprise an entrepreneurial mindset and skill set? My research and experience along with the examples of the innovative leaders profiled in this chapter suggest the following attributes are a good place to start:

1. Vision and Dissatisfaction with Present State

"Leadership is the ability to translate vision into reality."
—Warren Bennis

A common thread among every innovative leader profiled in this chapter is that each one had a clear vision for their institution that they cared passionately about. Each one was able to imagine a future state that was different from the present situation. Maria Klawe envisioned a world where young women were actively engaged in STEM field pursuits, something that mattered deeply to her. Michael Crow envisioned a time where financial barriers to a college degree no longer existed. In educational contexts, innovation is never an end unto itself. Through vision and foresight, leaders are able to help their campuses concisely foresee the future, identify opportunities that will transform the institution's fate, and foster positive change to more effectively, and fully leverage the mission. Effective entrepreneurial leaders are skilled at connecting vision and foresight to community aspirations, many of which are often unspoken. As Jonathon Swift wrote, "Vision is the art of seeing things invisible. Foresight is all about looking forward and anticipating things that others cannot yet see."

2. Perseverance and Focused Execution

"Success is going from failure to failure without loss of enthusiasm." —Sir Winston Churchill

In a study of the world's greatest innovators, persistence is one of the attributes present in each one.[23] You also see persistence at work in the innovative leader examples found in this chapter. Persistence is typically defined as the ability to keep going in pursuit of one's goals even when experiencing challenges, setbacks, or failure. Effective entrepreneurs seem to have an almost uncanny ability to know when to stop and when to keep going, driven by their vision of what is possible. Even though Cheryl Hyman's "Reinvention" program was initially met with skepticism, she kept going and pushed it through, convinced that Chicago City College students deserved better. Effective entrepreneurs also tend to not worry about failing; instead, they view failure as a necessary part of the process and as a means for learning and adapting. They understand that a failure-avoidance culture results in employees who are afraid to try new things; because they understand this, they are more likely to promote a culture of learning and experimentation. Maria Klawe operationalized her vision of creating an inclusive STEM culture for women by putting in place a series of actions that would ensure her success. Indeed, while entrepreneurial leaders nearly all have a vision, it's the ones who are also relentlessly focused on the activities that get them to their goal who are most likely to be successful.

PROFILE OF AN ENTREPRENEURIAL LEADER

Michael Crow—Arizona State University

Since becoming president in 2002, Crow has grown the university to more than 80,000 students while increasing persistence rates and the enrollment of high-need students. With a personal commitment to providing educational access for less-advantaged students, Crow has driven the university's ambitious expansion into online education including innovative new partnerships such as ASU's agreement with Starbucks which provides an online education to Starbuck employees, courtesy of the company and Arizona State. Also noteworthy is the Global Freshman Academy which enables high school students to begin taking online classes and defer payment until end of the semester when they can decide if they are happy with grade and want to pay for college credit.

See "ASU ranked most innovative school in US for the fourth straight time." ASU Now. Arizona State University. 9 September 2018. asunow.asu.edu/20180909-asu-news-ranked-most-innovative-US-school-fourth-time

3. Self-Belief and Internally Motivated

> *"When doing what we most love transforms us into the best possible version of ourselves and that version hints at even greater future possibilities, the urge to explore those possibilities becomes feverish compulsion. Intrinsic motivation goes through the roof. Thus, flow becomes an alternative path to mastery, sans the misery."* —Steven Kotler

Effective entrepreneurial leaders have a strong belief in themselves and in their vision for their organizations, a confidence typically gained from years of experimenting, failing, learning and adjusting, and adapting their vision. Entrepreneurial leaders are typically very self-assured, while also being unusually aware of their own strengths and weaknesses, and comfortable demonstrating what they know without hubris. Those who work with such leaders can often sense the individual's passion for the cause and their strong sense of fire within. Case in point: Amy Laitinen, former Obama administration education policy adviser who believed that adult learners were not well served by federal credit hour definitions and the corresponding impact for federal financial aid eligibility.[24] Laitinen was particularly perplexed about the lack of federal financial support for adult students in competency-based education (CBE) programs, which (instead of giving students college credit based on "seat time" in class) allows them to move at their own pace, typically in online classes, and advance by showing mastery of specific knowledge and skills ("competencies") on exams designed by subject-matter experts. CBE is particularly useful for students who have already garnered considerable knowledge on the job and can convert that knowledge into college credit by taking exams and building portfolios of their prior work that are judged by outside experts—"prior learning assessment," typically at a fraction of the time and cost of traditional degrees. While working at the think tank New America in 2011, Laitinen began researching this issue in earnest and discovered an obscure provision in a 2006 statute allowing for something called "direct assessment." Thanks to her dogged determination to spread the word about this loophole among her wide network, a growing number of colleges are now creating CBE-based curricula, and their adult students are now qualifying for federal financial aid with hundreds more exploring this option.

> ### PROFILE OF AN ENTREPRENEURIAL LEADER
>
> **Michael Sorrell—Paul Quinn College**
>
> Paul Quinn College was near closure when Sorrell became president in 2007. The 150-year-old historically black college had fewer than 250 students and a very high attrition rate. Seeing an opportunity in his back yard, Sorrell eliminated the football program (saving the institution $600,000 annually) and converted the field into a working farm with an eye toward leveraging the college community's location in a federally recognized food desert. Today, the farm is operated by Paul Quinn students who get paid for their work, and the farm's produce is sold to area grocers and restaurants, used on campus, or donated to local nonprofits. Through Sorrell's "New Urban College Model," students learn essential business skills while getting paid for relevant work that benefits the local community.
>
> ---
>
> *See Harris, John. "Michael Sorrell took Paul Quinn College from barely surviving to thriving." The Undefeated. ESPN Internet Ventures. 15 November 2018. theundefeated.com/features/michael-sorrell-took-paul-quinn-college-from-barely-surviving-to-thriving/*

4. Courageous Risk Taker

> *"Security is mostly a superstition. It does not exist in nature, nor do the children of men as a whole experience it. Avoiding danger is no safer in the long run than outright exposure. Life is either a daring adventure or nothing."* —Helen Keller

This one builds upon the previous points and will certainly not be a surprise. The term "risk-taker" has become somewhat synonymous with the notion of an entrepreneurial leader and is frequently promoted as a necessary attribute for success. Yet, the notion of the courageous and risk-taking entrepreneur is much more nuanced than this. While there is ample talk about the need for leaders to be courageous and take risks, leaders are not always inclined to model this. For one, our organizations are not typically structured to promote or easily accept a high level of "risk-taking." If people do not see their leaders taking risks or if they are not personally supported when trying new things, they will be less likely to take risks in doing something different in the future. It's also important to consider that, according to Babson College entrepreneurship professor, Leonard Green, the best entrepreneurs are "calculated risk-takers."[25] According to Green, this is a critical distinction and can mean the difference between success and failure. Successful entrepreneurs are adept at minimizing risk along the way by learning and adapting as they go. This is very different from the leader who bets it all on one roll of the dice where the odds and impact of success or failure are much more impactful. One of my deans at my institution provides a great example of courageous risk taking in action. As a leader of her school, she is typically "elbows deep in learning" right along with her faculty and program directors. When she suggests a new idea for the classroom, she is first in line to try it. She is truly a "human guinea pig" who is continually immersing herself in new learning opportunities. It's no wonder that her school is highly innovative and that her faculty follow her example.

5. Opportunity Oriented and Outward Looking

"To stay ahead, you must have your next idea waiting in the wings."—Rosabeth Moss Kanter

When entrepreneurial leaders look for new ideas, they are increasingly more likely to look outside the academy than to rely on the inspiration found within. Indeed, the best entrepreneurial leaders discipline themselves to look outwards and to be on the alert for ideas that can come from the most unlikely of places. Consider Ben Castleman. In 2011, he was researching the problem of "summer melt." As a doctoral candidate at Harvard, Castleman was intrigued with finding a low-cost way to address this issue which plagues many colleges year after year. Through his research, he found that the problem is most acute among low-income students who do not have access to the pre-college supports available to students from middle- and upper-class families. Stepping back from the problem, Castleman spent some time observing the behavior of high school students where he taught and had an "Aha!" moment. Realizing how much time his students were spending on their phones Castleman partnered with uAspire, a Boston-based nonprofit, to test the effectiveness of text message reminders directed to newly graduated seniors. The result: Students who lacked college-planning support and who received the texts were significantly more likely to enroll in the fall. Costing only $7.00 per student, Castleman has continued to refine his innovative idea, partnering with the Common App to reach 450,000 low-income students and, most recently, with Michelle Obama's Better Make Room campaign where he hopes to reach millions of high schoolers. [26]

6. Wired to Network

"Networking is not about just connecting people. It's about connecting people with people, people with ideas, and people with opportunities." —Michele Jennae

Much has been written about the notion of the "networked university." As defined by Jeff Selingo, the networked university involves a new kind of partnership involving multiple institutions sharing structures and resources while delivering essential services at a lower cost. The networked university is premised on the notion that all institutions are better served by working together and that the sum is greater than just one institution working in its own siloed space. [27] In his role leading the development of Georgia Tech's online master's in computer science, professor and associate dean Charles Isbell, provides a real-world example of this entrepreneurial leadership attribute in action. Motivated by the knowledge that an advanced computer science degree from a traditional on-campus program like Georgia Tech is out of reach for most potential students due to the cost and physical limitations, which made program expansion unrealistic, Isbell reached out to an unlikely partner: the for-profit Udacity. Working in tandem with Udacity's CEO, Sebastian Thrun, Isbell devised a less expensive online version of Georgia Tech's traditional campus-based graduate program. Now enrolling nearly 4,000 students, the program is highly successful: "It turns out, we're accessing a whole set of students who can succeed but otherwise would not have the opportunity," reports Isbell. Developing an appetite for networking in the typical academic organization requires an ability to look beyond institutional boundaries for partners and to consider opportunities which might mean giving up some control and ownership to realize a bigger goal than what might be achieved working on one's own.

PROFILE OF AN ENTREPRENEURIAL LEADER

Cheryl Hyman—City Colleges of Chicago

When Hyman introduced a new program—"Reinvention"—early in her presidency for the City Colleges of Chicago system, the critics were quick to weigh in. Finding a system that graduated less than 7% of its students, Hyman took the controversial step of pushing students out of the classroom and into the workplace. With a keen focus on job training, partnerships with Chicago area businesses, and a highly specialized curricula, Hyman's new program emphasized pushing students through remedial classes more quickly and getting them real-world experience. In just a few years, the graduation rate doubled, and promising gains were made with student retention.

See Smith, Ashley A. "The Reinvention of City Colleges of Chicago." Inside Higher Ed. 19 March 2018. www.insidehighered.com/news/2018/03/19/former-city-colleges-chicago-chancellor-discusses-new-book-and-controversial-reforms

7. Negative Capability and Comfort with Uncertainty

"I wanted a perfect ending. Now I've learned, the hard way, that some poems don't rhyme, and some stories don't have a clear beginning, middle, and end. Life is about not knowing, having to change, taking the moment and making the best of it, without knowing what's going to happen next. Delicious Ambiguity." —Gilda Radner

The poet John Keats first used the term "negative capability" to describe great artists like Shakespeare who had an unusual capacity to thrive in uncertainty. Specifically, he was referring to the ability to be comfortable with ambiguity and remain open to explore many possible outcomes versus rushing prematurely to a conclusion in order to ease the anxiety that can accompany such a state.[28] Consider Charlotte Yates, who was profiled in a Harvard Business Review article about entrepreneurial leadership.[29] Founder of the telecommunications firm Telwares, Yates described her early experience working in a corporate setting as different from many of her colleagues: "I didn't follow IBM's design process and their normal chain of command, because my task would have never gotten done," she says. "I didn't see myself as having a tightly defined box; I didn't see the boundaries. I was looking at a blank piece of paper and saying to myself, 'Now, what do I want to create here?'" Likewise, Paul LeBlanc, who has led Southern New Hampshire University since 2003, appears to relish his experience in leading through chaos and uncertainty. In a profile by *The Chronicle of Higher Education,* LeBlanc described the various changes his institution was in the midst of as akin to "breaking out of the higher-ed echo chamber." Hiring key staff from outside of higher education, using business lingo to build SNHU's culture, and instituting a highly flexible non-siloed and fluid organizational structure were just a few of the many innovations he led. Entrepreneurial leaders like Yates and LeBlanc are "chaos pilots," a term first coined in 1991 by Danish politician Uffe Elbaek, founder of Kaospilot—an innovative business school designed to teach students how to lead through uncertainty.[30] While chaos pilots have negative capability, they also have other essential leadership skills such as the ability to create the necessary structure that allows others to keep moving forward even in the midst of the most shaky climate. While chaos pilots often make others uncomfortable with their incessant challenging of the status quo, they are the ones who can see their way through organizational problems and uncertainty to a better future.

8. Focused on Doing the Right Thing and Asking the Right Questions

"What people think of as the moment of discovery is really the discovery of the question." —Jonas Salk

As provost and vice president for academic affairs in the University of Hawaii system, Linda Johnsrud discovered that her students were taking much longer on average to earn their bachelor's degrees. [31] She immediately realized the increased financial burden this created for students and their families with more out-of-pocket tuition and living expenses, more college debt, and delayed entrance into workforce. She also knew that many of these students were at risk for leaving the institution without a degree in hand. Johnsrud dug deeper and learned that an informal yet widespread advising practice involved encouraging students to take fewer than 15 credits per semester thus delaying their completion. In response, Johnsrud initiated a campaign, "15-to-Finish," targeted at raising awareness among students and advisors and help more students attain a degree. Since the program's launch, Hawaii's graduation rate has increase by 8% and 15 other states have implemented similar programs. Johnsrud's innovative solution came about because of her willingness to ask hard questions and examine information from a variety of perspectives. This ability to ask questions like "Why?" and "Why not?" is a skill that all effective entrepreneurs possess. People who are constantly questioning things tend to also be good at observing, making connections, and experimenting. Entrepreneurial leaders question everything. Her end goal was the right goal—to help her students across the finish line with less debt and financial strain—and, with that in mind, she kept asking questions until she found an effective solution. She did not settle for a surface or easy answer; instead, she looked for the root cause of the problem. Too often, leaders get detoured in their efforts to do the right thing by settling for incomplete answers and inaccurate information, or they are dissuaded by staff who try to shift the agenda when one digs too deeply.

9. Work with What You Have, Make It Up as You Go Along, and Just Do It

"Now is no time to think of what you do not have. Think of what you can do with what there is."—Ernest Hemingway

University of Virginia Darden professor Saras Sarasvathy has been studying entrepreneurial leaders for a very long time.[32] Her theory of "effectuation" came from her groundbreaking research involving in-depth interviews with 27 serial entrepreneurs. Her research was designed to answer the question: "What do entrepreneurs actually do?" Her meticulous research proved that, in contrast to managers, entrepreneurs tend to make it up as they go along, and they start with whatever they have at hand including who they are, what they know, and who they know. For example, if a cook were to act entrepreneurially, he or she would create a dish with whatever ingredients were available in the kitchen pantry versus cooking from a recipe. Going on, her theory suggests that entrepreneurs are really good at leveraging contingencies (or said another way, they make lemons out of lemonade) in large part because they are flexible and open to change, and they are networking machines. Most importantly, Sarasvathy's research confirms that this process can easily be learned. Michael Sorrell's decision to repurpose his institutions' football field in order to launch Paul Quinn College's New School Urban Model is a great example of Sarasvathy's "bird-in-hand" principle—he looked around his campus and saw opportunity in a football field that was costing the institution undue financial strain. Every institution has resources at hand that can be repurposed in new and innovative ways if leaders are willing to consider the possibilities and just do it.

10. Curious

> *"Remember to look up at the stars and not down at your feet. Try to make sense of what you see and wonder about what makes the universe exist. Be curious. And however difficult life may seem, there is always something you can do and succeed at. It matters that you don't just give up."* —Stephen Hawking

If one considers the most notable entrepreneurial leaders of recent times, one thing stands out above all else They are all highly curious people. Whether thinking about Amazon CEO Jeff Bezos, scientist Stephen Hawking, designer Vera Wang, or media mogul Oprah Winfrey, they all are deeply engaged in pursuing the new and better, constantly looking for new ideas and learning. Successful entrepreneurial leaders have a knack for asking the right people the right questions. They also are intensely interested in a wide variety of subjects including art, literature, history, and more, and they are able to connect the dots between disparate thoughts to create new possibilities. Consider Steve Jobs, who was influenced by the aesthetic quality of everything he came in contact with. One wonders whether Apple would have achieved such success in the marketplace without Job's relentless curiosity and devotion to beauty. Entrepreneurial leaders are also adept at admitting what they don't know and asking for help when they need it—including seeking wisdom from the crowd. One of the best examples I have ever seen of obtaining wisdom from the crowd comes from the television show "Who Wants to be a Millionaire," where one of the "lifelines" involves asking the audience for help with answering the question. I have rarely seen an audience get the question wrong. I once worked for a president who was a master at obtaining wisdom from the crowd. Whenever the institution was facing a difficult or sticky decision, he would revert to gameshow host mode, circulating around the campus and asking everyone he encountered—from faculty to janitors—a series of questions related to the problem at hand. In return, he would get a bushel of input and advice including opposing ideas and suggestions. This president maintained that the wide range of input helped him to better understand the full context surrounding the problem at hand and invariably led to better solutions and new ideas. Perhaps most importantly, by asking for input of everyone in the organization, he empowered others to be curious and to assume ownership for the well-being of the institution.

Assessment: Entrepreneurial IQ[33]

Take this brief assessment to learn more about your entrepreneurial leadership capabilities. Instructions for scoring this quiz follow the assessment, along with suggestions for how to enhance your skills in each of the ten attributes of entrepreneurial leadership.

WHAT IS YOUR ENTREPRENEURIAL IQ?

Circle the number next to each item with which you agree.

---

1. When trying to resolve an issue, I drive people crazy with my incessant questions.

2. When faced with seemingly insurmountable challenges, I have a deep, innermost conviction that I will succeed.

3. Most of my professional reading time is spent with higher ed related journals and resources.

4. I am comfortable jumping in to start something even if I don't have all the facts at hand.

5. When unforeseen obstacles throw me off course, I throw myself into creating a revised plan.

6. When confronted by a difficult problem, I have trouble seeing a positive outcome.

7. If there's something I don't know, I feel compelled to seek out the answer.

8. I spend a great deal of time thinking about how to make things better.

9. When working on projects with individuals from across campus, it's easy for me to give up control in pursuit of a bigger goal.

10. When considering options in decision making, I usually choose the option with the least amount of downside.

11. When considering solutions to a problem, I typically choose the path of least resistance and/or the solution that creates the least discomfort for people.

12. There have been occasions when I am so sure of my idea that I've been able to convince someone who was previously reticent.

13. I make a point to get out of my office each day and interact with people from across the campus.

14. I enjoy trying to make lemons out of lemonade.

15. Most of my ideas have failed to materialize due to poor execution.

16. When working through a problem, I like to explore as many options as possible before settling on a solution.

17. I systematically store information, clip articles, and keep records of knowledge, expertise, and facts that may help me further down the line.

18. When leading an initiative, I am easily dissuaded by the naysayers.

19. It's better to have a large network of people you know a little, than a small network of people you know well.

20. Some of my biggest professional successes have been born from personal risk.

21. When making critical decisions in my area, I rely upon my sense as to how a particular outcome will impact the viability of the institution.

22. When encountering failure in leading new initiatives, I prefer to stay on the same path and hope that things will eventually work out.

23. My professional network includes individuals from outside of academia.

24. Resource constraints are holding me back from being more successful in my work.

25. During some of my most stressful periods, I've been at my most motivated, optimistic, and productive.

26. I am comfortable working in an environment where responsibilities and priorities frequently shift.

27. When looking for a solution to a problem, I typically rely on those who are closest to the problem for input.

28. When telling others about my current projects and ideas, I prefer to tell stories rather than reel off facts.

29. I enjoy getting to know people from all walks of life.

30. When I am taking on a new initiative, I typically take time to think about what could go wrong and adjust my plan accordingly.

Scoring

In scoring, there are ten sections, each of which relates to one of entrepreneurial qualities discussed in this chapter. For each of the ten sections, there is a total of three points available.

VISION AND PASSION

Score one point each for questions 8 and 28.
Add a bonus point if you <u>did not</u> answer yes to question 18.

The visionary entrepreneurial leader embodies the values and mission of his or her organizations and is able to attract the attention of others for the cause. In the academic environment, this characteristic shines through in the best communicators – those who know that it's human stories about educational impact rather than dry facts that have the power to engage and who are able to connect these stories to a future that others can get excited about and believe in.

If you scored low here, spend some time developing your own personal vision statement as a starting point. What is important to you? What do you most value? Then try connecting your personal mission statement to your current institution and your role. Finding personal connections between your values and the mission of your institution is a great starting point for visionary leadership.

PERSEVERANCE AND FOCUSED EXECUTION

Score one point each for questions 5 and 25.
Add a bonus point if you <u>did not</u> answer yes to question 15.

When the going gets tough, the tough get going, and that's certainly true of entrepreneurial leaders, who not only weather the darkest of storms but often appear to emerge even stronger and more driven than before. Resilience is a key requisite for success; successful entrepreneurs are able to either see beyond the storm clouds or understand when to cut their losses and try a different path. Applied in an academic environment, the characteristics of a determined entrepreneur are demonstrable in an individual who is also skilled at mapping out an execution pathway, staying focused, and changing course as needed to reach the end goal.

If you scored low here, try experimenting with some mini-failures that have low risk. For example, if you are not techy at all, spend some time trying to put together a tech toy. See how long you can stay at it before giving up. Try something like this on a weekly basis to develop the perseverance muscle and to get comfortable with failure.

SELF BELIEF AND INTERNALLY MOTIVATED

Score one point each for questions 2 and 12.
Add a bonus point if you did not answer yes to question 22.

In order to navigate the volatility and ambiguity of this new era, the successful entrepreneurial leader must have rock solid belief in themselves and their vision. Where they see opportunities, they have the confidence to take action, and where they lack the knowledge required to make decisions, they take confidence from discovering answers among their networks. Applied in the academic setting, entrepreneurial confidence is likely to manifest in someone who is seen as self-assured and passionate about their beliefs, trusts their own judgement, and grows through active learning.

If you scored low here, choose something about which you are very passionate, and do something to demonstrate your passion. Perhaps you can share your passion with five other people in the next week, one each day. Also, you could write and post an online blog in which you describe the issue and why you care so deeply about it. Make it a practice to begin living out your beliefs today, and watch your self-confidence soar.

THE COURAGEOUS RISK-TAKER

Score one point each for questions 20 and 30.
Add a bonus point if you <u>did not</u> answer yes to question 10.

Most academic organizations are risk-averse and yet there is clearly more at risk for most institutions that do nothing. Experienced entrepreneurial leaders are comfortable taking calculated risks and often attribute some of their greatest successes to running with an initiative that had no guarantee of success at the outset. Risks are just as necessary in the academic world as they are in business, and those who take calculated risks are increasingly likely to be seen as willing to grow, committed to the organization, and embodying the traits of a potential leader.

If you scored low here, find something that you would like to try that you think might be good for your institution, such as a new teaching approach or a new technological intervention. Volunteer to be the first to try it out and then find a way to share your experience with others. Not only will you personally expand your learning but you will also model for others courageous risk-taking in action.

OPPORTUNITY AND OUTWARD LOOKING

Score one point each for questions 13 and 23.
Add a bonus point if you <u>did not</u> answer yes to question 3.

Entrepreneurial leaders never rest on their laurels, always looking for the next novel idea that's going to move their organizations on to the next level. Quick to act, entrepreneurs instinctively know the right time to bring an idea to life and that sharing fosters team engagement. In the academic world, the opportunistic entrepreneur is the one who's always asking: "How can we make this even better?" With a strong emphasis on quality, they enjoy keeping abreast of new developments and find inspiration in the most mundane and unusual places.

If you scored low here, try expanding your problem-solving capabilities. Choose an issue that your institution or your department is struggling to resolve. Talk to people you know outside of higher ed, and ask them how they might solve the problem. Most likely, they will suggest things you would have never considered, and you might just find a novel solution.

WIRED FOR NETWORKING

Score one point each for questions 9 and 29.
Add a bonus point if you did not answer yes to question 19.

The networked entrepreneurial leader knows that quality wins over quantity when it comes to networking. Always looking to deepen relationships, connectors are great listeners who love to solve problems for others. In the academic world, such types are often found roaming the campus making and nurturing relationships that come in handy for those cross departmental projects. These are also the individuals who have wide networks of contacts outside the institution at a variety of organizational types. Trusted communicators, they are sensitive to others' needs and approach relationships with longevity in mind.

If you scored low here, make a goal to begin widening your networks now. Consider attending a professional conference in a field that is only tangentially related to your academic area (or not at all!). Next time you are tasked with pulling together a team to work on a project, consider whether there might be a role for someone from outside your campus--perhaps an employer of your students or someone in the local community who can bring a fresh and valuable perspective to your work.

NEGATIVE CAPABILITY

Score one point each for questions 16 and 26.
Add a bonus point if you <u>did not</u> answer yes to question 6.

Successful entrepreneurial leaders have an unusually high comfort level with uncertainty and can easily and happily function, especially when the outcomes and expectations are not clear. These are the individuals who often wear multiple hats and step in and out of a variety of roles sometimes within just a single day. In the academic setting, these are the individuals most likely to challenge the status quo and be the occasional thorn in the administration's side. Highly creative, they tend to care less for hierarchy and authority than they do creating something that adds value and meaning to the institution's mission.

If you scored low here, try naming and reframing the feelings you experience next time you find yourself in an ambiguous situation. Stop and ask yourself, "What am I feeling right now?" and take a minute to acknowledge the feelings of vulnerability. Then reframe those feelings as opportunities.

For example, rather than viewing the ambiguity as a threat and something to be avoided what if you viewed it as an opportunity that would open new doors for you? Something that would be good for you and add value to your life and work?

Focused on Doing the Right Thing

Score one point each for questions 1 and 21.
Add a bonus point if you <u>did not</u> answer yes to question 11.

Effective entrepreneurial leaders have a keen sense for how each and every issue impacts the institution's viability. They tend to be instinctive, analytical, and highly organized when it comes to financial information and implications—often spotting hidden meanings in data which go unnoticed by others. Entrepreneurs are also able to balance their long-term vision with their short-term goals. Applied in an academic environment, these entrepreneurial qualities are evident in a person with deep and clear focus and efficiency, close attention to detail, and ability to see the bigger picture.

If you scored low here, try asking more questions the next time someone brings something to you for approval. Come up with at least five "Why?" or "Why not?" questions to ask about the issue under review. Consider how this issue might potentially impact the viability of the institution, and if you don't know, pick up the phone and call the CFO to ask. Finally, if your financial acumen is limited, consider attending a NACUBO webinar or conference.

Effectuationist Extraordinaire

Score one point each for questions 4 and 14.
Add a bonus point if you <u>did not</u> answer yes to question 24.

The effective entrepreneur typically does not have a well-defined plan of action when good ideas strike. What she does have is a keen sense about how to work with whatever resources are at hand, and she is comfortable with jumping in and starting something even if the road map is not clear or certain. Entrepreneurs are great at seeing the silver lining, even in the direst of circumstances, and are the ones who will frequently suggest a novel breakthrough solution to a perplexing issue.

If you scored low here, try this simple method for building one's entrepreneurial mindset. Start by identifying something you would like to have happen. Take a small step toward making it happen—just do it and don't worry about the outcome. Stop and reflect on what you learned. Then take another step forward that incorporates what you learned in previous step. Keep repeating these steps and be sure to take the time to pause and reflect on what you learned.

Here is an example: Perhaps you want to make some extra money by offering a course on Udemy.com. First step? Browse the udemy.com website to find courses in areas where you have an interest and some expertise. Pause and consider what you have learned and possible implications. Next step? Sign up to receive the course creation resources. Pause and consider what you have learned. Next step? Begin creating your course by completing each of the five steps found on the website. Don't worry about creating the best course ever at the outset—just jump in and get started. Lastly, tell a colleague what you are doing, so he or she will check in with you from time to time, which can be helpful for staying on track.

CURIOUS

Score one point each for questions 7 and 17.
Add a bonus point if you <u>did not</u> answer yes to question 27.

The successful entrepreneur is a lifelong learner on steroids. They instinctively know that the more they learn, the more effective they are likely to be, but they also tend to enjoy learning just for the sake of learning. Natural collectors of data and information, they have mental libraries of facts and figures stored away for future reference. They are highly inquisitive and can often be found asking questions—lots of questions—of whomever or whatever happens to come across their horizon at any given moment. In academic settings, the curious entrepreneurs are highly useful people to whom others are naturally drawn when they want to unearth obscure information.

If you scored low here, commit now to spend more time each day outside of your office. Try eating lunch with some students in the campus dining hall, and ask them to tell you about their experience on your campus. Try engaging on a regular basis in what producer Brian Grazer calls "curiosity conversations," which is cultivating the discipline to show a keen interest in others by asking questions and remaining open-minded to what you learn. Grazer claims that most of his best movie ideas originated in curiosity conversations.

What's Next

In this chapter, we discussed the importance of an entrepreneurial mindset for today's academic leader and outlined the skills and attributes that comprise such a mindset. As research has shown, a leader's entrepreneurial mindset can and often does drive the success of the institution. Yet, it is not easy to lead and sustain entrepreneurial efforts in an academic organization. The next chapter highlights some of the common and harmful myths that can hold a leader back and provides suggestions for how to avoid getting caught up in these potentially powerful myths.

> **KEY STRATEGIC QUESTIONS FOR ACADEMIC LEADERS**
>
> These questions are designed to help you assess your personal entrepreneurial mindset and leadership skill capabilities. Once you complete and score the assessment, be sure to take some time to consider which skills and attributes are most important to your career success and what steps you might take beginning today to cultivate your entrepreneurial leadership IQ.
>
> 1. In considering your entrepreneurial IQ assessment results, on which skill and attribute items did you score high? Do you agree with your scores? Why or why not?
>
> 2. On which skill and attribute items did you score low? Do you agree with your scores? Why or why not?
>
> 3. Consider people you know who are highly entrepreneurial. Are there additional skills or attributes that these individuals possess that you would add to the list in this chapter?
>
> 4. Choose one of the skills or attributes where you scored low. What action might you take to strengthen your skill in this area?
>
> 5. Of the entrepreneurial mindset skills and attributes discussed in this chapter, which ones are most critical for your professional role and success in your current institutional context? Why?

CHAPTER 3
FINDING THE ENTREPRENEURIAL SPIRIT WITHIN

Creative thinking skills are more important than ever if we are to deal with the vast and complex array of challenges facing many colleges and universities.

The higher education environment is clearly stressed as evidenced by a double dose of concerning projections offered by Moody's Investors Service and Fitch Ratings. [34] Both agencies declared a negative short-term outlook for higher education citing high operating costs and constraints on tuition revenue, among other factors. The solution? Revenue growth and flexibility were mentioned as being key to improved financial health for most colleges and universities, strategies that require the kind of entrepreneurial leadership approach discussed in the previous chapter.

My keen and longstanding interest in innovation was first fueled by my doctoral dissertation research, conducted in the early 1990s with a focus on small college resiliency. I studied the financial performance and management strategies of 100 small resource constrained institutions over a ten-year period to account for why some colleges thrived while others declined. I found that the most resilient colleges employed several strategies that, when taken together, helped explain their success.

Most significantly, each of these schools exhibited an entrepreneurial mindset, something that has been touted by prominent higher education thinkers[35] as a critical prerequisite for thriving in disruptive times. In fact, my research suggests that, at the end of the day, institutional resiliency may depend more on mindset than skill set.

7 Destructive Myths about Innovation

Having been in the trenches for more than thirty years, I also know that this mindset is not easy, especially for academic institutions. As legendary management consultant Peter Drucker concludes in his article "The Discipline of Innovation": "In innovation, there is talent, there is ingenuity, and there is knowledge. But when it's said and done, what innovation requires is hard, focused, purposeful work."[36]

In my experience, one of the major roadblocks in the way of our success is that over time, institutional leaders have accepted a number of harmful myths about innovation as truths. These myths also play a critical role in limiting our willingness to take risks and to pilot and scale up new initiatives. Here is my top seven list of these common myths–along with some thoughts about how to avoid getting trapped in them.

Myth #1: Innovation is too difficult

Leaders sometimes hesitate to initiate innovation in part because they think it will be too hard or that it will require bringing in an expert who is schooled in how to think and act innovatively. A variation of this myth is the belief that innovation costs too much. A provost friend of mine at another institution recently told me that she was holding back on initiating a curricular change effort for precisely this reason—it would be "too difficult" to get her faculty on board, and if she did get them on board, they would most likely come up with ideas her institution cannot afford to implement. "So why bother?" she concluded.

However, the science of innovation[37] suggests that many of us tend to overthink innovation on the front end, talking ourselves out of taking even those less risky, smaller steps forward which over time can set the stage for positive change. What to do the next time you are tempted to put something in your "too-hard" basket? Shift your focus from thinking about innovation as a singular event with groundbreaking outcomes to building a climate that teaches, rewards, and incentivizes innovative thinking.

In other words, rather than focusing on some big blitz, presidentially driven "innovation initiative" that immediately puts people on edge and leaves them feeling defensive, start instead by nurturing a climate where faculty and staff are enabled to leverage their existing natural curiosity on a daily basis, and where institutional structure and process allows for and welcomes wide sharing and cross-pollination of ideas from every corner of the campus. St. Olaf College was on the forefront in this regard with its launch nearly 20 years ago of the Center for Innovation in the Liberal Arts,[38] a dedicated campus resource for facilitating faculty conversation around innovative practice in teaching and learning.

Myth #2: Innovation "just happens"

People love to describe a kind of "eureka" experience when explaining the origin of a new, great idea; however, most innovations incubate slowly, sometimes over years or decades. According to author Steve Johnson,[39] many of the great innovations in history did not come about as a lightning bolt but instead were the result of years of small, incremental changes, a lot of trial and error, and repurposing of old ideas. For example, when Tim Berners-Lee first created the World Wide Web as a tool for scholars, he never imagined that it would evolve over time into a network central to the development of the Information Age, used by billions of people to interact on the Internet.

At my own institution, The American Women's College—an innovative, fully online educational program that is transforming the way adult women learn—emerged from a decade-old campus-based program serving adult women.[40] Most institutions have existing offerings that can be repurposed or reimagined to serve a new market of learners.

The challenge is to teach yourself how to look at something very familiar that exists in one form and see new possibilities, new markets. For example:

- What campus-based programs might have a broader market if delivered online or hybrid?

- What if you were to adapt your academic calendar to allow students more problem-based or experiential learning experiences?

- What inherent campus strengths might have broader value if lived out in new and unique ways?

Oberlin College has long been known as a creative place where students are challenged to simultaneously develop their intellectual and artistic gifts and passions. The institution built on this historic and long-standing strength when it established its new creativity and leadership program housed in the Center for Innovation and Impact. An initiative designed to fully and intentionally reflect Oberlin's commitment to artistic excellent and academic rigor while preparing students for leadership and civic engagement, the program offers academic courses, project funding, guest lectures, and experiential learning opportunities.[41]

Myth #3: Innovation happens in a vacuum

When institutions embark on innovative initiatives, the natural tendency is to separate the individuals doing the innovative work in order to give them space and room for the ideas to blossom, as well as to protect them from institutional constraints. Indeed, this can be an important condition for getting a new endeavor successfully launched. There is also risk, however, in isolating this innovation from the rest of the institution to the point that there is minimal engagement between the two.

As Johnson writes, worthwhile innovation initiatives are most likely to succeed over time when they can fully leverage existing organizational assets and capabilities. Just as important is the opportunity for ideas to connect with each other. It is no coincidence that great cultural innovations emerged from the Parisian café culture of the 1920s, where creatives from diverse backgrounds and experiences met in the same space for hours on end. According to those who write on this topic,[42] a key to innovation on an organizational level is the presence of a network that broadly facilitates shared interactions that allow ideas to diffuse, circulate, and combine with other ideas. Institutions that are replacing the traditional academic departmental structure with interdisciplinary clusters that bring faculty and students together across diverse disciplines—such as what is being pioneered at Plymouth State University—are creating space on their campuses for new ideas and ways of thinking to emerge.[43]

To what extent are you creating space and opportunity for faculty and staff to mix it up, especially around critical campus priorities? The next time you launch a new initiative, be sure to consider the composition of your group. Aim for a wide mix in terms of demographics, such as gender, age, and ethnicity, as well as experience and background. Some of the best new process ideas on our campus have come not from those who are "in the weeds" with deep knowledge and familiarity but instead from those who were able to look at the process from an entirely different perspective and with new eyes. So, make sure the group driving your effort is diverse.

Myth #4: Innovation is something only creative geniuses do

There is a tendency to idealize innovation—to think of individuals like Steve Jobs, Albert Einstein, and Marie Curie as different from the rest of us, as having a kind of genius that enables them to create. In truth, each of us is born with innate creative instincts. If you watch children play, you will see them inventing dozens of things within a short time span. However, by the time we grow to adulthood, our innate creative instincts have been tamed by the conventions of conformity. Similarly, in academic organizations, good ideas are often immediately killed in the interest of the intellect and the analytical process.

In his book *How to Fly a Horse: The Secret History of Creation, Invention, and Discovery* (Anchor, 2001), Kevin Ashton tells story after story of individuals who worked tirelessly to create something new, often failing miserably until something took hold. For instance, James Dyson, the inventor of a cyclonic vacuum cleaner, made 5,126 prototypes before hitting on the successful design. Or, consider the back story of how the structure of DNA was discovered due in large part to a series of pioneering women who persisted in their field despite barriers of discrimination. In studying these examples and drawing from his own life experience (which includes coming up with the now-pervasive term "the internet of things"), Ashton concludes that people who are presumed to be "genius" innovators most often earned their success through mundane problem-solving methods: hard work and trial and error.[44]

What this means is that any one of us and every one of us has the potential to innovate. If we can open up pathways on our campuses that encourage everyone's access to creativity within a climate that tolerates experimentation, the potential for innovation might just be limitless.

Myth #5: Innovation is top-down

A similarly defeating myth is the notion that innovation only happens when led by a dynamic, key leader who personally drives new idea creation. While there are certainly notable stories about turnaround leaders who transformed their institutions through sheer force of will and perseverance, sustainable innovation is much more likely in today's environment when leaders take a systematic approach to creating and nurturing an innovative climate from the ground up. The higher education context is simply too dynamic and too fluid for most leaders to respond fast enough as solo innovators.

In contrast to top-down innovation, which is typically fueled by a strong vision and driven by a small team of senior leaders, *bottom-up innovation* is fueled by the creativity of many, particularly those who are closest to the mission on a daily basis. The Khan Academy[45] is an example of bottom-up innovation in practice. Through the creation and dissemination of more than 3,000, 10-minute free instructional videos on just about any subject, the Khan Academy has turned education on its head. It has ignited the flipped education approach where instructors can utilize the video resources for at-home student learning while reserving precious in-class time for problem-based learning. This flexible model makes much more efficient and effective use of the instructor's resources and allows for user feedback. This way lessons are continually refined and improved to better serve those most directly impacted.

According to the research,[46] leaders who excel at supporting bottom-up innovation exhibit a unique set of practices, including "behaving like a shepherd and leading from the back" in addition to modeling "a balance between creativity and discipline and between patience and a sense of urgency."

Myth #6: You can never have too many good ideas

How many of us have participated in brainstorming sessions that went nowhere? We tend to believe that the more ideas we generate, the more likely we will uncover that one, really good idea. Yet, coming up with ideas is rarely the issue for most institutions. The challenge comes in determining which ideas are worth our precious time and limited resources.

Psychologist Keith Sawyer suggests that to be optimally effective, idea generation needs to sit in the middle of an eight-stage process—one that includes "asking the right question, becoming an expert, practicing mindfulness, taking time off from a problem so your subconscious can incubate, generating lots of ideas (this is the brainstorming part), fusing ideas, choosing the best ones, and finally, making something out of your great ideas."[47] At a minimum, leaders need to keep their mission and strategic priorities front and center as they are evaluating new ideas. Regardless of where it comes from, a cool idea should never be added to someone's to-do list until someone can clearly articulate how it relates to the mission and how it addresses a pressing issue that your institution is facing.

It's also important to consider how you will measure the impact of any idea you are considering. For instance, how might this idea add value for the student experience, and how will you know when you have been successful? If the idea does not lend itself to measurement, that may be an indication that it is not worth your time.

Myth #7: Innovation is always good

The other downside to idealizing innovation for its own sake is the belief that innovation always produces good outcomes. Really? Innovation is always good? How about the *New Coke* debacle? How might we feel about an innovation that threatens to end our profession? What impact might today's great idea have many years into the future?

Innovation is change. And with change, there are always winners and losers. If we are honest with ourselves, no one really likes to be on the receiving end of change. Neuroscientists tell us that uncertainty about the future produces a strong alert reaction in our brains which diminishes our ability to focus. In brief, our brains do not like uncertainty, and we try to avoid it at all costs.[48]

At the same time, many inventions were created with the best intentions only to lead to dangerous consequences. For example, tobacco was first used around first century BC by the Maya people of Central America as a helpful tool in sacred and religious rituals.[49] Likewise, I imagine that Karl Benz and Henry Ford never dreamed that automobiles would one day kill 40k people annually in the U.S.[50]

Leaders should never lose site of the human side of innovation and the fact that any successful idea has many potential outcomes that are impossible to predict and difficult to measure. Idealizing innovation and creativity—without planfulness, intentionality, and strategic direction to provide guidance as to which innovations are worthy of investment and effort—can be as harmful as risk aversion and remaining bound by the way we have always done things.

Still, the evidence is clear: higher education is experiencing great change and disruption. One way or another, our institutions are going to shift, either from inside or outside. Creative thinking skills are more important than ever if we are to deal with the vast and complex array of challenges facing many colleges and universities and maintain some control over our own destiny.

10 Ways to Cultivate Creativity

So, how do we break through the structural fixedness that keeps us tethered to our comfort zones and blocks us from seeing things in new ways? Here are ten suggestions for cultivating creative habits of mind that have worked for me and for colleagues who are similarly challenged by the demands of the role:

1. Make creative thinking a habit

Many of us believe that creativity is something you either have or don't. And yet, the research suggests that creative thinking is no different than any other behavior that we might want to change or develop.[51] Thomas Edison's creative thinking habits provide a great example of how creativity can be cultivated by anyone in nearly any industry. As illustrated by his notebooks, which span six decades, the keys to becoming a habitual creative thinker include: generate as many ideas as possible, discipline yourself to ask "why" and "why not," keep an idea journal, and adapt an exploratory frame of mind.[52]

Just as with other common habits that form because of repetition and intention, creativity *can* become one's default mode. The key is to make a commitment to work at it, to challenge yourself, and to implement daily practices that will be habit-forming over time. For example, I now keep a small notepad in my purse so that I can record ideas immediately whenever and wherever they come. A friend keeps an idea notebook on her desk and has disciplined herself to take five minutes at the end of each day to jot down all ideas—good and bad—that emerged throughout that day.

2. Nurture curiosity

Award-winning producer of such movie and television hits as *A Beautiful Mind, Apollo 13, 24, Empire,* and *Frost/Nixon,* Brian Grazer attributes his success in the film industry to the power of curiosity and says it's something he has worked at his entire life. In his recent book, *A Curious Mind: The Secret to a Bigger Life,* [53] he shares his belief that every conversation is an opportunity for generating game-changing ideas. He has disciplined himself to ask leading questions and to be alert to possibilities that might otherwise fly right by. Like Edison, Grazer has learned to remain open-minded and detached from personal opinions and assumptions, to be present, and to expect to be surprised.

Some of our best new program ideas at Bay Path have resulted from Grazer-esque curiosity conversations.

Several years ago, during an end of year celebration, I learned from one of our criminal justice and legal studies double majors about her plans to enroll in a cybersecurity master's program at a university in the region. I asked several leading questions about her decision to pursue this career pathway and eventually concluded that there was something to this. The result of this conversation? Bay Path University is now one of the leading universities in the country in the education of cybersecurity professionals at the undergraduate and graduate levels.

3. Formalize opportunities for idea creation

One of my colleagues at another institution has a standing agenda item for her weekly deans' meeting labeled "crazy ideas." Each week, someone is assigned to share an outlandish idea with her team, with the only rule being: "There is no bad idea." Invariably, the ensuing discussions lead to breakthrough thinking, and more than a few new programs have been generated because of someone's crazy idea. Alternatively, you might ask someone to restate a problem from different perspectives or turn an issue upside down to consider an implausible scenario.

The point here is that new ideas typically don't just emerge on their own. The higher ed environment is one where it's always easier to consider why something cannot be done versus considering what it might take to do something differently. There are many tools (see the examples in the following pages) that can be used to spark creative thinking and generate new ideas in group settings so that your entire group forms the habit of creative thinking. The key is to formalize the use of these tools so that creative thinking becomes an important and expected part of your ongoing meetings.

Generating New Ideas I

excerpted from mindtools.com

It is easy to get stuck in dead-end thinking patterns. Breaking these thought patterns can help you get your mind unstuck and generate new ideas. Here are some techniques you can use to break established thought patterns:

Challenge assumptions: For every situation, you have a set of key assumptions. Challenging these assumptions gives you a whole new spin on possibilities.

You want to start a new graduate program in management, but you don't think you can gain the support of the faculty. Challenge the assumption. Sure, everyone might not be on board, but might there be one or two faculty who could have an interest in this? All it takes is one champion to start something. And if you can't find someone on the inside, can you find an external resource to help get this started? Suddenly the picture starts looking brighter.

Reword the problem: Stating the problem differently often leads to different ideas. To reword the problem, look at the issue from different angles. "Why do we need to solve the problem?", "What's the roadblock here?", "What will happen if we don't solve the problem?" These questions will give you new insights. You might come up with new ideas to solve your new problem.

The story about provost Linda Johnsrud's innovative solution for enhancing persistence at the University of Hawaii (see Chapter 2) is a great example of this technique in action. Everyone assumed the typical culprits were at work in causing students to drop out. Yet, when Johnsrud reframed the question to better understand the problem from a wider view and pushed back against the easy assumptions, she came up with a surprising finding: the advising system was a key contributing factor to holding students back.

GENERATING NEW IDEAS I, CONTINUED

Think in reverse: If you feel you cannot think of anything new, try turning things upside-down. Instead of focusing on how you could solve a problem/improve operations/enhance a product, consider how could you create the problem/worsen operations/downgrade the product. The reverse ideas will come flowing in. Consider these ideas, – once you've reversed them again, as possible solutions for the original challenge. For example, let's say you are concerned about poor post-graduate outcomes for the students at your university. How about creating a Grade Inflation University?—a school that retroactively awards high grades to all graduates as a way to boost employment outcomes? Crazy idea, perhaps, but it might be just the thing to open up some breakthrough ideas that could move the dime.

Express yourself through different media: We have multiple intelligences but somehow, when faced with workplace challenges, we just tend to use our verbal reasoning ability. How about expressing the challenge through different media? Clay, music, word association games, collage, paint, there are several ways you can express the challenge. Don't bother about solving the challenge at this point. Just express it. Different expression might spark off different thought patterns. And these new thought patterns may yield new ideas. Check out the website *Information is Beautiful* (informationisbeautiful.net) for some great examples about how to do this.

Generating New Ideas II

excerpted from mindtools.com

Some of the best ideas seem to occur just by chance. You see something or you hear someone, often totally unconnected to the situation you are trying to resolve, and the penny drops in place. Newton and the apple, Archimedes in the bath tub; examples abound. Why does this happen? The random element provides a new stimulus and gets our brain cells ticking. You can capitalize on this knowledge by consciously trying to connect the unconnected. Actively seek stimuli from unexpected places and then see if you can use these stimuli to build a connection with your situation. Some techniques you could use are:

Use random input: Choose a word from the dictionary and look for novel connections between the word and your problem.

Mind map possible ideas: Put a key word or phrase in the middle of the page. Write whatever else comes in your mind on the same page. See if you can make any connections.

Pick up a picture. Consider how you can relate it to your situation.

Take an item. Ask yourself questions such as "How could this item help in addressing the challenge?" or "What attributes of this item could help us solve our challenge?"

> **GENERATING NEW IDEAS III**
>
> *excerpted from mindtools.com*
>
> Over the years we all build a certain type of perspective and this perspective yields a certain type of idea. If you want different ideas, you will have to shift your perspective. To do so:
>
> **Get someone else's perspective:** Ask different people what they would do if faced with your challenge. A president I once worked for does this brilliantly—he walks around campus and asks everyone he meets for their ideas about any number of topics.
>
> **Play the "If I were" game:** Ask yourself "If I were ..." how would I address this challenge? You could be anyone: a famous scientist, a media mogul, an Olympic medalist or Einstein.
>
> The idea is the person you decide to be has certain identifiable traits. And you have to use these traits to address the challenge. For instance, if you decide to play Einstein, you might want to bring traits such as creativity, big thinking and risk-taking when formulating an idea. If you are an Olympic medalist, you would focus on things such as perfection, persistence and execution detail.

GENERATING NEW IDEAS IV

excerpted from mindtools.com

Enablers are activities and actions that assist with, rather than directly provoke, idea generation. They create a positive atmosphere. Some of the enablers that can help you get your creative juices flowing are:

Belief in yourself: Believe that you are creative, believe that ideas will come to you; positive reinforcement helps you perform better.

Creative loafing time: Nap, go for a walk, listen to music, play with your child, take a break from formal idea-generating. Your mind needs the rest, and will often come up with connections precisely when it isn't trying to make them.

Change of environment: Sometimes changing the setting changes your thought process. Go to a nearby coffee shop instead of the conference room in your office, or hold your discussion while walking together round a local park.

Shutting out distractions: Keep your thinking space both literally and mentally clutter-free. Shut off the Blackberry, close the door, divert your phone calls and then think.

Fun and humor: These are essential ingredients, especially in group settings.

4. Connect the dots

I used to believe that creativity was all about coming up with original ideas, but what I have since learned is that the best new ideas typically come because of connections that someone has made between existing ideas. What this means is that any one of us can learn how to connect the dots.

When asked for his definition of creativity, Steve Jobs offered similar thoughts: "Creativity is just connecting things. When you ask creative people how they did something, they feel a little guilty because they didn't really do it, they just saw something."[54] A fellow provost at a neighboring institution keeps a large white board in her office to capture ideas that are generated at her monthly council meetings. She structures time each month for team members to review the sticky notes and see what connections or patterns they can find. According to this very wise provost, "some of their best ideas have been right in front of them on the board but invisible until someone connected the dots between two or three sticky notes."

5. Get out of the office

For most of us, very few if any new ideas are generated while sitting at our desks processing paperwork. When asked how he came up with the theory of relativity, Albert Einstein said, "I thought of it while riding my bicycle."[55] Those who exercise regularly can attest to the way our thinking changes when we are in the aerobic state of flow. Ideas emerge as if by magic, and the filters that sometimes keep good ideas out are relaxed. A friend of mine likes to hold walking meetings and claims that the outcome of these meetings is invariably more positive and productive than meetings held in his office. Given that an increasing body of research[56] confirms that exercise can in fact increase creativity, I think my friend is on to something.

Develop the habit of getting out of your office at least once a day. Schedule in time each day that gives you opportunity for those curiosity conversations with students or others on campus. A faculty member I know who was struggling to get her latest writing project going began spending time each week at our local Starbucks. She now credits that time spent soaking up the smell of coffee and the conversations all around her as the impetus she needed to get her creative juices going.

6. Embrace fear and failure

According to psychology professor and creativity researcher Dr. Keith Simonton, the number of creative breakthroughs one has is directly linked to the quantity of effort and a tenacious and persistent attitude. From his research on individuals across many occupational fields, Simonton found that creative individuals simply generated *more* ideas—including many that were dead-ends—and demonstrated extraordinary resilience and an acceptance of failure a part of the process.[57]

In her 2008 Harvard commencement speech, author J.K. Rowling extolled the benefits of repeated rejection and failure for igniting her imagination, eventually culminating in the *Harry Potter* series.[58] In Elizabeth Gilbert's latest book, *Big Magic: Creative Living Beyond Fear*,[59] she talks about the positive and empowering tone set by the boss of her publishing house, who opened meetings with the following words: "You will never get in trouble in this organization for failing, as long as you fail in increasingly interesting ways."[60]

Being creative is like throwing spaghetti against a wall and seeing what sticks. It takes courage as leaders—especially within academic organizations—to squelch the urge for the right answer and instead create a culture that values and encourages prolific and uninhibited spaghetti throwing.

7. Try on different hats

We all have habitual ways of thinking and problem solving, and we can easily get trapped by our own biases. One of my favorite creative thinking techniques was originated by Edward de Bono and is called the *Six Thinking Hats* model.[61] I have used this model personally when trying to work through a tough problem to which no solution seems obvious; I have also used it in meetings when discussing issues that are likely to result in arguments or confrontations. In brief, there are six different styles of thinking, and each style is represented by a different color hat. Each hat—or perspective—is valid and presents a unique way of considering the issue at hand. There are no value judgments associated with the perspectives that may arise when using a particular style of thinking or "hat." Here are descriptions of the six hats:

> **White hat:** When wearing this hat, you are concerned with data, and you want to gather all information, including past trends and gaps in data or knowledge with an eye towards filling the gaps.
>
> **Red hat:** Here you rely on your intuition, gut, and/or emotion. You are concerned with how others might react emotionally, and you want to understand the responses of those who may not fully know your reasoning.

Black hat: You are concerned with the potential negative outcomes that might result from an issue or decision. You approach things cautiously and try to see why something might not work.

Yellow hat: You bring the optimistic viewpoint and are able to see the benefits and value of any decision. You are the one who keeps things going when the group gets bogged down.

Green hat: When wearing the green hat, you ooze creativity. Your style is very freewheeling, and you do not censor ideas—yours or others. The more ideas the merrier.

Blue hat: You are the controller and direct activity according to what is needed by the group, for instance, if the group appears stuck, more green hat thinking might be required.

When used with a group of individuals, the Six Thinking Hats model can be powerful tool for opening up the opportunities for creativity and new ways of thinking about even the most stubborn issues.

8. Practice out-of-the-box thinking

Design thinking is another tool that can be very helpful for breaking through ingrained ways of thinking and opening up out-of-the-box and/or surprising solutions. Popularized in the early 1990s by the company IDEO, this approach is based largely on the methods and processes that designers use, but it has evolved from a wide range of fields including business, engineering, and architecture and can be applied to virtually any field or purpose. Design thinking's value for particularly vexing and ambiguous problems comes from the approach's human-centric focus and the non-linear progressive nature of the process, making it especially useful for higher education settings. By putting people first and focusing heavily on empathy (the first step in the process) design thinking encourages you to consider the real people you serve first and foremost and to make sure you truly understand the problem you are trying to address before searching for solutions.

At a high level, the design thinking process seems simple enough:

1) Understand the problem, making sure to fully consider the perspectives of those most directly affected, involving them as fully as possible, and asking the right questions.

2) Brainstorm and generate as many ideas as possible, holding nothing back and suspending judgment.

3) Explore, test, and experience possible solutions.

4) Repeat.

5) Implement the best possible solution that has been refined through the previous stages.[62]

Live testing of potential solutions and iteration of the process is what brings it to life and is what ultimately results in surprising and successful outcomes.

While this is an overly simplified explanation, I have found the design thinking process to be helpful for pushing one's thinking beyond the typical or expected possibilities. For example, let's say you want to better respond to your student's demands for economic security via a good first job after graduation. Using design thinking, you might work backwards from the first job versus working forward from the K-12 system (which is how higher education typically approaches problem solving). You would go deep into understanding the requirements of the entry level jobs in the fields that your school offers, including talking with employers of current and prospective graduates. You might consider overhauling existing program curricula, including general education, to create clear pathways that directly and fully address student and employer needs. You might consider embedding experiential opportunities that provide real and direct opportunities for relevant skill development. You will also most likely need to redesign your structure to increase more seamless structures between your students and employers. A tall order? Yes. Much of higher education may not be ready for such an approach. But for those institutions that are committed to serving those who are not well served by our current system and structure, such an approach may be exactly what is needed.

9. Adopt the beginner's mind

A few years ago, I took a course on mindfulness and was struck—deeply—by the notion of the Beginner's Mind. As explained in my course, this has to do with approaching a situation with an attitude of openness and curiosity—as if you were approaching it for the very first time. The concept comes from Zen teacher Suzuki Roshi who said, "In the beginner's mind there are many possibilities; in the expert's mind there are few."[63]

The concept sounds simple, and yet, in an academic organization—where we place high value on our experts who tell us how things "should be" or "must be"—it is anything but simple. Given the benefits of the approach, it's worth a try. Whether you're trying to solve a difficult problem, enhance your own creativity, or open up possibilities in brainstorming, the Beginner's Mind technique can provide you with fresh eyes and focus. When your mind is open, you are more receptive to ideas and possibilities, you will ask for help more readily, you view failure in a more constructive and less defensive way, and you will be less anxious (which removes a common block to creative thinking).

Here are some easy first steps for cultivating a Beginner's Mind:

- **See risks as experimentation**, and give yourself at least one full day to try something out. Trying out something new actually makes us feel good—it releases dopamine in our brains and can motivate us in helpful way. By giving yourself enough time to trying something new, you are less likely to become overwhelmed and give up.

- **Be kind to yourself.** Let go of the need to be perfect and get it right. Remind yourself that this is an experiment, and you are not being graded. Silence your inner critic. The point is to learn from this and have fun.

- **Make a game of this.** For example, see how many people you can approach to ask for advice about whatever you are trying out. Adopt the stance of a true beginner and find some mentors who can guide you. Asking questions is at the core of the beginner's mind. Keep a journal of the questions you ask and the responses you get.

10. Mix it up

In the same article I quoted above under Tip #4, Steve Jobs suggests that the best dot-connectors are those who have had a variety of diverse experiences: "A lot of people in our industry haven't had very diverse experiences. So, they don't have enough dots to connect, and they end up with very linear solutions without a broad perspective on the problem. The broader one's understanding of the human experience, the better design we will have." [64]

Perhaps it's not surprising that travel abroad[65] has been found to increase college students' creative thinking skills. The mere act of getting out of one's comfort zone to experience new sights and sounds can be transformational to one's mindset.

The same "mix-it-up" concept applies when you bring the outside in to your everyday work processes and experiences. For example, bringing in external professional experts who have differing points of view to work alongside faculty on academic program initiatives can result in new ways of thinking about how education is being delivered. Research[66] clearly demonstrates that better, more creative solutions emerge from diverse groups of individuals. So, the more we diversify our faculty and staff, the better our odds for creating cultures where creative thinking is likely to emerge.

What's Next

In spite of these myths that many of us carry around in our heads, I do believe it's possible to jump start your institution's innovation engine by adopting practices and nurturing habits and environments that are conducive for creative thinking and behavior. This starts by understanding the barriers that are at play on a particular campus and that often get in the way of entrepreneurial thinking and new initiatives. In my experience, the forces preserving the status quo are especially powerful within academic organizations and are institutionalized in ways that make change very difficult.

In the next chapter, I will review the most common barriers to innovation that are in play on most college or university campuses, and I will conclude the chapter with specific strategies that any academic leader can deploy to set the stage for innovation.

Key Strategic Questions for Academic Leaders

For academic leaders, the creative spirit is essential to nurture, especially if you want to play an important role in contributing to your institution's viability and success. However, the nature of the provost or dean's role leaves little time for creative endeavors and thought. These questions are designed to help you identify myths that may be holding you back and easy things that anyone can do to nurture the creative spirit within.

1. Can you think of a time when you have been held back by one of the seven myths described in this chapter?

2. As a general practice, which of these myths is holding you back from being more creative in your professional role?

3. Of these myths, which ones are you most easily able to address? How?

4. What other myths to innovation have you experienced in your professional roles?

5. How much time do you spend on a daily basis outside of your office versus tethered to your desk?

6. To what extent do you operate with a beginner's mind?

7. How do your current role and responsibilities impact your creative spirit?

8. Which of the creativity enhancing suggestions discussed in this chapter resonate most with you? What will you do?

CHAPTER 4
SETTING THE STAGE FOR INNOVATION ON YOUR CAMPUS

In Chapter 3, I discussed the difficulty of creating and nurturing innovation within an academic organization. Unfortunately, those who are well positioned and authorized by role and formal authority to lead change are often weighed down with workloads and responsibilities that can kill the creative impulse.

Perhaps it is no wonder then that, according to a national study,[67] the average tenure of a chief academic officer or provost is only 4.7 years, compared to the significantly longer 8.5 average tenure of all college presidents. According to this same study, the top frustrations for chief academic officers include lack of resources, difficulty cultivating leadership in others, curmudgeonly faculty, campus infighting, and unresponsive campus governance structures. Only 31% of respondents view "leading change and fostering innovation" as job priorities; most of their time is spent managing bureaucratic processes, paperwork, and attending endless rounds of meetings.

Why is it so difficult to create and nurture innovation within an academic organization? In my experience, significant change will never occur until the forces for change are greater in combination than the forces preserving the status quo. This is especially the case in most academic institutions where the forces for resisting change are often institutionalized in complex and powerful ways. These forces generally fall into ten categories which I have called "barriers to change."

While some of these barriers are at work in all organizational settings, I do believe they play out in unique ways in the individual campus setting according to the institution's culture, mission, and political dynamics. Academic leaders are wise to be aware of the potential and unique impact of these barriers on their campus and to anticipate how they might hinder the new academic program development process. The ten most common barriers to change are reviewed below followed by suggestions for mitigating the impact of these barriers as well as encouraging and building the capacity for entrepreneurship and creativity throughout your organization. This chapter concludes with two assessment tools that you can use to assess your institution's readiness for innovation and change and strengthen your innovation project management skills.

10 Common Barriers to Change in Higher Education

1. Risk avoidance

Faculty, staff, and administrators are no different from anyone else in being slow to exchange what they know and do, even if they are not happy with it, for the unknown, which has the potential of being far worse. The risk of being deskilled and rendered irrelevant is a powerful fear, especially for faculty, and is often the reason for resistance to new program ideas or delivery models. Ask any provost who has tried to implement a new delivery model, and you will typically hear a litany of frustrations due to the skeptical and (unacknowledged) fearful responses from faculty. Especially for those who have made their livings teaching in a traditional classroom setting, new pedagogical modes and delivery models can cause real anxiety and concern about long-term job security. Reporting on the challenges faced by two once venerable institutions in an Ithaca S+R publication, William Bowen and Lawrence Bacow observed:

> *"Rather than confront truly difficult decisions, and risk personal insult and damage, it may often seem easier for both presidents and trustees just to hope that the sun will shine tomorrow—whatever the official weather forecast—and to assume that if it rains eventually, as it almost surely will, it will rain on someone else's parade."*[68]

2. Zero-sum thinking

Most colleges and universities exist in a culture of competition among institutions, among programs, and even among faculty. The pull towards self-protection can be intense, resulting in a fear that if another department or faculty gets new resources, "there will be less for me and my department."

The widely reported collapse of the Duke University undergraduate curricular reform initiative[69] is a good example of this dynamic at work. After five years of hard work culminating in the development of an innovative new curriculum called Blueprint, the effort fell apart over faculty quibbling about specific elements, such as the criticism voiced by foreign language faculty over the proposed reduction in required foreign language coursework. New program ideas—regardless of how innovative or well-founded—can be viewed as something that will take away the resources or the attention that faculty believe they need to do their jobs. Subsequently, cooperation and consensus can be very difficult to achieve and is rarely rewarded.

3. Accreditation

As membership organizations, accreditors gear their standards and policies toward maintaining and increasing excellence in higher education *as it is understood* by those members. In other words, nearly all accreditation processes and standards are designed to maintain the status quo. While we are beginning to see the winds shift slightly in this regard—for example, in its most recent revision, NECHE added a standard dedicated to effectiveness[70]—notions of excellence remain mostly focused on input measures (e.g., mission statement, planning practices, governance structure, academic oversight, student policies, all things that are inputs to the learning process) not outcomes of it. Without changing the input measures, it's virtually impossible to change the business model, and to date, most regional accrediting bodies have stifled institutional efforts to launch new programs that stray too far from the norm. Case in point: The Higher Learning Commission (HLC)'s edict to Tiffin University and Bellevue University to shutter their innovative Ivy Bridge and Flexxive programs. Despite receiving approval for its program in 2013, Bellevue now remains five years later under program review with the Department of Education and has had its innovative engine severely throttled.[71]

4. Tradition and culture

Tradition can be an extremely powerful force—from within and outside of the academy—and can never be underestimated when planning change of any kind. An insightful 2012 article by Joseph Simplicio titled "The University Culture," points to the important role of university culture, and helps to explain why this force is particularly powerful on some campuses. Simplico suggests that each university has a unique culture "born from the institution's history and ... steeped in tradition," which "provides stability and continuity." He goes on to state that universities have guardians of this culture who are "veteran faculty members, entrenched staff members, and others with longevity and seniority" who "stand watch over the status quo, ... begrudgingly allow only the most necessary of changes, and ... usher in newcomers and indoctrinate them into the fold."[72] The far reaching hold of culture is obvious in the experience of Sweet Briar College. When the then-president and board of the long struggling small women's college announced their decision to close in 2015, the alumnae rallied to accomplish what many said could not be done.[73] They pursued legal action against the administration and won, resulting in the institution's reopening with a new president and board. Consider the words of Sweet Briar Board Chair and self-anointed "tradition guardian" Teresa Pike Tomlinson: "Sweet Briar's near collapse turned out to be a blessing because the school now has an alumnae network that its president described as 'like Patton's army.'"

5. Leadership

When considering the great higher education leaders across history, one is left with the image of a warrior leader—someone who has a strong-willed and charismatic personality, is able to serve as a kind of "mayor" of the campus and who leads decisively relying often on gut instinct. But in this new era of higher education with limited resources, a wary public and a need to do things more quickly and in partnership with others, a new style of leadership is certainly called for. In a prescient *New York Times* piece by Thomas Friedman, the author suggests that the paradigm shift taking place in corporate America calls for a new style of leader—a style more akin to gardening than waging war. I believe this analogy to be very apropos for the times in which we live for higher education as well. As the analogy goes, gardeners are skilled at seeding, pruning, inspiring, and cultivating ideas from others, knowing when and how to nurture growth as well as how to tend to the various and unique plots of land that makeup the garden. They have a keen sense of timing, knowing if they harvest too soon, they might disrupt the growth cycle. The notion of a gardener president is very much in keeping with the kind of entrepreneurial leader described in the previous chapter. Yet, until institutions and their boards are able to adapt their notions about effective leadership, particularly as they are searching for new leaders, change and innovation efforts may be hampered.

6. Internal systems, structures, and decision-making processes

The reward and budget allocation systems on most college campuses tend to reinforce the status quo with few, if any, rewards for taking risks. And top-down, control-based hierarchical structures discourage individual initiative and reduce autonomy. As *Hackathon* contributor Peter Russian observes about the challenges of today's world, "those closest to the front line are going to be better placed to understand the increasing demands of an informed customer [e.g. student] and need to be able to respond to those demands."[74] Yet, the traditional hierarchical and siloed structure found in most academic organizations makes it very difficult to organize for change in a way that is contextually responsive. Moreover, the pull of the academic discipline through which most traditional faculty have been socialized and to which they feel a continuing strong sense of loyalty can be a powerful deterrent to considering new ways of doing things, particularly when it comes to teaching and learning. For many faculty, professional identity—how one views oneself in the context of the academic discipline and how one defines professional status—serves as a powerful barrier to pedagogical reform and change. For example, what the academic discipline norms suggest and value, and what one's professional peers (most of whom may be external to one's home campus) think, are likely more important influencers for the individual faculty member than campus individuals and events.

7. Staffing and recruitment processes

Likewise, the search processes for most new academic positions tend to place greater weight on preserving the status quo. In her insightful book *Now You See It*, Dr. Cathy Davidson suggests that diversification of the faculty is one of the most powerful things an institution can do to enhance innovation. Per Davidson, new ideas and ways of thinking about teaching and learning will come "only through a purposeful mixing it up of perspectives, experiences and backgrounds," something that is impossible to achieve when we hire people "just like ourselves."[75] Likewise, the research on creativity confirms that the single most important ingredient for nurturing creating thinking is diversification.[76] Without a diverse range of experiences, knowledge, background, and education, groups are much less likely to produce creative results. According to the research, such diversification is particularly important at the senior level and those exerting the most significant influence on key institutional decisions.

8. Faculty governance

The traditional faculty socialization and tenure processes can also be a powerful barrier to change on today's college campus. Tenure track faculty play a particularly important role because of their oversight and control of the teaching and learning experience. Any effort to change how things are done may be seen by the faculty as a threat to academic excellence or integrity. Moreover, the very process of earning tenure, a process based entirely on rewarding and reinforcing the status quo for individual faculty members typically allows for minimal incentives for those who want to experiment with new and sometimes untested approaches. Plus, on many campuses, the very pursuit of tenure drives faculty members to focus on producing research—which is sometimes of questionable and limited value—to the exclusion of their teaching responsibilities and dedication to students. Perhaps not surprisingly, at its annual meeting of the Council of Independent Colleges in 2016, a panel of presidents drafted a list of "essential" and "negotiable" elements for the future of higher education institutions, including tenure on the "negotiable" list.[77]

9. Organizational silos

Many institutions, their leaders, and their faculty tend to work in silos, cut off from the broader inputs and influences that may shape their very future. If the institution is too internally focused and rigidly structured, its leaders may miss the signs of change within its fluid market context. In today's disruptive environment, academic institutions must be able to change quickly to meet the evolving needs of the communities they serve, including rapid realignment of skills and assets. The rapid acceleration in college closures and consolidations in recent years, as reported on by *EducationDive*,[78] provides a sad example of this reality. It is noteworthy that the path forward for some struggling colleges may be found in new and unusual partnerships. For example, the retailer Hobby Lobby recently purchased the 73-acre campus of Saint Gregory's University, a Catholic college in Shawnee, Oklahoma, that closed in late 2017 with the stated plans to operate the campus as a college. Likewise, after closing and subsequently reopening under new leadership in 2015, Sweet Briar College has established a partnership with the neighboring Virginia Center for the Creative Arts, an internationally renowned artists' colony for the visual, literary, and performing arts, located next door to the campus.

10. Success

Ironically, one of the toughest barriers to negotiate is *success*. Successful institutions tend to define quality by their own standards, with the status quo serving as a marker to exemplify quality. Hence, in good times, there is neither the imperative nor a sense of urgency to change anything. Yet, it's precisely when things are going well for an institution that its leaders need to look to the future. Stephen Remedios, Principal at the Boston Consulting Group's Leadership & Talent Enablement Centre, sees past success as one of the greatest decision biases: "When there's no threat on the horizon, and you've just had your best quarter in a while, adapting to remain relevant in the next quarter is the last thing on anyone's agenda."[79]

Identifying Your Key Barriers

The Identifying Key Barriers checklist found here provides a helpful starting point for thinking about the issues that are getting in the way and/or impeding change efforts for you and/or for your campus. The checklist also provides you with an opportunity to consider where you may be able to have the biggest impact in addressing one or more of these barriers. With some barriers—such as the impact of accreditation and related external constraints—there may not be much you can do. However, there are other areas where you may be able to more easily have an impact. For example, by mixing up the composition of committees and planning groups, one can quickly move the dime by broadening the range of perspectives that will inform group process and decision making. The key here to understand the barriers that may be at work in a particular change context and know where your time and energy might be best spent in moving things forward.

CHECKLIST: IDENTIFYING BARRIERS TO CHANGE

To what extent is each of the following barriers a factor in impeding change efforts on your campus?

	Major barrier				*Not at all*
Risk avoidance	1	2	3	4	5

How might you address this?

	Major barrier				Not at all
Zero-sum thinking	1	2	3	4	5

How might you address this?

	Major barrier				Not at all
Accreditation	1	2	3	4	5

How might you address this?

	Major barrier				Not at all
Tradition and culture	1	2	3	4	5

How might you address this?

	Major barrier			Not at all	
Leadership style	1	2	3	4	5

How might you address this?

	Major barrier			Not at all	
Internal systems, structures, and decision-making processes	1	2	3	4	5

How might you address this?

	Major barrier			Not at all	
Staffing and recruitment process	1	2	3	4	5

How might you address this?

	Major barrier				*Not at all*
Faculty governance	1	2	3	4	5

How might you address this?

	Major barrier				*Not at all*
Organizational silos	1	2	3	4	5

How might you address this?

	Major barrier				*Not at all*
Success	1	2	3	4	5

How might you address this?

Building the Capacity for Entrepreneurship and Creativity Across Your Campus

According to the research, successful innovative organizations *work* at it. They pursue innovation holistically and systematically paying attention to the many aspects of the organization that are important for creating and sustaining a culture that embraces new ways of thinking and responding. They establish a discipline around innovation, and they track metrics—religiously—to monitor their results. They also invest in innovation and structure processes and resources to ensure their efforts will be successful.

In higher education—where the status quo is being regularly challenged by new models and shifts in the business of educational delivery—academic leaders need to similarly make innovation a priority. However, in a field as dynamic as higher education where change and creativity can be hindered in surprising ways, any effort to institute change must take into consideration the unique organizational dynamics that are at play on a particular college campus. In my experience, effective academic leaders in higher education are those who adapt their approach to building an appetite and capacity for entrepreneurship to fit their organizational culture—globally (the culture of higher education as a whole) and granularly (the culture of their specific campus or academic department). What does that look like? Here are seven practices that have proven effective in a variety of higher education settings for strengthening an institution's capacity for innovation.

1. Practice and model creative leadership

Creative leadership encompasses both a philosophy and an action, the goal of which is to promote innovative thinking and mission-driven entrepreneurship. According to Puccio, Mance, and Murdock (2011),[80] creative leadership is "the ability to deliberately engage one's imagination to define and guide a group toward a novel goal—a direction that is new for the group, resulting in a profoundly positive influence on the organization and the individuals in that setting." Perhaps most relevant to higher education is one of the practice's core assumptions: *change is a given; it's on-going and open-ended and is something not to be endured or managed but instead nurtured and celebrated.*

Rather than being focused on the process of managing change, the creative academic leader is focused on building a more creative organizational culture. Rather than driving ideas for change downward, the creative academic leader works to foster an organic environment in which new ideas are welcomed and nurtured from anywhere in the organization. Rather than imposing change on those who don't want it, creative academic leaders invest time in strengthening their own personal creativity and entrepreneurial capacity while also modeling an attitude that celebrates innovation and creativity in those with whom they most closely work. Given the processes that creative leaders draw heavily upon—problem solving, cultivating, and refining new ideas including novel ones that go against the grain—this is a leadership style and set of practices that are in particular sync with faculty talent, training, and ways of thinking. For example, creative leaders believe that the best ideas emerge through the collision of ideas and perspectives. In an academic setting where vigorous debate abounds, a creative leader takes full advantage of the setting to provide a safe and supportive environment in which to reframe the clashes into creative and collaborative thinking and action.

2. Make innovation a priority

Building an innovative culture starts with letting everyone on the campus know that this is an important priority. If innovation is important, then you should treat it just like you do the other things that are important in a collegiate environment such as enrollment, financial management and so on. Can you imagine recruiting students today without a strategy or well researched plan? Likewise, if you are serious about nurturing innovation, start by crafting a specific strategy that clearly identifies what your institution is trying to accomplish and why. Then make sure you provide ample opportunity for discussion and input about the strategy with important constituent groups. Include the innovation strategy in your strategic plan or whatever document/process you use for future planning. Moreover, your innovation strategy should emanate from some kind of strategic imperative to respond to your institution's greatest marketplace and missional opportunities and threats.

Rather than just "doing innovation" for the fun of it, leaders need to provide a clear, compelling, and transparent context for the innovation strategy that clearly links the purpose and goals with your context and mission. For example, Southern New Hampshire University's 2018-2023 Strategic Plan is structured around five commitments, each of which responds to four priority areas: "strengthening what we do well; innovating for the future; building capacity for our new ambitious goals (building a platform that allows us to educate 300,000 learners by 2023): and game changing initiatives."[81] According to their website, SNHU's innovation strategy was widely vetted and grew out of a process whereby they thought deeply about their purpose and core values and collectively imagined the future world in which their students will work and study. SNHU's president, Paul LeBlanc, clearly practices and models creative leadership.

3. Invest strategically in innovation

One can usually tell what is important on any campus by looking at the budget to see how financial resources are being allocated. Particularly with new ideas, it's important to have a transparent funding approach and process that can make innovative ideas a reality. A common best practice adopted by many schools is the creation of a donor-funded pool of monies that can be tapped to support investments in innovative ideas and that ideally are outside of the annual budgeting process and resource pool.

For example, several years ago, Westminster College (Utah) established The President's Innovation Network (PIN),[82] comprised of individuals and corporate representatives who, collectively, annually provide the president with venture funding to be used in developing educational innovations or other strategic initiatives. In the PIN's most recent report (annual reports describing the investments and their impact for that year are posted on the President's website page), the fund supported twelve initiatives ranging from a $50,000 investment to launch a social impact incubator to a $40,000 investment to support Office of Diversity, Equity, and Inclusion programming and $25,000 to launch a Center for Innovative Cultures.

At my institution, the president established an annual award—The President's Award for Innovation—that is given at the annual Holiday Celebration to recognize a staff or faculty member who has demonstrated extraordinary creativity and innovative thinking in the course of their work at Bay Path. The recipient is selected by a committee of peers, receives a cash award, and is featured on a plaque with other award recipients in a highly visible space on campus.

These examples illustrate easy things that any institution can do to recognize and reward innovative thinking, as well as to free up resources that can be deployed outside of the normal bureaucracy and the barriers that exist therein.

4. Consider learning launches

Sometimes and especially in academe, baby steps can be a wonderful low-risk, less contentious way to introduce new ideas. When my institution was considering adapting our One-Day-Saturday campus-based program for adult women to provide a fully online delivery option, we were concerned that our market might not respond to an online format. After all, the high touch aspect of the campus-based program coupled with the strong community that developed among the adult women in each cohort were primary drivers for the program's high student satisfaction. Instead of converting all programs at once, we decided to do a learning launch and pilot one program to start. Drawing upon what we knew about the factors that contributed to our high graduation rates and strong program satisfaction, we designed one major and used it to test strategies for emulating the high touch and community in a fully online classroom. After cycling one student cohort through the program and evaluating their experience, we were confident enough in the results to move forward in converting other majors to online delivery. The learning launch was invaluable for testing assumptions about how our adult women best learn, for testing what and how aspects of the campus-based experience can be translated into the online experience, and for experimenting on a smaller, less-risky scale before assuming bigger risk.

There are a wide variety of ways that you can conduct learning launches. For example, before launching a fully developed new program in a new area, how about starting with a certificate or boot camp? These can be especially effective with technical and skills-based programs and allow you to test the market before going further. For academic leaders, the point here is to encourage faculty and staff to experiment in small, lower risk ways as a means of developing an appetite for innovation. Learning launches can also be a great way for individuals to experience failure and for the institution to learn how to accept and tolerate failure. Once someone has experienced some success if only on a small scale, the drive to create new things can be contagious.

5. Provide safe space for idea incubation

As discussed earlier in this chapter, the organizational bureaucracy can be a powerful barrier to innovation. Especially with new academic program ideas, resistance can quickly surface in one's colleagues if they fear that your new program is going to reduce the resources that are available to meet their program's needs. Unfortunately, I have seen more than a few excellent program ideas get squelched by well-meaning faculty who were trapped in a zero-sum thinking mode.

So, what to do? Borrowing from the corporate playbook, academic leaders are increasingly providing a safe space in which to vet and incubate new program ideas outside of the organization's structure and bureaucracy. This can be a particularly effective strategy if you can also fund the incubation with donor-or other external funding that does not impact current funding levels for other programs and initiatives. This is essentially how The American Women's College (TAWC) was launched at my institution. Given the significantly different delivery model, we concluded that the program needed a different structure and environment in which to operate during the launch. Consequently, we created a new academic division that reported directly to the president and was housed in an off-campus location. Most importantly, we created an entirely new and distinct set of operating standards along with a teaching and learning framework that reflected our best thinking about what this program needed to be successful. Looking back, I am certain that this program would not have gotten off the ground had it been launched within the traditional academic structure.

If you choose to go down this path, keep in mind that it's critical that you are highly transparent about what you are doing and why, especially with how you are funding the initiative and the results you are achieving. I also believe there is a point of diminishing return with incubated ideas. If you leave the incubated initiative separate from the rest of the institution for too long, you risk the initiative becoming entrenched in its own context and you lose the opportunity for organizational learning that can happen when you migrate the incubated idea or initiative back into the institution.

6. Establish an intentionality around innovation

If innovation is to take hold in a campus culture, leaders need to work at it in a very intentional and public way. Some presidents do this by identifying and leveraging external resources. For example, in developing its most recent strategic plan described above, Southern New Hampshire University engaged with the Institute for the Future[83] to facilitate a futures-driven planning exercise on how students will live and learn in the future.

Other institutions have designated a chief innovation officer or someone working in a similar capacity to champion and cultivate innovative initiatives as well as to engage the campus in innovative thinking and activity. There are obvious pros and cons to this approach. On one hand, if you have someone who is well respected and savvy at negotiating campus politics, this can be an effective means of nurturing and sustaining innovative thinking across the campus. On the other hand, the ultimate goal for leaders should be to cultivate many individuals to think like chief innovation officers versus relying on one individual to carry the day.

However innovative ideas get brought forward, it is important that senior leaders are actively engaged and publicly supportive of innovative initiatives wherever they may be lodged (including those ideas that are being developed outside of one's own immediate area). Leaders can facilitate innovation by providing resources for professional development in new and emerging areas, by creating cross-departmental and divisional opportunities for idea generation, by exposing faculty and staff to innovative practices at other institutions, and by making sure that people have the time, the training, and the resources to do the work of innovation.

7. Invest in a continued conversation

I have long admired the practice known as "hackathons" —brainstorming/problem-solving marathon sessions— originated by the software-coding community. In these hackathons, many talented people come together from different disciplines to work on a problem over a limited time period. These sessions are all about creating conditions for conversation, interaction, and collaboration —something that can be a powerful strategy for building your institution's capacity for innovation and creativity.

When Oberlin College and Conservatory established its Center for Innovation & Impact,[84] it operationalized in a persuasive way the institution's long-standing missional commitment to fostering creativity and academic excellence. The Center plays an important role in convening students, faculty, and staff around issues and initiatives that teach innovative thinking skills. The Center also offers academic courses, project funding, guest lectures, and experiential learning opportunities that are open to the entire Oberlin community including parents and alumni).

In a similar vein, several years ago, my institution established an annual signature event "The Innovative Thinking and Entrepreneurial Lecture," which is open to the campus and the general public. It is given by an individual who has been distinguished as an innovative leader.

However ones does it, the important thing here is to invest in mechanisms that facilitate communication and collaboration across the campus and between the campus and external world around activities and initiatives that foster new ways of thinking. Over time, the conversation itself can play an important role in sustaining a culture where innovative thinking and creativity become an expectation for "how we do business around here."

Checklist: Assess Your Institution's Organizational Readiness for Innovation

Innovation has been recognized as an increasingly important priority across all industries these days. According to a Deloitte Consulting LLP study on innovation activities,[85] organizations that are demonstrably successful innovators tend to use the same toolkit. Specifically, these organizations have built their innovation strategy around four key factors—approach, organization, resources, and metrics. Here is a checklist that incorporates these toolkit components—adapted for higher education organizations—for academic leaders to use to assess how their institutions' approach to innovation compares to the most successful innovators.

1. APPROACH

A. Innovation strategy—How clearly have you articulated your goals for innovation?

___ Does your institution's strategic plan or stated strategy include a goal for innovation that clearly identifies what you are trying to accomplish?

___ Does your institution's strategic plan or stated strategy include priorities based on strategic imperatives to respond to marketplace opportunities and competitors?

B. Pipeline and portfolio management—How have you organized innovative initiatives within your institution's infrastructure to ensure they are fully developed and well managed?

   __ Does your innovation strategy reflect long term goals balanced with modest risk?

   __ Have you fully and transparently integrated your innovation initiatives into work streams and decision making?

C. Process—Do you have a workable and transparent process for incubating, sorting, testing, and launching new ideas within your institution?

   __ Have you defined a process for incubating ideas, sorting and testing them, and launching those that are most successful that is relatively free from organizational constraints?

   __ Does your process allow for failure and learning from those innovations that miss their mark?

2. ORGANIZATION

A. Senior leadership—To what extent does the senior leadership team engage with innovation?

   __ Do your senior leaders serve as champions for innovation and new idea generation?

B. Governance—How and by whom are innovative decisions made?

___ Who in your institution typically makes innovative decisions? From which areas of the institution are innovative ideas most likely to emerge?

___ Do you have a clear and transparent process for encouraging, vetting, and implementing new ideas?

C. Collaboration—What mechanisms are in place for identifying and leveraging collaborative opportunities to deliver innovative ideas, with external partners and within and across institutional departments?

___ Does your institution's strategy include a priority for collaborating with external partners/experts or non-traditional resources?

___ To what extent does your institution's culture support collaboration across departments and functional areas? How easy would it be to launch an innovation that required collaboration between areas?

3. RESOURCES AND COMPETENCIES

A. Funding—What financial resources are dedicated to innovation, and how is this funding accessed? and the means for accessing the funding?

___ Does your institution set aside funding to support innovation initiatives?

___ Is there an easy process for accessing the funding that is widely available?

B. Human Resources—Recruiting and utilizing people in the right ways to leverage innovative initiatives:

___ To what extent do you intentionally recruit and hire individuals for faculty and staff positions who bring diverse talents and perspectives?

___ Do you have a process within your institution for cultivating and nurturing innovative thinking?

C. Innovation Resources and Tools—Resources and tools that are utilized to support an innovative culture or the implementation of innovative ideas

___ What resources do you use to manage new idea generation and development?

___ Do you have cutting-edge software, tools, or techniques to support innovation in high priority areas (e.g., admissions, advancement, data management, etc.)?

4. METRICS AND INCENTIVES

A. Financial and other rewards—Financial and other non-monetary incentives used to recognize innovative efforts:

___ How do you reward and recognize innovative efforts within your institution?

B. Metrics—Quantitate measures that are used to track progress:

　__ Does your institutional strategy include defined metrics for innovative initiatives?

　__ Are these metrics clearly and widely communicated across the institution?

　__ Do you routinely track and widely communicate progress in achieving these metrics?

Innovative Project Evaluation Guide[86]

The best ideas in the world can fail to launch if the organization is not ready or if good management processes are not in place. This evaluation guide has been designed to assist individuals who are thinking about implementing an innovation, and is intended to help you think proactive about issues that can either facilitate or derail your efforts.

FIRST, CHOOSE AN INNOVATION/PROJECT IN YOUR INSTITUTION TO ASSESS:

1. Describe the innovation:

2. My innovation is:
   ___ Contemplated
   ___ Underway
   ___ Completed

3. What is innovative about it/What is the opportunity for innovation?

4. Why do/did you want to do it?

5. Which definition of "innovation" are you using (choose one)?
   ___ Inventing something new
   ___ Generating new ideas only
   ___ Improving something that already exists
   ___ Spreading new ideas
   ___ Performing an existing task in a new way
   ___ Following the market leader
   ___ Adopting something that has been successfully tried elsewhere
   ___ Introducing changes
   ___ Attracting innovative people
   ___ Seeing something from a different perspective

6. At which stage is the innovation right now?
   ___ Ready
   ___ Developing support
   ___ Pilot
   ___ Implementation
   ___ Evaluation
   ___ Learning
   ___ Complete

ASSESS READINESS:

7. Does your institution your institution have sufficient skill and capacity to:
   ___ Recognize problems?
   ___ Define problems?
   ___ Identify solutions?
   ___ Develop an effective and viable strategy?
   ___ Recruit competent and talented faculty and staff?

8. Why have you or your institution decided that change is needed?

9. How important is this change to your area?

    not very important 1 2 3 4 5 *very important*

10. How important is this change to your institution?

    not very important 1 2 3 4 5 *very important*

IDENTIFY THE PROBLEM:

11. What is the problem you are trying to solve?

12. Has the objective of the innovation been clearly defined? What is it?

13. What will happen if you do not pursue this innovation?

DEVELOP SOLUTIONS:

14. Have you explored broadly for ideas?

15. How?
    ___ Website research
    ___ Competitor scan
    ___ Best practices scan
    ___ Consulted with colleagues
    ___ Other

16. Do you have enough of the right kinds of ideas?

17. Have you used creativity enhancement techniques?
    Examples:
    ___ Design Thinking
    ___ Edward de Bono's Thinking Hats
    ___ Mihaly Csikszentmihalyi's Flow Concept
    ___ Min Basadur's Creativity Process
    ___ Michael Kirton's Adaptor-Innovator (KAI) distinction
    ___ John Kao's Creativity Audit
    ___ Other

18. Have you benchmarked (compared your ideas with the best known practices in this area)?

DEVELOP SUPPORT AND GAIN APPROVAL:

Strategic Planning:

19. How will your institution determine that the innovation is worth doing?

20. How does the innovation align with or support your institution's strategy and priorities?

21. What benefits does/will the innovation offer:
    ___ Improving the bottom line (financial)
    ___ Greater effectiveness
    ___ Process improvement
    ___ Policy improvement
    ___ Better service to constituents
    ___ Greater responsiveness
    ___ Improved quality
    ___ Improved collaboration
    ___ Other

22. What risks are inherent in the innovation?

23. Have you identified, characterized, assessed, and measured the risks?

24. What is the worst thing that can happen if the innovation fails?

25. How will you reduce the likelihood or impact of those risks?

Communications:

26. Have you involved the areas and people who will be directly and/or indirectly affected?

27. Have you communicated your ideas to others? To whom? How?

28. Does your innovation have momentum? Why?

29. Is there anyone who may have a reason to not support this innovation? How valid are these concerns? How might you respond to this opposition?

30. What is most essential key to securing support across your institution for this innovation?

PILOT TESTING:

31. Have you decided to pilot the innovation?

    If no, proceed to "Implementation Stage" below.

32. Do you have what you need to pilot it appropriately?
    ___ Ideas
    ___ The right people
    ___ Support
    ___ Resources
    ___ Other

33. How and through whom will you pilot it?

34. Do you have a plan for learning from and building upon an unsuccessful/successful pilot? How?

IMPLEMENTATION STAGE:

35. Has adequate time been allocated for planning, implementation, and evaluation?

36. Do you have a project implementation plan?

37. Have adequate resources been assigned to the innovation?
    ___ The right people
    ___ Sufficient budget
    ___ Appropriate techniques
    ___ Necessary technology
    ___ Other

BUILD A TEAM:

38. Do you have the leadership required to see the innovation through to the point where it can be appropriately assessed?

39. How does senior leadership feel about this innovation?
    ___ Negative
    ___ Uninterested
    ___ Unaware
    ___ Mildly interested
    ___ Enthusiastic

    Why?

    How will you bring them along?

40. Who is the/champion for this innovation?

41. Who will be key to promoting the success of this effort? Who are the most essential project team members?

42. Is the infrastructure in place that is required?

43. Is there a structure to encourage cross-fertilization among disciplines, professions, functions, topic areas, departments, with outside organizations, groups, etc.? What is it?

EVALUATION STAGE:

44. What are the results (outputs and outcomes)?

45. Did you have a good experience with the innovation? How do you know?

46. What specific results did you achieve?

LEARNING STAGE:

47. What did you learn from this innovation effort?

48. What went well?

49. What would you do differently in implementing another innovation?

50. How will you celebrate success?

51. How will you celebrate failure and the opportunity to learn?

52. How will you create and retain an institutional memory from this innovation?

What's Next

In this first section, we explored the trends and forces that are creating disruption across the American higher education section. Understanding the forces that are at work in your own campus is a helpful starting point for identifying new initiatives including new program possibilities. Given the challenges facing higher education, entrepreneurial leadership skills are essential; however, most academic leaders come to their roles lacking the experience which can hone such skills. Chapters 2-4 provided tips and techniques that any academic leader can adopt to create a sense of urgency on his or her own campus as well to develop one's own personal entrepreneurial leadership IQ.

In Section II, we will apply these concepts as we review the art and science of academic innovation. Specifically, how might an academic leader approach new program portfolio development? What elements are essential to consider? What is important for long-term sustainability and success? These are just a few of the essential issues that will be covered in Section II.

> ### KEY STRATEGIC QUESTIONS FOR ACADEMIC LEADERS
>
> These questions are designed to help you assess which change barriers are most likely to get in the way of your new academic program development efforts and to consider what you might do as a leader to build your institution's capacity for innovation and creativity.
>
> 1. To what extent is each of the ten barriers to innovation at work on your campus or within your department?
>
> 2. Which barriers are most likely to get in the way of your efforts to bring forward change or new ideas?
>
> 3. Who are the self-appointed guardians on your campus? How might they influence your efforts to institute new programs?
>
> 4. Of the seven practices for building your institution's innovative mindset reviewed in this chapter, which ones resonate most with you? Why?
>
> 5. How would you describe your institution's approach to innovation?
>
> 6. Is this approach working well for your institution? Why or why not?
>
> 7. Considering the Assessing Your Institution's Innovative Readiness Checklist, how is your institution doing? Where are you strong? Where is there room for improvement?

Helpful Resources

Here is a short list of my favorite resources that I have found helpful in my work on academic innovation and entrepreneurship. While not exhaustive nor exclusive to higher education, this list provides a good starting point for increasing one's knowledge about the topics covered in Section I, as well as for adding some inspiration into your life.

Higher Education Demographics

Grawe, Nathan D. *Demographics and the Demand for Higher Education.* Johns Hopkins University Press, 2018. Written by a University of Chicago professor in Economics and a Carleton College, this book provides an easy-to-read and incisive analysis of the demographics shifts that are already underway and having a profound impact on enrollment.

The New Generation of Students: How Colleges Can Recruit, Teach, and Serve Gen Z. The Chronicle of Higher Education, 2018. Drawing on demographic trends, surveys, expert observations, and more, this special report by The Chronicle of Higher Education provides a valuable resource for all colleges and universities that want to better serve Gen Z.

Mrig, Amit, and Pat Sanaghan. *The Future of Higher Education: Will Higher Education Seize the Future of Fall Victim to It?* Academic Impressions, 2018. This white paper provides an insightful summary of the most compelling challenges facing higher education leaders along with helpful strategies for addressing these challenges.

EducationDive. www.educationdive.com/news/tracker-college-and-university-closings-and-consolidation/539961/ This real-time website is maintained by the nonprofit EducationDive and tracks major college and university closings, mergers, acquisitions, and other consolidations from 2016 to the present.

New Higher Education Models

Aoun, Joseph E. *Robot-Proof: Higher Education in the Age of Artificial Intelligence.* MIT Press, 2017. Written by the President of Northeastern University, this book provides a practical perspective on how colleges and universities might more fully leverage our technology-infused world to prepare students for the world in which they will work and live.

Craig, Ryan. *A New U: Faster + Cheaper Alternatives to College.* BenBella Books, 2018. This is a must-read for anyone interested in how the education system needs to change to better support the transition from an industrial economy to a knowledge economy. It provides an insightful perspective on what the future of higher education might look like.

Cook, Lisa, and Daniel Fusch. *Spotlight on Innovation: Colleges and Universities that are Making a Difference.* Academic Impressions, 2015. This report profiles the innovative experiences of four Department of Education First in the World grant recipients to improve college access and completion.

Mrig, Amit. *Small but Mighty: 4 Small Colleges Thriving in a Disruptive Environment.* Academic Impressions, 2015. In this white paper from Academic Impressions, read how four small colleges have bucked the national enrollment decline trend.

Creativity and Innovative Thinking

Kao, John. *Clearing the Mind for Creativity*. New World City Inc., 2011. This is a very short book that provides helpful exercises for achieving your own beginner's mind.

Neumeier, Marty. *The 46 Rules of Genius: An Innovator's Guide to Creativity*. New Riders, 2014. This book provides an easy-to-understand framework for the practice of creativity and how to nurture the innovator within.

Neumeier, Marty. *The Branding Gap*. Pearsons, 2006.
Neumeier, Marty. *Zag*. New Riders, 2006.
Neumeier, Marty. *The Designful Company*. New Riders, 2009.
Neumeier, Marty. *The Brand Flip*. New Riders, 2016.

This four-book whiteboard overview series gives you the tools you need to carve out and sustain a truly distinctive market position.

Grant, Adam. *Originals: How Non-Conformists Move the World*. Penguin, 2016. This highly entertaining read provides a new perspective on where new ideas come from and how to become a master at generating them.

Grazer, Brian. *A Curious Mind: The Secrets to a Bigger Life*. Simon and Schuster, 2015. This book makes a great case for the power of curiosity with easy to follow tips for igniting your own personal curiosity.

Puccio, Gerald, et al. *Creative Leadership: Skills That Drive Change*. Sage Publications, 2010. One of my favorite books on leadership, *Creative Leadership* helps readers enhance their creative talents and employ these skills as leaders. It includes a discussion of the important role creativity plays in leadership, an extensive account of the skills necessary to be an effective creative leader, and a range of historical and contemporary examples throughout that bring the Creative Problem-Solving model to life visually.

Brain Pickings (www.brainpickings.org/) is a compilation of cross-disciplinary and highly interesting information nuggets spanning art, science, design, history, and philosophy. Started by MIT Futures of Entertainment Fellow Maria Popova, the weekly e-newsletter is sure to inspire creative thought.

TED Talks (www.ted.com) encompasses inspiration on virtually every topic imaginable. Long considered a trusted repository of ideas in a wide variety of fields, these relatively short videos present ideas and inspirations from successful people from all over the world.

Information is Beautiful (www.informationisbeautiful.net) distils data, information, and knowledge into beautiful, useful graphics, and diagrams and provides you with an out-of-the-box means for learning better.

The *Innovation Masters Series* from Stanford University (scpd.stanford.edu/design/videos/index.php) provides a free series of webinars and lectures about design thinking and other innovative thinking topics, recorded on the Stanford Online YouTube Channel.

Innovative Leadership

Liedtka, Jeanne, et al. *The Catalyst: How You Can Become and Extraordinary Growth Leader.* Crown Publishing Group, 2009. This book provides a practical and easy to apply techniques and skills for growing an organization. The best take-away? The authors show you how any individual in an organization can be a positive catalyst for growth and innovation.

Couros, George. *The Innovator's Mindset: Empower Learning, Unleash Talent, and Lead a Culture of Creativity.* Dave Burgess Consulting, Inc., 2015. This is a great book for education leaders of any kind and full of ideas for creating more student-centered environments. Provides a helpful way for thinking about innovation as more than what we do but as something we are or can become.

Drucker, Peter. *Innovation and Leadership.* Harper Collins, 1985. Timeless wisdom in this easy to read book by the great guru of management.

Kim, W. Chan, and Renee Mauborgne. *Blue Ocean Strategy: How to Create Uncontested Market Space and Make the Competition Irrelevant.* Harvard Business School Press, 2005. While written for corporate leaders, this book provides one of the best roadmaps I have found for all organizational sectors for creating an actionable and defensible one-and-only market position.

Mrig, Amit, and Patrick Sanaghan. *The Skills Future Higher-Ed Leaders Need to Succeed.* Academic Impressions, 2017. This 30-page paper summarizes the skills most needed by today's academic organizations.

Christensen, Clayton. *The Innovative University.* Jossey-Bass, 2011.
Christensen, Clayton. *The Innovator's Dilemma.* Harper Business Press, 2011.

These two books by Clayton Christensen will school you in the theory of disruptive innovation and how it applies to higher education.

Buller, Jeffrey L. *Change Leadership in Higher Education.* Jossey-Bass, 2015. One of the few resources that I have found that speak specifically to "how to innovative" within the academic organizational setting and culture. It is highly practical with great examples and case studies.

Heifetz, Ronald, et al. *The Practice of Adaptive Leadership.* Harvard Business Press, 2009. One of the most popular change leadership books on the market, this book is filled with stories and examples with practical tools and easy to implement tactics for leading innovation and change in any organizational context.

SECTION II—THE ART AND SCIENCE OF LAUNCHING NEW ACADEMIC PROGRAMS

OVERVIEW

Academic leaders who are committed to driving entrepreneurial growth on their campus are wise to balance their approach to work by paying equal attention to both the art and science in planning and decision making. Especially with the process of new program development, the art aspects discussed in Section I must be balanced with a rigorous, transparent, and well-executed process for identifying, vetting, and operationalizing new program ideas and initiatives.

In Section II, we turn our attention to the science side of academic entrepreneurship by providing a step-by-step process for bringing new program ideas to life. While comprehensive in nature, this process can easily be adapted to fit the specific needs of any campus. Understanding that it's difficult at the outset to anticipate all the variables that will impact your new program's viability, Section II concludes with important considerations for remaining flexible and adaptable once your program is up and running.

CHAPTER 5
IS IT TIME TO LAUNCH THAT NEW ACADEMIC PROGRAM?

In Section I, we explored the trends and forces that are creating disruption across the American higher education landscape. The challenges facing higher education in recent times are certainly well documented and unsettling. Understanding the forces that are at work on your own campus is a helpful starting point for identifying new initiatives, including new program possibilities. Given the challenges facing higher education, entrepreneurial leadership skills are essential; however, most academic leaders come to their roles lacking the experience through which such skills are developed.

In my opinion, the current climate requires a new kind of leadership, especially within the academic arena. Especially for resource-constrained institutions (which is most of higher education these days), traditional management approaches such as strategic planning, resource prioritizeation, and/or cutting one's way to sustainability are no longer sufficient long-term solutions. In this current context, successful institutions are dynamically outward-looking and have developed a discipline around driving entrepreneurial growth in ways that extend and further leverage the mission. This is what having an entrepreneurial mindset is all about; from my experience, nurturing such a mindset at the institutional level requires both art (intuition, active listening, and keen attention to opportunities) and science (rigorous discipline and process).

Section I explored the art of new academic program development. There is an abundance of resources that any academic leader can utilize to develop an entrepreneurial mindset. There is also a growing body of resources available to help provosts and deans nurture innovative thinking on an institutional level.

What's critical is this: Academic leaders who are serious about driving entrepreneurial growth on their campuses need to adopt a management approach that balances the art with a rigorous and well supported process for identifying, evaluating, and operationalizing program ideas. This is the *science* part of academic entrepreneurship. An entrepreneurial mindset requires that academic leaders maintain a "yin and yang" kind of orientation to their work making sure to balance both the art and science in planning and decision making.

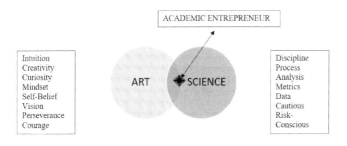

I consider myself an **academic entrepreneur**. Throughout my career in higher education, I have been focused on looking outward and asking key questions, such as: "How can we do this differently," "What do we do really well that might be leveraged in new and unique ways," and "What market opportunities exist that we are uniquely equipped to meet?"

At Bay Path University, where I have served as Provost since 2010, we undertake vision planning every three years and as part of this process, we routinely ask these questions as we review new opportunities that are both mission-centric and entrepreneurial. Through this process, we launched approximately 30 new graduate programs over the past decade and established the American Women's College (AWC), the first women's only fully online program in the country. We also initiated several curricular innovations that powerfully leverage our mission such as our Women as Empowered Learners and Leaders (WELL) program, a multi-dimensional signature learning experience that weaves together academic coursework, leadership skills, career preparation, and community service. One thing we learned over the years is that good ideas can come from virtually anywhere—anytime. That being said, we also learned that there are specific things you can do to foster creativity and new idea generation on demand. Here are five considerations for generating and evaluating new academic program ideas:

1. Become a positive champion for new program idea creation.

2. Institute a disciplined approach to brainstorming and competitor scanning.

3. Make sure you understand your constituent's learning needs.

4. Assess new program ideas against your existing program portfolio.

5. Screen new program ideas for viability before moving forward

1. Champion the generation of new academic program ideas

Many of the ideas discussed in Section I are all about fostering a culture where new ideas will flow more readily. This starts with having the confidence that you can generate new ideas that can change the trajectory for your institution. In an academic environment, where provosts and deans are sometimes surrounded by faculty who tend towards skepticism and analysis-paralysis, I cannot overstate the importance of maintaining a positive attitude about what is possible. You will always find individuals who are ready to point out the faults of every new idea. As academic leaders, new idea generation begins with believing in yourself and your ability to create exciting and viable new opportunities.

So, where do you start? You cannot be creative in a vacuum. At Bay Path, we like to say that there is no bad idea—just ideas needing to be vetted and considered in light of what is happening on campus and in the broader higher education context. This means staying in touch with what is happening "out there" and working hard to understand how current trends and ideas may affect our constituents and what they want from the programs we deliver on our campus—current and future.

For example: Bay Path offered a graduate program in forensic science for many years. The enrollments were small, and, regardless of the many things we tried on the recruitment side, we found it difficult to enroll more than seven to eight students in a given year. Concerned about the program's viability, and also aware of the difficulty some of our undergraduate science students were having in getting good jobs after graduation, our dean and a small group of science faculty applied for a grant from the Massachusetts Life Sciences Center. The grant funded an in-depth study of the market in our region and included interviews with industry experts and current employers of our graduates. What we learned in the process is that our programs were not adequately preparing our students with the laboratory skills they needed to be successful in 21st century work settings in the life science industry. Armed with this knowledge, our dean and faculty overhauled the curriculum, converting the master's in forensic science to a master's degree in applied laboratory science and operations. In just a few years, we have seen a marked difference in enrollment as well as in post-graduate job placements for our students in this field.

A key takeaway? *More knowledge means more and better ideas.* You simply can never know enough about the market context for your program offerings. To gain more knowledge, try the following:

- **Interview industry experts in the fields where you offer programs**. These are the people who will be hiring your graduates and they are generally futuristic in terms of knowing and evaluating the latest industry hiring trends and job demands.

- **Interview or survey employers of your students**. Find out what they think about your graduates' preparation, including any limitations in skills or knowledge.

- **Take a virtual field trip to an institution that has been recognized for educational innovation**. Visit an institution that has been recognized as a leader for out-of-the-box practice. For starters, check out the *Reimagine Education Award* winners for 2019.[87] Reimagine Education is a global competition that rewards innovative approaches aimed at enhancing student learning outcomes and employability, offering $50,000 in funding to the overall winner(s) and 16 *Oscars of Education*. It culminates in an international conference for all those seeking to shape the future of education.

- **Research the top most innovative schools in your region** on the *U.S. News & World Report Most Innovative Schools* annual ranking.[88] These are the colleges and universities that have been identified by college presidents, provosts, and admissions deans in a peer assessment as the schools to watch because of their cutting-edge practices and innovations in curriculum, technology, and other areas.

- **Go outside the academy**. While this is assumed in my first point above, the point cannot be overstated. Especially in this current climate where curricular relevancy is highly important, the boundaries between our institutions and the outside world need to be as transparent as possible. An easy way to do this is to bring the outside in by including industry professionals on task forces and planning committees as a start.

- Make it a practice to **regularly scan newsletters and online resources that report on important future trends**. Here are three of my favorites:

Education Dive
www.educationdive.com/topic/HigherED

This site provides busy professionals with a bird's-eye-view of the education industry in 60 seconds.

Institute for the Future
www.iftf.org/home

As the world's leading non-profit strategic futures organization, IFF's core research staff and creative design studio work together to provide practical foresight for a world undergoing rapid change.

EDUCAUSE
www.educause.edu/about

EDUCAUSE and its members contribute to thought leadership on major issues, help clarify the current environment, document effective practices, and highlight how emerging trends and technologies may influence the evolution of IT in higher education.

2. Develop a discipline around brainstorming and watching the institution's competitors

Brainstorming is a great way to generate lots of new ideas, quickly. For those who have experienced bad brainstorms, the term can sometimes elicit negative reactions. Brainstorming works best when you are focused on a specific outcome--such as in the example shared above, which started with our dean asking how we could get more students enrolled in our graduate program in forensic science. Brainstorming pioneer Alex Osborn[89] suggests that the best brainstorming outcomes happen when everyone involved has the opportunity to contribute freely, stating whatever comes to mind—and wildly. The more outrageous the ideas, the greater likelihood that you will generate breakthrough ideas. Brainstorming techniques pioneered by Osborn include:

- A moderator who also functions as a "policeman" for the session.
- A small group of six to ten people.
- Short sessions (no more than one hour).
- Rules for the brainstorming process.

The moderator acts as the official encourager, policing against improper behavior, and as the recorder of all ideas—on large sheets of paper or a whiteboard visible to the group. Words are written down as short phrases, exactly as given. Osborn's brainstorming rules include:

- No criticism of ideas—defer judgment on your ideas and others.
- Go for large numbers of ideas—the more the better.
- Stay focused on the topic.
- Build on each other's ideas—combining and using pieces of other ideas from the group is encouraged.
- Encourage wild and exaggerated ideas.

To get maximum value from brainstorming, it's important to take the time to edit the ideas list as soon after the session as possible—while the exchange is still fresh in mind. Unusable ideas or incomplete ideas are parked for future reference while a shorter list of ideas or combined ideas is moved forward for further vetting (see item 3 that follows). These techniques work even with a very small group, including just one person; although, the volume or create range of ideas is limited with a smaller group.

Sometimes the best, least expensive, fastest, and least risky way to develop a new program is to copy or improve upon a successful program that is offered by another institution. For example, when Bay Path decided to bring up a graduate program in genetic counseling, we looked carefully at the programs offered by other institutions in our region, examined the trend data on the profession, and (through an informal brainstorming session) identified two important things: First, we learned that telehealth is a big and growing employment market for genetic counselors. Second, we learned that no existing genetic counseling graduate degree significantly utilized technology in program delivery. Our decision to launch the first fully online graduate degree in genetic counseling leverages an important trend while preparing students to be successful in extending access to genetic counseling services 24/7.

Being intentional about "following the leader" when it comes to new program ideation may make some academic leaders uncomfortable. Indeed, given the demographic trends discussed in Chapter 1, the competition for many programs is already extremely tight. Adopting this discipline—of paying attention to what programs other institutions are launching and then considering how you might offer the same thing less expensively, or to a wider market using new technologies—provides mutual learning and benefit. By starting with a known program, you can save considerable time and money in the launch phase.

When considering whether to follow this approach, here are some things to keep in mind:

- When you are not one of the first to offer an existing program, it may be more difficult to scale for volume.

- This approach does not work as well when the new program idea depends upon proprietary technology, significant upfront capital investments, or the existence of stringent proprietary information protections.

- Market timing is everything—this approach works better with newer fields of study than with existing programs; it also works better if you are able to move fairly quickly in launching your adapted new program.

3. Take every opportunity possible to understand your constituents' learning needs—current and future

Some of our best new program ideas have come from what Brian Grazer has termed "curiosity conversations."[90] For example, the idea to launch a program in cybersecurity management originated several years ago when I was having a conversation with a soon-to-be graduate. A double major in legal studies and criminal justice, she told me she was going on for a graduate degree in cybersecurity at a neighboring institution. She also told me that she wished the program was offered online, but there were very few fully online programs in this field at the time. I proceeded to ask her a series of questions in order to better understand the connection between her undergraduate studies and this field about which I knew virtually nothing. By the end of our conversation, I had a "niggling" sense that this idea needed further investigation. Several months later, following a thorough feasibility study which confirmed the decision, Bay Path launched a fully online graduate program in cybersecurity management. Had I not taken the time to have this conversation and ask several deep questions, I would not have gotten to the point where my gut instinct kicked in signaling that there was something here to pay attention to.

In the business world, successful innovative companies are ruthlessly disciplined in their efforts to understand customer needs and experiences. In large organizations, it's not uncommon to find a division that is devoted entirely to customer satisfaction testing and assessment of target user needs and wants.

While in academic organizations, such a customer-centric focus may be met with uncertainty on the part of some academics who believe that the curriculum should be fully and entirely faculty driven, there are still easy things that one can do to more fully understand the actual experience of your students and how your programs are faring in the minds of important others such as those who influence students to choose your institution—easy things that can provide a steady flow of input for new idea generation include:

- **Staying close to your students—prospective, current, and graduates.** How often do you ask your students what they want/need that they are not getting from your institution? What do you know about students who are accepted at your institution and go elsewhere? Are they going elsewhere to study in areas where you do not offer programs? The National Student Clearinghouse[91] provides a wonderful means for tracking where your non-matriculated students in specific majors eventually enrolled. How often do you take the time to sit down and talk with your students? Do you conduct regular student satisfaction surveys and if so, do you analyze the results by specific programs? It is just as important to understand the positive experiences of your students as it is to understand the areas where they have complaints.

- **Staying close to those who hire and educate your students once they leave your institution.** How often do you seek input from the employers of your graduates or department faculty in graduate programs where your students enrolled? Bringing employers together occasionally—either virtually or on campus—is a great way to monitor how well your programs are up to date with employer needs; not to mention, it gives you a quick means to get industry intel that could generate new program ideas.

- **Staying close to your sales force—the admissions team, for instance.** Your campus admissions team serves as the front door to your institution, and your recruiters can be a valuable source of information for why students enroll or don't enroll in your programs. Your admissions team is also aware of which programs students are asking for that you currently do not offer—keeping track of these requests and reviewing the list on a regular basis can provide you with a sense about market demand for certain programs and feed new program ideas. Because admissions staff are typically out in the field, they are also a good source for finding out what programs are "hot" and which institutions are offering similar programs that may be more attractive in the market. The point here is to make your admissions team your partner in the new program idea generation process.

- **Staying close to those who supply you with your students—for example: high school teachers and guidance counselors, and community college faculty and transfer counselors.** Your student pipeline providers can also be a wonderful source of easy intel about how your institution and your programs are viewed by prospective students and faculty. Ask them what programs they see their students looking for and which institutions are they choosing to study particular fields? What trends are they seeing in student enrollment behavior?

However you collect this kind of information, it's important to keep a written record so that you can note trends that may develop over time. I have a colleague at another institution who keeps a market intel notebook. She has disciplined herself to jot down notes whenever she receives information that could have relevance for new program ideation. According to my colleague, her notebook has served as a valuable source for surfacing new program ideas at her institution.

4. Understand how this new program will fit within your existing portfolio of program offerings

Once you have a list of new program idea possibilities to work from, you can begin to evaluate each idea from a more practical standpoint. At Bay Path, we typically begin by considering new program ideas utilizing two factors:

- Fit with mission
- Market context

For example, start by considering how this new program will fit within your existing portfolio of programs by asking:

- Does it create a new market niche or segment?
- Is it an addition or extension of an existing program?
- Does this new program build upon or improve an existing program?
- Does this new program reposition an existing program?

With limited resources, it's critical to consider all opportunities in light of the mission. Specifically:

- What impact will this new program have on mission?
- Will this program limit or enhance our mission impact and in what way?
- What will happen if we do *not* do this?

"Mission creep" (i.e., diverting precious resources to efforts that detract from our mission) is just as important a concern as missing opportunities that will enable us to expand and strengthen the mission's impact. As a single-gender focused institution, the women's mission is always front of mind when we consider new opportunities even in areas where we will enroll women and men.

For example, when we developed the MFA in Creative Nonfiction Writing program, one of only a handful of programs of this type offered were fully online; we included several creative nonfiction forms that have particular appeal for women—stories of the spiritual journey, food and travel writing, health and wellness narratives, women's stories, narrative journalism, the personal essay, and the memoir. While discussions about mission tend to rely more heavily on intuition (the "art") and historical precedence at most institutions, bringing market data analysis (the "science") into consideration helped us identify a financially smart opportunity that is leveraging our mission in new and powerful ways.

A second key set of criteria for vetting a new program idea involves assessing whether we can develop a market niche in a specific area. For example:

- What is the market context?

- Do we have the capability to carve out a niche?

- Does this niche make sense for us and is it attainable?

- Do we have a built-in market?

Through the feasibility study, which is described in the next chapter, extensive information is gathered about the market context including a full competitive scan. For example, when we developed the American Women's College, we knew that a majority of adult learners were women. In developing this country's first fully online degree completion program for women only, we leveraged our built-in market and historic expertise in educating women through our One Day A Week Saturday Program for Adult Women and filled a niche by creating a convenient, affordable, women-centric means for adult women to get their college degree entirely online.

Quite honestly, many of our best new program ideas have emerged initially as a "gut instinct" (the art). But because the market niche questions are an important element in the feasibility study, we have a process (the science) in place to ensure that our gut instincts are well vetted and we avoid an overreliance on the "if we build it, they will come" trap.

Assessing the potential market niche for a new program underscores the importance of fully understanding the market strengths, limitations, and potential gaps for your existing program portfolio. Reviewing the market context on a regular basis for each of your programs—individually and collectively—is one of the most important things an academic leader can do. Because the market context is highly dynamic, understanding each program's relative position vis-à-vis the competition is especially critical.

I have found the Ansoff Matrix[92] to be a helpful visual tool for mapping existing and new program possibilities as well as for analyzing and planning for new program growth. Developed in 1957 by applied mathematician and business manager H. Igor Ansoff, this tool is still used by business organizations to analyze and plan their strategies for growth. The matrix shows four strategies that can be used to help a firm grow and also analyzes risk associated with each strategy. I have adapted the matrix in the diagram shown here to illustrate how the tool can be used for new program planning in an academic organization. By considering where a new program idea fits within the four groups shown here (i.e., market penetration, market development, program development, or program/market diversification), you can assess the potential risk of adding the program as well as consider less risky possibilities that might be readily available, such as making easy revisions to existing programs. The point here is that most colleges and universities have a wider range of options available for growing enrollments than they realize. Using a tool like the Ansoff Matrix helps broaden your thinking and possibilities.

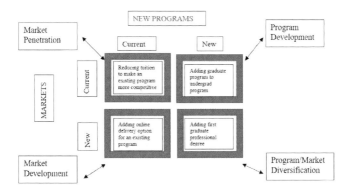

Here are definitions of each element:

Market Penetration

This strategy is concerned with increasing the market share of existing programs in their current markets. If the market and demand for a particular program is growing, it may be enough to simply maintain your share of enrollment. For example, by trying out new marketing and promotion strategies, decreasing tuition pricing, or acquiring a competitor, you may be able to attract new students. With programs that exist in saturated markets (e.g., the MBA in many geographic regions), this approach has its limits and may not be effective.

MARKET DEVELOPMENT

This approach involves seeking new markets for an existing program. This strategy works best when the demand for the specific program is strong and not tied directly to institutional brand or visibility. An example of this approach is expanding access of an existing program beyond your immediate geographic region by adding an online or hybrid delivery option.

PROGRAM DEVELOPMENT

This strategy involves developing new programs that cater to existing students. When an institution has notable strength in a core program area, as well as a clear and accurate understanding of its existing student markets, this approach can be highly effective. For example, by adding a new graduate program in an area where you have a strong undergraduate program, you can expand your market reach and grow overall enrollment.

DIVERSIFICATION

With this strategy you aim to grow enrollments by developing new programs in new market areas that are outside your existing program portfolio. This is the riskiest of the four strategies but may be a good choice if the program is in an emerging and/or growing field and the market is not saturated. An example of this is when a traditional liberal arts college brings up its first graduate degree in a professional area where it does not offer undergraduate programs.

5. Screen new program ideas to select the most viable

The final consideration has to do with those things that can contribute in subtle yet significant ways to the reasons why a new program fails to launch. In my experience, there are three factors that are most important to assess when evaluating the viability of new program ideas:

- Operational feasibility
- Strength and nature of internal support
- Potential for failure versus success

OPERATIONAL FEASIBILITY

Questions that help you assess whether you have the operational capacity to undertake a new program and do it well include:

- What does success look like?
- What will it take to be successful?
- How long will it take to be successful?
- What existing institutional assets might we draw upon to launch this effort?

For every new academic program we develop at Bay Path, our feasibility study includes a four year financial proforma that enables us to realistically address these questions. The proforma incorporates assumptions about enrollment, revenue, personnel, and operating expenses and allows us to understand what net profit margin is required for the program to be financially viable, within what time frame and at what cost.

Finding ways to tap into existing resources is an important consideration. For instance, because we have an extensive infrastructure in place to support online learning, we always ask whether a new program might be delivered online—knowing that the support costs are already built into the budget. The rigorous discipline we have established around new program development through the feasibility study and proforma process (the "science") has proven invaluable in understanding what it will truly take to successfully launch a new initiative.

INTERNAL SUPPORT

In considering new program possibilities, it's important to gauge the initial level of internal support as early in the process as possible. Key questions include:

- Do we have a champion(s) for this program?

- What role might this champion play in the development, launch, and maintenance of the program?

- What benefits and limitations are associated with this champion?

- Is anyone likely to resist this initiative, and if so, for what reasons?

Particularly in an academic environment, it is important to understand how a new program might fit within the political context of the institution. The success of our recently launched fully online master's degree in accounting is due in no small measure to the fact that the program was developed and launched by our chair of the undergraduate accounting program, an individual who has tremendous respect among her colleagues and extensive professional contacts and networks within our region.

Being disciplined in asking these key questions (the science) is one more way to ensure you are not missing something that could impact the success of the new program launch. At the same time, most provosts and deans who have been in the role for a while have a keen sixth sense (the art) about the political context and what internal factors might facilitate or doom a potential new program.

FAILURE POTENTIAL VS. OPPORTUNITY ASSESSMENT

A final consideration involves assessing the potential for failure against the potential for success. Questions that help you assess both the probability and impact of failure include:

- What might go wrong?

- How likely is it that this will happen?

- If this happens, what is the impact?

- How much failure can we tolerate and for how long?

At the same time, we try to assess the potential demand for the program as well as what broader opportunities this program might provide for the institution. While not a perfect science, having both aspects on the radar as we consider new program possibilities contributes to better decision making and reduces the potential for myopic thinking.

From my experience, both the art and the science are critical for ensuring financially sound, entrepreneurial growth. Having a rigorous process that draws on both allows you to avoid the opposite dangers of getting caught in "analysis paralysis" (always examining the data and never reaching a decision) or making avoidable errors because you are flying by the seat of your pants.

Such a discipline also helps you move from "dream it—> build it" to calculating what it will take to be successful. At the end of the day, dreaming and calculating do not need to be mutually exclusive pursuits. I believe that true entrepreneurial thinking, when applied in an academic context, can help institutions fully tap their mission-centric, innate potential. When art and science are applied in tandem, an entrepreneurial mindset can contribute to a deepened commitment to the educational mission of the institution.

What's Next

In this chapter, we considered five ways that you can generate and evaluate new program ideas. While good ideas can come from anywhere at any time, there are specific things that academic leaders can do to generate fresh thinking and ideas on demand. We also discussed the importance for academic leaders who want to drive growth to adopt an approach that balances the art with a rigorous and well supported process for identifying, evaluating, and operationalizing program ideas—this is the science part of academic entrepreneurship. In chapters 6-8, we will take a deeper dive into the science by providing a step-by-step process for bringing new academic programs to life.

KEY STRATEGIC QUESTIONS FOR ACADEMIC LEADERS

These questions are helpful to ask if you are looking to be more strategic about managing your academic program portfolio. In my experience, these are critical, first-step questions to help ensure you stay focused on those things that matter most to your institution's financial viability.

1. As you consider your approach to planning and management, how are you doing in balancing the art and science? Which aspect comes more naturally for you?

2. Do you have a good working knowledge about how much revenue each of your current programs contributes to the bottom line? Do you know which programs are the strongest contributors versus the least strong?

3. Have you done a program portfolio assessment to understand the relative strength and limitations of each program in terms of revenue contribution, mission alignment, and institutional reputation contribution?

4. To what extent do you understand what your students—prospective, current, and graduates—want from your institution? Do you have mechanisms in place for obtaining information from your students about their learning preferences and needs?

5. How do you ensure that your programs are relevant and meeting the needs of industry and graduate schools?

CHAPTER 6
THE SCIENCE OF BRINGING NEW PROGRAMS TO LIFE— THE FEASIBILITY CHECKLIST

Once you have generated and thoroughly vetted your idea for a new academic program, how do you implement and bring that idea to life? This is where things sometimes break down in academic organizations; the best ideas in the world can easily get swallowed up when the pressure to retain the status quo is fierce.

Management author and speaker Jim Collins suggests in *Great by Choice: Uncertainty, Chaos, and Luck—Why Some Thrive Despite Them All*[3] that organizational luck and success can be leveraged by cultivating a discipline around process and metrics. Indeed, he suggests that this discipline is key for maximizing whatever luck might naturally come one's way. A clearly articulated and transparent process can also go along ways toward breaking down the resistance one might encounter to new program ideas.

This has certainly been the case at Bay Path University where we have developed a rigorous process and template for evaluating the feasibility of new program ideas that we use across all divisions. This process has enabled us to remove some of the subjectivity that accompanies new academic program decision making, relying instead on a set of objective key elements and metrics that are applied equally to all new program possibilities. This process also ensures that the art for which we have no shortage is balanced by the science—a well-supported process for identifying, evaluating, and bringing good ideas to life.

A clearly articulated and consistently applied process provides a pathway for consideration and approval that ensures alignment with Bay Path University's governance process and evenness across divisions and programs—while allowing for agility and speed in enacting change that enhances our academic programs and student success. Such speed and agility do not come at the expense of constructive discourse within the governance structure. An essential element of the process is promoting and ensuring discussion and conversation about proposed changes within and among Bay Path's academic schools and divisions.

Overview of the Process

Our process begins with something called the "P Form." The P Form is required for all curricular modifications including, but not limited to: new courses; addition/elimination of courses; modifications to existing courses (including course number, title and/or descriptions); the discontinuation of courses; adding or discontinuing degree programs, majors, and minors/concentrations; and for changes to the student learning outcomes for a program/major. While curriculum change is often "batched" with multiple changes requested at the same time, separate P Forms are required for each change to preserve the historical record of curricular change at Bay Path and to promote clarity and transparency in the process.

Proposals for curricular change (P Forms) are classified within one of three approval categories: expedited review, non-expedited review, or new academic program approval. Because many current changes are of a minor nature (e.g., correcting errors, updating course titles, minor wording changes to course descriptions, etc.), an expedited review allows for quick consideration and changes, with opportunities for a more complete review if deemed necessary. Other changes, however, require more comprehensive reviews within the Bay Path governance structure, including feedback loops for discussion.

Proposals for new program approval require the most documentation and the most extensive review process; even still, the entire process—from beginning to end—can often be competed in less than one year. Required P Form components for new degree program proposals include:

- P Form Cover Sheet
- Feasibility Study
- Competitive Program Analysis
- Market Data Summary
- Curriculum Map
- Advising Sheet
- Proforma Budget

A sample P Form template for a new degree program is included in Appendix A. The diagram on the next page illustrates the process from beginning to end.

Some Critical Notes

A few things about how the process works that are important to keep in mind:

- **The process is premised on the belief that the curriculum is dynamic and responsive to internal and external needs**, consistent with the University's mission; a "one size fits all" approach to curriculum is unproductive and restrictive.

- **While anyone can serve as an originator for a new degree program** (including an individual faculty member, dean, provost or the president), typically, a new program comes up through an individual department and is approved first at the school level followed by the Senior Administration, Provost's Cabinet, full faculty, and finally the Board of Trustees. Regardless of who originates the P form, the life cycle and process are the same.

- **The process is iterative as illustrated by the two-way arrow on the right side of the diagram.** What this means is that a new program proposal can, and often does, go back and forth between these various stages as potential issues are identified and sent back to the originator for revisions. Because of the fluidity of the process, most issues are worked through before the proposal gets to the full faculty and/or Board of Trustees.

- **Registrar and Vice Provost review early in process is critical.** Having a technical review of the proposal early ensures that the program is doable from an administrative and infrastructure perspective. Frequently, changes will be recommended at this stage to strengthen or clarify proposal content. If the program will carry external accreditation or licensing of any kind, this early review also ensures that demands associated with these agencies are factored in to decision making.

- **Early senior administrative review allows for the integration of the new program and its needs into the institutional planning and budgeting process**. For example, if the School of Education, Health, and Human Sciences brings forward a proposal to start a doctorate in physical therapy (DPT), the capital needs will be significant and should be factored into long-range facility planning, among other things.

- **Because there is NO university-wide curriculum committee, new program proposals are vetted very deeply at the School level where the curricular expertise typically resides**. Not only does this allow for a quicker timeframe for decision making but also ensures that program proposal does not get off track or unnecessarily watered down in order to gain the approval of faculty in other areas.

- **When launching a program that is entirely new to the university, and campus expertise does not exist, a consultant will typically be hired**. The consultant works with the dean of the school where the program will reside in developing a feasibility study and completing and submitting the P form.

- **All new program proposals must be approved by both the Finance and Academic Committees of the Board prior to being reviewed by the full Board.** Having the Finance Committee of the Board review on the front end ensures support at the highest level of the institution as well as confirmation of the financial feasibility for the new program. Typically, both committees and the full board review and vote on the proposal at the same meeting.

- **An Implementation Team** comprised of the key players who will need to support the program implementation is convened shortly after approval by the Board of Trustees. This team typically includes the academic program director, dean, and representatives from the registrar's office, admissions, and marketing among others. This team confirms the timeline and oversees the launch of the new program.

The 10 Elements of the Feasibility Checklist

In the remainder of this chapter, I will review the checklist elements which comprise the feasibility study which accompanies the P Form for new program proposals. Specifically:

1. History and context of program, and its fit with culture.
2. Relationship to institutional mission.
3. Program rationale and market niche.

4. Student demand and target market.
5. Program description and structure.
6. Staffing, structure, and other necessary resource requirements.
7. Instructional delivery and schedule.
8. Student recruitment, advising, and learning support.
9. Student and program evaluation and assessment.
10. Implementation timeline.

In Chapter 7, we will review the financial resource requirements that must be addressed as a part of the feasibility study. Finally, in Chapter 8, strategies for operationalizing and sustaining new programs will be reviewed.

1. History and context of program and fit with culture

There are three important questions that are important to address in this first section:

- What is the history of the discipline represented by this program?

- How does this historical context shape the culture of the discipline?

- Will this program contribute positively to the institution's culture and if so, in what ways?

See the following sample, from the Master of Fine Arts in Creative Nonfiction Writing new program proposal.

Providing a historical context is especially useful for those reviewers who are not familiar with the discipline associated with the program. As is the case here, the history can also be useful for making a connection to the institution's history, culture, and mission—something that can strengthen the case for the program.

PROPOSED NEW PROGRAM FEASIBILITY STUDY

Master of Fine Arts in Creative Nonfiction Writing
Bay Path University

History, Context, and Cultural Fit

The history of creative writing in the academy is a story of two booms, both in the nineties: the 1890s and the 1990s. The 1890s saw a massive boom in publishing, and by 1900, the New York Times estimated there were more than 20,000 professional writers in the United States. The invention of the cylindrical press made possible the mass circulation of inexpensive books, newspapers, and periodicals, significantly raising the literacy rate among Americans and providing increased publishing opportunities for a new generation of creative writers. For example, in 1885, there were only four magazines in the United States with a circulation of over 100,000 each. The combined circulation of these magazines was a mere 600,000. In 1905, twenty general magazines had a circulation over 100,000, with a total circulation of 5.5 million. That nearly 1,000% increase in the circulation of the nation's top magazines in just a 20-year period meant more work for graduates with strong writing skills. Likewise, the fact that smaller magazines boomed during the same period (e.g., from just 1885 to 1890, 1,000 new periodicals were founded) meant more paying markets for young creative writers. Newspapers increased in size and number, and paperback books flourished as well, ensuring that creative writing would become a respected profession and legitimate academic discipline.

Proposed New Program Feasibility Study

The second creative writing boom, most properly identified as a 1990s phenomenon, coincided with the Internet boom and its then-nascent online publishing surge. The MFA in creative writing came of age during this period, with an increase in the number of academic programs from 28 in 1989 to more than 130 in 2010. A slowing economy contributed to the growing popularity of such programs. Many whose job seemed in jeopardy, or whose employment completely evaporated, returned to school, often choosing a program in creative writing. Others, believing that they had always had a story to tell and a book to write, chose the same option. For nonfiction writers, the subgenre of the memoir blossomed and provided the impetus for prospective students to tell their stories to a growing and interested audience.

Historically, women's colleges were among the few institutions of higher learning to give preferential treatment to creative writing instruction. In the early 1900s, a higher percentage of women's colleges offered creative writing workshops than men's colleges. In *A History of Professional Writing Instruction in American Colleges*, Katherine Adams gives the example of Newcomb College, a women's college in New Orleans that began offering creative writing courses in 1908. Meanwhile, its affiliated men's university, Tulane, took 31 more years to offer its first creative writing course. This trend is still evident today, albeit in different terms: Women apply to MFAs at a higher rate than men, are admitted at a higher rate, get more post-MFA fellowships, and (once in the post-MFA job market) perform better than men in terms of getting hired full-time. Burgeoning research suggests women also publish more regularly than men (as would be expected, given the foregoing data) in small-to-midsize literary magazines, as writer Seth Abramson noted last year in a blog entry titled, "The Suburban Ecstasies."

> **PROPOSED NEW PROGRAM FEASIBILITY STUDY**
>
> As a pioneer in innovative graduate academic programs for both men and women, Bay Path College seeks to empower its students as both lifelong learners and leaders. The innovative, professional, life-changing dynamics of the no-residency MFA in Creative Nonfiction Writing fit perfectly within these Bay Path College priorities. Just as other Bay Path College programs are designed to bend to the shape of students' lives, the no-residency MFA in Creative Nonfiction Writing enables busy adults to pursue their passion for creative writing without putting their lives on hold.

ANALYSIS

In this example of a section from the Bay Path University proposal to add the MFA in Creative Nonfiction Writing, attention is given to making the case for how this program fits the institutional mission. As illustrated here, there is a strong connection between the historical context out of which MFA degrees emerged and the historical mission of women's colleges. When bringing forward new programs that represent a departure from the commonly held understanding about the institution's educational mission (Bay Path's mission has long been understood to be professional and career focused), this kind of table setting verbiage can be helpful for gaining the necessary support.

2. Relationship to institutional mission

With limited resources, it's essential to consider how a new program might relate to the mission as well as extend or leverage the mission in new ways. Mission creep (i.e. diverting precious resources to efforts that detract from our mission) is as important a concern as missing opportunities that will enable you to expand and strengthen the impact of your mission. Here are key questions to ask as you assess the fit of any potential new program with your institution's mission:

- How does this new program reflect and further leverage the current mission's emphasis or elements?

- How might this program advance our strategic priorities?

- How does this new program relate to or further leverage existing offerings?

- How might this program fit with the culture of our institution?

- If we pursue this, how will other programs be impacted?

It's important to keep in mind that new programs can extend the mission in new and important ways. For example, even though we did not offer an undergraduate program in English or writing per se, we believed that the MFA in Creative Nonfiction Writing would leverage the women's mission of Bay Path because of the program's unique curricular design. See the following sample of this section of the feasibility study.

PROPOSED NEW PROGRAM FEASIBILITY STUDY

Master of Fine Arts in Creative Nonfiction Writing
Bay Path University

Mission

Bay Path College's mission as The New American Women's College for the Twenty-first Century ensures the uniqueness and importance of its no-residency Master of Fine Arts in Creative Nonfiction Writing. Women's colleges have been, and continue to be, remarkably generative environments for such programs. At Bay Path College, the issues of women and men who have not yet discovered their creative voices will serve as the foremost themes of writing projects. The design of these programmatic themes embraces significant innovation. Such innovation not only builds technological, analytical, oral, and written communications skills but also leads to the exploration of and the empowerment of self. This journey of empowerment is at the heart of and delineates the uniqueness of the Bay Path College no-residency Master of Fine Arts in Creative Nonfiction Writing. The program primarily seeks to involve its students in finding their creative voices through expressive nonfiction on the topics of their choice, or on tracks including women's stories, travel, and the stories of nourishment through food and spiritual awareness. As such, the Bay Path College no-residency Master of Fine Arts in Creative Nonfiction Writing becomes the unique aesthetic means by which its students can discover the intimate treasures of the human spirit.

ANALYSIS

Just as it's important to connect your new program to your institution's historical context, it's equally essential to explain how this program will enhance your mission. All regional accrediting bodies ask for documentation of missional connection when reviewing new program approvals. As illustrated here, the MFA is uniquely designed to leverage the institution's women-serving mission in compelling ways through its attention to women's ways of writing.

3. Program rationale and market niche

Addressing the "Why?" may be the single most important question to get right when considering the merits of a new program possibility.

- Why should we do this?

- What is most compelling about this possibility?

- Why does this program deserve to exist on our campus?

- What market niche will it fill and for whom?

- What evidence can we find of a need and/or a gap in the market for this program?

- Who else offers something like this?

- Might this be a signature program for us?

Answering these questions requires digging deep to understand the potential market context for your new program. At minimum, it's important to gather data about the competition and to understand how your program might best be differentiated from existing programs. See Appendix B at end of this chapter for a competitor scan template that you can use to get started.

It is also important to understand the industry outlook for graduates of this proposed program. Questions to ask here include:

- What is the occupational outlook for graduates in this field of study?
- What types of jobs will graduates be qualified for upon graduation?
- What is the demand for graduates in this field in our region? Nationwide? Internationally?

We use a variety of sources for getting industry outlook and competitor market data. Three of my favorites include:

The Bureau of Labor Statistics Occupation and Industry Projections

www.careeronestop.org/toolkit/careers/careers.aspx

This free website allows you to create a customized report for any of nearly 900 occupations, including national and state data on wages; employment; knowledge, skills, and abilities (KSAs); education and training; and links to more resources. While this source is a bit dated (one year or more), it's a good starting point for assessing market demand for new programs. Based on our initial scan of this website, we decided to launch the M.S. in Genetic Counseling. As shown (see the following page) in a screen shot from the website, the projected growth rate for genetic counselors is strong.

OCCUPATIONAL OUTLOOK HANDBOOK

Home ▼ | Subjects ▼ | Data Tools ▼ | Publications ▼ | Economic Releases ▼ | Students ▼ | Beta ▼

OOH HOME | OCCUPATION FINDER | OOH FAQ | OOH GLOSSARY | A-Z INDEX | OOH SITE MAP | EN ESPAÑOL

Occupational Outlook Handbook >

Occupation Finder

Search: Use the drop-down menu in one or more columns to narrow your search.
Sort: Use the arrows at the top of each column to sort alphabetically or numerically.

Show 25 entries

Showing 1 to 15 of 15 entries (filtered from 818 total entries)

OCCUPATION	ENTRY-LEVEL EDUCATION	ON-THE-JOB TRAINING	PROJECTED NUMBER OF NEW JOBS	PROJECTED GROWTH RATE	2017 MEDIAN PAY
	Master's degree			Much faster than av	
Computer and information research scientists	Master's degree	None	5,000 to 9,999	Much faster than average	$75,000 or more
Genetic counselors	Master's degree	None	0 to 999	Much faster than average	$75,000 or more
Healthcare social workers	Master's degree	Internship/residency	10,000 to 49,999	Much faster than average	$35,000 to $54,999
Marriage and family therapists	Master's degree	Internship/residency	5,000 to 9,999	Much faster than average	$35,000 to $54,999
Mathematicians	Master's degree	None	0 to 999	Much faster than average	$75,000 or more
Mental health and substance abuse social workers	Master's degree	Internship/residency	10,000 to 49,999	Much faster than average	$35,000 to $54,999
Mental health counselors	Master's degree	Internship/residency	10,000 to 49,999	Much faster than average	The annual wage is not available.
Nurse anesthetists	Master's degree	None	5,000 to 9,999	Much faster than average	$75,000 or more

Gray's Program Evaluation System (PES)

www.grayassociates.com

This annual subscription service helps you assess student demand, employment, competition, and strategic fit by program. The PES includes current data on such things as qualified inquiries, Google search volumes for the largest 200 academic programs, all Title IV completions, geo-enhanced, BLS jobs, wages, and employment projections, current Job Postings from Burning Glass Technologies, and job placement rates. With this data, you can score and rank programs on such things as student inquiry volume and growth, jobs, job growth and wages, competitors' size and growth by program, degree level, and market saturation.

CEB Talent Neuron

www.gartner.com/en/human-resources/talentneuron

TalentNeuron is an online market intelligence subscription portal with real-time labor insights, including: custom role analytics, dashboards, and presentations. Available data include information on key roles by location, occupation, and skill set as well as information about hiring and which skills and roles are in demand. When developing the curriculum for a new program, this is an excellent source for reviewing outcomes against what skills and knowledge employers are looking for in particular fields.

For every new program recommendation, the feasibility study requires a program competitor analysis. See the sample from a Bay Path proposal for a new Master of Fine Arts in Creative Nonfiction Writing program on the following pages.

College	Degree Title	Curricular Emphasis	Tuition and Fees	Credit Requirements
Vermont College of Fine Arts Montpelier, Vermont	MFA Creative Writing	Creative Nonfiction, Fiction, Poetry	$37,852. 4-semester total. ($8783 per semester. $680 per semester residency fee.)	64 credits
Bennington College (Bennington, Vermont)	MFA Creative Writing	Poetry, Fiction, Creative Nonfiction	$36,337. ($17,580 annual tuition. $1,175 one-time graduation and enrollment fees.)	64 credits
Lesley University (Cambridge Mass)	MFA Creative Writing	Fiction, Nonfiction, Poetry, Writing for Stage and Screen, Writing for Young People	$34,284. ($7,140 per semester tuition. $350 per semester residency fee.)	48 credits

Mode of Delivery	Program Distinctiveness	Geographic Market	Enrollment
Four, 10-day residencies	Dual and Cross Genre Study. "Non-hierarchical learning environment."	New England	20
Four, 10-day residencies	Each student works with at least four outstanding writers in genre of choice. Motto, "Make yours a writing life."	New England	18
Four, 9-day residencies	Emphasis on interdisciplinary study across genre lines.	New England/Boston metro	25

Analysis

This section of the MFA Feasibility Study presents comparison data on those programs offered elsewhere that are considered to be important competitors for the new program. This chart only contains a few of the institutions from the competitive scan and are included here to illustrate the elements for which data are collected on each program as part of the feasibility study. It's particularly important to consider total pricing, program length, delivery, and curricular features and distinctiveness. In reviewing these data for other MFA programs, we identified important gaps including that there was no fully online MFA program with our intended curricular focus, and there was no MFA program in the country that focused on women's unique ways of writing. Our program was then designed to fill these gaps and create a market niche for the new program.

PROPOSED NEW PROGRAM FEASIBILITY STUDY

Master of Fine Arts in Creative Nonfiction Writing
Bay Path University

Program Rationale and Market Niche

A void exits in Western Massachusetts for a different type of Master of Fine Arts in Creative Nonfiction Writing. There is no low-residency MFA program west of Pine Manor College, south of Bennington College, north of Western Connecticut State, or east of Bard College. Only one other no-residency creative writing program exists in the country, at the University of Texas at El Paso, and this program concentrates on poetry and fiction. Albertus Magnus College in New Haven, CT., touts its MFA as no-residency, yet it requires students to come to the campus three Saturdays per semester (a dozen visits throughout a course of study); thus, travel and any lodging expenses remain a reality for both students, faculty, and staff, and the college still must physically host twelve days of study. Western Massachusetts, known for its fine academic options and as the home of a large creative population, has yet to tap into this innovative and increasingly-sought-after learning model.

Mount Holyoke once held a vibrant and well-known writers' conference and remains the site of the annual conference held by the local chapter of the National Writers Union. The University of Massachusetts holds the Juniper Institute, a nationally recognized annual writing conference. Amherst and Smith are well known for their literary histories and faculties, including stellar visitors. The Eric Carle Museum in Amherst has just paired with Simmons College to offer an MFA in Writing for Children, an MA in Children's Literature, and an MFA/MA in Children's Literature. But none of these local academic institutions have incorporated a program of low- or no-residency MFA. On this side of the Mount Holyoke Range, choices for the study of creative writing are fewer and farther between.

Proposed New Program Feasibility Study

Appendix A provides comparative programmatic data for those colleges and universities in the eastern United States that offer low- and no-residency graduate creative writing degrees. The data contrasts curricular emphases, credit requirements and costs, mode of educational delivery, and program distinctiveness. It makes clear the need for a graduate creative writing nonfiction program that is laser focused on a single genre that presents the greatest number of career opportunities. This genre is creative nonfiction, which, because of its roots in the real world of human experience and its applicability to current popular publishing trends, will provide graduates with a truly relevant educational experience. The data in Appendix A also delineates how Bay Path's women's mission will attract the largest subset of potential applicants (mature women) who wish to hone and market their writing talents. Finally, among the colleges in the eastern region of this country offering similar programs, Bay Path will occupy a position toward the lower end of the total cost for completion range. Given the program's unique curricular and structural focus, in tandem with the competitive pricing, and given the success of our niche-focused graduate programs (in business administration; communications and information management; higher education administration; nonprofit management and philanthropy), there is every reason to believe that Bay Path College will occupy a strong position within the MFA in Creative Non-Fiction Writing market.

Analysis

Above, you can see sample content for the Program Rationale and Market Niche element of the Feasibility Study. This narrative explains the results of our competitor scan analysis (discussed above) and documents the rationale for the program from a market perspective. As illustrated here, the narrative provides important context for the market data; the narrative connects the dots for the reader between the data and the program's purpose, something that is a critical to gaining support for your new program.

4. Student demand and target market

In considering a new program possibility, it's important to develop a clear sense of who the program will serve. Such information can be gleaned through the competitive analysis you conduct with existing programs—or through focus group or survey research that you conduct with prospective students. For example, when we were considering launching our M.S. in Nonprofit Management degree, we convened a focus group with nonprofit leaders in the region to gain their input on the program.

- Who do you envision as your typical student? What demographics do they represent? What level of educational preparation will they need to be successful in this program?

- Why might someone be motivated to enroll in this program? What career, educational, or personal goals might he or she have that this program will help meet?

- What would compel a typical student to choose this program over one offered elsewhere?

- If this is a graduate program, are there existing undergraduate programs that will serve as a pipeline for this program? If so, what would these undergraduates be looking for in a graduate program? Might it be possible to structurally connect this new program to the undergraduate feeder program (e.g., as a 3+2 or 4+1 program)?

PROPOSED NEW PROGRAM FEASIBILITY STUDY

Master of Fine Arts in Creative Nonfiction Writing
Bay Path University

Student Demand/Target Market

The target market for the program is comprised of any college graduate whose writing potential is of high caliber and who seeks to bring that promise to another level while earning a master's degree. The three most common reasons potential students apply to graduate programs in creative writing, including low-residency models, are a desire to improve their writing, to be part of a community of writers, and/or to earn a degree that will enable them to teach. Often, all three reasons come into play. Perhaps the most paramount of these reasons has been the first – to improve – but in recent economic times, more and more potential students are seeking teaching as a second career and view the low-residency model as a practical means by which to earn the necessary advanced degree. There is interest in programs that offer residencies reduced beyond the typical two per year, as evidenced by Albertus Magnus' "residencies" of three Saturdays per semester, but a true no-residency program can draw from international student (and faculty) pools. Also, the Bay Path program will include courses on teaching writing. In most programs, teaching is observed in a workshop or seminar, rather than having that work explained, dissected, and practiced regularly.

Proposed New Program Feasibility Study

Potential students are those motivated by any of the above factors of bettering writing, joining a community, and preparing for a teaching career. The no-residency format will attract additional applicants who lack the time or funds to devote two years to exclusively attending a traditional program, or up to 22 days a year to attend a low-residency one.

Too few writers graduate from MFA programs with experience in or knowledge of publishing. This program will offer a two-course track on the process of getting published. The first course, "Introduction to Publishing," will demystify the journey through examination of the steps necessary to generate agent/editor interest; the structure of the publishing industry (including the burgeoning virtual publishing world); the roles played by agent, editor, publicist, sales representatives, and other key figures; and the all-important work an author can do after publication to give his or her book the best chances for commercial success. The second course, "Working in the Industry," will provide first-hand experience in the publishing world, via a semester-long internship at a publishing house, an independent bookstore, in an editor's office or at a literary agency; after which, a detailed paper on the experience must be written. While not every student might see publication as the ultimate goal, it can be an attractive means by which a writer can support herself and thus adding to the program's competitiveness.

A second two-course track that will make the program appealing is "Teaching Creative Writing." According to the Association of Writers & Writing Programs, between 1975 and 2010 the number of undergraduate and graduate writing programs increased more than tenfold, from 79 to 852. This explosion created thousands of teaching positions for writers. Bay Path writing graduates will be trained to fill these positions, and, as such, the marketability of the program will be augmented.

> **PROPOSED NEW PROGRAM FEASIBILITY STUDY**
>
> The no-residency MFA program will offer "Learning to Teach," a course focusing on the pedagogy and practice of teaching creative writing, and "Teaching to Learn," an actual teaching practicum.

ANALYSIS

Above, you can see sample content for the Student Demand and Target Market element of the Feasibility Study. With this element, it is critical that the narrative paint a picture of the typical student(s) who is likely to enroll in this new program and why. Further, the narrative should connect the dots between students' aspirations and motivations for enrolling in this program and the curricular design and focus. Without this information in hand, you will be shooting in the dark when you go to develop your student recruitment and marketing plans.

5. Program description and structure

Asking new program originators to prepare a detailed description about the program ensures an important reality check before the proposal gets too far along in the process. By answering the following questions early on, the viability of the proposed program is very apparent to the program developers and enhancements can be made to strengthen the proposal.

- What is the educational philosophy that underpins this program?

- What are the program outcomes?
- What is the curriculum, and how does it connect to the outcomes?
- How does the curriculum and its outcomes align to emerging occupational trends and potential job knowledge, skills, and abilities?
- Are there external accreditation or licensure requirements, and if so, what are they? Does the curriculum adhere to these requirements?
- Are there existing faculty who are qualified to teach this curriculum?
- Does the curriculum align to existing curricula in other programs? If so, does the program take advantage of these curricular synergies?
- What makes this curriculum distinctive?

For this section of the feasibility study, proposals must include program and student learning outcomes, degree requirements including number of credits, course descriptions and sequencing (if appropriate), and a curriculum outcomes map which illustrates the relationship between each course and the program outcomes. A template for a curriculum outcomes map can be found in Appendix C at the end of this chapter.

By using a resource such as TalentNeuron (discussed earlier in this chapter) you can ensure that the curriculum and its outcomes are relevant and responsive to real-time industry demands for essential skills and knowledge. Doing so gives you a powerful marketing message to highlight in program promotion.

It's important to take the time to consider any new program in light of existing offerings. Many times, synergies can be found that will make it possible to launch new programs with less expense. For example, when we were considering the curriculum for a master's degree in genetic counseling, we integrated several courses from our existing graduate program in clinical mental health counseling, saving course and staffing expense while also using the "borrowed" coursework to create a distinctive emphasis for the new program. Finding ways to differentiate the curriculum while the program is still in development helps strengthen the potential for success.

PROPOSED NEW PROGRAM FEASIBILITY STUDY

Master of Fine Arts in Creative Nonfiction Writing
Bay Path University

Program Description and Structure

The Bay Path MFA in Creative Nonfiction Writing program is a 39-credit hour program which can be completed in two years. Upon completion of the program, students will demonstrate significantly enhanced nonfiction writing skills and possess an understanding of the publishing industry well enough to make writing part or all of their careers. As such, the Bay Path no-residency Master of Fine Arts in Creative Nonfiction Writing will include, but not necessarily be limited to, the following student learning outcomes:

- Develop and hone skills in writing, editing, and revision in creative nonfiction.

- Recognize and write on the subject of the student's choosing, or along the program tracks of women's stories, travel and food, and spiritual nourishment.

- Demonstrate knowledge of the history of nonfiction and how the student's own work fits within that literary tradition.

Proposed New Program Feasibility Study

- Analyze and write with care about literary texts of considerable difficulty.

- Recognize critical positions and literary arguments, including the student's own critical and aesthetic position.

- Demonstrate the ability to read and respond thoughtfully and critically to work by other MFA students.

- Demonstrate knowledge of how to effectively perform in the online classroom setting.

- Demonstrate understanding of the theory and practice of literary publishing, including the practice of submitting work to literary journals and/or publishing houses.

- Demonstrate knowledge of the genres of creative nonfiction writing from the perspective of a teacher.

- Produce a creative writing teaching lesson and unit plan.

- Write a 150-page thesis of publishable quality.

Students in this program benefit from a curriculum built with their goals in mind: to focus on their own writing while gaining extraordinary insight into the theory and history of the genre; to work closely alongside published and esteemed writers; and, perhaps most importantly, to gain teaching and publishing experience that will serve as a foundation for a career as a working writer, teacher, editor, or publisher.

An essential element of the curriculum is the three-semester mentorship seminar and lab through which students are paired with published mentors and small groups of peers for writing practice and critique. Content courses will be taught each semester in an electronic classroom environment.

PROPOSED NEW PROGRAM FEASIBILITY STUDY

Through online courses, video conferencing, talks and panels, recorded lectures, mentor/mentee communications, and extensive writing and reading assignments, the basics and complexities of creative nonfiction will be studied. Well known authors will be scheduled for periodic online "chats" in both the mentorship seminars and content courses. Finally, students will have the opportunity to travel internationally with other students and faculty on a creative writing field seminar to generate creative work in new settings.

NO-RESIDENCY MASTER OF FINE ARTS IN CREATIVE WRITING REQUIRED COURSES: 39 CREDITS

MFA 600, 601,602	Mentorship Seminars I, II, III	6 credits
MFA 603, 604, 605	Mentorship Labs I, II, III	3 credits
MFA 625, 630	Creative Nonfiction Writing I and II: Form and Theory	6 credits
MFA 620, 621, 622, 623, 624	Craft and Reflection Workshops (must take 3)	6 credits
MFA 690, 691	Thesis I and II	6 credits
MFA 670, 675, 680, 685	Professional Track in Teaching or Publishing	6 credits
MFA 640, 644, 610	Electives	6 credits

COURSE DESCRIPTION

The Foundational Courses
MFA 600 Mentorship Seminar I

This course represents the first step in the program-long process of working toward the major project (i.e., the student's 150-page thesis). This online writing delivery system allows students, under the direction their faculty mentor, to accomplish collaborative work through the medium of the Bay Path College online educational delivery system.

ANALYSIS

As illustrated in this sample content, Bay Path's MFA program includes a highly individualized online writing mentorship lab in addition to an annual field seminar in Dingle, Ireland, both of which have proven to be popular curricular innovations. Providing this level of detail about the program structure, delivery, and curricular content is essential for estimating the full range of resources that will be required to support and sustain this program. For example, the mentorship seminars (which are organized in small groups of 5-6 students with one faculty mentor) are highly personalized and expensive to deliver as compared to the traditional classroom. While important for the program's coherence and quality, this feature required many adjustments with the financial assumptions in order to make the program financially viable.

6. Staffing, structure, and other necessary resource requirements

This sixth element addresses the question about what it will take to launch and sustain the program. At Bay Path, we tend to start small in resourcing new programs, holding off on "permanent" resource investments until the program demonstrates minimum viability. All new program proposals require a four-year financial proforma that incorporates the following key resource considerations:

- How will the program be staffed? How many faculty or staff will be required? What are the qualifications and what minimum level of compensation will be required? How easy will it be to hire for this program? Are there existing faculty or staff who can support this program?

- What physical space will this program require? How much and what type of space is needed? When, where, and how will the curriculum be delivered, and what does this mean for physical space needs?

- What equipment and technology are needed?

- What library and other learning resources are required and how will they be delivered?

- What will it cost to successfully market and recruit for the program?

- Are there resources already in place that could be tapped in support of this program?

- What demands will this program place on the institutional infrastructure that will impact the institution's budget?

- If this program carries external accreditation or licensing, what required support must be included in the financial projections for this program, now and going forward? Will these externally imposed requirements constrain the institution in ways that might impact its financial viability? The following sample table from the MFA feasibility study illustrates the kinds of resources that must be considered.

Resources	Costs/ Amounts
Library and Digital Resources	Additional library resources costing approx.-imately $8,000 are needed during first year of program. See proforma for specific anticipated library resource expenses in subsequent years. Given the online nature of the program, digital resources will be purchased and built into the courses in FY 2014 & 2015.
Marketing	New marketing dollars will need to be allocated for the launch and ongoing marketing of this program. Because of the significant online component, it's recommended that a microsite, similar to what was created for online degree completion program, be created and maintained. Preliminary annual marketing spending for this program is estimated at $50,000.
Program Budget	A budget for the Program Director will need to be developed and resourced. The parameters of this budget are prescribed by the proforma and include such expense items memberships, events, meetings, and travel.
Technology	Use of campus infrastructure, which includes computers and Wi-Fi. Instructional design services will be purchased in FY 2014 and 2015 in order to build out the courses. Program will need support from Center for Online Learning.
Program Administration	The currently vacant English faculty position will be used to create a program director position. This position is already in the budget. Given the year-round structure of the program, the program director will be hired on an 11-month contract. A part-time assistant director position will be created to assist with student advising and to oversee the teaching track.

Faculty	With the exception of courses taught by Program Director and Assistant Director, all courses are taught by adjunct faculty. MFA 600,601,602 pay rate is $5,000 per section. MFA 603,604,605 pay rate is $1000 per student. Pay rate for all other adjunct faculty-taught courses is $3,000 per course (for 3-credit courses) and $2,500 (for 2-credit courses). See proforma for more detail.
Facilities	Since the program will be delivered entirely online, no classroom space is needed. An office is needed for the program director and assistant director.
Accreditation Requirements	This program does not carry any external accreditation.

ANALYSIS

This section of the Feasibility Study illustrates the categories where we typically estimate the expenses that will be incurred in launching and running the program. The narrative that is provided for each is useful context for understanding key assumptions. For example, the narrative details about faculty staffing are useful for calculating the staffing expenses that are included in the financial proforma. Estimating marketing expenses can be tricky as it's difficult to know exactly how difficult the marketing context will be until the program is launched and you can see how the market responds. As a general rule of thumb, we estimate higher marketing expenses for a program that is delivered online in order to support the higher costs of digital marketing. We typically estimate anywhere from $50,000-$75,000 in marketing expenses (excluding staffing) to support an online program launch and $50,000 annually thereafter to support ongoing marketing efforts.

7. Instructional delivery and schedule

With every new program, it's critical to consider how the curriculum will be structured and delivered and what the ideal geographic market might be for the program. This is where the Ansoff Matrix discussed in Chapter 5 and competitive scanning of programs offered elsewhere can be valuable. Important questions to ask include:

- How will this program be delivered and why?

- What is the intended geographic market(s) for this program? Based on what you have learned about this market(s) and its learning preferences what is the ideal program delivery?

- What is the course length and why?

- If the program is designed to align with existing curricula, will your plans for delivery and scheduling support this?

- Do your plans for delivery and scheduling provide a competitive market advantage for this program? If so, in what way?

This last point is a particularly important one to consider. One of the least risky ways to launch a new program is to bring up something that is doing well at other institutions in your region and for which you can confirm strong market demand using a different mode of delivery or scheduling. This was certainly the case for the MFA program as well as for the Master of Science in Genetic Counseling. In the case of the latter, our decision to launch an entirely online graduate program in this burgeoning field opened up a large market and provided us with a compelling competitive advantage. Three years in, prospective students continue to report that the fully online delivery is the primary reason why they applied to the Bay Path program.

8. Student recruitment, advising, and learning support

Likewise, it's important to consider the processes, requirements, and support needed for recruiting and retaining the students who will study in your new program. Nearly all regional accrediting agencies have specific standards that pertain to these concerns. Critical questions to consider can be grouped into three categories:

STUDENT RECRUITMENT AND ADMISSIONS

- What are the requirements for admittance into the program?

- Are these requirements in keeping with expectations for program rigor and student achievement?

- Are your admittance requirements and decision-making processes in keeping with federal laws?

- Who will make admittance decisions and what is the process?

- How will you publicize your admittance policies and processes?

- Will you allow for transfer credit from other institutions? If so, have you created a written policy?

- Who will recruit students for this program and what methods will be used?

- Has a student recruitment plan been developed?

STUDENT ADVISING AND LEARNING SUPPORT

- How will students in the program be advised?

- Have you created student advising resources such as planning guides?

- Have you created a student handbook for this program that outlines policies and helpful information that is specific to the students in this program?

- How will students register for classes?

- What will happen to students who encounter academic difficulty? What support will you provide?

- Have you created policies regarding student academic progress? If so, do these policies align with financial aid policies and guidelines?

INSTRUCTIONAL METHODS AND SUPPORT

- What instructional methods will be used in the program?

- How will faculty be prepared to use these methods to support student learning?

- What instructional support is needed to support student success?

- How will this instructional support be made available to students?

- Might your instructional methods provide a competitive advantage for your new program?

An often-overlooked opportunity is instructional methodology. You can sometimes create a unique market niche for your program by simply structuring the teaching and learning process in a distinctive way. Case in point: When we converted our adult women's "Saturday-One-Day-a-Week" on campus program to online, we developed a one-of-a-kind instructional methodology called SOUL which stands for *Social Online Universal Learning*.[94] Based on our research about what adult women need to be successful in the classroom and complete their degrees, we created a learning approach that pairs highly innovative learning analytics with personalized instruction and support services. Key features of this model, which was selected in 2014 as a FIPSE "First-in-the-World" grant recipient, are shown here:

- **SOUL Connect (EXT097)** – This important on-boarding program helps each new TAWC student get oriented in the program and strategize with her Educator Coach to prepare for the academic journey ahead.

- **Accelerated Pace** – SOUL facilitates immediate interventions and critical supports whenever a student begins to struggle so she can complete her courses despite their accelerated pace.

- **SOUL KP (KnowledgePath)** – The SOUL KnowledgePath customizes instruction to the unique needs of each student by suggesting learning modalities that are most likely to help her in that subject. Available modalities include text, videos, audio clips, and interactive exercises.

- **Wrap-around Support** – Each student is partnered with a dedicated Educator Coach. If a student begins to struggle, SOUL's learning analytics and predictive models alert the Educator Coach who then can reach out to the student with specialized support before she falls behind.

- **SOUL Communities** – SOUL provides students with virtual learning communities to engage and network with other TAWC students who share their goals and professional interests. Program directors and faculty members facilitate these online interactions, so students typically learn about professional associations, read articles on topics in their chosen fields, join practice-based discussions, and explore relevant job postings.

- **SOUL Connect for Educators** – Through this program, our faculty learn how to use analytics to inform both their class instruction and student support.

9. Student and program evaluation and assessment

As with the previous element, regional accrediting agencies typically have stringent expectations that must be addressed in regard to student and program evaluation and assessment. Important questions to consider for both include:

STUDENT EVALUATION AND ASSESSMENT

- How will student learning be evaluated?
- What direct assessment methods will be used?
- What indirect methods will be used?
- How will this program document student learning and achievement?
- Will letter grades be used to evaluate student learning? If so, what grading system and criteria will be used?
- How will this program utilize student learning evaluation data to improve the program?

PROGRAM EVALUATION

- What methods will be used to evaluate this program and the achievement of program outcomes?

- How will this program gain ongoing external input on program success?

- How will this program utilize program evaluation data for improvement?

PROPOSED NEW PROGRAM FEASIBILITY STUDY

Master of Fine Arts in Creative Nonfiction Writing
Bay Path University

Student Evaluation and Assessment

The evaluation of student work and progress will be conducted by the faculty responsible for the individual courses. Such evaluation will be completed in a variety of formats appropriate to the course and topics, including: papers, group work, projects, and presentations. The thesis projects will serve as an omnibus evaluation for the program because of its integrative nature.

A comprehensive assessment plan will be developed by the Program Director and reviewed by the Bay Path Assessment Committee prior to the launch of the program. Assessment of learning outcomes will be accomplished via direct and indirect means. Direct assessment is based on an analysis of how students performed, achieved, or behaved in demonstrating how they met the learning outcomes of the program. Indirect assessment is based upon an analysis of reports about student behavior by third parties, such as employers, regarding how well students have met the learning outcomes.

Direct Methods of Assessment

Assessment of student's work in individual classes will be accomplished by the faculty in those classes. Assessment will be built into the individual course syllabi. Individual course syllabi will have outcomes that are linked to and in some cases coincidental with the program outcomes above. Program objectives will be assessed primarily through the capstone experience and the three signature assessments that will be built into the program at three specific points, near the beginning, midway, and capstone. These will be assessed via such tools as:

Student work

Student work is the most widely used method of direct assessment at the course level. Assignments flow from the course learning outcomes, which align directly with the program learning outcomes. Bloom's Taxonomy is used to measure student grasp of concepts and higher order thinking skills as they progress through the program. Faculty members evaluate student learning on each assignment. Students in the program will be evaluated on their ability to demonstrate knowledge as well as their ability to apply their knowledge and concepts to practical writing applications. In addition:

- Students will regularly work with professors one-on-one during the online courses involving intensive focused discussion regarding theme, content, and form, along with analysis of the work on the micro-editing level. Such work will catalyze students' ability to create strong work. Students will frequently hand in two or three drafts, and sometimes more, before a piece is considered finished.

- Students will develop and then write a nonfiction thesis. With the mentor's guidance over the course of two semesters, the student will bring the thesis through multiple drafts, repeatedly drawing out and critiquing the project for refinement in form and language. To hone aesthetic sense and skill, students will read ancillary works and produce an aesthetic statement of purpose.

Proposed New Program Feasibility Study

- In nonfiction writing elective courses, students will read a wide range of contemporary nonfiction and its antecedents, analyzing the work from a writer's perspective. The students' ability to evaluate and contextualize the literary selections will be assessed during online discussion and by review and critique of written assignments.

- Eportfolios will also be used as a tool for direct assessment. Such tools are also particularly useful regarding student recruitment, development, retention, and eventual career placement.

Grade Distribution Analyses

Creative writing is a subjective and relative process, as is the evaluation of creative writing. As is the case for most MFA in Creative Writing programs, this program does not assign letter grades or group rankings. Course work is assigned a passing or failing grade. There is also a low pass option for exceptional circumstances.

Faculty submit a grade for the semester's work at the end of each semester. Grades for semester projects are based on the quality of the writing and on whether the student has completed all required assignments according to the semester plan. A faculty member who decides to fail a student must submit reasons to the Director in writing. Since students work very closely with their mentors throughout the semester and receive midterm updates assessing the quality of their work to that point, the final grade should yield no surprises. The meanings of the three grades are as follows:

Pass: The student and the writing have satisfactorily met graduate-level standards.

Low Pass: The student will be placed on academic probation for the next semester.

Proposed New Program Feasibility Study

Fail: The student has not met program standards and will not be re-enrolled. A student may appeal the failing grade by submitting to the Director a portfolio of work with an explanatory cover letter. The Director will review this material and make a recommendation in consultation with the Faculty Advisory Board. Students who have failed are permitted to re-apply. The faculty mentor will also submit a written evaluation of the student's work, including the enhancement project and creative thesis, at the end of each semester.

This evaluation is of the greatest importance in acknowledging and delineating the student's growth as a writer. In judging the quality of the writing, the faculty mentor will consider whether the writing is at graduate level using the following criteria:

Evidence that the writer has not just reported what happened but has transformed experience and observations into art. Indicators of that transformation include:

- Fresh phrasing, concrete, specific, precise, and vibrant language.

- Well-crafted sentences.

- Work has fresh insights that could not have been learned without reading the piece.

- Evidence that the essay has a deeper concern than its apparent subject.

- Writer shows skill with pacing and orchestration of details to achieve certain effects.

Indirect Methods of Assessment

This assessment will typically be done with third parties who are able to observe the performance of our students and thereby make a judgment regarding how well they have mastered the material in the program. Indirect evaluative processes will include analysis of reports and interviews given by publishing or educational employers regarding how Bay Path College graduates have met the learning outcomes among other things.

Course Evaluation Surveys

These surveys consist of numerous questions and are completed at the end of the course by students. These survey data provide a subjective sense of whether the student feels he or she has learned the subject matter and explores in greater detail subjects related to instructional effectiveness. The surveys, over time, will measure correlation between student satisfaction and technology and faculty effectiveness, as well as the self-perception that students have attained knowledge.

Faculty Course Evaluations

Each term, faculty members could complete an evaluation of their course. They could respond to course content, student ability, and perception of their own teaching ability in the course. Data from these evaluations would be evaluated along with student evaluations of the course to inform decisions related to faculty development and training, course enhancement, course sequencing, and the like.

Exit Surveys

Exit surveys are an indirect measure of learning outcomes. These surveys corroborate assessment results from other methods indicating that students take what they learn in the program and apply it to enhance their lives personally and professionally.

PROPOSED NEW PROGRAM FEASIBILITY STUDY

Program Review

The new Director will convene a Program Advisory Council to consist of creative nonfiction writers, including several who represent the major tracks the program: women's stories, travel writing, and nourishment through food and spirituality. Ideally, this board will number approximately ten members and will meet via the Internet on a regular basis to provide information, assistance, and advice to the Director on such matters as:

- Program advocacy
- Marketing and student recruitment
- Resources development
- Employment trends
- Placement, internships, and contact with the profession
- Participation in the program review process

A formal review of the no-residency Master of Fine Arts in Creative Writing will be built into the third year of operation. By this point the program will have produced one graduating class and will have had two full years of operations to evaluate and consider for continual improvement. Assuming that the initial courses are offered in Fall 2014, the program review will begin in September 2016, or as soon thereafter as deemed practical by the Program Director, Dean, and Provost.

This review will be comprehensive, dealing with all aspects of program design, delivery, admissions, marketing, assessment, student satisfaction, placement, and alignment with employment trends.

> **PROPOSED NEW PROGRAM FEASIBILITY STUDY**
>
> The review will involve a written self-study addressing these issues with supporting data and documentation. The self-study will be reviewed internally and externally by a group of experts. The Program Review Report with recommendations and commendations will be due no later than May 1, 2017.

ANALYSIS

The sample content shown above illustrates how the Bay Path MFA documented its plans for student and program evaluation and assessment. All regional accrediting bodies now require a great deal of detail about your assessment plans with an emphasis on making sure you are utilizing direct assessment and external review to the greatest extent possible. They also will want to see that you have established mechanisms for incorporating the feedback you receive to improve your program going forward. You will note that the example here specifies our plans for direct assessment and external program review and outlines how this information will be utilized for ongoing program improvement.

10. Implementation timeline

The final element involves mapping out the steps required for implementation of the new program. If specialized accreditation or licensing is to be obtained, the requirements and timeline for doing so should be incorporated into the master timeline. If start-up funding is going to be required to launch this program, it's critical to have a full and realistic understanding about the timeline and any potential issues that might delay the program's launch. For example, when we launch programs that carry specialized accreditation such as for occupational therapy, we need to carefully coordinate the approval process timeline for four different parts of the approval process: the internal institutional timeline, the Massachusetts Board of Higher Education (MBHE), NECHE (our regional accreditor), and ACOTE (the accrediting agency for occupational therapy programs). The process for these other entities is not always clear and straightforward. For instance, for both NECHE and the MBHE we may sometimes be able to seek an expedited review or bypass the process altogether depending upon the structure and level of the new program being proposed.

With specialized accrediting agencies it's also important to understand the sequencing of the approval process timeline with the other approvals being obtained. For example, some specialized accreditors will require that all other approvals be obtained before submitting your application while others may allow you to apply at the same time or even before you have these other approvals in hand. The important thing here is to make sure you fully understand what approvals are required on the front end and incorporate all processes and timelines into your implementation plan. This is why we require an up-front review of the program by a senior academic affairs staff member designated to stay on top of accreditation and licensing matters across the University.

Depending upon what approvals are required, you will also want to map out other steps including marketing and recruitment, staff and faculty recruitment and hiring, course development, and other process steps as appropriate.

Sample Implementation Process and Design Template

The Implementation Process and Timeline Template shown below includes the full range of process steps that are typically required by my institution when obtaining approval for a new program. This template can easily be adapted to meet the unique needs of an institution according to its specific regulatory and internal approval processes.

Page 2 of this template includes several questions that are important to ask for every external regulatory approval that you must obtain. This information will significantly impact your overall timeline and needs to be considered at the outset of your process when you are making important assumptions, such as program expenses (need to capture all accreditation related expenses, new and ongoing), estimated program launch (if you are off by even a few months, this can greatly influence your financial results), and the overall timeline (if you must obtain multiple external approvals, it's important to understand timing details and coordinate appropriately).

Bay Path University Implementation Process and Timeline	
Action Item	**Date Completed**
P Form and Feasibility Study Completed	
Sponsoring School Approval Obtained	
Registrar Review Completed	
Vice Provost Review Completed	
Senior Administration Approval Obtained	
Provost Cabinet Approval Obtained	

Faculty Assembly Approval Obtained	
Board of Trustees Approval Obtained	
Specialized Accreditation Approval Obtained (Note: Delineate the Required Steps and Timeline Below)	
Massachusetts Board of Higher Education (MBHE) Approval Obtained (Note: Delineate the Required Steps and Timeline Below)	
NECHE Approval Obtained (Note: Delineate the Required Steps and Timeline Below)	
Marketing and Promotion Plan Developed and Launched	
Student Recruitment Process Launched	
Program Budget Finalized and Approved By CFO	
Program Director Hired or Appointed	
Faculty Hired or Assigned	
Student Handbook Created	
Facility Needs Finalized	
Technology Needs Finalized	
Library and Other Learning Materials Obtained	
Curriculum Developed and Finalized	
Program Assessment Plan Completed and Submitted to Assessment Committee	
Course Syllabi Developed and Approved by Program Director	
Courses Built in Learning Management System (LMS)	
First Cohort Enrolls	

Implementation Process and Timeline—Page 2

Specialized Accreditation Approval:

Does this program require specialized accreditation?

Yes | No

If yes, what is the name of the accrediting agency?

What steps are required to obtain this accreditation? (Provide as much detail as possible.)

What fees (upfront and ongoing) are required for this accreditation?

Is a site visit required?

Yes | No

If yes, when does the site visit take place?

What approvals must be in place before submitting the application for accreditation?

What documentation is required for the accreditation application?

Massachusetts Board of Higher Education (MBHE) Approval

Does this program require approval by the Massachusetts BHE*?

Yes | *No*

If yes, does this program qualify for the expedited review process*?

Yes | *No*

What fees are required for MBHE approval of this program?

Explain:

NECHE Approval

Does this program require approval by NECHE*?

Yes | *No*

Explain:

Have you accounted for the required accreditation fees in the program's proforma?

Yes | *No*

*If unsure about the answer, consult with the Vice Provost.

What's Next

When developing and launching new academic programs, it's impossible to capture *all* variables on the front end. Until the program is up and running, you never truly know how the market will respond and what this will mean for your program's viability. However, having a discipline around new program development ensures that we consider as many as possible "what if's" on the front end, while maintaining a culture of flexibility and market responsiveness once the program is launched. In the next chapter, we will review one additional very important feasibility study component: the proforma. Most new programs succeed or fail based on their capacity to attract sufficient numbers of students and to generate sufficient financial resources. While there may be exceptions (such as, a program that is so mission-centric that the institution maintains it regardless of enrollment), the vast majority of programs need to meet some kind of bottom-line expectation. This is increasingly true in the current environment. Making clear, realistic, and well-supported financial assumptions about any new program is a critically important priority. In Chapter 7, we will review helpful principles and assumptions for ensuring that your new program financial plans are sound.

> **KEY STRATEGIC QUESTIONS FOR ACADEMIC LEADERS**
>
> These questions are helpful to consider with other colleagues in your institution, particularly your CFO and president. Having a disciplined approach that ensures that new programs are sufficiently integrated into your broader planning and budgeted processes as early as possible, will require the full support of both individuals. These questions will help ensure you are on the same page and that your program development efforts receive the level of institutional attention they need to be successful.
>
> 1. How would you evaluate your institution's ability to successfully launch new academic programs? What improvements are needed?
>
> 2. To what extent does your institution follow a disciplined approach to new academic program planning?
>
> 3. Where does new program planning typically get bogged down on your campus? What might you do about this?
>
> 4. Is your new program planning process integrated with the institution's strategic planning and budgeting process?
>
> 5. How and at what point are your CFO and president involved in the new program planning process? Is this workable for you and for them?
>
> 6. How do you ensure the full participation and support of your board in the new program planning process?
>
> 7. Are there any elements that you would add to the feasibility study presented in this chapter?

Appendix A: Template for a New Program Feasibility Study

The following is the template for the new program feasibility study form that must be completed at Bay Path in order to get the approval process moving. This form includes all the elements discussed in Chapter 6. This form is available electronically at my institution and can be electronically completed and submitted.

BAY PATH UNIVERSITY

New Program Proposal | Executive Summary

Degree Title:

Level of Degree:

Delivery:

Number of Credits:

Cost of Degree:

Launch Date:

Calendar:

Description:

Include summary information about the degree program, including student learning outcomes, required resources, budget, and approvals.

ACADEMIC ENTREPRENEURSHIP

FEASIBILITY STUDY FOR CONSIDERATION OF [ENTER NAME OF DEGREE] [ADD DATE]

Table of Contents

Proposed Program Degree and Title
Overview
History and Context of [Enter Name of Field/Discipline]
Mission of Bay Path University
Program Rationale and Market Niche
Student Demand and Target Market
Program Description and Structure
Staffing
Instructional Content
    Calendar – [Enter Short Title of Desired Calendar]
Program Schedule and Advising Sheets
    Curriculum Map and Course Descriptions
        Foundational Core Courses
        Elective Track(s)
            Track #1 – [Enter Name]
Students
    Student Admissions
    Student Learning
    Method of Instruction
    Student Advising
Student Evaluation and Assessment
    Student Work
        Class Participation
        Methods of Evaluation and Grading
Program Evaluation
    Course Evaluation Surveys
    Faculty Course Evaluations
    Exit Surveys

Employer Surveys
　　Mid-program Satisfaction Survey
　　Graduate Survey
Program Review
Required Resources
Program Budget
Tuition
Next Steps

Appendix A. Programs That Offer [Enter Degree Name] in [Enter Geographic Area of Interest]
Appendix B. Advising Sheet
Appendix C. Curriculum Map
Appendix D. Gray Associates Data: [Enter Geographic Ares Included]
Appendix E. Colleges and Universities that Offer the [Enter Degree Name]
Appendix F. Workforce Data for [Enter Degree Name]
Appendix G. Proforma Budget

Proposed New Program Feasibility Study
[Enter Name of Degree]

Proposed Program Degree and Title:
[Enter Degree Name]

Overview:

- *Description of the new program.*
- *How many credits?*
- *Residency requirements?*
- *Program objectives?*
- *Delivery of the program?*
- *Calendar the program will run on?*

History and Context of the Field:

- *What is the traditional history of these types of programs?*
- *How does that fit with Bay Path University's culture?*

Mission of Bay Path University:

- *How does this program meet and serve the Bay Path University mission?*
- *How does the program connect with/respond to the priorities of the current or next Vision plan?*

Program Rationale and Market Niche:

- *Provide evidence of a need and gap in the market for this program.*

- *What is the occupational outlook for graduates in this field of study? (Gray Associates data)*
- *What types of jobs will graduates be qualified for upon graduation?*
- *What is the demand for graduates in this field in Massachusetts/Connecticut and other New England states? What were the results of the Gray Associates analysis? What does it mean for the attractiveness and competitiveness of the program? Add the screen shots of the Gray Associates data for each market as an image.*
- *What other colleges or universities offer a program like the one proposed? Include a comparison table as an appendix (with the Microsoft Excel table inserted as an image).*

College/ University Name		
Degree Title		
Curricular Emphasis		
Tuition and Fees		
Credits Required		
Mode of Delivery		
Program Distinctiveness		

- *How will Bay Path be distinguished in the marketplace by the new offering? Why will students choose Bay Path over other programs? Depth and substance are needed here. It must be more than the advantage of a low tuition model.*

Student Demand/Target Market:

- *Describe the typical student who will be served by this program.*
- *Why are they looking for this type of program?*
- *How will it assist students in reaching their goals?*
- *Where are the potential target markets for recruitment?*
- *For graduate programs, are there Bay Path feeder programs that could be structured as a 3+2 or 4+1? How will take program be structured?*

Program Description and Structure:

- *Description including program student learning outcomes*
- *Course sequence*
- *Course descriptions*
- *Include curriculum map as an Appendix (refer to in text)*

Staffing and Structure:

- *Faculty (full-time and/or adjunct) needs and expertise requirements*
- *Support staff needs*

Instructional Content:

- *Which of the following calendars will be used?*

- ○ *Traditional Semester Calendar (15 weeks, August to May)*
- ○ *Graduate Full-Term Calendar with Summer*
  Fall semester: August to December
  Spring semester: January to May
  Summer semester: May to June/July
- ○ *Graduate Full-Term Calendar without Summer*
  Fall semester: August to December
  Spring semester: January to May
- ○ *Graduate Accelerated Calendar*
  Fall Session 1: October to December
  Fall Session 2: January to February
  Spring Session 1: February to April
  Spring Session 2: April to June
  Summer Session 1: June to August
  Summer Session 2: August to October
- ○ *Other (please provide details and rationale)*

- *Will the program utilize 50% of courses currently offered from no more than three other programs at Bay Path? If yes, which ones? Why were they selected?*
- *What is the course schedule (by semester)?*
- *What courses are included? Include name, proposed number and course description. Please also identify whether the course is new or existing. An example is below:*

DNP 515 (3 credits): Healthcare Informatics – NEW

This course focuses on the collection, organization, analysis, and dissemination of information in nursing and health care. Students explore nursing informatics, the information system life-cycle, telemedicine, and the use of technology to enhance nursing care delivery and patient safety. Students learn how to design, use, and manipulate large and small patient databases for the analysis of patient outcomes.

- *Describe any concentrations or tracks within the degree program, including course sequence and required courses.*

Students

- *Student Admissions*
  - *What are the admissions requirements?*
  - *Special requirements for transfer credits?*
- *Student Learning*
  - *Does Bay Path have experience in delivery degree programs in this way so that students are set up for success?*
- *Methods of Instruction*
  - *What methods of instruction will be used?*
- *Student Advising*
  - *How will students in the program be advised?*

Student Evaluation and Assessment – *Standard language available*

- Student work
  - *How will student work be evaluated? Discuss the assessment plan and the use of direct assessment methods as the primary tool, with indirect assessment of student learning used sparingly.*

Program Evaluation – *Standard language available*

- *How will the program be evaluated? Please include language about student course evaluations and faculty course evaluations. Additional topics to address may include the following:*
    - *Exit Surveys*
    - *Employer Surveys*
    - *Mid/End Program Satisfaction Surveys*
    - *Graduate Survey (in addition to the Graduating Student Survey)*

Program Review – *Standard language available*

- *In the absence of specialized accreditation, what will the approach be to include external viewpoints in a program review process?*

Required Resources

- *Include a table that lists the required resources and their projected costs. A sample follows:*

Resources	Costs/ Amounts
Library and Digital Resources	Additional library resources will be needed, especially during the first year of the program. See proforma for specific anticipated library resource expenses. Given the online nature of the program, digital resources will be purchased and built into the courses in FY 2018 and 2019.

Marketing	New marketing dollars will need to be allocated for the launch and ongoing marketing of this program. Because of the significant online component, it's recommended that a microsite be developed similar to what is available for other online graduate programs.
Program Budget	A budget for the program director will need to be developed and resourced. The parameters of this budget are prescribed by the proforma and include such expense items as memberships, events, meetings, and travel.
Technology	Use of campus infrastructure, which includes computers and Wi-Fi, will be required.
Program Administration	Given the year-round structure of the program, the program director will be hired on a 12- month contract. The program director will have an office in the Ryan Center.
Faculty	Most courses will be taught by the program director and two full-time faculty members. Courses not taught by full-time faculty will be taught by adjunct faculty. The pay rate for adjunct faculty-taught courses is $3,000 per 3-credit course.

Tuition:

- *What is the proposed tuition for the program? How does it compare to that of other institutions offering similar programs?*

Timeline for Implementation

- In narrative form, describe the steps required for the implementation of the proposed program.

Specialized Accreditation

- *Is there specialized accreditation associated with this program? If so, explain the process in detail, including timeline and fees.*

Program Budget:

- *Describe the proforma, including the number of students in each cohort, projected revenue and expenses. Include a summary table like the one the follows:*

Item	FY18	FY19	FY20	FY21
Net Revenue				
Net Expenses				
Net Surplus (Deficit)				

Next Steps:

- *Include a table of actions and target dates, like the following sample. The specific steps will be determined by the review process required by the Board of Higher Education, NEASC, and specialized accrediting body.*

Action Item	Date
Program concept design developed and vetted	
Approval by [Name of School/Division], Provost's Cabinet, and Faculty Assembly	
Board of Trustees approval	
Massachusetts Board of Higher Education (BHE) Expedited Review Process initiated	
Massachusetts BHE approval expected	
[Specialized Accreditation Body] submission	
Marketing and student recruitment campaign launched	
NEASC Substantive Change request submitted	
Program Director hired	
First cohort enrolled	
[Specialized Accreditation Body] site visit	

Appendix B

The following is the template that accompanies the feasibility study and includes all the competitor data discussed in Chapter 6 that we consider in determining the program's market niche and tuition pricing. This data is typically gathered internally either by the Dean's office responsible for the program or by the consultant or faculty member who has been tasked with completion of the Feasibility Study. The Gray's Associates PES is used to gather some of this information in addition to scanning websites and direct calls to the institution's admissions office.

Competitor Profiles for [ENTER NAME OF DEGREE]

1. Provide one chart for each market: Longmeadow, Concord, New England, Mid-Atlantic, National

Market	Institution	Campus	Sector (Public / Private)	Award Level (Bachelor's, Master's, Doctorate)	CIP Code (XX.XXXX)	Tuition (Specify by credit, semester or flat rate)	Delivery (Distance or Campus)	Total Number of Credits Required	Calendar (Semester/ Quarter)	Program Distinguishing Features	Enrollment

Appendix C

The following is the template that accompanies the feasibility study and is used to map the program's student learning outcomes with each curricular component in the program, including every course. This information is extremely useful when seeking external accrediting approvals, as it addresses questions about how the curriculum aligns with outcomes and how student learning will be achieved in concrete ways.

[Program Name]

Program Curriculum Map

Successful graduates from this program will be able to......

Student Learning Outcomes → Courses ↓						

Curriculum Map Key: Place a letter in the appropriate box where the program goal is Introduced, Reinforced, and/or Mastered.
- **I** = Introduced; program student learning goal is introduced
- **R** = Reinforced; provide practice opportunities for the program student learning goal.
- **M** = Mastered; demonstrated mastery of the program student learning goal.

Some courses may have two letters (I/R or R/M) or all three (I/R/M).

***Foundation Course:** A course that provides base skills needed to be successful in the program (please use an X on the map). *Not all programs will have or require foundation courses.*

CHAPTER 7
FINANCIAL MODELING AND BUDGETING FOR NEW PROGRAMS

In the previous chapter, we discussed the importance of cultivating a discipline around process and metrics to new academic program development and success. Gaining a clear and accurate sense as to what it will take to launch and sustain your new program before you enroll your first student is a critical prerequisite and a helpful exercise for surfacing and testing important assumptions.

At Bay Path University, all new academic program proposals must include a **four-year financial proforma**, which is typically developed jointly by the dean, the chief financial officer, and the provost. Through this process, we invariably surface financial assumptions, strategies, and program operational plans or outcomes that, when checked more thoroughly, prove to be unworkable or in need of revision. For example, in developing a new graduate program a few years ago we discovered that our "creative" approach to structuring the curriculum was not financially viable without some major tweaking.

The financial proforma serves many useful purposes—the most important of which is estimating the program's net financial contribution and impact. If sufficiently robust, the proforma enables you to think systematically about what will be required (both short- and long-term) to ensure the program's success. The proforma also helps you think through upfront variables like pricing and marketing expenses to consider how much risk you are willing to assume for factors that are often outside of your control due to the competitive context in which your program resides.

At my institution, an important financial principle undergirding all new graduate program development is this:

At a minimum, a new program needs to be able to support itself while also contributing resources back to the institution. Specifically:

- By "support itself," we mean that the program's revenue contributions must offset and ideally outpace the expenses required for operation.

- The extent of net contribution expected by a new program and the timeline for meeting financial projections is determined by considering the program's importance to the institutional mission and the institution's projected long-term financial equilibrium.

For example, we may be willing to assume a greater upfront resource investment and a longer break-even timeline for a program that will contribute significantly over time. Or, we may be willing to consider a more modest and perhaps even a "break-even" net contribution for a program that contributes to our mission in a significant way. Obviously, you must also consider the contribution of each program against the whole to ensure a balance that enables the institution to maintain its financial equilibrium.

A second important principle for new program proformas involves the timeframe for your financial projections. From my experience, a minimum of three years is necessary for capturing the full range of variables that may potentially impact the program's financial potential.

In developing a financial proforma for a new academic program, there are four primary components that are included in the template that we use:

1. Enrollment and Pricing Assumptions
2. Revenue Projections and Assumptions
3. Expense Assumptions
4. Bottom Line Result Projections

I describe each component below, using data to illustrate what comprises each component.

1. Enrollment and Pricing Assumptions

Tuition pricing, as in the per credit rate (see Chart A), for individual programs is informed by the competitor analysis that we complete as part of the feasibility study.

CHART A

Enrollment and Pricing Assumptions	FY 2017	FY 2018	FY 2019	FY2020
Per Credit Rate	$795	$815	$840	$865
Total Credit Hours	210	528	714	750
Full Time Equivalent	7	18	24	25
Head Count New Only	18	20	25	25

Specifically, we research the primary competitors within the geographic reach of the program's market, taking into account discounts, scholarships, and other pricing differences by program. We also consider the difficulty of entering the market and the extent of competition. Our initial tuition price point typically reflects our best thinking about the minimum tuition price needed to obtain a breakeven position for the program as quickly as possible.

For example, when we launched the MFA in Creative Nonfiction and the M.S. in Genetic Counseling, we set the initial tuition pricing near the bottom of the range for our closest competitors albeit for different reasons. For the MFA program, we considered that the typical student would be financially challenged and without access to tuition reimbursement benefits. Moreover, we assumed a lower lifetime earning potential for the graduates of this program. We also chose a lower initial price point for the M.S. in Genetic Counseling but did so because we were entering a market where the competition included schools with strong brand reputation and programs that were well established. On the following four pages, see examples for these two programs.

Bay Path University MFA Tuition Pricing Competitive Scan

College	Title	Curricular Emphasis
Note: This chart is a sub-set of a larger scan which was conducted		
Vermont College of Fine Arts (Montpelier, Vermont	MFA Creative Writing	Creative Nonfiction, Fiction, Poetry
Bennington College (Bennington, Vermont)	MFA Creative Writing	Poetry, Fiction, Creative Nonfiction
Lesley University (Cambridge, Massachusetts)	MFA Creative Writing	Fiction, Nonfiction, Poetry, Writing for Stage and Screen, Writing for Young People
Goddard College (Plainfield, Vermont)	MFA Creative Writing	Fiction, Nonfiction, Playwriting, Graphic Novel, Poetry, Screenwriting and Young Adult Fiction
Bay Path University (Longmeadow, Massachusetts)	MFA Creative Nonfiction Writing	Creative Nonfiction
Pine Manor College (Chestnut Hill, Massachusetts)	MFA Creative Writing	Fiction, Creative Nonfiction, Poetry, Writing for Children and Young Adults

Bay Path University MFA Tuition Pricing Competitive Scan

Tuition and Fees	Credit Requirements	Mode of Delivery
with 15 institutions offering creative nonfiction MFA degrees.		
$37,852. 4-semester total. ($8,783 per semester. $680 per semester residency fee.)	64 credits	Four, 10- day residencies
$36,337. ($17,580) annual tuition. ($1,175 one-time graduation and enrollment fees.)	64 credits	Four, 10- day residencies
$34,284. ($7,140) per semester tuition. ($350 per semester residency fee.)	48 credits	Four, 9-day residencies
$36,184. ($8,235) per semester tuition. ($787 Room, Board, technology/semester)	48 credits	Four, 8-day residencies
$27,787 (total). Optional charge for the elective Ireland seminar trip. No fees.	39 credits	Entirely online, no residencies
$26,700. ($6,000) per semester tuition. $425 fees per semester	60 credits	Four, 10- day residencies.

Bay Path University MS Genetic Counseling
Tuition Pricing Competitive Scan

College	Title	Accreditation Year--ACGC
Note: This chart is a sub-set of a larger scan which was conducted with 20		
Boston University School of Medicine (Boston Metro)	Masters in Genetic Counseling Training Program	2022
Brandeis University (Waltham, MA)	Master of Science Program in Genetic Counseling	2016
Long Island University- CW Post (Brookville, NY)	Clinical Genetics Program	2019
Mt. Sinai School of Medicine (NYC Metro)	Master of Science Program in Genetic Counseling	2016
Sarah Lawrence College (Bronxville, NY)	Joan H. Marks Graduate Program in Human Genetics	2017
Bay Path University (Longmeadow, MA)	Master of Science Program in Genetic Counseling	2018

ACADEMIC ENTREPRENEURSHIP

Bay Path University MS Genetic Counseling
Tuition Pricing Competitive Scan

College	Title	Accreditation Year--ACGC
Note: This chart is a sub-set of a larger scan which was conducted with 20		
Boston University School of Medicine (Boston Metro)	Masters in Genetic Counseling Training Program	2022
Brandeis University (Waltham, MA)	Master of Science Program in Genetic Counseling	2016
Long Island University- CW Post (Brookville, NY)	Clinical Genetics Program	2019
Mt. Sinai School of Medicine (NYC Metro)	Master of Science Program in Genetic Counseling	2016
Sarah Lawrence College (Bronxville, NY)	Joan H. Marks Graduate Program in Human Genetics	2017
Bay Path University (Longmeadow, MA)	Master of Science Program in Genetic Counseling	2018

Getting it right with the program's pricing is tricky and sometimes, no matter how much good competitor research you do, the initial price point does not generate the enrollment you need. Additionally, the markets for most programs tend to be highly dynamic—compelling initial price point can quickly become an enrollment barrier. This is why it's important to schedule an annual review of your program after launch with a particular eye on the market context and to be willing to adjust your pricing as needed to remain competitive. This is an especially critical exercise to conduct when considering whether to increase the tuition from year to year and at what percentage increase. For the purpose of the proforma, we typically estimate an annual tuition increase of 3% knowing that this assumption will be reviewed annually and most likely adjusted.

Here are some key questions to ask when setting the pricing for a new program:

- Who is likely to be our key competitors and what are they charging for their programs (be sure to include tuition, fees, and the cost for all other required program components as well as scholarships offered by your competitors)?

- How competitive is the market for this program (this is where the Grays Evaluation PES system data discussed in Chapter 6 can be very helpful; it gives you inquiry totals for programs by CIP code).

- Will we be able to offer scholarships or discount the sticker price?

- Is this a program area for which we will need to compete on price?

- How hard will it be to gain a foothold in the market for this program? Do we need to use pricing to do so?

- Who is the typical student who will enroll in this program and what kind of financial resources are they likely to have? Will they have access to tuition reimbursement or are they likely to be self-supporting?

- How much of an annual tuition increase do we think this program can sustain?

Total credit hours is a calculation that sums the total credits projected to be taken by each student in a given year. Chart B illustrates the template that we use to project student enrollment per term and the total student credit hours for years one and two of the proforma. The total student credit hours estimated is obtained by multiplying the number of credits for each course by the projected head count enrollment and then summing the totals for all terms. Note that the credit hours are projected for the duration of the program, meaning that you will need to estimate an average retention rate for students. In the example shown here, and based on retention performance in other similar graduate programs, we estimated that 90% of the students who start the program in a given year will graduate within 2.5 years.

CHART B

Semester and Year	Course Number	Credits	Projected New Enrollment	Projected Returning Enrollment
FY 2016 - 2017	(assumes tuition rate of $795/credit)			
Session 1 (Oct)	600	3	18	
	630	3	0	
Session 2	605	3	18	
	635	3		
Session 3	610	3	17	
	640	3		
Session 4	615	3	17	
	645	3		
Total FY17				
FY 2017 - 2018	(assumes tuition rate of $815/credit)			
Session 5 Jul/Aug	620	3	17	
	650	3		
Session 6 Aug/Oct	625	3	17	
	670	3		
Session 1	600	3	20	
	630	3		16
Session 2	605	3	20	
	635	3		16
Session 3	610	3	19	
	640	3		16
Session 4	615	3	19	
	645	3		16
Total FY18				

Cohort 1
Cohort 2

ACADEMIC ENTREPRENEURSHIP

Semester and Year	Total Student Credit Hours	Number of Sections	Adjunct Cost	Projected Gross Tuition Revenue
FY 2016 - 2017				
Session 1 (Oct)	54	1	Director Taught	$42,930
	0			$0
Session 2	54	1	$3,000	$42,930
	0			$0
Session 3	51	1	$3,000	$40,545
	0			$0
Session 4	51	1	$3,000	$40,545
	0			$0
Total FY17	**210**		**$9,000**	**$166,950**
FY 2017 - 2018				
Session 5 Jul/Aug	51	1	$3,000	$41,565
	0			$0
Session 6 Aug/Oct	51	1	$3,000	$41,565
	0			$0
Session 1	60	1	Director Taught	$48,900
	48	1	$3,000	$37,440
Session 2	60	1	$3,000	$48,900
	48	1	$3,000	$39,120
Session 3	57	1	$3,000	$46,455
	48	1	$3,000	$39,120
Session 4	57	1	$3,000	$46,455
	48	1	3,000	$39,120
Total FY18	**528**		**27,000**	**$428,640**

You will also need to make decisions here about total enrollment capacity for the program and expectations for growth over time. In the example shown here, we estimated that with current available resources, to ensure a sufficiently high-quality program, we could manage a total enrollment of 40 students at any given point in time. We started with a smaller enrollment in year one in order to give us a year to work out new program issues and increased the entering cohort size to 20 in year two. Assuming a 90% persistence rate, the total enrollment for the program was estimated to range from 34-36 over the first three years of the program. This information gave us a good foundation for estimating bottom line revenue expectations, which are discussed below.

Key questions to consider when calculating student credit hours include:

- How many credits are students likely to take in a given session?

- Given the estimated rigor of the curriculum, what is the ideal credit hour load for a typical student?

- What is the ideal class size for the courses and how many sections of each course will be required?

- Are the credit hours assigned for each course and curricular component appropriate for the estimated rigor and requirements of the learning experience?

- What retention rate should we expect for this program? What percentage of students who begin in a given year are likely to complete the program and within what time frame?

- What is the ideal total student enrollment? At what enrollment point is program quality likely to be impacted and why?

2. Revenue Projections and Assumptions

The proforma also incorporates key revenue assumptions, which when reviewed in tandem with the other elements provides us with a good understanding about what it will take for this program to be financially viable. Determining the potential revenue flow for this program starts with calculating gross tuition revenue for each year of the proforma in addition to estimating all other possible sources of revenue. Additional sources of revenue might include income from fees that are specific to the program or charges for ancillary program components, such as a required residency experience for an online program. At Bay Path, we typically wrap all additional fees into a single tuition price and then work to make sure that the price point is as competitive as possible which provides a strong promotional message (e.g., "no extra fees").

In the example that follows (Chart C) for Fiscal Year (FY)17, we have projected a total of $166,950 in student tuition revenue. This is calculated by mapping out the course flow for this year (see preceding Chart B), multiplying the total student credit hours by the per credit tuition charge and summing the totals for all terms. Note that the example here also includes assumptions about annual tuition increases for this program (3%) and carries over the other assumptions about student retention, class size, and student credit hour loads. In the subsequent

FY2018, 2019 and 2020, these assumptions have been considered to calculate a projected revenue total of $428,640 (FY18), $599,760 (FY19), and $648,750 (FY20).

CHART C

		FY 2017	FY 2018	FY 2019	FY2020
Revenue Assumptions					
	Student Tuition	$166,950	$428,640	$599,760	$ 648,750

In building the proforma and working through these various assumptions, we typically go back and forth many times, adjusting assumptions and calculations until we reach a bottom line that is feasible. Determining what a feasible bottom line is for each program depends upon several factors including how mission critical a particular program is as well as how strong the long-term financial projections for the program. This is discussed in greater detail later.

3. Expense Assumptions

Chart D illustrates the wide-ranging expenses which must be captured in the proforma. The most significant expense is typically compensation and benefits which include the faculty (part-time and adjunct) cost by term and year in addition to other required staffing. Chart B shows our method for projecting faculty staffing needs and costs on a term by term basis. By assigning faculty to each curricular component on the front end you can make a fairly good estimate about staffing charges over the duration of the program. In the case of programs that carry external professional accreditation, it's important to know and factor in accrediting agency's minimum staffing requirements. For example, with health science programs you will typically find a minimum staffing ratio of some kind that must be met. These commonly are tied to program enrollment and will need to be adjusted accordingly.

At Bay Path, we assess a 10% overhead charge for each new revenue-producing program, typically beginning in year two. This allows us to account for the institutional infrastructure costs that are incurred as enrollments grow but can be difficult to isolate. For example, with each new online program there is additional burden for the Center for Online Teaching and Learning (COTL). These overhead charge funds are pooled and then used to fund new hires (such as, an instructional designer in the COTL) or to pay for items that are needed to strengthen the institution's capacity to support more students. Requests for use of these funds can be made by any Vice President through the annual budget process with the final decision made by the CFO and president.

An additional critical expense category to consider is marketing costs, which are determined according to the program's competitive context and geographic reach. For example, we will project higher marketing costs for a new program that will be offered entirely online and for which the reach is national or international, versus an on-campus program that has only a local reach. With the increased usage of digital methods for program marketing, marketing expenses have burgeoned in recent years. We now typically project a spend of approximately $50,000-$75,000 annually for new program marketing exclusive of staffing or personnel costs. Chapter 9 provides more guidance on how to develop a robust and cost-effective marketing plan to support your new program.

It is also important to consider whether the program will incur any capital expenditures (e.g., a build-out of existing space or equipment), whether there are any accrediting or other regulatory costs associated with the program, and what ongoing faculty and program staffing support are needed. For example, we typically budget an average of $1,500 per full-time faculty member to support annual conference attendance in addition to modest funds for office support.

CHART D

	FY 2017	FY 2018	FY 2019	FY2020
Expense Assumptions				
Compensation and benefits:				
Program Director	$ 90,000	$ 91,800	$ 93,636	$ 95,509
One graduate assistant	$ -	$ 4,750	$ 4,750	$ 4,750
Adjunct Faculty Wages	$ 9,000	$ 27,000	$ 30,000	$ 30,000
Benefits	$ 23,400	$ 26,125	$ 26,884	$ 27,352
Sub-total comp & benefits	$ 122,400	$ 149,675	$ 155,270	$ 157,611
Overhead Charge (10%)	$ -	$ 42,864	$ 59,976	$ 64,875
Bookstore	$ 1,000	$ 500	$ 500	$ 500
Postage	$ 500	$ 600	$ 700	$ 800
Printing/Copying	$ 1,000	$ 1,200	$ 1,300	$ 1,400
Honorarium (guest author lectures)		$ 5,000	$ 5,000	$ 5,000
Purchased Services				
Library	$ 7,500	$ 5,000	$ 5,000	$ 5,000
Marketing	$ 50,000	$ 75,000	$ 75,000	$ 75,000
Memberships/Dues	$ -	$ 1,000	$ 1,200	$ 1,400
Events	$ -	$ 500	$ 500	$ 500
Meetings/Conventions/Registration	$ -	$ 1,000	$ 1,500	$ 1,850
Travel (e.g. Experiential learning trip)	$ -	$ 2,000	$ 2,000	$ 2,000

As with calculating the starting tuition price point, getting a realistic estimate for new program expenses takes work and lots of conversation with the faculty who will be associated with the new program. I have found that each new program has its own unique culture and this culture can impact the budget, sometimes in profound ways. For example, when we were developing the budget for the M.S. in Genetic Counseling, we learned from the program director that the accrediting agency, ACGC, strongly encourages all programs to support their students' attendance and participation at the ACGC annual meeting. Hence, we built this expense into the budget on the front end. While it can be helpful to set consistent guidelines for the various expense categories and lines, it's also necessary to remain flexible so that you can respond to the unique idiosyncrasies of each individual program.

4. Bottom-Line Projections

Chart E ties the components together with an estimate for the program's net cash flow. This is calculated by subtracting the total expenses (Chart D) from the total revenues (Chart C) and subtracting any capital expense (if relevant). Unless there are compelling extenuating circumstances, we aim for a positive net cash flow for all new programs by year two. We also calculate the operating margin for each new program and aim for a margin of at least 25% by year two. The operating margin is calculated as follows: surplus/deficit divided by total revenues. A program that can sustain an operating margin of at least 50% by year four is considered to be a strong net financial contributor.

CHART E

Projected Results	FY 2017	FY 2018	FY 2019	FY2020
Total Expenses	$ 182,400	$ 284,339	$ 307,946	$ 315,936
Surplus (Deficit)	($15,450)	$144,301	$291,814	$332,814.10
Operating Margin	-9%	34%	49%	51%
Capital Expense	$ -	$ -	$ -	$ -
Net Cash Flow	($15,450)	$144,301.00	$291,814.00	$332,814.10

As noted earlier, determining a feasible bottom line for your new program depends upon a variety of things, most of which can be surfaced by working through a quick risk and opportunity assessment prior to making the final decision to launch. In my experience, there are five critical things to weigh as part of this assessment:

- Mission impact
- Market potential
- Launch barriers
- Failure potential
- Opportunity potential

Mission impact

It is critical to understand how a new program might potentially impact the mission of the institution, either positively or negatively. For example, when we made the somewhat risky decision to launch The American Women's College, we did so because we believed that this new program would leverage our women's mission and provide access to new markets that we otherwise could not reach. Indeed, we concluded that the launch of this new program was critically important for the long-term future of the institution. As a result, we were willing to assume a higher up-front investment cost and a lower operating margin in order to give this new program time to settle and find its course.

On the other hand, a program that is not related to the institution's mission can easily siphon valuable resources and dilute the brand with little to no return benefit. An exception here would be a new program that leverages hidden strength or promise or provides a school on the brink of going under with a safety net. An example of the latter is the story about Paul Quinn College and President Sorrell's launch of a "new urban college model" discussed in Chapter 2.

Important mission-related questions to consider include:

- What impact will this new program have on our mission?
- Will this program detract from our mission impact? How bad would that be?
- Will this program enhance our mission impact? If so, in what ways?
- What might happen if we do not launch this program?

Market potential

It is also important to consider the strength of the market as determined by the feasibility study discussed in the previous chapter. Specifically, reviewing the evidence that you gathered about program rationale and target market as well as student demand and market niche will give you a sense about what it will take to successfully launch this program. For example, our review of these elements for the M.S. in Genetic Counseling degree feasibility study found that there was virtually no competition within 90 miles and that the student demand far exceeded the number of available spots at programs across the country. This information gave us great assurance in moving forward with the modest up-front investment needing to be made to support the program's launch.

Important questions to ask here include:

- How broad and how deep is the target market?
- Is there a built-in student market that you have evidence for?

- Can we establish a market niche with this program? Does this niche make sense? Is it attainable?
- How strong is the competition for this program?
- Given the competition, what will it take to gain a foothold in the market? How long will this take? Can we afford this?

Launch barriers

While several things can hamper the launch of a new program, I have found three to be particularly troublesome: lack of internal support, inadequate up-front investment resources, and poor planning. First, I have found that the most brilliantly designed programs can fail to launch if there is no individual champion(s) for the program or, even worse, if campus players block the launch. Having a credible and well-respected champion for a new program can go a long way towards ensuring its success on the front end. For instance, I have no doubt that a major reason for the successful launch of our M.S. in accounting was the appointment of a highly respected accounting faculty member as program director. Because she was a known entity and trusted by faculty and staff alike, the halo effect kicked in—"they liked her; they liked the program"—and she was able to easily gain the cooperation of individuals and offices across the campus to support the launch. On the other hand, having a champion who is not respected leading a new program launch effort is one of several reasons why some may try to intentionally or furtively block a program's launch. Key questions to consider include:

- Do we have an effective champion for this new program?
- What role will this champion play going forward?
- What benefits and/or limitations are associated with this champion?
- Who might have a reason to block the launch of this program, and why?
- What might we do to address the concerns of those who may block this program's launch?

A second reason that some programs fail on the front end is due to a lack of inadequate up-front investment resources. As outlined below, there are several potential sources for new program start-up funding. Your responses to the other risk and opportunity factors will largely determine your comfort level with pursuing one or more of these sources.

NEW PROGRAM START-UP FUNDING SOURCES

1. Grant Funding. This can be a particularly good source if your new program will meet a labor shortage in your geographical region. Here are 6 sources to get you started:

- Ask your **board members** who they know and whether they have access to grant funding through foundations, corporations in the community, or family foundations they may be able to access through social contacts or business colleagues.

- Spend an hour using **Google** to search for foundations that specifically fund projects like the new program you are considering. You can use Google to find foundation websites, as well as lists of grants received by other organizations.

NEW PROGRAM START-UP FUNDING SOURCES

- Many major metro areas and other locales have regional associations of Grantmakers. Depending upon the focus of your new program, your **local funding group** may have a reason for supporting the launch of your program.

- Some areas also maintain a **regional foundation directory** that keeps a listing of organizations that makes grants in the area. Check with your local community foundation to see if such a directory is available.

- The **Foundation Center** is an incredible online resource that provides easy, low-cost access to an online database of funders. If you can't afford the fee, check with your regional foundation center to see if you can use their access.

- If you are seeking grants from the federal government in the United States, you can use The **Catalog of Federal Domestic Assistance** and **Grants.gov** to research available grant programs, view guidelines, and in many cases, submit online applications for grant funding. Many state governments offer similar online resources, as do national governments outside of the United States.

2. Corporate Funders as Program Partners. If your new program offers potential benefits for area businesses or corporate entities, consider approaching them about a potential partnership. This can be a good source if your program is meeting a critical employment shortage.

3. Private Donors. Your campus advancement team can often be a great source for start-up funding. Make them your partner early in the planning process by letting them know what you are working on and asking them if anyone in the institution's donor base might have interests that align with this new program.

New Program Start-Up Funding Sources

4. New Enterprise Fund. Establish a "pot" of funding by setting aside monies in each year to be used for covering start-up costs for new strategic initiatives. Schools that use this strategy typically have a committee that makes decisions about funding levels and focus. Most funds require evidence that the program will be self-sustaining within a specified number of years.

5. Unrestricted Endowment or Budget Surplus/Reserve Funds. Depending upon the assessment of potential benefit described below and especially if the evidence is compelling that your program will generate a strong positive cash flow within a fairly short time period, you may want to consider tapping unrestricted endowment funds or institutional budgeted reserve funds to support new program start-up.

6. Budget Reallocation. When new external funds are not available, you may consider reallocating existing operating budget funds to generate the required amount. This can be done by cutting all operating budgets by a set amount depending upon how much funding you need and using the "freed-up" funding for start-up expenses.

7. Planned Budget Deficit Spend. This last strategy which essentially involves "overspending" the operating budget to fund your start-up costs should be considered as a last resort and only when the evidence that the program has strong revenue enhancing promise is overwhelmingly affirmative.

Third, new programs can fail to launch due to poor planning. This is particularly the case when a campus does not think through or plan for the implementation details. By taking the time to conduct a thorough feasibility study and develop and vet a detailed and realistic proforma you will increase the odds for a successful new program launch. Having such a plan may also enable you to assume more risk on the front end if necessary, assuming the plan is credible. It is especially critical that new programs be integrated into the institution's budgeting and planning processes right from the beginning. At Bay Path, once the proforma is approved it is immediately integrated into the budget and all financial, staffing and other assumptions are integrated into the operating and capital budgets as appropriate.

Failure potential

It's well worth it to take the time to think through possible failure scenarios and the potential impact of each. Generally speaking, you want to weigh the probability of those things that could go wrong against the potential impact on the institution. For instance, one possibility is that the institution will not be able to generate enough enrollment and not meet the financial proforma revenue target. Let's say the financial hit in year one for a 10% enrollment shortfall is $150,000. Can the institution afford to absorb this level of revenue loss? When it comes to enrollment projections, it's helpful to think through a range of possibilities like this, estimating the range of potential revenue loss for each one.

The following diagram can be used for mapping each possible failure scenario in terms of likelihood and impact.

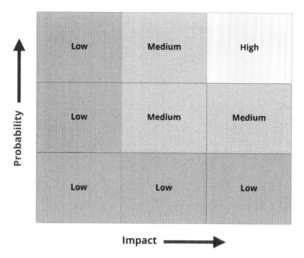

Questions to ask for each scenario include:

- What could go wrong?
- How likely is it that this will happen?
- What evidence do I have that this is a possibility?
- If this happens, what is the potential impact and for whom?
- If this happens, what is the worst that can happen and how bad would this be?
- Regarding this new program launch, how much financial and other failure can the institution afford to tolerate?

Opportunity potential

At the same time, you want to consider the full range of opportunity that this new program brings. Opportunity can be thought of in terms of several factors including:

- Mission reinforcing and expanding
- Revenue stream diversifying and strengthening
- Institutional reputation enhancing

Regarding mission, a new program that leverages your mission in new and dynamic ways can provide significant benefit, especially if the institution's viability is strengthened in the process. For example, Georgia Tech was founded in 1885 as a public research university and institute of technology with a long history of educating students for an information economy. When the school expanded one of its core existing graduate programs in computer science to include a new low-cost and fully online delivery option, it quadrupled its program enrollment generating a strong positive cash flow. The success of this initiative has led Georgia Tech to similarly expand other core graduate programs.

There are numerous grids that can be useful for mapping opportunity potential factors. Here are three that I have found useful.

Demand/Cost Potential Assessment

High-Demand/Low-Cost Programs	High-Demand/High-Cost Programs
Programs with growing enrollments and positive return on investment	Programs with growing enrollments and negative return on investment
Low-Demand/Low-Cost Programs	Low-Demand/High-Cost Programs
Programs with declining enrollments and positive return on investment	Programs with declining enrollments and negative return on investment

(Vertical axis: FTE Trends; Horizontal axis: Program Cost Trends)

With the Boston Consulting Group (BCG)-inspired matrix shown above you can assess where your new program is likely to fit in terms of enrollment and cost. Enrollment is assessed using the enrollment estimates and your bottom-line projections from the proforma. Generally, you want to hold back on programs that land in the low-demand/high-cost box unless you have a compelling reason for moving forward such as an endowed program with strong mission fit and funding that will last into perpetuity. On the other hand, your ideal new program will land in the high-demand/low-cost box. It's helpful to map all existing programs using this grid so that you have some sense as to what the institution can tolerate when considering the enrollment and expense capacity for a new program.

Questions to ask using this matrix include:

- Once your program is up and running, where does the feasibility study estimate it will land on this matrix?
- Will this program diversify and/or strengthen the institution's revenue stream? If so, in what ways?
- If this new program does not strengthen the institution's revenue stream, what other reasons make its existence compelling?
- Can the institution afford to add a program in this particular position?
- What is the minimum return on investment that is needed for this program to be viable?

With the Demand/Quality matrix shown on the next page, you are concerned with the potential opportunity this new program provides for enhancing your institution's reputation. As with the previous matrix demand is assessed using the enrollment estimates from the proforma. Quality is a more subjective measure and can be assessed using any number of input or output factors including projected student outcomes and quality of students and faculty. You will want to hold back on programs that land in the low-quality/low-demand box as the potential benefit would be very limited. On the other hand, a program that you have evidence to believe will be a high-quality/high-demand offering should be a high priority and worth any up-front risk, assuming you can afford the resources required to make it a strong program.

Demand/Quality Potential Assessment

In using this matrix, consider such questions as:

- What is the likelihood that this program will occupy a unique and compelling niche in the marketplace?
- Might this program be an area of distinction for the institution?

- What branding opportunities might this program generate?

- Do we have what it takes to deliver a high-quality program, and if so, can the institution afford the commitment of resources for this program?

- What is the student demand likely to be for this program? Will the level of quality impact the demand?

- If this program is projected to trend towards low-quality/low-demand are there other reasons for its existence?

Demand/Quality/Revenue Potential Assessment

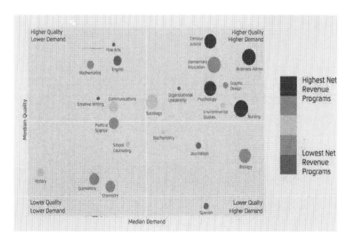

This third matrix combines quality, demand, and revenue in one assessment. The example shown here is from an assessment conducted by an institution that was trying to determine whether to add a new program in criminal justice. They placed all their existing undergraduate programs on this grid and then added criminal justice using the information gathered through the feasibility study. Based on this assessment, they concluded that criminal justice would be a significant positive contributor in terms of strengthening the mission, reputation, and revenue.

What's Next

Conducting feasibility studies and developing financial proformas for our new academic programs has been key to Bay Path University's success in launching more than 25 new graduate programs over the past decade. I cannot overestimate the value of taking the time to work through the various feasibility study elements and to test the proforma against the factors discussed in this chapter. I have also found it essential do this work in tandem other campus staff, including, most importantly, the CFO and senior staff in admissions, marketing, and advancement. When everyone on campus owns the new program and has a vested interest in its success the odds for a successful launch are enhanced. This also ensures that the program will not exist as an outlier but instead will be integrated into the campus infrastructure right from the beginning. Getting the program off-the-ground is just one aspect of successful new program development. Operationalizing the program to ensure its long-term viability is equally important and is the focus of the next chapter. In Chapter 8, we will review a number of key factors that can impact your ability to sustain your new program for the long haul.

Key Strategic Questions for Academic Leaders

These questions are helpful to consider in collaboration with your CFO and other senior officers whose support will be important for ensuring the success of any new program. These questions provide a useful framework for positioning your academic programs within the broader institutional infrastructure and resource base.

1. How does your institution assess the financial viability of new and/or existing academic programs?

2. What up-front funding resources might your institution have access to for supporting new program development?

3. To what extent do you regularly scan your competition in terms of tuition pricing and unique program niches?

4. Does your annual financial planning and budgeting process allow for review and adjustment of financial assumptions that were made when program was originally launched?

5. Is your new program planning process integrated with your institution's budgeting and capital/facility planning processes?

6. Do you have a mechanism and process in place for regularly assessing the financial and academic performance of all of your programs?

7. Is your advancement staff aware of your new program plans?

8. How does your institution assess the potential risk and opportunity for new programs?

Appendix A

This template can be adapted to develop the financial proforma that will support your new program and that should be an essential component of any new program Feasibility Study.

	NEW PROGRAM PROFORMA TEMPLATE					
		FY	FY	FY	FY	FY
Enrollment and Pricing Assumptions	Per Credit Rate					
	Total Credit Hours					
	Full Time Equivalent					
	Head Count New Only					
Revenue Assumptions	Student Tuition					
	Student Fees					
	Other:					
Expense Assumptions	Compensation and Benefits					
	Program Administrator Salary					
	Other Professional Staff Salary					
	Full Time Faculty Salary					
	Adjunct Faculty Salary					
	Benefits					
	Sub-Total Comp & Benefits					
	Overhead Charge _____ %					
	Bookstore					
	Postage					
	Printing/Copying					
	Honorarium					
	Purchased Services					
	Library					
	Marketing					
	Membership/Dues					
	Events					
	Meetings/Conferences/ Registrations					
	Travel					
	Other:					
Projected Results	Total Expenses					
	Surplus (Deficit)					
	Operating Margin					
	Capital Expense					
	Net Cash Flow					

Appendix B

This template on the following pages is used to map out every course and any other credit bearing components of your new program. It's important to map out the entire program for one full cycle. This enables you to accurately estimate staffing expenses and total student credit hours which you will need for projecting gross tuition revenue. You will also need to make assumption about class size (in order to estimate the number of sections needed for each course) and retention rates from year to year.

COURSE FLOW AND PROJECTED GROSS TUITION REVENUE WORKSHEET

Semester and Year	Course #	Credits	Projected New Headcount Enrollment	Projected Returning Headcount Enrollment	Total Student Credit Hours	# of Sections	Adjunct Faculty Stipend	Projected Gross Tuition Revenue

Appendix C

This checklist is one that academic leaders and other new program developers can use to ensure you capture and address all of the elements discussed in Chapters 6 and 7. It can be useful to reference at the beginning of your process and again at the end to make sure you have not missed anything important.

NEW ACADEMIC PROGRAM CONSIDERATIONS CHECKLIST

New Program: _____

STRATEGIC ISSUES
How will this program advance our mission, vision, and strategic priorities?
To what extent does this program build upon existing curricula?
Do we have a champion who will live and breathe this program? What evidence is there that this individual will be a positive and effective champion?
How will this program be delivered and to whom?

To what extent will other faculty groups and departments be supportive of this new program?

To what extent will this new program draw resources away from other critical areas and priorities?

If we pursue this new program, what other programs or priorities must wait?

MARKETPLACE CONTEXT ISSUES

To what extent might this program become a signature program—something that attracts regional, national, or international attention?

Is this program unique in our particular marketplace context? If not, what do we know about the competition?

If other institutions are already offering this program, do we have the potential to occupy a unique niche? Is this niche realistic and attainable? How long will it take?

How broad and how deep is the market for this program?

How might we best test potential program demand?

ECONOMIC AND RESOURCE ISSUES

Where is this program likely to map in terms of high-low cost, high-low quality, and high-low revenue?

What resources will be required to deliver a quality program?

What existing resources and assets might we utilized to deliver this program?

How much profit margin do we need from this program?

Can we offer this program less expensively than our competitors?

Are there accreditation requirements that we must consider?

Will the institution provide adequate upfront investment, or must this new program break even in first year?

RISK TOLERANCE ISSUES

In pursuing this opportunity, what could go wrong? How likely is it that this could happen?

How much failure can the institution tolerate?

Do we have access to start-up funding if needed?

Who might have a reason to block this program?

What opportunity does this new program present? Will it enhance the institution's mission, revenue, or reputation, and if so, in what way?

To what extent does the potential for positive impact outweigh the potential risk?

OTHER ISSUES TO CONSIDER:

CHAPTER 8
OPERATIONALIZING AND SUSTAINING NEW ACADEMIC PROGRAMS

In the first three chapters in this section, I outlined a blueprint for new academic program development and stressed the importance of a balanced approach. Understanding that it is impossible to capture all variables on the front end, the potential viability of a program is difficult to assess until that program is up and running. While having a discipline around new program development ensures that you will anticipate most of the important potential impact issues, maintaining a culture of flexibility and responsiveness once the program is launched is equally critical for the program's success. As the great American novelist Thomas Berger once wrote, "The art and science of asking questions is the source of all knowledge." Indeed, cultivating a spirit of question asking and wide-eyed vigilance as a program is embedded within your organizational culture and context, while not easy, is nevertheless a foundational pre-requisite for long-term viability.

Over the past decade, we have successfully implemented and sustained more than 25 new graduate programs at Bay Path University. Having learned a great deal through this process, I have found a handful of key factors that are important to keep in mind for the program's sustainability over time:

1. Think long-term with up-front investments.
2. Leverage untapped potential.
3. Start small, invest conservatively on the front end, and build as you go.
4. Maintain a spirit of adaptability.
5. Integrate Kaizen principles and practices.

Let me provide more context for each of these considerations.

1. Think Long-Term with Up-Front Investments

In considering new program investments, ask yourself whether an investment might have a broader and/or longer-term purpose? This is where one must push through the common tendency that exists on many of our campuses to think and act in a silo-enhancing way. By pushing ourselves to think outside of the silos and to see resources from a boundary-spanning perspective, we open a wide range of possibilities for the present and future viability of our institutions. For example, when we launched our first fully online graduate program in non-profit management and philanthropy in 2007, we also at the same time established a Center for Online Teaching and Learning. Given that our longer-term strategy involved expanding our online presence across several programmatic areas, an investment of this kind on the front end and with our very first online program made sense. Consequently, each new program that has been brought forward since 2007 has been reviewed to assess whether online or hybrid delivery might be an appropriate option. Likewise, when we hire program directors, we often look for individuals who have teaching expertise across more than one area. As much as possible, investments in personnel, facilities, and other areas should be defensible in terms of their potential adaptability within a broader context.

Key questions to ask when considering up-front investments to support a new program include:

- If considering a facility investment, might this space serve a broader purpose on our campus?

- Might this facility be useful for generating ancillary revenue from other sources to support the institution's operations?

- When evaluating candidates for new positions, what abilities or talents does this individual bring to our campus beyond what is needed for the specific role he or she has applied for?

2. Leverage Untapped Potential

In my experience, every campus has untapped potential and capacity—human, physical, and curricular resources—if one is willing to look for it. As with my previous point, this requires maintaining a broader institution-wide perspective about resources and being willing to ask deep and hard questions when considering resource investments to support new programs. With new program development, such untapped potential can be a valuable resource that enables you to build and achieve results more quickly and often with less risk than if you were bringing up a program entirely from ground zero. At Bay Path, we leveraged our historic expertise in educating adult women through campus-based programs by establishing the fully online American Women's College, an entity that provides essentially the same curriculum as the existing Saturday One-Day-A-Week program for adult women, through a new, innovative delivery and support model. Likewise, we recently established an OT Bridge program with a curriculum that builds off of our long-standing graduate program in occupational therapy. Utilizing some existing curricula, the OT Bridge program meets a critical professional pathway gap for individuals who have an associate degree in occupational therapy or physical therapy and want the master's degree—without the duplication in content that one typically finds between the associate and upper level content in this field.

Important questions to ask when looking for untapped resource potential include:

- Do we have existing curricula—either at the undergraduate or graduate levels—that relates to this new program to any extent?

- If so, how might we create synergy between our existing program and this new offering?

- Are there existing faculty and/or staff that have expertise that could benefit this new program?

- What existing institutional resources and capabilities might be leveraged to support this new program?

3. Start Small, Invest Conservatively, and Build as You Go

Because our Board of Trustees expects that we will break even as soon as possible, we have developed a discipline around starting small and investing only in the most critical expenses necessary until the program is up and running and we can better assess the full potential. This means we typically start with one full-time, dedicated program director or chair and a cadre of adjunct faculty for new graduate programs. Unless the program has external accreditation requirements which specify minimum staffing levels, our program proforma ties personnel additions in subsequent years directly to enrollment growth. By making this understanding transparent during the proforma development and subsequent budget process, the angst that sometimes accompanies program staffing decisions is lessened. Understanding that staffing increases may be directly tied to enrollment growth can also provide an incentive for program staff and faculty to be more directly involved with student recruitment. Once the program is up and running, we closely monitor net contribution results and make decisions about staffing additions as part of the annual budget process. Once we see signs of financial viability, we ramp up our investment while continually reviewing results and adapting as we go. For example, if a program takes off much more quickly than projected, we will adjust both staffing and revenue expectations and add staffing resources more quickly. The important point here is to stay flexible, monitor your results closely, and adapt assumptions as the results warrant.

To ensure you are not overspending on the front end, consider these questions:

- What is the minimum amount of staffing required to support this program at a reasonable level of quality?

- How can staffing from other departments and areas be utilized to "fill the gap?"

- Have we considered alternative staffing models such as "non-tenure track" or a "professor of practice"[95] appointment in lieu of the traditional full-time tenure track faculty hire?

- Is there evidence to support the immediate need for all requested resources?

- Once fully mature, what is the ideal staffing for this program?

- While keeping in mind program quality expectations, what is an appropriate timeline for increasing staffing?

4. Maintain a Spirit of Adaptability

Maintaining a spirit of adaptability once a program is up and running sounds like an easy thing to do, and yet, in most of our institutions, the pull towards the status quo is a difficult thing to resist. This is where the principles discussed in Chapters 2 and 3 become particularly important for academic leaders. For example, Saras Saravathy's notion of effectuation reviewed in Chapter 2 is all about adaptability—being flexible and making it up as you go. But, how do you do this when the forces resisting adaptability can sometimes seem overwhelming? Having and adhering to a disciplined process for ongoing review of all programs with clearly articulated performance targets is a good starting point. For instance, once a new program is launched on our campus, we typically review the results on an annual basis paying close attention to enrollment and revenue; and we make changes immediately if the review warrants it. At Bay Path University, when we launched our M.S. in Applied Data Science, the program missed its enrollment target by a wide margin in the first year. After reviewing admissions and marketing data, we adjusted the curriculum to add a "generalist" track catering to individuals using data for decision making as generalists in a wide variety of fields. While the original curriculum was designed to attract data science specialists, we found that the market was much bigger than this and that our particular niche was with generalists who are now enrolling in large numbers. Had we not had a process that forced us to review and revise assumptions so quickly after the launch, I'm not sure this program would have survived. In my experience, leading the way in maintaining a spirit of adaptability is a critical part of academic leadership. The diagram on the next page captures the range of traits that academic leaders need to nurture if you're going to help your institution stay relevant in adapting to your environment.

Until a program is up and running, it's virtually impossible to fully know its marketplace potential. For that reason, one must be vigilant in monitoring program results and be quick to make changes in response to these results as warranted. In nearly every new program that we have launched, we have made changes in program design and content after the initial launch based on what we learned about market demand and student learning needs.

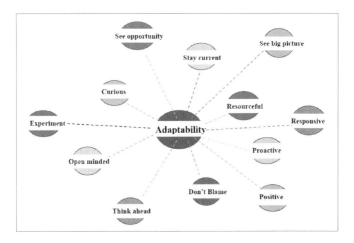

There are several important questions to ask here:

- Do we have a process in place for annual review of program results and implications?

- What criteria will be most important to review in order to assess the performance of new programs?

- If the results are off target from the proforma, what do we need to know, and where can we get the information?

- What changes might be necessary in response to our review?

- What will it take to make these changes?

5. Integrate Kaizen Principles and Practices

Kaizen is a Japanese philosophy originally adopted by Asian car makers and now a pivotal concept for the continuous improvement movement across the globe. Gradually making its way into higher education in recent years, Kaizen refers to collaborative activities that continually improve organizational functions and processes. As illustrated on the following pages, there are several "Kaizen-esque" practices that can be employed to ensure that you remain clear-eyed in assessing the program's performance over time.

Especially during the first year of new program implementation, it can be helpful to have a series of questions that you ask to ensure you are accurately interpreting market response to your programs.

For example:

- To what extent does the demographic profile of your enrolling students match your preliminary assumptions about who would enroll?

- If there are significant differences, what do they mean?

- What factors have been most significant in your students' enrollment decision?

- Why did they choose your institution generally and this program specifically?

- How strong is the funnel performance for this program (e.g. yield of applicants, accepted, and enrolled)?

- To what extent are your students' learning expectations being met?

- How satisfied are they with their experience in this program and at your institution?

Having an external board of advisors made up of industry professionals who you utilize to observe, ask key questions, and assess performance with you and your faculty can also be extremely helpful.

Kaizen Best Practices, Adapted for Academic Program Development

1. Focus on the process. Kaizen is based on a philosophy of small, incremental, continuous improvement. When developing and evaluating new programs, Kaizen would have you remain flexible and adaptive, focused on the big picture. The end result—the program—is never more important than the process that resulted in the program. If the program does not hit its mark, look to the process to discover the reasons.

2. Engage employees in the decision-making process. Kaizen believes that the best solutions happen when those closest to the problem are involved and when multiple perspectives are brought to bear. Once new programs are launched involve all those impacted by the program—directly and indirectly—in ongoing evaluation of the program. By empowering faculty and staff to problem solve and troubleshoot as you go, they will have a vested interest in supporting its long-term success.

> ### KAIZEN BEST PRACTICES, ADAPTED FOR ACADEMIC PROGRAM DEVELOPMENT
>
> **3. Go after low-hanging fruit.** The Kaizen approach to management focuses on small, incremental improvements which enables change to happen more quickly and creates a momentum that can facilitate future and bigger change. Kaizen practice does not accept excuses or get bogged down in looking for blame; instead, the emphasis is on just making things happen. With new program development and evaluation, it's important to keep pushing faculty and staff along and not let them get derailed by over-analysis or the need to "get it right."
>
> **4. Assume improvement is always needed.** According to the Kaizen philosophy, improvement has no limits. Never settling for "good enough" or the status quo, Kaizen practitioners assume that every aspect of an organization or process can be improved. Employees are encouraged to look at established policies and methods with a fresh eye. Instead of thinking up reasons why something can't be done, they're urged to ignore conventional limitations and figure out how it can be done. This is particularly important to keep in mind with new programs that appear to be highly successful at the outset.
>
> **5. Go to the source—the "Gemba."** Gemba is a Japanese term meaning "the real place." As applied in practice, the idea of Gemba is that problems are visible and the best improvement ideas will come by going to the source of the problem. The example shared above about the M.S. in Data Science is a great example of this. We asked many questions of many different people until discovering that our original assumptions about the program's target market were incomplete.

> **KAIZEN BEST PRACTICES, ADAPTED FOR ACADEMIC PROGRAM DEVELOPMENT**
>
> **6. Look for the root cause.** With Kaizen, before making decisions you want to ask "why" five times to get to the root cause of the problem. A variation of this practice is the 5W and 1H method which involves asking a series of *Who? What? Where? When? Why?* and *How?* questions until you uncover the heart of the problem. With evaluation of new programs that are not meeting their targets, it's important to resist easy answers that may reflect faulty assumptions.
>
> **7. Know your customer.** Understanding who your customers are and what they want and need from you is an important Kaizen practice. With Kaizen it is all about creating customer value, something that is hard to do if you do not know your customer very well. As it relates to new program development, taking the time to fully understand your target markets is critically important. If things miss the mark, look first to your students—those who enrolled and those who did not—as the initial step in your assessment.
>
> **8. Be transparent.** A core Kaizen principle is to make performance and improvements tangible and visible by using metrics and real data and disciplining yourself to monitor and publicize the results. This is one way of keeping yourself honest and looking beyond any preconceived notions which can color your interpretation of data. Especially when evaluating the performance results of new programs, it can be helpful to share the data broadly and involve many in interpreting meaning.

What's Next

Even with the best developed plan, it's virtually impossible to anticipate all of the variables that can impact the long-term viability of a program. Indeed, until a new program is fully up and running and the bugs have been worked out so to speak, it's difficult to fully understand how the program is playing out in the marketplace. While having a discipline around new program development ensures that you will anticipate most of the important potential impact issues, maintaining a culture of flexibility and responsiveness once the program is launched is equally critical for the program's success.

In this final chapter of Section II, we reviewed five principles that are important to keep in mind for the program's sustainability over time: 1) Think long-term with up-front investments; 2) Leverage untapped potential; 3) Start small, invest conservatively on the front end, and build as you go; 4) Maintain a spirit of adaptability, and 5) Integrate and practice Kaizen principles. As reinforced throughout this chapter, cultivating a practice of question asking and wide-eyed vigilance as a program is embedded within your organizational culture and context is an essential pre-requisite for long-term viability.

In Section III, we will delve more deeply into three areas that can impact program viability—short-term and over time—if not considered early in the program development process. These include program marketing and promotion, the regulatory context, and infrastructure and resource planning. With each of these areas, we will review important issues that can hinder your success as well as best practices.

Key Strategic Questions for Academic Leaders

These questions are intended to help you think through what it's going to take to sustain your new program. These are meant for personal self-reflection as much as for discussion starters that you might use with your team. For example, these questions can stimulate helpful conversations about your institution's culture and what you might do to enable a more collaborative and boundary spanning approach to planning. How would you evaluate your institution's ability to successfully launch new academic programs? What improvements are needed?

1. When you consider available resources for a new program or initiative, do you have a boundary-spanning or a silo-reinforcing mentality?

2. What synergies currently exist between the programs and the staffing resources on your campus? Why is this the case?

3. Do you have a process in place to support a more collaborative approach to resource management?

4. How much flexibility do you have with your staffing models? Are you entirely dependent upon a full-time tenure-track model for faculty staffing? Have you considered alternative models?

5. How adaptable is your campus culture?

6. To what extent do you model adaptive leadership within your campus community?

7. Which of the Kaizen practices most resonate with you? Why?

Helpful Resources

Growth Strategy Tools and Resources

Heath, Mia. *Ansoff Matrix for Beginners*. CreateSpace Publishing, 2016. This text is a very quick and easy to read summarizing the core elements of Ansoff's growth strategy.

An online free guide to the Ansoff Product Market Growth Matrix can be found here: www.ansoffmatrix.com

Collins, Jim, and Morten Hansen. *Great by Choice*. HarperCollins Publishers, 2011. This book answers the question: Why do some organizations thrive in uncertainty, even chaos, and others do not? Based on nine years of research and rigorous analysis, management guru Jim Collins and co-author Morten Hansen outline the principles for building a great enterprise in dynamic times—applicable for all organizational sectors.

Market and Industry Scanning Resources

Bureau of Labor Statistics Occupation and Industry Projections:
www.careeronestop.org/toolkit/careers/careers.aspx
This free website allows you to create a customized report for any of nearly 900 occupations, including national and state data on wages; employment; knowledge, skills, and abilities (KSAs); education and training; and links to more resources.

Gray's Program Evaluation System (PES): This annual subscription service helps you assess student demand, employment, competition and strategic fit by program. The PES includes current data on such things as qualified inquiries, Google search volumes for the largest 200 academic program, all Title IV completions, geo-enhanced, BLS jobs, wages, and employment projections, current Job Postings from Burning Glass Technologies, and job placement rates. With this data you may score and rank programs on such things as student inquiry volume and growth, jobs, job growth and wages, competitors' size and growth by program, degree level, and market saturation. See: www.grayassociates.com

CEB TalentNeuron: TalentNeuron is an online market intelligence subscription portal with real-time labor insights including custom role analytics, dashboards, and presentations. Available data include information on key roles by location, occupation, and skill set as well as information about hiring and which skills and roles are in demand. When developing the curriculum for a new program this is an excellent source for reviewing outcomes against what skills and knowledge employers are looking for in particular fields. See: www.gartner.com/en/human-resources/talentneuron

National Student Clearinghouse: studentclearinghouse.org. Among its many service areas, the one I have found most useful is the Research Service which provides services and reports that draw on the Clearinghouse's unmatched information resources about student-level educational outcomes nationwide.

Education Dive provides busy professionals with a bird's-eye-view of the education industry in 60 seconds. See: www.educationdive.com/topic/HigherED/

Institute for the Future (www.iftf.org) is the world's leading non-profit strategic futures organization. IFF's core research staff and creative design studio work together to provide practical foresight for a world undergoing rapid change.

EDUCAUSE (www.educause.edu) and its members contribute to thought leadership on major issues, help clarify the current environment, document effective practices, and highlight how emerging trends and technologies may influence the evolution of IT in higher education.

Infrastructure Planning

Cort, Cliff, et al. "The Challenge of Making Buildings Flexible: How to Create Campuses that Adapt to Changing Needs." *Planning for Higher Education Journal*, vol. 45, no. 4, July-September 2017.

Curricular Planning

Beach, Robert, and Ronald Lindahl. "Instituting a New Degree Program: A Case Study of University Planning." *Planning for Higher Education Journal*, vol. 45, no. 4, July-September 2017.

Financial Modeling and Planning

Integrated Resource and Budget Planning at Colleges and Universities. Edited by Carol Rylee. Society for College and University Planning Publishers, 2011. Looking for tools to help make your next planning or campus project easier? The Society for College and University Planning's Resource & Budget Planning Advisory Group has generated practical analyses of and insights toward tools and processes that can help you today and with projects to come.

The Higher Education Consortia (HEC) provides an integrated platform of products and services that facilitate unit and institutional improvement to four-year colleges and universities. The Consortia advances the national dialogue in higher education by providing insights into the changing environment of instructional costs, productivity, and scholarly activity. See: ire.udel.edu/cost

Barr, Margaret, and George McClellan. *Budgets and Financial Management in Higher Education.* Jossey-Bass Publishers, 2018. This text helps new administrators understand and become more pro-ficient in their financial management role within an institution. Grounded in the latest knowledge base and filled with examples from across all types of institutions, it provides an understanding of the basics of budgeting and fiscal management in higher education; defines the elements of a budget, the budget cycle, and the steps for creating a budget; suggests ways of avoiding common pitfalls and problems of managing budgets; and contains effective strategies for dealing with the loss of resources

Townsley, Michael K. *Financial Strategy for Higher Education: A Field Guide for Presidents, CFOs and Boards of Trustees.* Lulu Publishing Services, 2014. This is a good basic resource with lots of checklists and templates. It includes start-up program budget templates along with sample capital project tables and helpful wisdom about tuition pricing and discounting.

Kaizen Principles and Practices

Kaizen Institute (www.kaizen.com) has been in existence since the 1980s and provides training and consulting for organizations around the world on Kaizen and continuous improvement. The website includes good free resources.

Tom Curtis's online blog and website provides lots of great examples for easy to do Kaizen practices. See: onimproving.blogspot.com/2014/08/parking-nudge.html www.slideshare.net/onimproving

Dennis, Pascal. *The Remedy: Bringing Lean Thinking Out of the Factory to Transform the Entire Organization*. Wiley Publishers, 2010. While focused on a business organization, the examples provided for how to apply Kaizen-type principles have relevance for higher education leaders.

Maurer. Robert. *One Small Step Can Change Your Life: The Kaizen Way*. Workman Publishing Company, 2014. This essential guide to Kaizen—the art of making great and lasting change through small, steady steps—was written by Dr. Robert Maurer, a psychologist on the staff of both the University of Washington School of Medicine and Santa Monica UCLA Medical Center and an expert on Kaizen who speaks and consults nationally. This book outlines the role that fear plays in every type of change—and Kaizen's ability to neutralize it by circumventing the brain's built-in resistance to new behavior—Dr. Maurer then explains the 7 Small Steps: How to Think Small Thoughts, Take Small Actions, Solve Small Problems, and more. He shows how to perform mind sculpture—visualizing virtual change so that real change comes more naturally—why small rewards lead to big returns by internalizing motivation, and how great discoveries are made by paying attention to the little details most of us overlook.

Group Process and Creative Problem Solving (CPS)

This free online article explores what CPS is and its key principles. A model is provided that can be used to generate creative solutions.

www.mindtools.com/pages/article/creative-problem-solving.htm

And this free website offers an abundance of resources to help you get the most of brainstorming:

www.brainstorming.co.uk/tutorials/historyofbrainstorming.html

SECTION III—OPERATIONALIZING ACADEMIC PROGRAMS

OVERVIEW

The traditional assumptions that framed academic program planning in the not-so-distant past no longer work in this new era characterized by constraints and fluidity. Most colleges today are operating in a highly evolving and networked context. Most institutions can no longer afford to treat their academic program portfolios as an afterthought or as something that resides apart from the rest of the institution and the broader world in which the institution is located. Entrepreneurial academic leaders have a holistic and systems-oriented perspective that informs decision making around new program planning and resourcing. In Section III, we will unpackage this perspective by delving more deeply into three areas that can impact a new program's viability—program marketing and promotion, the regulatory context, and infrastructure and resource planning. In each area, we will review important issues that can hinder your success, and we will also highlight best practices that can be utilized to leverage resources and opportunities, sometimes in surprising and unexpected ways.

CHAPTER 9
POSITIONING YOUR NEW PROGRAM FOR SUCCESS

When I first began my career in higher education over 35 years ago, the idea of marketing and branding was just beginning to take hold. Back then, higher education marketing focused primarily on the look, message format, and the logo. Indeed, I can recall long and protracted arguments about logo design—to what end, I still do not know. I can also recall the deep skepticism I encountered from faculty when discussing a more significant role for marketing. The idea of being intentional about messaging to position the institution and its programs in a particular way was a foreign notion to many faculty and some administrators; most simply didn't understand what marketing was, some feared what this might mean for the integrity of the institution, and some thought this was just another one of those passing fads.

How times have changed. The importance of marketing and branding for one's institutional reputation, enrollment success, and overall viability is a much more readily and widely accepted notion today. For institutions that are launching new academic programs, the role and value of marketing is especially critical. Especially in this current climate, a comprehensive and well-researched marketing plan can make the difference between success and failure for a new program. Even for small, resource-constrained institutions there are easy and relatively low-cost things that you can do to build a strong foundation in the program's market context. That is what this chapter is all about.

This chapter provides a basic orientation for everything you need to know to create a marketing and recruitment plan for your new program. Specifically, we will address the following questions:

1. What is marketing, and why is it so important for the success of new programs?
2. What tools and approaches are useful for understanding your program's target market?
3. What are the components of a comprehensive new program marketing plan?
4. What high impact marketing practices are most effective?
5. What is branding, how is it different from marketing, and what is its value for new program development?
6. What role does social media play in the launch of new programs?
7. What adult and graduate student recruitment practices are most effective?
8. What key metrics are important to track to evaluate the effectiveness of your marketing efforts?
9. What is a marketing playbook and what value does it add?

This chapter concludes with guidelines for developing a marketing playbook for your new program, along with a sample playbook plan for a new graduate program that was launched at my institution. In brief, a marketing playbook is a short document that should inform marketing and recruitment decisions as well as help all internal audiences get on the same page in terms of program messaging and markets.

1. Defining Marketing and its Value

According to the American Marketing Association, "Marketing is the activity, set of institutions, and processes for creating, communicating, delivering, and exchanging offerings that have value for customers, clients, partners, and society at large."[96]

For new program marketing, the key words in this definition are: *"creating, communicating, delivering, and exchanging offerings that have value."* Your new program should provide value to the students who enroll, to the employers who hire your students, to your institution that houses the program, and to the broader world in which your program graduates will work and live. Ideally, your new program will add something that does not already exist, or it will improve upon something that does exist, thus deepening the value. All good higher education marketing starts from this important foundation; if you are not able to articulate the value that your new program adds, for whom, and how, your marketing and enrollment results are likely to suffer.

A second part of the AMA definition that bears attention are these words: *"the activity, set of institutions, and processes."* At its core, marketing is a management process that connects the needs, interests, and wants of constituents with "the something" that benefits them, namely, your new program. Marketing is often confused with advertising and while both are important, advertising is just one component of a multi-pronged process. Some also believe that good marketing "just happens." In my experience the best marketing results come from a comprehensive process that is strategic, highly intentional, and well managed.

It should be clear from these definitions that marketing is all about what your institution is doing to build relationships with important constituent groups beginning with prospective students for your new program. This is where marketing's value comes into play. For a college or university to remain viable, it must build and maintain positive relationships with those upon whom it's dependent for carrying out its educational mission. No students—no mission. Hence, the process of marketing begins with learning what your prospective students want and need from you and making sure your new program delivers on this.

The dynamic context described in Chapter 1 makes it clear that effective marketing and enrollment results are more critical than ever. Yet, in the face of a rapidly changing market context, many institutions are challenged to know how best to spend their limited resources. Taken together, there are four forces that are responsible for this complicated context:

- **The evolution of prospective student shopping behavior.** The context in which students search for programs and colleges has changed dramatically just in the span of a few years. Tried and true methods for generating leads and inquiries are no longer as effective due to the advent of online search capabilities and the increase in stealth applications.[97] Moreover, what prospective students are looking for is changing. A 2016 Google study found that today's students are more likely to search by category (e.g. program, degree) than by specific brand. This is especially true for today's adult student.

- **The proliferation of new marketing technologies and channels**. With the explosion of marketing technologies and methodologies, institutions face a bewildering array of choices. Figuring out where and how to get started is a much more complex decision than it used to be. Note: According to the online marketing repository Chiefmarter.com, in 2015, there were 350 marketing companies of record compared to 7,000 plus in 2018. In addition, digital touch points options are expanding at a dizzying pace. Consider this recent short list of options[98]:

  o Web—must work on desktop/laptop, tablet, smartphone, etc.

  o Mobile—native apps, SMS, AR/VR experiences, etc.

  o Beacon-triggered and geolocation-based mobile experiences.

  o Chatbots—screen-based and voice-based, across a variety of devices.

  o Wearables—smart watches and more purpose-specific wearables.

  o AR/VR glasses and headsets—from Google Cardboard to Occulus and HoloLens.

- Connected TVs with an explosion of OTT content and services.
- Connected cars—Android Auto and Dash are two platform examples.
- Digital out-of-home signage and digital kiosks—including augmented reality features.
- APIs as a digital interface for citizen developers with tools like IFTTT.
- New point-of-sale experiences—Amazon Go is an example of how far this can go.
- 3D printing for digitally delivering physical items to prospects/customers.

While this list is most likely beyond the capacity of most institutions for new program marketing, it's helpful to know what options are out there. While innovative today, many of these marketing channels will become affordable options in the not-so-distant future.

- **The depth, breadth, and sophistication of the competition.** The frenzied state of competition that most institutions reside in, not to mention the fact that everyone seems to be launching new programs these days using increasingly sophisticated marketing tools and methods, makes good marketing all that more critical and also more complex.

- **The increased complexity of the marketing function has resulted in new marketing structures and roles.** Organizing and staffing the marketing function has increased in complexity as well. The competencies and skills needed to effectively market in the current climate are different than what was the case even five years ago. In launching new programs, institutions may need to be creative about how they will access the expertise they need for effective program marketing.

2. Target Market Research Tools and Approaches

Management guru Peter Drucker once commented that "The aim of marketing is to know and understand the customer so well the product or service sells itself."[99] In these few words, Drucker captures the essence of target market research—the goal of which is to get to know your markets, to appreciate who is going to be interested in your new program and why, to understand as deeply as possible what your prospective students want and need from your program.

According to the American Marketing Association, target market research is "the systematic gathering, recording, and analyzing of data about issues surrounding the marketing of goods and services." The important word here is "systematic." Without an effort to regularly and methodically research the target markets for your new program you will not have a clear enough understanding about how best to market your program or recruit for your program. You can't be successful promoting something that you don't understand.

Good market research data adds value in a number of other important ways including:

- Influencing program and curricular design on the front end.

- Determining program viability and demand.

- Eliminating frustration, distrust and subjectivity.

- Saving you time and money and help you avoid costly mistakes.

- Informing strategies related to market segmentation and market positioning.

- Identifying and analyzing your program's competition.

- Informing decisions related to tuition pricing, delivery modality, marketing messaging, and advertising strategy and channels among other things.

Target market research does not need to be costly; nor does it need to be complicated. For example, it can be as simple as interviewing prospective students to learn what they are looking for in programs like the one you want to launch. A few basic target market research techniques include analyzing industry and labor demand data, studying your competition, and analyzing demographic data about prospective students.

Whatever method you use, your primary focus sis to gather enough information so you have a good idea about the student who is likely to enroll in your new program and his or her demographic profile, interests, needs, and wants. Market research to support new programs should answer questions such as:

- Who is likely to enroll in this program?

- How would you describe or profile this student?

- Where are they located?

- What is their educational background?

- Why would this student enroll in our program? What is she/he hoping to gain from the program?

- Most importantly, is the program as designed going to meet the interests, needs, and wants of the prospective student—at the best place, at the right price, and in the right amounts?

An easy way to remember the key phases of target market research process is the "STP and Stakeholder Analysis" model.[100] STP is an acronym for Segmentation, Targeting, and Positioning.

Here are definitions for each element as adapted for higher education:

> **Segmentation**. Segmentation involves differentiating your market on the basis of demographic variables (e.g., gender, age, and education), geographic variables (e.g., state, region, and distance from campus), psychographic variables (e.g., interests and values) and behaviors (e.g., media habits and brand loyalty). There is no one right way to segment a market. It depends entirely on what will make the most sense for your institution and for the nature of the program you are launching. For example, your market segmentation for a new entirely online physical

therapy program that will have a national reach is going to be very different than for an entirely campus-based graduate program in education designed to serve the educators in your immediate region.

Target Markets Identification. Once you identify your market segments, you will need to decide which ones to target and which ones to put to the side. Questions to ask about your market segments: (1) Does this segment have strong revenue and growth potential? (2) Is this segment relatively inexpensive to reach with marketing efforts? (3) Is this segment currently being served by competitors, and if so, how many and how strong is the competition? and (4) Does this segment have needs and interests that our institution and this program are well suited to meet?

Note: If you discover that your new program does not fit a definable segment of the market, you might need to reevaluate your program to determine whether it can be retooled to better align with a specific target market.

Positioning. Positioning has to do with crafting the right messaging about your program so that the segmented markets will respond and understand the potential value and benefit that the program offers for them. A best practice here is to draft a segmentation profile for your ideal prospective student, including: name, age, occupation, likes, dislikes, etc. This personalizes your target market and helps you create effective messaging.

Stakeholder Analysis. The success of any new program ultimately depends on your ability to gain the support of and manage the expectations of key people. Effective stakeholder management can have a significant and immediate impact on whether your program flourishes or goes under. Because you cannot satisfy the diverse needs of all stakeholders, it's important to identify which stakeholders are the most important and then keep them in mind when making day-to-day and long-term strategic decisions about the program. Here is a tool that can be useful for identifying who your program stakeholders are and the potential each one has to influence your program's success:

Stakeholder			
Importance (L, M, H)			
Potential contribution to program's success			
Expectations of the program			
Ability to influence others (L, M, H			
Power over the program's success (L, M, H)			

Market research is not a perfect science; however, as discussed in Chapter 7, understanding your market on the front end of your new program's launch is critically important. There are as many ways to conduct market research as the day is long. Some easy places to start include:

- **Use free online resources** to search local demographic data, competitors, view site maps, industry outlook, and much more.

- **Develop simple surveys** to use with prospective students, potential employers, and so on. You will be surprised what you can learn just by asking a few questions.

- **Review local maps**. They are a great way to understand a geographic area and the local resources, including other institutions, and to put a "market" in perspective.

- **Use economic development agencies** and professional associations affiliated with the new program you're launching. They can be powerful resources available to help find all types of market and demographic information and can sometimes be a particularly good source of information about the depth and breadth of the market.

- **Review Census and Labor Department** data and publications.

- As I mentioned in Chapter 7, **know who your competitors are and study them carefully**. Who are they serving? How is their program structured and delivered? What do people say about the quality of their program? Plus, any other market information you can find out.

Beyond this, there are four basic categories for which you want to collect key data:

- Labor and Demographic Analytics
- Competition
- Marketing
- Primary Data

The following table provides examples and a rationale for each data type within each category along with suggestions for where you can find the data. See the resource listing at the end of Section III for more information about the data sources.

Key Data & Sources: Labor and Demographics Analytics		
Data	**Why**	**Data Source(s)**
Number of jobs Job growth	Forecast program demand and growth potential	BLS, NCES, City/State, Burning Glass, EAB, Gray Associates, Emsi
Key skills as identified by employers	Inform curriculum and marketing	Emsi, City/State
Large/key employers in targeted markets	Outreach to key employers	Emsi, Burning Glass, EAB, City/State
Demographic trends for key student markets	Help forecast demand and market segments	National/city/state reports, NCES, Gray Associates, LinkedIn

Academic Entrepreneurship

Key Data & Sources: Competition		
Data	**Why**	**Data Source(s)**
Institutions offering the program; Enrollment in competitor programs; Completion data	Estimate market size, forecast demand, identify key competitors, evaluate trends	IPEDS, City/State, Gray Associates, Emsi, Chmura
Curriculum; Unique features Tuition; Admission requirements; Market positioning	Identify areas of competitive overlap, opportunity and advantage	Competitor websites, secret shopping, education guides

Key Data & Sources: Marketing		
Data	**Why**	**Data**
Key marketing channels	Inform marketing strategies and tactics	Ruffalo Noel Levitz, Learning House, EAB, Education Dynamics
Key decision drivers (and messaging suggestions)	Craft relevant and compelling messaging and content	Ruffalo Noel Levitz, Learning House, EAB, Education Dynamics
Cost of acquisition Average yield rates	Determine marketing spend and inform ROI	Internal data, RNL, EAB, UPCEA
Program name and course titles	Ensure market traction	Google Trends and key word analysis

Key Data & Sources: Primary Data		
Data	**Why**	**Data Source(s)**
Prospective student insights: decision drivers, curriculum, desired outcomes	Inform decisions regarding curriculum and marketing	Prospective students
Employer and influencer insights: skills demand, curriculum, credentialing	Inform decisions regarding curriculum and marketing	Advisory boards, donors, employers, alumni, business groups, etc.

When it comes to data acquisition an important consideration is whether to do the work in-house or outsource? In making this decision, consider:

- The scope of the work/project.
- Your internal capacity.
- How much time this will take and whether you can afford the time.
- Whether you possess internal expertise to do this well.
- Whether the data come from primary or secondary sources.[101]
- Your culture.
- Cost.

Increasingly, many institutions combine external data solutions and tools with internal research. The following list provides a great starting point for information that can be obtained using internal staff. Most of the secondary source information from these organizations is available online and free or at a very minimal cost.

SECONDARY RESEARCH SOURCES

The ecosystem of secondary research resources is large and ever expanding. Here is a summary listing:

Government: Federal, state, city sources, including education/higher education entities and commissions. *Examples: Bureau of Labor Statistics, IPEDS, National Center for Education Statistics, National Student Clearinghouse.*

Professional Associations. *Examples: NACUBO, Council on Graduate Schools.*

Discipline-Specific Accrediting Organizations. *Example: ACOTE.*

Consulting and Service Firms Focused on Higher Education. *Examples: Ruffalo Noel Levitz, Academic Impressions, Education Advisory Board.*

Philanthropic Organizations. *Examples: LUMINA, Bill and Melinda Gates Foundation.*

Think Tanks and Academic Centers. *Example: Georgetown Center for Education and the Workforce.*

State/Regional Economic Agencies. *Example: Massachusetts Economic Development and Finance Agency.*

> **Higher Education Press.** *Examples: The Chronicle of Higher Education, Inside Higher Ed, Academic Impressions Daily Pulse.*
>
> **Investment Firms.** *Example: TIAA-CREF.*

Checklist: Market research data

Use the following checklist to review the range of data sources that are available to help you develop your new program's marketing plan and determine its potential marketplace niche.

Market Potential (External)

- ☐ **Number of Jobs/Year National:** Three-year average of the number of jobs associated with the degree/degree level (SOC and CIP codes). Note trends.

    Why: Programs with strong regional and national job markets should see relatively higher demand.

    Source: Labor data analytics solutions (EMSI, Gray, Chmura, etc., EAB)

- ☐ **Number of Jobs/Year Regional:** Three-year average of the number of jobs associated with the degree/degree level in surrounding states (SOC and CIP codes). Note trends.

    Why: Programs with strong regional and national job markets should see relatively higher demand.

    Source: Labor data analytics solutions (EMSI, Gray, Chmura, etc., EAB)

☐ **Regional Ratio:** The percentage of jobs in-region vs national.

Why: Research suggests most students choose a program within a 50-mile radius. Programs with a strong regional ratio should aggressively target regional markets. Programs with a weak regional ratio may need to target national markets, which will likely increase cost of acquisition.

Source: Labor data analytics solutions (EMSI, Gray, Chmura, etc., EAB)

☐ **Salary:** Average median salary for all job categories associated with the degree/degree level. Calculated from O*Net, Payscale, and Burning Glass.

Why: Higher median salaries suggest a potential marketing opportunity/message for the program.

Source: Labor data analytics solution (EMSI, Gray, Chmura, etc.), O*Net, Payscale, and Burning Glass.

☐ **National Growth:** Calculated three-year job growth.

What it means: National growth rates suggest level of demand. Rapid growth suggests increasing demand. Decline suggests potential oversaturation of qualified employees and less demand.

Source: LinkedIn.

☐ **Regional Growth:** Forecasted three-year job growth from LinkedIn.

What it means: Growth rates suggest level of demand. Rapid growth suggests increasing demand. Decline suggests potential oversaturation of qualified employees and less demand. Variance between regional and national growth rates can help determine marketing spend.

Source: LinkedIn.

- **Skill demands and top employers:** Develop list of key skills within content area and large volume employers.

  What it means: Key skill areas helps inform curriculum, and knowing large employers can facilitate marketing, internship/career placement, partnership development, etc.

  Source: EMSI, Chmura, etc.

Competition (External)

- **Credentials in Field:** Percent of employees in strongly aligned job fields who possess an equivalent degree to proposed offering.

  Why: A higher percentage indicates the credential is commonly held in the industry. A lower percentage indicates the credential is not commonly held and program may be misaligned to the market.

  Source: O*Net, Emsi, and Bureau of Labor Statistics (BLS) data.

- **Degree output:** IPEDS data on total degrees nationally awarded at level and in the field.

  Why: Programs with high degree outputs suggest degree is known/accepted and has established demand. Compare outputs with number of jobs to determine market saturation level.

  Source: IPEDS, Gray, Emsi, Chmura

☐ **Competitive profiles:** Develop competitive profiles for all regional competitors and key national competitors that includes student headcount, curriculum overview and map, admission standards and application fees, tuition and scholarships, academic calendar, modality, faculty composition (tenured, adjunct, etc.), market positioning strategy, etc.

Why: Competitive information is crucial to inform program and curricular decisions, points of differentiation, and marketing strategy. Further, programs with little regional competition can more easily gain market share. Strong competition likely requires greater marketing investment.

Source: Website research, IPEDS, Gray, Emsi, Chmura.

Marketing

☐ **Keyword research:** Research name of the program, as well as likely search terms related to it, (e.g., master's degree in XYZ, graduate degree in XYZ, XYZ masters, certificate in XYZ, XYZ program, etc.).

Why: Keywords that score/rank highly suggest greater organic web traffic and provide guidelines for what keywords to purchase for paid search (e.g., Google Adwords, etc.).

Source: Google Trends and Google Analytics, Yahoo Keyword Planner, etc.

☐ **Audience Analysis questions:** What are audience motivations for program? How does the program appeal to those motivations? What are audiences' desired outcomes of education? What messaging points are most relevant to audience? What macro/industry forces are impacting the audience?

Internal considerations and questions

- **Capacity –** What are capacity constraints related to enrollment? To what extent can the program leverage existing faculty/staff/facility infrastructure?

- **Modality –** In what modalities can the program be delivered?

- **Growth capacity –** To what extent can the program be quickly scaled?

- **Institutional priority –** To what extent is the program key to the institution and the department?

- **Financial commitment and proforma –** What are start-up costs, and how quickly will the program provide a net contribution?

- **Barrier to entry –** How high is the barrier to entry for this program? Can competitors easily offer like programs?

- **Outcomes –** Does the program lead to clear professional outcomes, e.g., a career path for traditional undergraduates or salary increase for post-traditional learners?

Source: Chris Nicholson, Ph.D., University of Denver

3. New Program Marketing Plan: Components and Essentials

In their eagerness to get out the door with their new program, some colleges omit the very important step of drafting a marketing plan to support the new program. The marketing plan serves as the blueprint that outlines how you will communicate the value and benefit of your new program. As such, it provides an organizing framework that makes transparent the assumptions you are making about the program including who will enroll and can be very helpful in ensuring that everyone is on the same page.

7 P's of Marketing

A comprehensive marketing plan for a new academic program will typically use a mix of marketing elements known as the *7 P's of Marketing* as a framework.[102] I have adapted these elements here to be useful for developing a plan to support your new program.

PRODUCT

In traditional marketing the product is the thing you are selling, namely your new program. Your competitors are the other institutions that offer the same or similar programs. In considering your product, you want to articulate the tangible and intangible benefits that your new program provides including understanding who will benefit and in what specific ways. Too many higher education institutions frame their program marketing in terms of program features versus benefits which is shortsighted. A clear articulation of program benefits serves as a foundation for nearly every other marketing decision.

PRICE

This second "P" refers specifically to the tuition price you set for your new program but more broadly must also consider the bottom line profit margin your program needs to achieve in order to be sustainable. Developing a coherent, defendable, and realistic pricing strategy for your new program is one of the most important decisions you will make. Tuition pricing should not be set according to simply what is needed to cover the program's expenses. Instead, your starting price point should be determined by considering several factors including competitor program pricing, your institution's reputation and prestige profile, how unique and in demand your program is and the extent to which your program will lead to higher paying jobs, among other things.

PLACEMENT

This "P" has to do with where your program will be delivered. For example, will your program be offered online and serve a national or international market, or will it primarily serve a region defined as within 90 miles of your campus? The decisions you make here will impact other decisions including pricing, promotion and process. For instance, if you decide to roll out an entirely online program, you will need to segment your target markets geographically in order to reach those individuals most likely to be interested in your program.

Promotion

Promotion is the "P" that most people think about when they consider marketing. Indeed, promotion is a very important part of the overall marketing mix. In a nutshell, promotion consists of all the various ways and methods you will use to get the word out about your new program. Common promotional methods include direct mail, advertising, publicity and public relations, personal selling, sponsorships, website, and, an increasingly important method, social media and digital/interactive promotion. Two traditional methods often overlooked by higher education institutions are product giveaways and customer referral incentives. When adapted for higher education, both methods can be particularly powerful when launching a new program. See more about these methods later in this chapter.

People

Especially in higher education, the individuals delivering the product, aka program, have an inordinate impact on how students evaluate their experience. The people here include all the individuals who touch your prospective students including recruitment staff and the individuals who deliver the learning experience, namely your faculty. Professionalism, courtesy, trustworthiness, approachability, and preparedness are just a few of the characteristics that can create loyalty and satisfaction on the part of your students.

Process

This "P" has to do with the "how" your program is delivered, and all of the processes involved in recruiting, enrolling, and educating your students. It is worth it to take the time to review these processes including using secret shoppers to experience your program's recruitment process and give you feedback. How easy is it for students to get answers to important questions about the program? How user friendly is your website? Are program policies and procedures made transparent to students on the front end? Are policies and procedures reasonable and defendable? Process is an increasingly important consideration for institutions wanting to increase adult student enrollments as adult students are particularly likely to value responsiveness and a high degree of service.[103]

PHYSICAL EVIDENCE

This final "P" is all about your students' satisfaction. Because education is an intangible, students will look to a wide range of things in assessing the quality of their experience with you. It is important to think through on the front end what evidence you will look to on a regular basis to stay in close touch with your students' experience. At my institution, program directors often meet with their students in person on a regular basis—individually and in groups—and they actively solicit feedback on their experience. This section should also articulate the goals that have been set for the program including enrollment, financial and academic as the program's ability to meet the stated goals provides one piece of evidence about its performance in the marketplace in which it operates.

Core Components of a Marketing Plan

Using the 7 P's as a guide, you can develop a marketing plan to support the roll-out of your new program. A comprehensive plan should minimally include the following components:

Program Description

Your plan should start with a good description of your program, including: its degree and program name, mission, program and learning outcomes, curricular strengths and differentiating aspects, bragging points, calendar and schedule details, and delivery details including how it will be delivered (e.g. campus-based, online, or hybrid).

Target Markets

For this section, include details about who the program is intended for such as segmented market descriptions (include important demographics about each segment) and insights about each market (e.g., motivating factors, resistance considerations, decision criteria, career fields, etc.).

Pricing Strategy

Your plan should include details about the set tuition price point for your program, any available discounts or scholarship opportunities, and a tuition pricing comparison for your key competitors (this should provide justification for your set pricing point). Include a few bullets outlining the justification for your tuition price point (e.g., program has few competitors, market demand is very high and so on). In terms of the marketing plan, you will also want to consider other indirect costs to the student, such as ancillary program fees, textbook, and other program resource costs, as well as transportation, time, and convenience costs.

Program Delivery, Placement and Geographic Target

This element overlaps with your description of the program and target markets. Even still, it's important to spell out the specifics about how the program will be delivered and which geographic markets are most likely to be good sources of students and why. For example, if you are rolling out an entirely online graduate program in occupational therapy, you may target a specific region of the country where there is a good supply of practitioners and very few program competitors. Being clear about this at the outset will help you make better promotional strategy decisions.

Promotion Strategy

Your marketing plan should spell out the specific methods you plan to use to promote your program including your strategies for each market segment. It's also critical to articulate in writing the key program benefits—overall and as relevant to each market segment—and program selling messages (which should answer the question: "Why should someone enroll in this program, at your institution, at this point in time?"). In terms of decisions, you will have to consider which methods you want to use as well as what image you want your program to reflect in its market context. Even with limited funds, it's important to take the time to think through basic elements such as how will the program be represented on your institution's website and who and how will your students be recruited? This should all be spelled out in the promotion strategy section of your plan.

Competition

This section includes everything you have learned about your program's key competitors including their pricing and discounting strategies (know their bottom-line cost) and their program strengths and weaknesses. It is particularly important to know what differentiates each of your competitors, what makes their program unique and attractive to prospective students? How does your program improve upon what your competitors are offering? Know this, and spell it out in this section of your plan.

COMPETITIVE ANALYSIS

For this section, I suggest you include two things: 1) a grid that lists the competitors identified above with key program features and a comparison to your program, and 2) a SWOT analysis[104] that clearly articulates your program's strengths, weaknesses, opportunities, and threats. Here are sample grids for each:

SAMPLE PROGRAM COMPARISON ANALYSIS

	School A	School B	School C	School D
Program name				
Bottom line cost				
Delivery				
Distinctive features				
Weaknesses and limitations				
Competitive advantage				
How does our program compare?				

Sample Program SWOT Analysis

Strengths	**Weaknesses**
Cutting edge curriculum No GRE required Quick completion Faculty practitioners with strong reputations in their fields	Too many pre-requisites for first semester courses Tuition higher than competition Institution has no reputation in this field
Opportunities	**Threats**
Growing industry Region is a hotbed for this field	Many schools launching similar programs right now

Marketing Budget

The final piece has to do with what your marketing plan is going to cost in order to be fully operationalized. This cannot be done until you have developed your promotional strategy and delineated the various methods and approaches that you plan to use. It is important to develop a marketing budget that is realistic and based on hard evidence about what it is going to take to enroll the desired number of students for your program. Your marketing budget spend will depend upon many things including how much market demand there is for your program, your delivery methods (online programs tend to require more marketing spend), and your specific marketing promotion mix. You will also want to identify metrics that you will use to assess the return on your investment (ROI). See more later in this chapter about metrics and assessing ROI.

Below, the new graduate program marketing launch process[105] and corresponding plan for my institution's new applied data science master's degree illustrates how these principles can be applied. This information corresponds with the marketing playbook example for the same graduate degree that is included at the end of this chapter. Note that the marketing playbook content for the M.S. in Applied Data Science clearly articulates and directly responds to many of the elements discussed above. At my institution, the playbook is created as a first step and serves as an important guide for the ensuing decisions about which marketing channels to use and how best to position the program vis-à-vis the competitive context.

NEW ACADEMIC PROGRAM MARKETING LAUNCH PROCESS

(Bay Path University)

These are the steps that are typically followed at Bay Path University in creating a marketing plan to support the launch of a new academic program. This entire process typically takes anywhere from 3-5 months, depending upon whether the program staff have been hired or appointed. The development of the marketing plan is led by the director of enrollment marketing who works closely with the academic program chair or director, the dean of the school in which the program will reside, and the recruitment and admission team to create the final plan. Most of the information described below is gathered internally although market research tools as described elsewhere in this chapter are consulted as appropriate. Depending upon the program, surveys or focus groups may be conducted to test messaging and positioning assumptions.

PROGRAM APPROVALS

1. Marketing obtains and reviews the approved P Form and Feasibility study.

2. Marketing obtains confirmation from the Registrar and Analytics that coding for the new program has been added to Jenzabar (Registrar) and Hobsons (Analytics).

PROGRAM RESEARCH

1. Marketing convenes planning launch meeting to review program information (which typically resides in the feasibility study):
   - Program Information:
     - Create opening paragraph describing the program and field.
     - Create a 3-5 word slogan/call to action for the program.
     - Create program selling points.
     - Program outcomes, what students will learn/gain.
     - Start dates.
       - What month(s) will have start dates each academic year?
     - Course delivery.
       - 100% Online, Online/On Campus, 100% On Campus

- Cohort model or not, are courses sequential?
- Which campuses have on campus options
- Full-time, part-time, or both
  - Program Options
    - What are the courses, credits per course, course descriptions?
    - Are there tracks, concentrations, licensure options? If so, description, credits, and curriculum needed
  - Faculty
    - Program Director/Chair (need biography, title, headshot, contact info, digital signature)
    - Faculty/Adjunct Faculty (need biography, title, headshot, contact info)
  - What are the tuition and enrollment goals?
  - Who is the admissions recruiter?
2. Marketing works with Program Director to complete the marketing playbook, which will answer the following:
   - What is this program's one-and-only position? What distinguishes it from the competition?
   - What are the key marketing and promotional messages for this program?

- What are the target market demographics? (e.g., audience groups, age, education degree and major, experience, salary, etc.)
- What audience insights are important to know for this program?
- Who are the top five competitors and what is our advantage/disadvantage?
- SWOT Analysis: Strengths, Weaknesses, Opportunities, Threats?
- Program Kudos or Accolades?
- Career and Job Outlook (state, region and national)?
- What do current students and alumni say about their experience in this program?
- Important People, Success Stories, and Facts to Know?
- Recruiter Tips?
- Other Facts?
- What industries and organizations are affiliated with the degree?
- What conferences should be attended by admissions, if they are exhibiting, coordinate advertising, attendance list rental, if available?

MARKETING TOOLS/PRE-PLANNING

1. Marketing ensures that start dates are added to inquiry forms and applications.

2. Marketing coordinates the selection and purchase of compelling imagery for marketing materials and

website that aligns with our playbook information about messaging and program brand.

3. Marketing works with communications office to build website pages and content for new program:
    - Create copy that differentiates program as well as selling features in collaboration with program director
    - Add curriculum and schedules
    - Include faculty bios
    - Admissions requirements page
    - Program outcomes page
    - Create back-end SEO and tagging
    - Industry facts to sell program for homepage
    - Links to reputable industry websites and facts
4. Build ad landing page for program (shortened version of website pages).
    - Build inquiry form for program
    - Add program to chat live
    - Build keyword list for bidding
    - Build ad copy for pay-per-click creative
    - Build geography targeting
5. Create program information sheet:
    - Derived from approved website content
    - Once approved send to printer, disperse to appropriate campuses and admissions counselors

6. Add degree to program listing sell sheet.
7. Establish communication plan for CRM (customer relationship management system).
    - Build communication emails
    - Schedule emails for all stages of the funnel
8. Create program director video.
    - Introduction of program director, discuss background, the program, what students will learn, career plans, etc.
    - Make into different length video clips to use on social media and website
9. Create program director Q & A for website and mailings.
    - What do you love about the program? What's the value of the degree? Why should students choose the school for this degree?
10. Program director introduction letter.
    - This letter introduces themselves and the program, and is typically sent to affiliated organizations, alumni, current students, faculty at other institutions, etc.

MARKETING PLANNING

1. Identify key target markets (e.g., geography, demographics, professions, affiliated organizations, etc.). This is informed by the marketing playbook and market research.
2. Research specific organizations that fit your key target market; make contact with representative and receive copies of all media kits needed to plan.

- This will help determine if they have the following advertising opportunities available:
  - Subscriber/Member mailing/email list rentals
  - Digital Advertising
    - Website Display Advertising
    - E-newsletter Advertising
  - Print Advertising
    - Publications, Journals, Conference Programs

3. Establish Marketing Plan for fiscal year (July-June).
   - Mark all start dates for the program on plan to align marketing strategies.
   - Plan is a blend of industry-specific advertising, traditional advertising, and branding.
   - Plan based off of program-targeted assessment for major media areas:
     - Direct Mail (Letters, Posters, Postcards)
     - Radio (Local, National, Digital)
     - Online & Digital (PPC, display, e-newsletters, and social media)
     - Print (Publications, Journals, Conference Programs)
     - Billboard (Vinyl and Digital design)
     - Television (Local, National, Cable, Digital, Broadcast)

4. Frequently assess ROI of efforts and interest activity, change plan/add additional buys based on assessments.

MARKETING PLAN SAMPLE

(Bay Path University—Master of Science in Applied Data Science Program Launch)

Following the program's launch, the marketing team (which includes the marketing director, program director, dean, and assigned recruiter) meet monthly to assess results and make changes as needed to the playbook and the annual marketing plan. See the following example of a marketing plan that was created to support the launch of a new graduate degree program in applied data science.

ACADEMIC ENTREPRENEURSHIP

*Planning not booked	JUL	AUG	SEP	OCT 22-Oct	NOV	DEC	JAN	FEB 25-Feb	MAR	APR	MAY	JUN	COMMENTS	QUANTITY & CRITERIA
START DATE:														
DIRECT MAIL:														
Business Large Mailer	x												Art MFA, LDN, CBT, CBM, COM, INF, ADS, MBA, MAPP, SPP, HCM Inquiries and features & with county past 3 years; Grad admissions lists from SC; TAPPG/OBC/PMG Current Students and Alumni from past 3 years from Accounting, Applied Computer Science, Business Administration, Business Analysis, Communications, Community Health, Computer Science, Conductor Security, Digital Forensics, Digital Marketing Management, Entrepreneurship, Food Industry Management, Information Assurance, Interior Design, Leadership & Organizational Studies, Marketing, Operations Management, Small Business Development, Strategic Human Resource Management, SoftBT MT ATD, HR Zip codes $40,000 - 150,000 income, 25 minute drive around Longmeadow & 15 minute drive around Sturbridge & Concord (Qty 6,686, every household (TGT-A, 170,800)	8/27 Q 212,234
ADS postcard		x											GRE Lists, ADS Inquiries past 3 years, Biomechanical list	8/20 Q 9912
Poster Mailing Letter/MMO			x										BO, BUSINESS, A LSG, MFA, HCM, CHI Career Services/New England Colleges and Universities	9/4 Q 367
Business Large Mailer			x										MFA, LDR, CBT, CBM, COM, INF, ADS, MBA, MAPP, SPP, HCM Inquiries, Again, Accept, LM/CR past 18/20	9/18 Q425
Business Jan OH & Feb Start Letter						x							Art MFA, LDN, CBT, CBM, COM, INF, ADS, MBA, MAPP, SPP, HCM, HCA, magnetic, Apps, Accepts	12/14 Q 1044
Business Large Mailer						x							Towns Inc. rep's 30 mile radius around Hartford and Springfield every other SOLOMON SOUND - college graduates	12/14 Q 27,000
RADIO:														
WFCR 88.5 FM (NEPR)	x	x	x										Drive- & Streaming 200-17/50/15 SP/Sk/3M	M-F Radio News, SA-F 7a-10a 2014
WBUR 90.9 FM (NEPR)	x	x	x										On-Air 17/30/18-06/26/18;	# NCPR Morning Edition Shows, 5 WCN 3h Three Consumers Marketplace Shows, 20 Adds each W-News Network
WMRQ 104.1 FM	x	x	x										30 Second Ads: M-F 6a-10a, 3p-7p (7/30/18-9/07/18)	Adds 25-48 Year Old, New Music, Employee, Wholetime, & Orators
WKSS 95.7 FM	x	x	x											
WRNX 100.9 FM	x	x	x											
WBWL 101.7 FM	x	x	x											
WWYX 92.5 FM	x	x	x											
WKCI 101.3 FM	x	x	x											

ONLINE:															
Search Engine Marketing (SEM)		x	x	x	x	x	x	x	x	x	x	x	x	x	Reach Local Search Campaigns
Chat Live		x						x	x	x	x			x	Reach Local Chat Element on Website
Display (CRM Retargeting)								x							320x50, 320x100, 300x600, 468x60, 728x90, 320x480, 300x250 Search RET (Target inquiries and apps for high cost programs - MGT and MSA)
Display (Search Retargeting)								x							All of MA and Hartford DMA
Display (Site Retargeting)							x	x							300x50, 120x600, 336x280, 468x60, 320x50, 300x600 Site RET – Targets all users who have recently searched for keywords relevant to each program
Display (Category Retargeting)							x	x							All of MA and Hartford DMA
															300x50, 120x600, 336x280, 468x60, 728x90, 300x600 Category Contextual (Target users who have recently been viewing content containing keywords relevant to the programs)
Display (Lookalikes Retargeting)							x	x							All of MA and Hartford DMA
															300x50, 120x600, 336x280, 468x60, 728x90, 300x600 Lookalikes (similar online profiles to CRM matched ones)
KDnuggets Custom HTML E-blast	26-Jul	13-Sep				x	x								Custom HTML
KDnuggets.com	x	x				x									300x250 Banner Homepage
ARMA Custom E-blast		6-Aug								9-Apr					IDM/INF/EDP/DASR/RIM/ADN
Information Management (ARMA)													x		CM/INF/EDP/ADS
BusinessWest Daily Enews		8/22, 8/24, 8/29	9/6, 9/20, 9/26	28-Nov											8/22 9/12 BiZ DM, 8/24 9/12 BiZ DM, 8/29 IADS, 9/6 9/12 BiZ DM, 9/20 (10/3 BiZ DM), 9/26 10/3 BiZ DM)
Business Hobsons Email		9/6, 9/7, 9/12													9/6 BMSR - 4,2995, 9/7 BMCR - 2,180, 9/12 (2017-2018) All Stage Business Programs 2,997
Business Hobsons Email			x												GRE purchased lists: ADS, ACE, and Business
Massive			x												Business 728x90, 300x250, 320x50 Oct Start Reminder
Hobsons Text			x												inquiries, Apps, Accepts, Reminder for Oct Start
LinkedIn			x												Business 1200x627 Oct Start Promotion
PRINT:															
Information Management (ARMA)					x								x		Full Page B&W/INF/EDP/ADS
Go Local		x	x												Full Page Color (Branding) / AchessED LPN Diagnos. Sept. Open House, Promotions
BusinessWest Magazine		OH	BRAND		BZ OH	BZ OH									
BILLBOARDS:															
Chicopee I-90 E/O Exit 5, Baskin Dr, Faces E (D)	ADS														
Worcester I-290 S/O Exit 11 (V)	ADS	ADS	ADS												
Peabody Rd I-95 @ 271 Newbury St (D)	ADS	ADS	ADS												
Hartford I-84W Capitol Ave (D)	ADS				ADS										
Hartford I-84 @ Farmington Near Exit 37 (D)	ADS														
Hartford I-915 Exit 34 (D)		ADS													
Hartford I-91 S/O Reserve Rd Exit 29 (V)			ADS		ADS										
Hartford I-91 @ Colt Bld. S/O Whitehead Hwy (D)															

ACADEMIC ENTREPRENEURSHIP

SMALL BLADES:									
West Farms Mall		x		x	x	x	x	x		Grand Re-opening, 2 Ceremonies, 2 musicians in Mall
CAMPUS TV SLIDES:									
All Campus TVs	ADS		BIZ OH	ADS	ADS	ADS	ADS	ADS		
TELEVISION/DIGITAL TVS:									
Comcast Spotlight Cable	x	x	x	x	x		x	x		Campus specific commercials with course offerings and open houses
Premium Digital TV (Aspyu/Online	x	x	x	x	x		x	x		Phone, Sports, Specials in the following cities: Lowell, Woburn, Springfield, Brockton, Enfield (all towns in these zones listed on the TV tab)
WFSB CBS Hartford	x	x	x	x	x		x	x		All cable networks: Javen, Boston, Worcester, Lowell, Newburn, Springfield, Brockton, Enfield (Part of Comcast Spotlight)
WVIT NBC Hartford	x	x	x	x	x		x	x		Campus specific commercials with course offerings and open houses
WWLP NBC Springfield	x	x	x	x	x		x	x		News
CW Springfield	x	x	x	x	x		x	x		Campus specific commercials with course offerings and open houses
WWLP Video Pre-roll		x								News, Prime, Sports, Specials
WSHM CBS Springfield	x	x	x	x	x		x	x		On-me, suedaes (this is owned by WWLP)
WGGB ABC Springfield	x	x	x	x	x		x	x		Promode / Open House (Part of WWLP)
EGGB FOX Springfield	x	x	x	x	x		x	x		News, Prime, Sports, Specials (Part of WesternMass News)
WesternMass News Video Pre-roll	x	x	x	x			x	x		News, Prime, Sports, Specials (Part of WesternMass News)
WesternMass News Storm Closings		x			x	x	x	x	x		Promode, Open House (Part of WesternMass News)

4. High Impact Marketing Practices

There are an abundance of marketing strategies, tools, and approaches that one can use to launch your new program. Here is a short list of strategies that are relatively low-cost, easy to implement, and impactful. This list is not meant to be exclusive—a more detailed listing of marketing strategy resources is included at the end of Section III. The strategies listed below are designed to be used in conjunction with each other and as part of a broader marketing plan. Implementing a good mix of strategies utilizing multiple methods and channels ensures the best outcome possible. In tandem, these strategies create a synergy that helps builds recognition for your program in the marketplace.

Formalize and legitimatize the role of marketing in program ideation, design, and launch.

It should be obvious by now that I believe strongly that marketing considerations need to be on the agenda from the very beginning of the program development process. Unfortunately, this is not often the case in many colleges and universities. Without an understanding of the market context in which the program will reside, it's difficult, if not impossible, to design a curriculum and make decisions about other program elements such as delivery model in alignment with what the market wants. There are very few programs and institutions where the notion of "if you build it, they will come" applies anymore. A team-based approach to program development that includes academics working alongside marketing and enrollment professionals ensures everyone is on the same page from the beginning and that the program development process receives a steady flow of realism. Marketing and enrollment professionals will have important input to add to the process that academics might otherwise miss. Conversely, marketing and enrollment professionals will gain a deep understanding about the program that will help them be more effective in marketing and recruiting for the program. By establishing good working relationships on the front end, you set the stage for sustaining the information flow back and forth which can be vitally important once the program launches. Your enrollment professionals are your eyes and ears on the ground; they will know first-hand what prospective students think about your program, why they enroll and why they choose to go elsewhere. This is critically valuable intel to mine and reference on a regular basis.

Map and leverage program influencer relationships.

Remember that stakeholder analysis tool we discussed earlier? Well, this is where the tool comes in very handy. One of the easiest and least expensive ways to get the word out about your new program is to leverage an army of individuals who are familiar with your program, who believe in it and who can help spread the word through their own personal and organizational networks. For many institutions, and this is certainly the case at Bay Path, prospective students who are referred by "insiders"—meaning current students or graduates of the program or others who are affiliated with the program and institution—wind up enrolling at a significantly higher rate than students who come to us through other marketing sources. Make a list of the individuals who have the potential to influence others on behalf of your program. Consider current students and alumni, board members, faculty and staff, community liaisons, and so on. Then develop a strategy for each group that makes it easy for them to share your program with others. Host a reception each year for your key influencers. Keep them close and well informed about your program after it's up and running. Let them know how much appreciate their help. Many schools have had success with a referral incentive program. For example, if you are launching a new graduate program in education, consider offering one free course in any of your graduate programs to school administrators in your region who refer one or more enrollees in a given year.

Stay close to your students.

This is a simple but very effective way to learn about your primary market: your students. Starting at the very beginning, and as soon after they deposit as possible, ask your students why they selected your program, what other programs they considered, why they chose your program over the competition, and what they hope to gain from their experience in the program. After they enroll, and at regular intervals, find ways to continue to get feedback with a focus on the entire experience they are having with the program and with your institution. Are there aspects of the experience they would change? If so, what are they, and why? What do they like and dislike about the program and your institution? Are there expectations being met? There are a variety of ways to get this information, including: paper and pen or electronic surveys, small group and one-on-one meetings, informal gatherings, etc. The important point is to genuinely care about how your students are experiencing your program, to take the time to ask them, to listen deeply, and then respond as appropriate. As you find ways to make improvements in response to student feedback, make sure you publicize this fact. Nothing demonstrates your interest and concern more than knowing that you care enough to respond to student feedback.

Feature faculty as thought leaders.

While faculty may not be comfortable being placed in a direct marketing or recruitment role on behalf of their program, they can be highly effective in other significantly beneficial ways. At my institution, many of our programs host free, online webinars featuring program faculty who share content on a topic that relates to what they teach in the program. These webinars are marketed as a part of the overall marketing strategy for the program. Our faculty love the opportunity to share their expertise about something that they are passionate about, and prospective students and other attendees get an opportunity to sample the program in a no-risk, no-obligation context. Webinars, short workshops, and other program content-centered venues are a wonderful way to draw people in to your program and build your inquiry pool.

Establish an annual signature event.

With new programs in fields where you do not have an established reputation, consider holding a signature event that brings experts in the field to your campus as speakers and workshop facilitators. When my institution launched our programs in cybersecurity some in the region were initially skeptical. This was a very new area for our institution, and we did not have a foundation to build on.

We did two things on the front end that quickly put any concerns to rest. First, we established a program advisory board and recruited the best minds in the region to serve on the board as market experts. With the advisory board's help, we also established a signature event: The Cybersecurity Summit, an annual event which attracts cyber professionals from across the region who come to network and to hear from national experts in the field on hot topics.

Start a blog.

Blogs are informational websites that generally reflect the personality of the author; they are updated frequently and written in a conversational, informal style. Blogs are effective communication vehicles that, if tailored to narrowly-focused groups and relevant program-related topics, can introduce your program to new individuals on a daily basis. It is estimated that there are over 100 million active blogs. According to marketing statistics by Hubspot.com,[106] over 46% of people read blogs every day. Now for the clincher: 82% of marketers who blog daily acquired a customer using their blog, as opposed to 57% of marketers who blog monthly -- which, by itself, is still an impressive result. Think about those numbers for a minute. Blogs are popular and powerful. Additionally, reading other blogs can familiarize you to a vast array of resources, reflections, and opinions that may prove useful for your marketing strategy. Consider having your program's chair or director or a faculty member create a blog about something they are passionate about and that is related to your program. The bottom-line: starting and/or participating in a blog can be an excellent approach for building visibility for your program and extending your reach.

Write an article.

Similarly, ask faculty and program staff to write articles that deliver valuable content about something that will have interest to the general public but also relates to your program. Local newspapers and media outlets are always looking for fresh, interesting articles for their readers. Articles that benefit the community in some way, and mention your program's name at the same time, are a wonderful source of free advertising. Start by considering what hot topics your community is grappling with and find a link to your program. Perhaps you are bringing up a new program in drug and alcohol counseling, and your institution resides in a region that has been hard hit by the opioid crisis. Ask a faculty member or program chair to pen a short article that provides guidance for family members who have a loved one who is struggling with addiction. The key here is to prepare an easy-to-read article that is interesting and has a community or regional connection. An advertisement, disguised as an article, will never get published.

Make sure your program has an online presence.

Like it or not, the Internet has become an integral part of our everyday lives. It makes sense then that you would want to market your business online. Fast becoming a mandatory market strategy, positioning your business on the Internet is a must. The Internet's global footprint will give your business the ability to reach potential customers that without it would be impossible. For example, a family is vacationing to the area where your business is located, and they want to know area restaurants. Your restaurant would want to make sure that its menu, phone number, and address can be found online. Because this family also has a dog, a dog grooming business would want to ensure its hours of operation, costs, and product offerings are available at the touch of a keyboard. Consider online advertising services like Google AdWords, which can help you reach more of your target market at an affordable pay-per-click rate.

Build and curate engaging social media content.

Social media is an increasingly important component of one's marketing plan and strategy. Even for small, resource-constrained institutions, a social media strategy is a critically important component. To begin, you will need to identify the social media channels that make the most sense for your program along with content themes that you want to emphasize. This is where social media audience research comes in to play (more on this later). Once you know who you are trying to reach using social media, you can create and disseminate appropriate content using the relevant channels. An easy way to get started is to ask your students to create and share content on their social media. For example, have your students create short videos depicting some aspect of their experience in your program. Instagram Stories, Facebook Live, and other in-the-moment media are great outlets for user-generated content.

Research your social media audience.

Just because nearly 80% of adults use Facebook does not mean your prospective students are hanging out there. Understand who your audience is and which social media channels attract which demographics. For example,

Facebook's most popular demographics include: women users (83%), 18-29-year-olds (88%), urban- and rural-located users (81% each), those earning less than $30,000 (84%), and users with some college experience (82%).[107] You can get similar demographic usage statistics online for the other social media channels including Instagram, Twitter, etc. You may also want to consider adding a question to your inquiry and application materials that asks which social media channels the individual regularly uses. Keeping track of this information over time, particularly for those who eventually enroll in your program, gives you a quick way to know which social media channels may be most closely in sync with your target markets.

Find ways to engage with prospective students in non-threatening contexts.

Social media channels are networks. This means that their primary purpose is to create a space where individuals can connect, discuss topics, and share content. Maintaining an active presence in this space takes time and intentionality but this is something that can pay big dividends when it comes to building a reputation and brand for your program. Relationship management is a big part of student recruitment, and social media provides a wonderful opportunity for interacting, responding, and gauging interest in a way that is not possible through more traditional marketing channels. As you consider your social media strategy, keep in mind the importance of posting content when your target market is most likely to be online (this information is available along with the demographic data mentioned above at various online sources), and also when someone at your institution is available to interact and respond. According to the Sprout Social Index, most social media users believe that brands should respond to social media messages within four hours. Make sure you have someone designated to monitor and interact on whichever social media channels you select.

Build an in-house student pipeline flow.

Another easy low-cost way to build a student market for your program is to connect it in some way to an existing undergraduate program (if a graduate program) or vice versa. While this may not work for all content areas, it's worth considering if your new program has curricular overlap or connection to a program that already exists. For example, when we launched our new graduate program in health care management, we worked with the undergraduate program in health services administration to link these two programs. Two courses in the new graduate program were identified as being appropriate for upper-level undergraduates and were embedded in the undergraduate major as required courses. The courses are allowed to count toward the credit total required for graduation at the baccalaureate level while also counting toward the credits required for the graduate degree. Once students experience the graduate program first-hand, they are more likely to continue with the remaining courses. New programs can be connected to existing programs in any number of ways. The important thing is to structure the connection in such a way that you pull the students into your new program.

Integrate your marketing messages and efforts.

No matter what marketing channels you wind up using, it's critical to make sure the messaging you disseminate about your program is consistent across all that you do. This includes direct mail, paid advertising, website, social media as well as the personal selling that will be done by admissions recruitment staff and others who communicate on behalf of the program with prospective students. Why is this so important? Coherence in messaging provides clarity and reinforcement of your most impactful selling points, something that is increasingly important in a crowded marketplace. A first step in achieving coherence is to make your messaging and marketing efforts as transparent as possible. This is where a written marketing plan and marketing playbook for your program can serve as valuable tools for getting everyone on the same page and making messaging and marketing goals explicit. See the end of this chapter for a sample playbook.

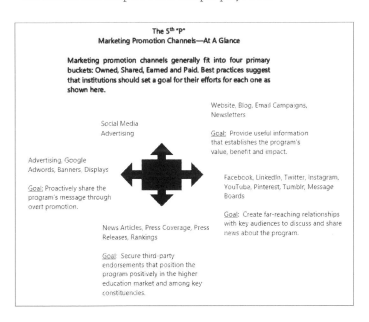

5. Brand, Branding and Positioning

Brand, branding, and positioning are very important concepts when it comes to the success of your new program. They are also concepts that are not well understood and are frequently confused with other concepts like advertising and public relations. In fact, while brand, branding, and positioning go hand in hand, they have distinct meanings that are important to understand, particularly as you are launching your new program. Even the smallest and most resource-constrained institution needs to consider how it wants to be viewed by the external world. This is what brand is all about. In the simplest of terms, your program's brand is its personality—it answers the question, "Who are you?" Your program's brand is also its reputation and vice versa. Your program's brand is the basis on which others will evaluate and differentiate your program vis-à-vis other programs. And, your program's brand will determine the expectations that others have of your program. No wonder Sir John Hegarty, Founder of BBH, wrote, "A brand is the most valuable piece of real estate in the world; a corner of someone's mind."[108]

Your program's brand is the total of all experiences and perceptions that someone has with your program—it's what is lived out on a daily basis. It is the thing that causes an emotional response in others—a gut feeling, if you will. Others own your brand—this is an important point. You do not have direct control of the perceptions that others hold about your program.

Branding, on the other hand, consists of the things you do, the activities you undertake to influence these perceptions.

What influences brand perception? Practically everything —your website, your communication (email, social media and so on), the physical and environmental setting of your program, behaviors and attitudes of faculty and staff, advertising, messaging, decisions and actions taken by program staff, and on it goes. In a nutshell, branding is all about aligning what you want others to think about your program with what they actually think based on the sum of their experiences with your program. Just as your personality is determined over time based on your individual attributes and actions, the same is true for the brand position that your program will occupy. Intentionally or not, your program will claim a brand position. To whatever extent you can be clear about the brand position you want your program to hold including the attributes you want your program to be known for, and then be deliberate about managing your actions so as to convey a consistent image to others through all that you do, your program will be well served.

The importance of brand in higher education is illustrated by the results of a survey[109] administered to thousands of adult college students asking about their decisions to enroll at a particular institution. The single most important factor for both populations is the academic reputation of the institution (80% of adult undergraduates and 80% of adult graduate students cited this factor as very important in their ultimate decision). Moreover, according to higher education marketing consultant, Jim Black, "delivering on the promise of the brand is the single most important aspect of branding a higher education institution."[110] As Black points out, the benefit of branding in a higher education context comes from the focus it brings. If done well, your brand provides a sharp filter through which everything is vetted (e.g., strategic directions, resource allocations, hiring decisions, and curriculum development). Particularly in fluid times, a well-defined brand can strategically focus your efforts and help you be more effective.

There are a variety of ways to develop and implement a branding strategy for your new program. Two key elements of nearly all approaches include identifying your program's uniqueness and determining what makes it stand out from your competitors. This is where brand positioning comes into play. According to L. Jean K. Harrison-Walker of the University of Houston-Clear Lake, positioning has to do with "how and institution is perceived in the minds of consumers, relative to competitors."[111] In arriving at one's brand position, Harrison-Walker suggests that academic institutions are well served to consider four of the basic P's of marketing as points of comparison with others in the same competitive marketplace:

- Product (the program features, attributes and benefits).
- Price (tuition, fees and bottom-line cost to student).
- Promotion (marketing and communications).
- Place (delivery system including program size, class size, faculty-student ratio, delivery model and so on).

Harrison-Walkers advises institutions to consider their brand position relative to their competitors based on program attributes (e.g. formal or friendly, competitive versus relaxed), user groups (e.g. tech professional versus data generalist), and contexts for use (e.g. technical job focus versus graduate school gateway).

Developing a brand positioning statement—this is different from a tagline—can be a great way to get clarity around your program's brand and its position in the marketplace. Typically used internally only, a positioning statement is useful for shaping program messaging and making decisions that will impact how others perceive your program. Creating an effective position strategy begins with identifying your program's uniqueness and determining what makes it stand out from your competitors as discussed earlier. According to the traditional business literature, there are four essential elements of a first-rate positioning statement:

1. **Your Audience**: Who is your program designed to reach? What is their demographic? What are their attitudes? What are their pain points?

2. **Your Market**: What is your market category? How does your brand better relate to your audience, in comparison to your competition?

3. **Your Brand Promise**: Think back to your audience's pain points, and then ask yourself, how does your brand solve those problems? *In the eyes of your audience,* what are the greatest benefits your brand offers?[112]

4. **Your Evidence**: What irrefutable evidence can you offer to demonstrate that your brand delivers on its promise?

After thoughtfully answering these four questions, you can craft your positioning statement:

> For [your audience], [program name] is the [your market] that best delivers on [your brand promise] because [program name] and only (your program name) is [your evidence].

According to Harrison-Walker, a brand positioning statement should be feasible to execute over the long term and target the desired student population. For example, a program that positions itself as valuing close faculty student mentoring relationships would not want to grow so large that this attribute cannot be effectively lived out. Harrison-Walker identifies five possible perspectives a college or university might use to position itself vis-à-vis its peers, including corporate examples for comparison:

Angle	Corporate Example	Higher Education Example
Position by Attribute	Charmin is the soft bathroom tissue.	Brown University is the relaxed, open-minded Ivy League college.
Position by Use	Nyquil is the night-time cold medicine.	Cornell University is the university-of-choice for hotel administration majors.
Position by Product Category	I Can't Believe It's Not Butter positions itself as butter.	The University of Phoenix is a corporate university that positions itself as a member of the traditional university community.
Position by Price/ Quality	Grey Poupon distinguishes itself as a top of the line mustard; Malt-o-Meal is recognized as the economy brand cereal.	The University of Michigan is referred to as the "Harvard of the West" for its academic rigor and high tuition.
Competitive Positioning	Avis positioned itself as the "number two" rental car company to associate itself with Hertz as the number one competitor. They claimed that as number two, they would try harder to please the customer.	Marion College changed its name to Indiana Wesleyan University to associate itself with other elite Wesleyan universities in the country.

While defining your brand and developing your brand positioning statement are two important steps for securing your program's future, there is a third branding-related consideration that is perhaps the most important one of all. All the work discussed thus far is of no avail if you do not put a plan in place to ensure that your program's brand and positioning statement are consistent and coherent with the lived experience of students, faculty and others who experience your program. A program that delivers on its brand promise will enjoy positive, long-term relationships with its constituents, and these relationships will help the program build and solidify its reputation over time.

Questions to Ask to Assess the Strength of your Program's Brand Positioning Statement

1. Will it help inform your program marketing decisions?
2. Does it effectively differentiate your program from the competition?
3. Is it believable?
4. Is it flexible enough to allow for growth over time? (In other words, does it position your program for long-term success?)
5. Does it paint a clear mental image?
6. Does it speak **directly** to your core target markets?
7. Is it consistent across all aspects of your brand?
8. Does it motivate your audience?
9. Is it easily understood?
10. Will it stand up to your competitors?
11. Is it *unique*? (Is it different from your competitors' brand positioning?)
12. Is it *memorable*?
13. Can you *OWN* it?

Source: This list is adapted from:

www.cultbranding.com/ceo/create-strong-brand-positioning-strategy

Jim Black offers these five steps for delivering on the brand promise:[113]

1. Define the brand promise.

The definition must be based on the institution's personality—congruent with what the institution espouses to be and, more importantly, consistent with institutional behavior. Most colleges and universities have clearly articulated core values, which should be fundamental elements of the brand promise definition. These values and thus, the brand promise must be relevant both to internal and external constituents. Employees, for example, must passionately believe in and care about the promise for it to be authentically delivered through the educational experience and student services. Relevancy does not equate to standardized adoption, but instead it translates to individualized interpretations and behavior associated with the promise. Hence, the promise must be malleable enough to be accepted and practiced by different subcultures within an institution as well as individuals with their own unique beliefs and values. In the academy, this is the only practical way to strike a balance between the objective of universal adoption and maintaining a modicum of autonomy. Collectively, the college or university community must define desired expectations and behaviors associated with the promise.

2. Live the brand promise.

Consider the role of all faculty, staff, and administrators as "institutional trust agents." In reality, every encounter people have with the institution is a "moment of truth." You have thousands of institutional moments of truth every day. Whether the encounter occurs in the classroom, in an administrative office, through a campus event, online, in person, or on the phone, each experience either fosters or erodes institutional trust. Think for a moment about your own personal and professional relationships. Is there a single valued relationship in your life that is not built on a foundation of mutual trust? Our students, their families, the school's alumni, and others we serve are fundamentally the same. They will desire a relationship with an institution only if they trust you.

3. Operationalize the brand promise.

The promise must be personified through our services, business transactions, human interactions, information delivery, and learning experiences. It must be embedded in the culture and become a part of our institutional DNA. It must be viewed as a covenant between the institution and those we serve—never to be broken. Finally, it requires an unfaltering focus on identifying and eradicating promise gaps using some combination of people, processes, pedagogy, and technology.

4. Deliver the brand promise consistently.

To achieve consistency, institutions must (1) clearly define the desired constituent experience and (2) ensure the employee experience is aligned with the desired constituent experience. For instance, if a staff member feels mistreated by the institution, it will be virtually impossible for that individual to effectively represent the brand promise to the students they serve. So, to improve consistency of promise delivery to our constituents, we must first create an environment for employees that is conducive to feeling passionate about the organization and its promise. The campus environment must be one that values the contributions of individuals and proactively enhances human capacity.

5. Convey the brand promise.

Too often, higher education organizations permit their constituents to form impressions of the institution in an information vacuum—usually based on anecdotes, media coverage, and the negative experiences of the few. Effectively conveying the promise requires an ongoing internal and external campaign. It requires careful management of constituent expectations, the promotion of promise delivery successes, as well as intentional efforts to build institutional loyalty over time.

Black also emphasizes the need for ongoing brand monitoring as well as a system for evaluating the effectiveness of your brand message and promotional tactics over time. We will review metrics that you can use to do just this in the final section of this chapter along with other key metrics that are useful for assessing program recruitment and marketing effectiveness.

KEY BRAND PRINCIPLES

1. *Branding is the most valuable real estate in the world*—a corner of someone's mind (1), whether they are your core customer, or not.

2. *All successful branding is based in a truth*—it's also the easiest way to implement and maintain your communications because truth is natural, memorable and genuine. It's also expected.

3. *Branding is internal before it's external*—your staff need to be your greatest ambassadors. The mistake is to think branding is only about broadcasting externally.

4. *Branding is not a department*—it's the responsibility (and representation) of your entire organization, from receptionist to CEO.

5. *Branding is cultural*—it's the collective attitudes and ideas of a group of people. Your brand is as much about individual behavior as it is about collective behavior.

6. *Mission, vision, and values are internal*—these are a great internal guide but no one outside the organization really cares. They will only be interested in the value you provide them.

7. *Your brand is not just what you say it is*—it's what other people say it is; the challenge is managing the gap. And never underestimate the power of perception because it can be more persuasive than the truth.

8. *Your brand is not your logo*—your logo is the shorthand visual reminder; your brand is the relationship you have with your customer. Brand is who you are and how you act, identity is how you look (2). And everything you do is communication.

KEY BRAND PRINCIPLES

9. *Branding makes an organization visible and understood*—the logo and communications material are a window to your brand. Consider how you want to be seen. If you're not clear about your own brand, don't expect that others will be, either.

10. *Your brand is your filter*—use it to help decide on everything, from hiring staff to making acquisitions or pursuing initiatives. It's all about finding the right fit.

11. *Don't just have a positioning*—have a position. Taking a stand will help define the brand purpose.

12. *A brand is a long-term and evolving objective*—it requires dedication and commitment. Building and maintaining your brand cannot be outsourced. It's not a short-term exercise.

13. *More than ever, your customer or end user is at the heart of your brand*—whether you like it or not. Put simply: Your brand is the promise you make; the customer experience is the promise you keep. (3)

14. *If your brand is to have value, what you do must have value*—branding is the articulation of that value.

15. *It helps if you can explain your brand purpose in a few words*—for example: one word equity, single-minded proposition, unique selling proposition. This makes it easier for staff and customers to remember your brand purpose.

(1) Hegarty On Advertising (Thames & Hudson), Sir John Hegarty, page 39.

(2) Ian Anderson, The Designers Republic, UK.

(3) Proto Partners, website (Company / What We Believe)

Source: "Branding Principles." TheSumOf. 2019. thesumof.com.au/branding-principles/

6. Social Media, Digital Marketing, Website, and Mobile Device Optimization

In recent years, branding and marketing have changed with nearly lightning speed. Nowhere are these changes more evident than in the online space. As a result, no new program marketing plan is complete without a social or digital component. The terms—social and digital--are interchangeable and have to do with the use of social media and digital marketing platforms more generally as well as the institution's website and mobile device optimization. All are critical components to consider for getting the word out and building strong constituency support and loyalty for your new program.

Here are some quick tips for leveraging the social and digital components:

- Given that your institution's website is a primary mode of digital communication with potential applicants, make sure that your program's information is up-to-date and reflects the information students will be most interested in:
    - Academics: Program details, outcomes, success stories
    - Money: Costs and Financial Resources
    - Enrollment: Application Process, Recruiter Contact, Admissions Events
- Because the way students use your website will change throughout the recruitment process, be sure to create website content that targets students

at different points in the enrollment cycle. For example, students that are at the front end of the process are looking for basic information about the program including job and industry related stats, third-party endorsements, video content about the program, and relevant photos. As students get to know you and your program, they will want more detail about your faculty, current student, and alumni. Particularly when students are at the point of commitment, it's important to reinforce the program's value and return on investment. Student and alumni success stories, job placement, and graduate school placement information are particularly powerful information points.

- It is also important to make sure your website is search optimized which means managing website content in such a way that you improve your website's rankings in search engines. In today's crowded online market, search results matter. Here are a few techniques which you can employ on your own to improve your program's website search placement:[114]

    o Publish content that readers will be searching for—make sure it is relevant!

    o Update your program website content on a regular basis and highlight trending topics.

    o Use metadata when posting content including relevant title, detailed description, and relevant keywords.

    o Make your program's site link-worthy by using program keywords instead of "click here" for links within the text.

- o Use alt tags to describe visual media and improve its discoverability.
- Given the propensity of smartphones for online searching, it's also important that your program's website, forms and other processes by which prospective students will engage with you are mobile-optimized. According to a study about the impact of mobile browsing on the college search process, mobile marketing strategies must ensure that information is quickly accessible, rewarding (e.g., it delivers a perceived benefit), and easy-to-navigate.[115]

A final tip involves being highly intentional and strategic in the management of your program's social media initiatives. A 2014 Salesforce Marketing Cloud report suggests that an effective social media plan should identify appropriate audiences, define goals and objectives, conduct social media "listening," plan engagement tactics and content creation, and measure efforts.[116] See a sample new program social media plan below.

Sample New Program Social Media Campaign

Step	Actions	
Prepare to get social	Build a social media team	Research best practices
Choose audience	Identify program target audiences' demographics, interests, expectations	Answer audience questions: How do they seek information? How do they use social media? What challenges might they be trying to solve?

Define objectives	Establish objectives: make sure they are specific, measurable, attainable, realistic and time-bound	Potential objectives could: increase inquiries, increase applicants, raise program visibility, enhance program reputation
Social media listening	Understand target audience Gauge impressions about program brand Find potential applicants	Keep tabs on competitor programs Collect student feedback Identify influential program advocates and detractors
Plan engagement tactics	Provide a glimpse of student life (through videos, podcasts) Share good news and success stories about program, students and faculty	Foster student-to-student or student-to-faculty interaction Help students connect with each other Provide real-time responses to student questions and concerns
Plan for content creation	Choose themes and topics (ask students, admissions staff, faculty, join higher ed LinkedIn groups, follow higher ed news sources, discover keywords in web analytics, monitor competitor programs)	Select media types (blog posts, e-newsletters, webinars, videos, vlog or podcasts) Develop content calendar to stay on track Distribute content
Measure results	Focus on metrics that relate to your objectives: awareness, attention and reach	Measure and optimize conversations

7. Best Adult Student Recruitment Practices

In my experience, graduate and adult admissions and recruitment often get the short end of the stick on many college and university campuses. While the science of recruitment has been widely embraced and operationalized at the undergraduate level, graduate recruitment is often not managed with the same level of direction or precision. This is often the case at the very institutions that are looking to the graduate and adult markets as a remedy for declining or flat undergraduate enrollments.

10 Roadblocks to Graduate and Adult Recruitment

Ruffalo Noel Levitz Senior Vice President, Craig Engle has identified ten roadblocks to successful graduate and adult recruitment that are helpful to use to assess your institution's commitment to adult and graduate student recruitment:[117]

ISSUE 1: THERE IS LITTLE INFLUENCE FROM "THE TOP"

Graduate recruitment is often seen as the territory of individual academic programs and their faculty members. Without the active involvement and strong support of executive leaders in graduate recruitment, it is difficult to secure the level of resources needed to build a strong graduate recruitment program.

Issue 2: Graduate recruitment is decentralized

Graduate program directors tend to have no training or experience in the fundamentals of recruitment. As a result, follow-up and faculty commitments are inconsistent, communications, and web content are uneven, and database management is virtually non-existent.

Issue 3: A desire to shape the class, not grow it—creating a disconnect between the two

Shaping is sometimes seen as a separate or more desirable goal than growing enrollment. The two do not have to be mutually exclusive. Growth can bring significant benefits to graduate programs, such as more qualified and diverse students and increased revenue.

Issue 4: Ignoring the top end of the funnel

Most graduate recruitment efforts do not focus as much as they should on prospects and inquiries, instead starting the process at the applicant stage. Graduate and professional programs need to take a lesson from undergraduate admissions and proactively build their inquiry pools through travel, solicitation, referral, and self-initiated avenues.

Issue 5: An inadequate database to track all funnel activities

Having a robust, organized data process is crucial. This includes four points:

1. A centralized database that is accessible to all relevant parties.
2. Training for staff on proper data entry and tracking.
3. The ability to account for different program start dates, data fields, and other items that may vary from program to program.
4. Creation of management reports that allow the program directors to compare and project new student enrollment.

ISSUE 6: LACK OF A STRONG ANNUAL PLAN

A graduate recruitment plan needs to have these elements:

- A situation analysis
- Goal setting
- Strategies for goal achievement
- Action plans

ISSUE 7: LITTLE PERSONAL RELATIONSHIP BUILDING WITH PROSPECTIVE STUDENTS

To get the graduate and professional students you want, you must let them know they are wanted. Building relationships early is the best way to engage prospective students and move them toward applying and enrolling.

ISSUE 8: COMMUNICATION MANAGEMENT

Build a communication flow that provides students with information that is most relevant to each stage—resist the temptation to overwhelm students with everything all at once.

Issue 9: Scholarships and financial aid

As employer benefits decline, institutions will need to discuss providing more merit and need-based assistance. Graduate and professional students have different needs and expectations than undergraduates, requiring a different level of expertise and sensitivity by the financial aid office.

Issue 10: Not enough coordination among faculty/graduate directors

Admissions staff and faculty need to come together to:

- Develop individual and a master graduate recruitment plan.
- Identify the admissions office and department responsibilities.
- Create print and online communication flows and establish standards.
- Commit to using data so that efforts can be tracked and evaluated.
- Support and coordinate campus visit efforts.

In a survey co-administered by The National Association of Graduate Admissions Professionals (NAGAP) and Noel-Levitz profiling marketing and student recruitment practices for master's level graduate programs, 10 highly effective graduate program recruitment practices were identified.[118]

- Awarding assistantships with a work obligation attached.
- Follow up by phone with incomplete applications.

- Search engine optimization to ensure program appears in search results.
- Availability of distinct graduate program web pages.
- Campus visits for admitted students.
- Phone calls to admitted students from faculty.
- Follow up by email with incomplete applications.
- Institutional aid awarded based on student financial need.
- Open house and campus visit days to generate inquiries.
- Distinct web pages to enhance international student interest.

8. Metrics and Return on Investment

Good marketing and effective student recruitment require good data. You can't know whether you're making the right decisions and using the right strategies on behalf of your program unless you measure your performance. Given the amount of marketing resources typically needed to effectively promote and recruit students for your new program, it's very important that you keep track of what works and what doesn't—and make changes accordingly. At the end of the day, marketing and recruitment efforts should be viewed as an investment in your program—versus a cost—and you will want to understand the relationships between the costs of your various activities and the revenue generated.

While a full overview of marketing metrics and ROI is beyond the scope of this book and chapter, there are a few basic metrics with which all academic leaders should be familiar. At minimum, these are important metrics to have on your radar when assessing the effectiveness of your marketing and recruitment efforts. Generally speaking, the most essential metrics that matter fall into four basic categories:

- Recruitment yield and cost
- Marketing cost
- Website visitor engagement and conversion
- Social media and digital return on investment

Begin by making sure you are able to track your spending and performance for recruitment separate from marketing and that you also are tracking the results for your specific marketing channel strategies and activities. For instance, you will want to know the results from user engagement with your website and other social media tools as separate metrics. I generally believe that if you are spending institutional dollars to promote your program you have an obligation to measure the impact of that spend, even if in a very simple way.

Recruitment yield and cost

As a starting point, you will want to know the yield rates for all individuals who inquired about your program and progressed to deeper levels of involvement culminating in a deposit and enrollment. A typical enrollment funnel analysis tracks yield at five levels:

1. Inquiry to Applicant

2. Applicant to Admitted
3. Admitted to Enrolled
4. Inquiry to Enrolled
5. Applicant to Enrolled

Why is this important? Knowing your yield by funnel level percentage helps you set more realistic enrollment goals over time and also helps you pinpoint potential marketing and branding opportunities and limitations. For example, if you know that 60% of your inquiries typically apply to your program, and 35% of those applicants typically enroll, you would need to generate at least 250 qualified inquiries and 150 completed applications to reach an enrollment goal of 50 students.

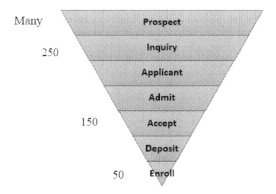

Prospect: A recruiting record exists for a specific term and level.
Inquiry: A specific interaction has been initiated by prospect.
Applicant: An application has been submitted for specific term and level.
Admit: Institution has extended offer of admission.
Accept: Applicant has accepted offer.
Deposit: Applicant has made a deposit to confirm acceptance of offer.
Enroll: Deposited applicant enrolls in course(s).

By understanding yield performance, you can better target specific recruitment and marketing efforts and set goals that are realistic and attainable.

Tracking enrollment performance at these various funnel levels also gives you a sense about where your marketing and recruitment efforts are doing well and where you may need improvement. For example, if you generate a high number of inquiries who do not apply to your program, that is a signal that your marketing messaging may need refinement (i.e., your messaging may not be in sync with what inquiries find when they look more closely) or you may need to focus more personalized outreach to move inquiries to the applicant stage. Low yield at the top of the funnel typically suggests a branding or messaging issue whereas low yield at the bottom of the funnel (applicant to enrolled) typically suggests the need for greater personalization and outreach with applicants. The important point here is to understand how inquiries are moving down the enrollment funnel and to target specific recruitment and marketing strategies at each stage depending upon your yield rates.

You will also want to track your recruitment costs in the aggregate (as well as by inquiry/lead, applicant, admit, and enrolled) and compare to national benchmark data so that you have a basic sense as to whether your investment in this area is sufficient. A few things to keep in mind when making sense of your enrollment yield and recruitment cost data:

1. Metrics tend to be institution-specific; when starting a new program, compare your yield and cost metrics to existing similar programs as a starting point.

2. Use national benchmark data as a comparison but with caution (see the *Helpful Resources* at the end of Section III). I have found that yield performance can vary widely among graduate and adult programs depending upon the field of study and market context.

3. Consider your program's context (e.g., program type and level, delivery mode, competition, target markets, etc.). If you are launching a new online program with a national marketing, your costs will be higher, and your yields will most likely be lower. Context is everything when interpreting your metrics.

4. Be conservative until you have a few years of experience and can benchmark against historic trend data for your specific program.

A sample recruitment plan for new graduate programs can be found in Appendix B.

Marketing costs and conversion rates

You will want to track your total marketing spend on an annual basis for your new program as well as the conversion rates by marketing promotion source. This means it will be important to have a reliable means for capturing and recording how your prospects come to you in the first place. Most institutions now have access to customer relationship management (CRM) tools. The important point is to make sure you have good systems and processes in place for capturing and recording accurate data about every prospect including first source code and relevant demographic data. While there are a wide range of CRMs to choose from, the best solutions enable you to integrate and personalize all your communication with prospective students that your communication is seamless, individualized, and mobile-ready. See the sample worksheet the follows for capturing your marketing spend:

Cost of Acquisition by Marketing Channel and Conversion Rates				
	Cost Per Inquiry	% Enrolled	% Applied	% Completed Accepted
Direct Mail				
Paid Advertising				
Open Houses				
Website				
Referral				
Social Media				

An additional common benchmark to consider here is the total marketing spend as a percentage of either gross or net revenue for the program. As a general rule of thumb, 10% is considered a good average for this benchmark. For-profits average approximately 20-25% spend as percentage of revenue; whereas, nonprofit institutions average 3-5%.

Website Visitor Engagement

When determining the effectiveness of your program's website pages, there are three popular metrics: session duration, pages per session, and bounce rates. Traditionally, longer sessions, with more pages per session, and a low bounce rate suggests higher user engagement. According to Google Analytics, the average session duration in higher education is 2.21, the average number of pages per session is 2.24, and the average bounce rate is 54%. Once you have these data in hand, you can set conversion goals using Google Analytics. A conversion goal typically measures completed steps in the admissions process such as:

- Campus visit registration
- Information request
- Starting the application

You will also need to define what constitutes "conversion." For example, some schools call it a conversion when a website user reaches the "thank you" page after submitting a form. How can conversion goals help you improve your program's website pages? Once you start tracking data with conversion goals, you can ask a whole set of new questions about your website performance such as:

- Which pages or content elements are most helpful in conversion?
- Which pages or content elements are least helpful?
- Based on this, what content changes should we make?
- What is the session duration for visitors who convert?
- How can I test to get more conversions?
- What devices are people converting on?

Social and Digital Media Return on Investment

Finally, assuming you are using social media to promote your program and have established goals for your efforts, you will want to assess whether your efforts are paying off. Here are a few basic metrics that are important to monitor and have on your radar:

SOCIAL MEDIA FOLLOWERS

Especially if your goal involves extending your program's reach, you will want to keep track of the number of individuals who follow your program on the social media channels where you are active. By keeping track of followers by channel, you will be able to see which channels work the best for your program. For example, let's say you have invested considerable time on LinkedIn but do not see any follower activity there; however, your YouTube profile seems to be much more popular. You may want to cut back on LinkedIn and put more effort into the channels that are paying off for you.

FOLLOWER GROWTH

If increasing your follower numbers is an important key metric, you will want to see your follower number increase over time. This metric tells you whether you are gaining traction or whether your followers are leaving you. Again, you can target in on faster-growing profiles and put more effort there. Monitoring follower activity and growth is very easy. You can do it with a simple spreadsheet that you update each month.

Top engaging social channels

This one is a little more complex, but if you are using social media to strengthen engagement with students, this is really important. Many people use social media to drive traffic to their website. Google Analytics enables you to track social media referral activity and then compares this with the average time someone spends on one of your website pages. As the thinking goes, someone who spends more time on your site is typically more engaged, and you have a better chance of eventually enrolling them.

Top referring and converting social channels

Similar to the previous metric, you want to know which platforms are performing best for your program. For example, you can track the raw number of unique visitors or sessions to your program's site. You will want to consider things like bounce rate (whether your visitors leave soon after arriving), which pages and content hold visitors for the longest time, conversion rate (whether they apply or enroll), and average time on your site. You also will want to know if your social media marketing efforts are leading directly to enrollments. If so, you have a demonstrable return on investment.

There are a variety of tools available for tracking multiple social networks. Hootsuite[119] is one of the best free tools that I have encountered. Hootsuite enables you to track multiple social networks in one place and monitor specific search terms in real time which can be handy for tacking mentions of your program in the digital space. The only way to know if social media marketing makes sense for your program is to be clear about your goals and then track those metrics which will best tell you want works and what doesn't. At the end of the day your overall goal should be to increase your commitment to those things that are working and stop doing everything else. Find the social channels that work the best for your unique program and post your top content in those places, making sure the content you place has clear calls-to-action (e.g., "Apply now!").

9. The Marketing Playbook

Throughout this chapter we have talked about the importance of coherence in your program's marketing messaging and communication. At its core, coherence is the thing that makes your program marketing impactful and helps you stand out in a crowded marketplace. Coherence in marketing also provides a helpful framework for living out your program's brand with consistency. One of the best ways I have found to ensure consistency is with the marketing playbook. In brief, a marketing playbook is a brief document that you develop about your program that provides key information that is drawn from the feasibility study and marketing plan, including such elements as:

- Brand position description
- Brand positioning statement
- Key general messages (about your institution)
- Key program-specific messages
- Target audience descriptions (including demographics and behavioral insights)
- Key competitors and their differentiating strengths and limitations

- Program's bragging points
- SWOT Analysis
- Important people to know
- Recruitment tips including specific outcome stories and data points

Ideally, the playbook is developed jointly involving input from the program's academic staff as well as marketing and recruitment staff. Once developed, a second section can be added outlining the annual marketing plan which should utilize the playbook as a foundational guide. For example, the target audience demographics and behavioral insights should be referenced in making decisions about how and where to market the program. At minimum, the second section of the playbook should include:

- Enrollment goals
- Marketing goals and strategies by channel

See the marketing playbook template on the next page. A complete sample playbook for a new graduate program at Bay Path University can be found in Appendix A.

What's Next

The importance of marketing and branding to the success of your new program cannot be taken for granted. Especially in today's crowded marketplace, a well-researched and comprehensive marketing and branding plan—if effectively executed—can have a significant impact in a successful launch and long-term sustainability. This chapter provided a basic orientation to the most

MARKETING PLAYBOOK: PROGRAM NAME

KEY GENERAL MESSAGES
- University is ranked XX by YY
- Complete your credential completely online – no campus attendance required
- Convenient part-time format allows you to advance your career without putting it on hold
- No standardized test required
- Earn a graduate certificate and/or take a course before you earn your masters

PROGRAM SPECIFIC MESSAGES
- Gain end-to-end knowledge of SCM, including the six pillars of SCM (design, procurement, planning, manufacturing, logistics, and sustainability)
- Industry driven curriculum equips early-career and mid-career students with the knowledge and skills for supply-chain leadership roles
- Customize elements of the curriculum (practicum) and work one-on-one with faculty to tackle real-world supply-chain issues
- Strong industry connections across curriculum, from faculty to guest speakers. Highly personalized with faculty as career mentors
- Applied curriculum allows you to practice knowledge and skills you learn immediately

TARGET DEMO
DEMOGRAPHICS: Age: 25-45; Geographic: state/region/US Salary: $30K+ Education: Bachelor's +; majors in XX, YY, ZZ
KEY AUDIENCE: Early career professionals; BA/BS in XX, YY
KEY AUDIENCE: Early to mid-career professionals with experience in field. Job titles include: XX, YY; military
KEY AUDIENCE: Early to mid-career professionals in tangential industries/fields: education, NGOs, environmental, healthcare

AUDIENCE INSIGHT
MOTIVATION: Career pivot, enter new field, increase earning potential, solve societal and environmental challenges
RESISTANCE: Cost, value, unsure of career outcomes
DECISION CRITERIA: Time to completion, convenience, cost, professional value/boost, enter fast growing field
CAREERS: Logistics companies, consulting, consumer packaged goods, transportation, distribution

SWOT

S	- Cutting edge curriculum - Finish quickly, no GRE - Faculty as ind. leaders	W	- Course constraints with pre-reqs
O	- Growing field - Partnership oppt's - Regional hotbed for indust.	T	- Increasing com, market saturation?

COMPETITION
Michigan State, Georgia Tech, USC

RANKING/AWARDS
Top, Best program…

PEOPLE TO KNOW
Faculty;
Students;
Alumni;

RECRUITER TIPS
- Six pillars of SCM
- Choose from 4-course for 6 course certificates
- No GRE, waive application fee
- Begin course as non-degree student
- Industry-driven curriculum.

---

essential elements of this plan including discussing key tips for using social media and measuring your marketing and recruitment results.

Just as with higher education marketing and branding, accreditation exists in a context that is also very fluid. Still, it is a very important consideration for program developers to keep in mind as you are bringing new programs to life. In the next chapter, we will take a quick tour through the world of accreditation, highlighting those issues that are most important to have on your radar as a part of your planning process. While not an exhaustive review, Chapter 10 will provide a basic overview of the roles, purposes and levels of accreditation, along with process and planning considerations that you need to know.

Key Strategic Questions for Academic Leaders

These questions are designed to help you think through your approach to marketing and recruitment as well as whether you are committing sufficient time and resources to this component. These are excellent questions to ask in a small group that includes representatives from your marketing and recruitment staff along with the individual who is assigned to lead your new program.

1. Do you have a written marketing plan to support your new program?

2. Do you have a written recruitment plan that spells out goals according to the student markets identified in your marketing plan?

3. How was your marketing plan developed and did it include input from marketing and recruitment staff as well as from program faculty and academic staff?

4. What marketing and recruitment resources have been committed to support your program?

5. Does your marketing plan fully address the 7 P's?

6. What market research did you conduct and what does it suggest about how best to market your program?

7. Have you developed a brand positioning statement for your program?

8. Do you have a website and social media plan for your new program?

9. What mechanisms will you put in place to ensure ongoing monitoring of and responding to marketing and recruitment results and ROI?

Appendix A

This sample playbook illustrates the use of this tool to support the launch of Bay Path University's new Master of Science in Applied Data Science. The development of this playbook (and all others) is led by the Executive Director of Graduate Marketing and Analytics in collaboration with program faculty and staff, the dean, and recruitment staff. This playbook corresponds with the marketing plan shown earlier in this chapter.

MARKETING PLAYBOOK SAMPLE
Bay Path University
Master of Science in Applied Data Science

DEGREE TYPE	Master of Science
TRACKS & CREDITS	Generalist or Specialist Track (36 Credits Each)
START MONTHS	Oct, Feb
DELIVERY	Fully Online
DEPARTMENT	School of Science & Management
DIRECTOR	Dr. Ning Jia
DEAN	Dr. Tom Loper

1. What is this program's one-and-only position? What distinguishes it from the competition?

Our curriculum is custom-made for the job skills desired in the market with the necessary foundation, as well as advanced/hot topics in data science (most schools put together a data science program by borrowing courses from different departments without careful consideration of student learning experience/outcome or the market demand).

- Original foundational courses remain for students seeking in-depth knowledge.

- Alternative foundational courses are added for students lacking in mathematical background— There will be no math requirement at admission.

- Courses in hot topics, such as text mining and deep learning, are added. Traditional topics, such as time series analysis and database management, are added. All but one (deep learning) of these topics are accessible to both tracks.

- An introductory course in data science is added, which both prepares the students in math and programming skills and also gives a general overview of data science and its many applications as a whole.

- Geographically:
    o As a non-research school, we are the only one of two schools near the Boston metropolitan area (the other being Merrimack) that offers a true data science program (vs. Data Analytics type programs;

BU Bentley, Babson, Northeastern, and many others have such programs).

- Locally, there are not many other data science/analytic type programs; we can shift our focus from harder data science to target more general audience.

• Two tracks to complete the degree (students can decide on the track after taking the first core course):

- *Feedback:* Students like the two-track option. They are talking about the two tracks; the lights are coming on about the fact that Data Science requires a team effort. They may not be sure which side of the team they ultimately want to be on, but our program will help them figure that out.

- *Generalist Track:* Utilize your industry expertise in collaboration with data science specialists to prioritize opportunities provided by big data. Learn how digitization, big data, machine learning, and AI are being used in organizations. Your knowledge and perspective will make you an invaluable resource on an applied data science team.

- *Specialist Track:* Utilize your math, statistics, and computational aptitude skills to mine large data sets and streams. Learn how to use industry specific algorithms, machine learning, even deep learning to help industry professionals uncover new market opportunities, greater efficiencies, optimal performance, and so much more.

2. What are the key marketing and promotional messages for this program?

- Maximize Value with Data.

- Go Beyond Business Analytics.

- Two tracks to the program help you figure out which side of the data science team you want to be on; we'll provide you with a framework regardless of your background and experience.

- Well-designed and comprehensive, we cover skills that are actually demanded in market.

- Strong faculty background in both academia and business—faculty are very accessible and devoted to students learning outcome.

- Great student job prospects—students are getting better positions/business opportunities while still going through the program.

- Bay Path University's MS in Applied Data Science has been recognized by *datasciencegraduateprograms.com* as being the best master's in data science in the state of Massachusetts!

- The M.S. in Applied Data Science has been ranked 12th in a list of the top 50 data-science programs nationwide by onlinecoursereport.com.

- Taught in a small, highly dynamic, and interactive 100% online community.

- Our extraordinary team of faculty have many academic achievements, as well as, decades of industry experience.

- Gain hands-on application, using popular database tools, such as: Python, SAS, R, and SQL.

- Comprehensive curriculum encompassing both classical statistical methods and cutting-edge machine learning methods, to analyze both "small" and "big" data.

- Option to attend full-time or part-time while continuing with family life, work, and other commitments and students usually complete their degree in 1-2 years.

- Access to mentoring, tutoring, library resources, academic resources, and career services will assist students in becoming independent and successful learners.

- Financial Aid is available; no GMAT or GRE required.

3. What are the target market demographics? (audience groups, age, education degree and major, experience, salary)

- Adults (Men and Women).

- Bachelor's degree, some experience with data, or STEM-related bachelor's degree.

- Ages 25-49.

- Geography:
    - Massachusetts (local Springfield/Holyoke DMA where main campus is located), specifically Boston, MA
    - Hartford, CT

- 10 best Cities[120] to find a data science job: Raleigh, NC; Boston, MA; Portland, OR; San Diego, CA; Dallas, TX; Denver, CO; Hartford, CT; Atlanta, GA; St. Louis, MO; Toronto, Canada.

4. What audience insights are important to know for this program?

- Motivations: career-changers; career-risers
- Resistance
- Decision Criteria: cost, location, course format, accessibility to faculty/staff/resources
- Information Sources
- Careers
- Duties and Skills
- Name recognition of schools

5. Who are the top 5 competitors and what is our advantage/disadvantage?

MERRIMACK—MS IN DATA SCIENCE[121]

This is the only other "small" school in Boston area that also offers a degree in actual data science.

Our disadvantage:

- Merrimack has a huge online campaign (possibly other type campaign too in the Boston area).

- Merrimack has name-recognition in Boston area.
- Merrimack's program is online.
- Merrimack's tuition is $27,680.

Our advantage:

- Our curriculum is better designed. Merrimack's program has only 8 courses and does not cover some of the hotter topics.
- Merrimack does not have strong academic reputation in Boston area, and the course offerings look light on the data analysis part.
- We have better student/faculty profiles for our website.
- Depending on how we advertise, Concord is much more central location than Andover, where Merrimack is located.

BENTLEY UNIVERSITY—MASTERS IN ANALYTICS[122]

This can be a strong competitor for people seeking an easier degree than a data science degree.

Our disadvantage:

- Bentley has a wide variety and great offering in management and business analytics-related topics.
- This is also a well-established program (99 is 2017 class size, 70% are full-time, but has part-time option), with elaborate marketing campaigns and many admission dates.

Our advantage:

- Bentley's program is not a data science program, with only mostly introductory stats/data mining courses;

- Bentley's program is on-ground; although, enough classes are run in the evenings, so students can be part-time.

- Bentley's tuition is $46,200 for this degree. But given the Boston location and job prospects, students may not be very price-sensitive.

- Other notables: The average age of Bentley students is 26; 69% are international (their recent marketing campaign is in Morocco), 62% female. Well-designed website/campaign.

BU—MS in Computer Information Systems concentration in Data analytics[123]

This can be a competitor for people with IT background seeking a degree related to data science.

Our disadvantage:

- BU has strong name-recognition; although, this degree is offered at a lesser campus (MET).

- This program can be both online and on-ground.

Our advantage:

- BU's curriculum focuses mostly on information systems, although usually that is very job-promising. The data analytics-related courses are very light.

- The website is not well-designed, not great online-campaign.

Northeastern—MS in Data Science[124]

Can attract stronger students with more serious background.

Our disadvantage:

- Northeastern has much bigger name-recognition.
- Wide course offering spanning many schools (engineering, science, business). Strong faculty.
- Northeastern has coop program to places students in internships.
- Tuition is $49k. But again, students may not be price-sensitive.

Our advantage:

- Northeastern's program is on-ground (most students tend to be international), but most classes are in the evenings. For part-time students, this isn't an easy commute.
- Northeastern's program is solely built on courses from various schools, without a systematic build-up for data science.
- Other notables: Northeastern has two placement exams in math and programming skills, based on the outcome students may need to take additional courses. $1532 per credit.

HARVARD EXTENSION SCHOOL—GRADUATE CERTIFICATE IN DATA SCIENCE[125]

Our disadvantage:

- Harvard (and its extension school) has big name-recognition.

Our advantage:

- Harvard's program is just for a certificate. Courses are very light.

- Harvard's program is on-ground.

- Other notables: Harvard newly started a MS program in data science:[126] This may mainly serve as a side degree for students pursuing other (largely PhD) degrees. But it is important indication that top institutions are starting to see data science as an important field.

BOTTOM LINE:

In the Boston area,

- We need to figure out how to market our school as a local school to Boston.

- Many schools have data analytics or business analytics type degrees, and they are finding their niches already.

- We need to focus on the true data science nature of our program and its coverage of both deeper statistical knowledge and the hotter topics.

In the Western Mass region,

- We can focus on the fact that we have the easier version of the two tracks and figure out how to promote this other track.

6. SWOT Analysis

Strengths	**Weaknesses**
Well-designed curriculum, focus on business application, fully online.	Lack of reputation/ establishment.
Opportunities	**Threats**
A lot of jobs in data science, going fully online gives us potentially a large market. Expansion of pre-req's to allow for more students to apply.	Schools like Western New England. Other programs offer similar courses in hybrid formats for students with lesser qualifications

7. Program Kudos or Accolades

- Bay Path University's MS in Applied Data Science has been recognized by *datasciencegraduateprograms.com* as being the best master's in data science in the state of Massachusetts!

- The M.S. in Applied Data Science has been ranked 12th in a list of the top 50 data-science programs nationwide by *onlinecoursereport.com*.

8. Career and Job Outlook (state, region and national)

- Amazing at all these levels—many new jobs in data science, many old jobs with stronger data analytics element, and these jobs are not going away.

- *Companies compete for experienced professionals*— Thanks to all of the new educational programs, and all of the students flocking to analytics and data science,[127] there are increasing numbers of inexperienced quantitative professionals out there. However, hiring groups are generally most interested in candidates that have at least some business experience, preferably in a specific domain, so that they can guide more junior team members. But, the pool of people with 4+ years of experience is slim relative to the demand, so if you're looking for someone with more experience, it *will* be difficult.

- Almost all companies are now aware that data-driven decision making is critical if they want to succeed. Many are still trying to staff with the talent shortage in full force.

9. What do current students and alumni say about their experience in this program?

- "This program has already helped me with my career goals, because, before I even finished my degree at Bay Path, I received a job offer with Pfizer, Inc. This program grounded me in three key data science programming languages like SAS, R, and Python, which I use every day in my job. From building reports and presenting facts to study teams during clinical trials, this program enhanced my data exploitation and visualization skills using marketplace software programs." — Eric Ngomba G '18

- "In order to accomplish my career advancement I need to enhance my basic tool knowledge (SQL,R,Python), gain more confidence and skill in statistical approaches, and strengthen my way of handling data both visually and mentally. This program will help with my ultimate career goal of becoming a data scientist." —Kristen Rezac G '19

- "This program will allow me to establish an important skill set that is certain to be in demand across industries going forward." —Stefan Magel G '18

10. Important People, Success Stories and Facts to Know:

- Dr. Jia received her PhD in Mathematics from the University of Minnesota and has held statistician and actuarial roles at Dana Farber Cancer Institute, The Hartford Financial Services Group, and Affinion Group. In these positions she has applied and developed advanced statistical methods and mathematical models to tackle big data problems, and innovative ways to investigate not-so-big data problems that lead to direct business or scientific applications. She has given presentations at many universities and international conferences on both mathematical and statistical subjects. A committed educator, Dr. Jia has taught at the University of Minnesota, Virginia Tech, and Harvard University, and she has volunteered at the Children's Hospital in Minneapolis and in the Hartford School District.

11. Recruiter Tips:

- People interested in the degree probably already know the importance of data science and job outlook. We should focus on why they should study at Bay Path instead of other schools.
- Good points to stress:
    - our great curriculum
    - our great faculty team
    - our student job-outcome

12. Other Facts

DATA SCIENCE MEETUPS & COMMUNITIES IN MASSACHUSETTS

The Greater Boston area has many things: universities, bars, students, and data science meetups. There are groups centered on specific tools (e.g. Apache Spark[128]), foci (e.g. Machine Learning[129], AI[130], Cognitive Computing[131], etc.), and fields (e.g. Bio-Entrepreneurs[132]). As well as those just mentioned, here are 5 more to explore:

1. *Big Data Developers* (BDD)[133]: BDD was formed with the backing of IBM. The free meetups are intended to give developers and data scientists the chance to work on solutions and tools in IBM's Big Data portfolio.

2. *Boston Data Mining* (BDM)[134]: Home to 3,500+ members, BDM is sponsored by Strata + Hadoop World, WeWork, and Open Data Science. It's based in Cambridge and hosts talks & events on all kinds of topics related to data mining/science. A similar group is *The Data Scientist*.[135]

3. *Boston Predictive Analytics*[136]: Founded in 2010, BPA organizes a number of lectures, tutorials, and workshops (especially in R). Topics can cover everything from machine learning to social media.

4. *Western Mass Statistics and Data Science*[137]: Targeted towards folks in the Pioneer Valley and Five College Area, this group has evolved into an all-purpose meetup, hosting and cross-listing public talks and events.

DATA SCIENCE CONFERENCES & WORKSHOPS IN MASSACHUSETTS

Thanks to its position on the coast, major data science conferences (e.g. Strata+Hadoop World,[138] IEEE ICDM & DSAA,[139] SIGKDD,[140] JSM,[141] etc.) and focused forums (e.g., PAPIs.io[142]) often stop in Boston. Check

KDNuggets[143] for info on upcoming events. If you're pursuing a master's degree or PhD in the Bay State, you may also be interested in:

1. *Big Data Innovation Summit*[144]: The BDIS is just what you might think: a place to meet other experts interested in product innovation, data science and machine learning, big data strategy, and BI. Speakers come from big names like MIT, Facebook, and TripAdvisor and there are plenty of interactive workshops and networking sessions.

2. *Boston Data Festival*[145]: Sponsored by ODSC (see below), this event is packed with training sessions and geared towards encouraging new talent. One of BDF's aims is to help attendees achieve their career goals—whether that's developing a big data start-up or getting hired by a major firm.

3. *Hewlett Packard Enterprise (HPE) Big Data Conference*[146]: This annual conference gives attendees the chance to hang out with HPE engineers and meet a lot of other industry practitioners interested in technical developments.

4. *MIT Sloan Sports Analytics Conference*[147]: If you're into analytics and sports science, this is the place to be. Along with workshops and talks, there's a Startup Trade Show, a First Pitch Case Competition, a Hackathon, and a whole lot more.

5. *Open Data Science Conference (ODSC) East*[148]: ODSC regularly alights in Boston for its annual weekend conference. There are talks, in-depth workshops, tutorial sessions, and lots of networking opportunities, as well as a popular Saturday Afterparty.

OTHER FINDINGS

- Because of all the state encouragement and university research we've mentioned, Massachusetts is fertile ground for data science jobs. A 2016 WalletHub report on the *Best & Worst Metro Areas for STEM Professionals*[149] ranked the Boston-Cambridge area #6—behind names like San Jose, Austin, and Seattle. Those jobs are being generated by numerous employers, both large and small:

- MIT and Harvard form the nuclei of a major technology hub in Cambridge. Google and Amazon have offices here, right down the road from the Microsoft N.E.R.D Center.

- Universities are also fueling start-ups and data science businesses. An *Innovation that Matters 2016* report[150] from the U.S. Chamber of Commerce Foundation and 1776, a start-up incubator, ranked Boston #1 for fostering entrepreneurial growth and innovation.

- GE moved its headquarters to Boston in 2016, and it's deeply invested in big data. Stitchdata's 2015 study on *The State of Data Science*[151] noted that the company had 50+ data scientists on staff.

- In addition, Massachusetts is world-renowned for its medical institutions. If you're intrigued by the intersection of data science and biotechnology/healthcare, you're in the right place. According to *Research America*,[152] Massachusetts ranks #2 in states that receive the most NIH funding and #1 in funding from the Agency for Healthcare Research and Quality.

- We found 14 universities in Massachusetts offering Master's in Data Science programs (and/or closely related programs, like M.S. in Analytics / Master's in Business Analytics). They are as follows:

BABSON COLLEGE | WELLESLEY, MASSACHUSETTS

MBA with Business Analytics Concentration
OFFERED BY: F.W. Olin Graduate School of Business
DELIVERY: Campus
LENGTH: 41-55 Credits

BAY PATH UNIVERSITY | LONGMEADOW, MASSACHUSETTS

Master of Science in Applied Data Science
OFFERED BY: Graduate school
DELIVERY: Campus or online
LENGTH: 36 Credits
PRE-REQUISITE TECHNICAL COURSEWORK: math, statistics

BENTLEY UNIVERSITY | WALTHAM, MASSACHUSETTS

Emerging Leaders MBA - Business Analytics
OFFERED BY: Graduate School of Business
DELIVERY: Campus
LENGTH: 55 Credits

Emerging Leaders MBA - Information Systems and Technology
OFFERED BY: Graduate School of Business
DELIVERY: Campus
LENGTH: 55 Credits

Graduate Certificate in Business Analytics
OFFERED BY: Graduate School of Business
DELIVERY: Campus
LENGTH: 12 Credits

Graduate Certificate in Marketing Analytics
OFFERED BY: Graduate School of Business
DELIVERY: Campus
LENGTH: 15 Credits

Master of Business Analytics
OFFERED BY: Graduate School of Business
DELIVERY: Campus
LENGTH: 33 Credits

Master of Science in Marketing Analytics
OFFERED BY: Graduate School of Business
DELIVERY: Campus
LENGTH: 33 Credits

Master of Science in Information Technology
OFFERED BY: Graduate School of Business
DELIVERY: Campus
LENGTH: 39 Credits

Part-Time Professional MBA - Business Analytics
OFFERED BY: Graduate School of Business
DELIVERY: Campus
LENGTH: 45 Credits

Part-Time Professional MBA - Information Systems and Technology
OFFERED BY: Graduate School of Business
DELIVERY: Campus
LENGTH: 45 Credits

PhD in Business - Business Analytics Specialization
OFFERED BY: Department of Mathematical Sciences
DELIVERY: Campus
LENGTH: 4 Years

BOSTON UNIVERSITY | BOSTON, MASSACHUSETTS

Applied Business Analytics Graduate Certificate
OFFERED BY: Metropolitan College
DELIVERY: Online or On Campus
LENGTH: 16 Credits

Data Analytics Graduate Certificate
OFFERED BY: Metropolitan College
DELIVERY: Online or On Campus
LENGTH: 16 Credits

Master of Arts in Remote Sensing & Geospatial Sciences
OFFERED BY: Earth & Environment Department
DELIVERY: Campus
LENGTH: 32 Credits

Master of Science in Applied Business Analytics
OFFERED BY: Metropolitan College
DELIVERY: Online
LENGTH: 48 Credits

Master of Science in Computer Information Systems - Data Analytics Concentration
OFFERED BY: Metropolitan College
DELIVERY: Online or On Campus
LENGTH: 40 Credits

Master of Science in Computer Science - Data Analytics Concentration
OFFERED BY: Metropolitan College
DELIVERY: On Campus
LENGTH: 40 Credits

Master of Science in Statistical Practice
OFFERED BY: College of Arts & Sciences
DELIVERY: Campus
LENGTH: 32 Credits (1.0 to 1.5 years)

ACADEMIC ENTREPRENEURSHIP

BRANDEIS UNIVERSITY | WALTHAM, MASSACHUSETTS

Master of Science in Strategic Analytics
OFFERED BY: Graduate Professional Studies
DELIVERY: Online
LENGTH: 30 Credits

Master of Arts in Computational Linguistics
OFFERED BY: Mitchom School of Computer Science
DELIVERY: Campus
LENGTH: Two Years

CLARK UNIVERSITY | WORCESTER, MASSACHUSETTS

Master of Science in Business Analytics
OFFERED BY: Graduate School of Management
DELIVERY: Campus
LENGTH: 11 Units

Master's in Business Administration - Information Management and Business Analytics Concentration
OFFERED BY: Graduate School of Management
DELIVERY: Campus or Hybrid
LENGTH: 15.5 Units

HARVARD UNIVERSITY | CAMBRIDGE, MASSACHUSETTS

Data Science Certificate
OFFERED BY: Extension School
DELIVERY: Campus
LENGTH: 4 Courses

Harvard Business Analytics Program
OFFERED BY: Harvard Business School, John A. Paulson School of Engineering and Applied Sciences, Faculty of Arts and Sciences
DELIVERY: Online
LENGTH: 9 Months

Master of Science in Computational Biology and Quantitative Genetics
OFFERED BY: School of Public Health
DELIVERY: Campus
LENGTH: 80 Credits/18 Months
PRE-REQUISITE TECHNICAL COURSEWORK: technical bachelor's degree

Master of Science in Computational Science and Engineering
OFFERED BY: School of Engineering and Applied Sciences
DELIVERY: Campus
LENGTH: 1 Year

Master of Science in Health Data Science
OFFERED BY: School of Public Health
DELIVERY: Campus
LENGTH: 60 Credits
PRE-REQUISITE TECHNICAL COURSEWORK: technical bachelor's degree, computer science, math

MASSACHUSETTS INSTITUTE OF TECHNOLOGY | CAMBRIDGE, MASSACHUSETTS

Master of Business Analytics
OFFERED BY: Sloan School of Management
DELIVERY: Campus
LENGTH: 1 Year
PRE-REQUISITE TECHNICAL COURSEWORK: math, statistics, computer science

Master's in System Design & Management
OFFERED BY: School of Engineering and the MIT Sloan School of Management
DELIVERY: Campus
LENGTH: 92 Credits

ACADEMIC ENTREPRENEURSHIP

MERRIMACK COLLEGE | NORTH ANDOVER, MASSACHUSETTS

Master of Science in Business Analytics
OFFERED BY: School of Science and Engineering and the Girard School of Business
DELIVERY: Online
LENGTH: 32 Credits

Master of Science in Data Science
OFFERED BY: School of Science and Engineering and the Girard School of Business
DELIVERY: Online
LENGTH: 32 Credits
PRE-REQUISITE TECHNICAL COURSEWORK: technical bachelor's degree

NORTHEASTERN UNIVERSITY | BOSTON, MASSACHUSETTS

Graduate Certificate in Data Analytics
OFFERED BY: College of Computer and Information Sciences
DELIVERY: Online
LENGTH: 4 Credits

Graduate Certificate in Urban Informatics
OFFERED BY: Interdisciplinary
DELIVERY: Online
LENGTH: 12 Credits
PRE-REQUISITE TECHNICAL COURSEWORK: statistics

Master of Professional Studies in Informatics
OFFERED BY: College of Professional Studies
DELIVERY: Online
LENGTH: 45 Credits

Master of Science in Bioinformatics
OFFERED BY: College of Science
DELIVERY: Campus or Online
LENGTH: 32 Credits

Master of Science in Health Informatics
OFFERED BY: College of Computer and Information Science
DELIVERY: Campus or Online
LENGTH: 33 Credits

Master of Science in Urban Informatics
OFFERED BY: Interdisciplinary
DELIVERY: Online
LENGTH: 32 Credits
PRE-REQUISITE TECHNICAL COURSEWORK: statistics

Online Master of Professional Studies in Analytics
OFFERED BY: College of Computer & Information Science
DELIVERY: Online
LENGTH: 1 Year (full-time) or 2 Years (part-time)

PhD in Personal Health Informatics
DELIVERY: Campus
LENGTH: 5 Years
PRE-REQUISITE TECHNICAL COURSEWORK: technical bachelor's degree

SUFFOLK UNIVERSITY | BOSTON, MASSACHUSETTS

Master of Science in Business Analytics
OFFERED BY: Sawyer Business School
DELIVERY: Campus
LENGTH: 31 Credits

UNIVERSITY OF MASSACHUSETTS AMHERST | AMHERST, MASSACHUSETTS

Certificate in Statistical and Computational Data Science
OFFERED BY: College of Information and Computer Sciences
DELIVERY: Campus
LENGTH: 15 Credits

Graduate Certificate in Business Analytics
OFFERED BY: College of Management
DELIVERY: Online
LENGTH: 18 Credits

Master of Science in Computer Science with Concentration in Data Science
OFFERED BY: College of Information and Computer Sciences
DELIVERY: Campus
LENGTH: 30 Credits
PRE-REQUISITE TECHNICAL COURSEWORK: computer science

UNIVERSITY OF MASSACHUSETTS-BOSTON | BOSTON, MASSACHUSETTS

Graduate Certificate in Business Analytics
OFFERED BY: College of Advancing & Professional Studies
DELIVERY: Online
LENGTH: 4 Courses

Ph.D. in Business Administration - Information Systems for Data Science Track
OFFERED BY: College of Management
DELIVERY: Campus
LENGTH: 48 Credits
PRE-REQUISITE TECHNICAL COURSEWORK: math, computer science

WORCESTER POLYTECHNIC INSTITUTE | WORCESTER, MASSACHUSETTS

Graduate Certificate in Data Science
OFFERED BY: Data Science
DELIVERY: Campus
LENGTH: 15 Credits

Master of Science in Data Science
OFFERED BY: Data Science
DELIVERY: Campus
LENGTH: 33 Credits
PRE-REQUISITE TECHNICAL COURSEWORK: computer science, statistics, math

Ph.D. in Data Science
OFFERED BY: College of Arts & Sciences
DELIVERY: Campus
LENGTH: 60 Credits
PRE-REQUISITE TECHNICAL COURSEWORK: technical bachelor's degree

DATA SCIENCE MEETUPS & COMMUNITIES IN CONNECTICUT

Pick a city, any city, and you're likely to find a data science meetup to suit your interests. Along with the five we've listed here, you may also want to explore hands-on groups like NewHaven.IO[153] and Connecticut R Users Group[154], where you'll have a chance to play.

1. *Connecticut Big Data*[155]: This large group of data geeks meets monthly to explore technical tools *and* big data from a business perspective. Professionals, students, and enthusiasts are welcome to attend.

2. *CT Predictive Analytics*[156]: CT is one of the biggest meetups in the state with 400+ members in fields such as healthcare, pharmaceuticals, media, marketing, and insurance. Presentations are heavily focused on practical tools and techniques.

3. *Data Scientists in Stamford*[157]: If you're wedged between New Haven and NYC, this meetup is here to help. Topics cover everything from

predicting the stock market using genetic programming to the limitations of data science.

4. *Hartford Artificial Intelligence and Deep Learning*[158]: Sponsored by H2O.ai and founded in February 2017, this group aims to explore areas related to the intersection of AI and big data. Locals can also investigate the *Hartford Tech Meetup*.[159]

5. *New Haven Data Science*[160]: Folks in New Haven Data Science are often treated to talks and workshops that focus on the data science toolkit—Automated Machine Learning, Text Analytics, Health Care Fraud Detection, you name it. Members also participate in events like Civic Hack Days.

DATA SCIENCE CONFERENCES & WORKSHOPS IN CONNECTICUT

Because NYC is just around the corner, Connecticut is not often on the map for data science conferences (e.g., Strata+Hadoop World,[161] Predictive Analytics World,[162] IEEE ICDM,[163] SIGKDD,[164] etc.). However, there are smaller events where you can grow your skills and network. These include:

1. *Hartford Tech Summit*[165]: Though it's not specifically focused on data science, the HTS is a useful place to start building business contacts. Most topics address the latest IT trends and knowledge.

2. *Innovation Summit: The Connecticut Technology Council* (CTC) organizes an annual conference for entrepreneurs and start-ups. The day includes networking, investor meetings, informational workshops, and more. Check out CTC's Events Calendar[166] for further opportunities.

3. *UConn Events*[167]: UConn often hosts workshops (e.g., Introduction to SAS) and larger events related to big data (e.g., 2017 Conference on Lifetime Data Science). Check the events calendar in your department or school (e.g., School of Business) for more ideas.

4. *Yale Customer Insights Conference*[168]: Organized by the Yale School of Management, this conference is a mix of global leaders in business, academia, and society who are using data to drive growth. Topics cover everything from marketing strategy and consumer choice to product innovation.

5. *Yale Day of Data*[169]: This is a very useful link to bookmark! Every year, Yale's big data centers and research groups get together to host an interdisciplinary symposium. The event includes workshops, keynotes, presentations, and lightning talks.

OTHER FINDINGS

- A lot of data-driven companies tend to live in a high tech corridor that runs from Hartford and Farmington through to New Haven, Bridgeport, and Stamford:

    o Hartford is blessed by major insurance names like Aetna, Hartford Financial Services Group, and Cigna, as well as institutions that are deeply invested in medical care and research.

    o Outside of the center city, you'll also discover companies such as VLink Inc. and the well-known Jackson Laboratory for

- Genomic Medicine, which is right next door to UConn Health in Farmington.
- Thanks to the efforts of initiatives like the Yale Entrepreneurial Institute[170] and the Office of Cooperative Research,[171] a variety of Yale-grown start-ups[172] are now clustered in the New Haven area. The city is also home to young but fast-growing companies such as Arvinas (pharmaceuticals), SeeClickFix (digital communications), and Continuity (compliance management systems).
- Gartner is headquartered in Stamford and employs almost 2,000 IT research analysts and consultants in the service of its clients.
- In addition to traditional job sites, it's worth checking the Marcum Tech Top 40,[173] which lists Connecticut's fastest growing tech companies, and Innovation Hartford's map of start-ups throughout the state.[174]

CENTRAL CONNECTICUT STATE UNIVERSITY | NEW BRITAIN, CONNECTICUT

Graduate Certificate in Data Mining
OFFERED BY: Department of Mathematical Sciences
DELIVERY: Online
LENGTH: 18 Credits
PRE-REQUISITE TECHNICAL COURSEWORK: statistics

Master of Science in Data Mining
OFFERED BY: Department of Mathematical Sciences
DELIVERY: Campus
LENGTH: 33 Credits
PRE-REQUISITE TECHNICAL COURSEWORK: statistics

QUINNIPIAC UNIVERSITY | HAMDEN, CONNECTICUT

Master of Science in Business Analytics
OFFERED BY: School of Business
DELIVERY: Online
LENGTH: 33 credits

UNIVERSITY OF BRIDGEPORT | BRIDGEPORT, CONNECTICUT

MBA - Analytics Intelligence Concentration
OFFERED BY: Ernest C. Trefz School of Business
DELIVERY: Campus
LENGTH: 30 Credits

UNIVERSITY OF CONNECTICUT | STORRS, CONNECTICUT

Master of Science in Business Analytics and Project Management
OFFERED BY: School of Business
DELIVERY: Campus
LENGTH: 33 Hours
PRE-REQUISITE TECHNICAL COURSEWORK: math

UNIVERSITY OF NEW HAVEN | WEST HAVEN, CONNECTICUT

MBA - Business Intelligence Concentration
OFFERED BY: College of Business
DELIVERY: Campus
LENGTH: 30-54 Credits

YALE UNIVERSITY | NEW HAVEN, CONNECTICUT

Terminal Master of Arts in Statistics
OFFERED BY: Department of Statistics and Data Science
DELIVERY: Campus
LENGTH: 8 Courses

Appendix B

Appendix B provides a sample of the Bay Path University recruitment plan template that is customized for each new graduate program launch. This template includes the elements that are common across all graduate programs (see the objectives section and the introductory content) as well as those sections that are customized to meet the recruitment needs of each graduate program, and the program's identified markets, and its program niche.

TABLE OF CONTENTS

Introduction
  Historical Information
  Alignment between national trends, practices, and objectives

Objectives:
  Objectives
  Priorities and responsibilities
  Timeline and outcomes

Plan of Action
  Steps to perform the action
  Projected dates
  Systemic controls

Assessment
  Results
  Impact of strategies and intervention
  Accountability

Review
  Success

Introduction

Graduate students are vital to the overall viability of Bay Path University. Indeed, Bay Path is positioning itself as a leading higher educational institution in the Western Massachusetts area and beyond by providing a wide-ranging portfolio of graduate programs that are consistent with the region's workforce and high demand job market need areas. Globalization and technological innovation have brought about long-term changes within the economy, altering the higher education demands which impact recruitment strategies that must occur at the graduate level in order to train students to be able to obtain and preserve meaningful careers.

NATIONAL ENROLLMENT LANDSCAPE

National trends in graduate applications to United States graduate schools have shown a slight decrease overall in recent years, largely in response to an improved job economy. However, graduate school applications to private, not-for-profit higher education institutions have increased, a reflection of the increased attention being paid to expanding tuition revenue streams by private colleges and universities. Between fall 2007 and fall 2017, graduate applications grew at an average annual rate of 4%. The average annual increase over the ten-year time period was most significant for applications to master's degree programs, among women, and in the fields of mathematics, computer sciences, health sciences, and engineering as reported by the Council of Graduate Schools in "Graduate Enrollment and Degrees: 2007 to 2017."

Among U.S. citizens and permanent residents, increases in first-time graduate enrollment were greater for Hispanic/Latinos (5.6%) than Black/African Americans (2.2%), and Asian/Pacific Islanders (4.5%) most recently. However, American Indian/Alaska Natives and Whites have experienced decreases in first-time enrollment (-6.5% and -0.2%, respectively) during this period. First-time graduate enrollment of international students decreased 3.7% between Fall 2016 and Fall 2017. it's the second decrease since 2003, though the five-year average annual increase (4.7%) and ten-year average annual increase (5.6%) rates remain high. By contrast, first-time graduate enrollment reported a 1.1% increase among U.S. citizens and permanent residents between Fall 2016 and Fall 2017; though lower than last year (3.2%), it's still a healthy increase.

By broad field of study, the largest one-year increases (2016 to 2017) in graduate applications occurred in the broad fields of business (4.5%), public administration and services (1.9%), education (1.8%), and mathematics and computer sciences (1.7%). Graduate applications decreased over the one-year period in engineering (-7.3%), arts and humanities (-1.8%), physical and earth sciences (-0.6%), and biological and agricultural sciences (-0.4%). While the decline of graduate applications in arts and humanities appears to follow the trend from the last five years, the decline in engineering appears to be a deviation from the five-year average annual rate of change (1.0%) and ten-year average annual rate of change (5.6%).

GEOGRAPHIC LANDSCAPE

Bay Path University serves students at all levels of their educational attainment in the Western Massachusetts and northern Connecticut region (and online through its burgeoning online programming in multiple fields of study). Western Massachusetts' population is concentrated in the cities and suburbs along the Connecticut River, in an urban axis surrounding Springfield that is contiguous with greater Hartford, Connecticut (i.e., the Knowledge Corridor.) A secondary population concentration exists in the Housatonic-Hoosic valley due to the industrial heritage of Pittsfield and North Adams and the development of tourism throughout that valley. This far-western zone is linked to New York City and Albany, New York, more than with the rest of Massachusetts; however, both populated zones are ultimately part of the Northeast megalopolis. The rest of Western Massachusetts is lightly populated, particularly the Hilltowns where densities below 50 persons per square mile are the rule.

The decline of manufacturing as the region's economic engine since World War II—and, in particular, since the controversial closing of the Springfield Armory—was counterbalanced in Western Massachusetts by growth in post-secondary education and healthcare. This created new jobs and land development as well as had gentrifying effects in many college towns. State and community-funded schools (e.g., University of Massachusetts Amherst and Westfield State University) were conspicuous in their growth, as were the region's highly regarded liberal arts colleges, including Williams founded 1793, Amherst founded 1821, Mount Holyoke founded 1837, and Smith founded 1871. The current list of Western Massachusetts colleges and universities includes:

- Amherst College
- American International College
- Bard College at Simon's Rock

- Bay Path University
- Berkshire Community College
- Cambridge College
- Conway School of Landscape Design
- Elms College
- Five Colleges Association
- Greenfield Community College
- Hallmark Institute of Photography
- Hampshire College
- Holyoke Community College
- Massachusetts College of Liberal Arts
- Mount Holyoke College
- Smith College
- Springfield College
- Springfield Technical Community College
- University of Massachusetts Amherst
- Westfield State University
- Western New England University
- Williams College

In terms of demographics, while the number of people calling Western Massachusetts and northern Connecticut home isn't changing much, the population is becoming more racially and ethnically diverse. The increase in the population of Hispanics in the region is especially significant, with a stagnating and decreasing population of white individuals.

Currently, Bay Path University offers graduate programs that directly respond to the workforce needs in the region—both current and future. These programs are offered online and/or at one of four campus sites across the Commonwealth:

> MS Accounting*
> MS, EDS Applied Behavior Analysis*#^$
> MS Applied Data Science*
> MS Applied Laboratory Science and Operations+
> MS, EDS Clinical Mental Health Counseling#^$
> MS Communications*
> MS Communications and Information Management*
> MFA Creative Nonfiction Writing*
> MS Cybersecurity Management*
> MS Developmental Psychology#^$
> MSED, EDS Early Childhood Education#^$
> MSED, EDS Elementary Education#^$
> MS Genetic Counseling*
> MS Healthcare Management*
> MS Higher Education Administration*
> EdD Higher Education Leadership and Organizational Studies*
> MS Information Management*
> MS Leadership and Negotiation*
> MBA Entrepreneurial Thinking and Innovative Practices*+
> MS Nonprofit Management and Philanthropy*+
> MSN Nursing*
> DNP Nursing Practice*
> MOT Occupational Therapy#
> MOT Occupational Therapy Bridge#
> OTD Occupational Therapy*
> MS Physician Assistant Studies#
> MPH Public Health*
> MSED EDS Reading and Literacy Instruction#$
> MSED, EDS Special Education#^$
> MSED, EDS Special Education Administrator#$
> MS Strategic Fundraising and Philanthropy*+

Online Delivery
+ *Londmeadow Campus*
# *Eastlongmeadow Campus*
^ *Sturbridge Campus*
$ *Concord Campus*

BAY PATH UNIVERSITY ENROLLMENT AT A GLANCE

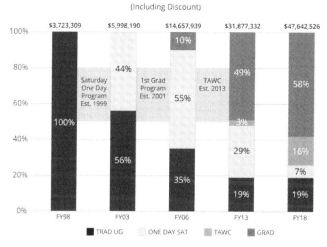

When looking at the enrollment trends historically at Bay Path, graduate students have become an increasingly larger and more significant part of the overall student enrollment and student community. As shown here, the percentage of net tuition revenue contributed by graduate programs has grown from 10% of the total in 2006 to nearly 60% in 2018.

This trajectory is due in no small measure to the effective graduate recruitment and marketing management systems that have been put in place over the past decade. Graduate education at Bay Path University has the potential to increase its enrollment even further by using the graduate recruitment action plan outlined for each new program to assist in achieving the intended objectives that support growth and advancement of graduate education.

The two charts that follow will be completed for each new program and will serve as a guide for shaping the program-specific recruitment strategies that are undertaken.

Proforma New Student Enrollment Headcount Goals--Total				
FY 2019	FY 2020	FY 2021	FY 2022	FY 2023

Enrollment Funnel Goals--Total				
FY 2019	FY 2020	FY 2021	FY 2022	FY 2023
Inquiries	Inquiries	Inquiries	Inquiries	Inquiries
Completed Applications	Completed Applications	Completed Applications	Completed Applications	Completed Applications
Accepted	Accepted	Accepted	Accepted	Accepted
Enrolled	Enrolled	Enrolled	Enrolled	Enrolled
Yield % Applicant to Enroll	Yield % Applicant to Enroll	Yield % Applicant to Enroll	Yield % Applicant to Enroll	Yield % Applicant to Enroll
Yield % Accepted to Enroll	Yield % Accepted to Enroll	Yield % Accepted to Enroll	Yield % Accepted to Enroll	Yield % Accepted to Enroll

New Student Enrollment Goal by Market Niche—Year 1 (FY 2019)			
Market Niche	Headcount Goal (should add up to total headcount goal above)	Key Market Insights Important for Enrollment Decision	Important Marketing and Promotional Messages for this Market
1.Example: Professionals who work in area hospitals within 25-mile radius.	25	Career advancement important. Convenient and flexible course delivery. Strong program reputation in region. Hands-on and relevant skills-based curriculum.	Degree completion in 15 months or less. Highly credentialed faculty with many years of clinical experience. Fully online delivery option available.
2.			
3.			
4.			
5.			

ACADEMIC ENTREPRENEURSHIP

	Enrollment Strategies by Market Niche—Year 1 (FY 2019)		
	Note: Key enrollment strategies should be identified for each student market, along with an enrollment goal and strategy cost.		
Market Niche	Enrollment Strategies per Market Niche	Anticipated Result	Budget
1. Example: Professionals who work in area hospitals within 25-mile radius.	1. Establish minimum of three partnerships with local hospitals to include $1,000 annual tuition discount for employees who enroll in program.	10	$10,000
	2.		
	3.		
2.	1.		
	2.		
	3.		
3.	1.		
	2.		
	3.		
Enrollment Strategy by Admissions Funnel—Year 1 (FY 2019)			
Note: Key enrollment strategies should be identified for each level in the admissions funnel, including: inquiry/lead generation, application generation, and deposit/matriculation yield, along with strategy cost for each.			
Inquiry/Lead Generation*	1.		
	2.		
	3.		
Application Generation*	1.		
	2.		
	3.		
Deposit and Enrollment Yield*	1.		
	2.		
	3.		

Tactical strategies for achieving each of the above enrollment funnel headcount goals should be considered for each the marketing channels that have been identified in the marketing plan. See the following examples of strategy categories for each level.

EXAMPLE OF INQUIRY GENERATION STRATEGIES

- Website
- Paid search
- Direct mail
- Email
- Specific organization outreach

- Conferences, exhibits, and sponsorships
- Organizational partnership/recruitment
- Radio
- Outdoor
- Alumni Outreach
- Online, on-demand information session
- GRE name buys (for graduate programs as appropriate)

EXAMPLE OF APPLICATION GENERATION STRATEGIES

- Recruiter personal outreach
- Communication flow
- Email blasts
- Online, on-demand information session
- Waive app fee promotion
- Lead scoring for targeted, aggressive inquiry nurturing

EXAMPLE OF YIELD (APPLICATION-TO-ENROLLED) GENERATION STRATEGIES

- Recruiter personal outreach
- Advisor outreach
- Communication flow
- Faculty/Program Director phone call/email

While the following objectives apply to the recruitment of students for all graduate programs, each objective is customized to meet the specific targets and niche for each program:

Objectives

In an effort to identify, recruit, and enroll a diverse graduate student population, the Office of Graduate Recruitment will implement technology, superb customer service, and intentional strategic recruitment to meet the following objectives for each new program:

1. Increase efficiency and effectiveness of recruiting activities.
2. Provide effective management of the recruitment, admission, and enrollment, of graduate students.
3. Identify current and future trends to forecast graduate school admittance.
4. Recruit, retain, and graduate a diverse student body.
5. Support and market the quality of graduate education and its programs.
6. Grow strong, mutually beneficial partnerships that engage our local, national, and global communities.

OBJECTIVE 1

Increase efficiency and effectiveness of recruiting activities. Provide effective management of the recruitment, admission, and enrollment of graduate students.

A. Use of technology, assessments, and best practices to strategically recruit, enroll, and graduate students; provide personal service while increasing the size of graduate enrollment.

B. Apply web-based technology solutions and social media for continuous improvement of service daily.

C. Analyze enrollment data to strategically cultivate enrollment growth.

D. Develop domestic academic and nonacademic pipelines for recruitment.

E. Provide training and support for Graduate Program Directors (i.e., facilitating Graduate Council Meetings and attending program New Student Orientation).

F. Establish enrollment targets to develop appropriate recruitment strategies.

Objective 2

Identify current and future trends to forecast graduate school admittance.

A. Understand the primary drivers that impact enrollment and use this information to influence Strategy and resource decisions. Drivers = applications = percentage of completed applications = admit rate = enrolled / yield.

B. Review and analyze the National Student Clearinghouse trends data, and other sources such as FAFSA data to create a pathway to attract, recruit, and enroll the "right fit" students.

C. Use a forecasting model to capture historical trends; establish a goal for the following term by outlining drivers including total applications received and total applications completed.

OBJECTIVE 3

Recruit, retain, and graduate a diverse student body.

A. Adopt innovative, high-contact recruitment models, including those that employ alumni of color and international alumni, to attract a diverse student body from all areas of the state, the nation, and the world.

B. Graduate directors and other interested faculty will be informed on best practices for recruiting, retaining, and graduating graduate students.

C. Graduate assistantships will be used when appropriate to recruiting and graduating a diverse population of graduate students when allocating institutional financial support to programs, departments with special emphasis put on supporting graduate education for the Western Massachusetts region.

D. Purchase GRE Names.

OBJECTIVE 4

Support and market the quality of graduate education, and its programs.

A. Cultivate the relationship with current undergraduate students in order to entice them to attend a graduate program at Bay Path.

B. Work with administrative units to remove obstacles and provide roadmaps for the development of innovative programs.

C. Promote positive communication with various office entities (i.e., School of Science and Business, School of Education and Health and Human Sciences, School of Liberal Studies, Financial Aid, Student Affairs, and the Registrar's Office). Communicate with the Financial Aid Office to learn about the students that have sent FASFA forms to Bay Path but have not yet applied for the University.

D. Provide streamlined and responsive administrative processes for graduate programs.

OBJECTIVE 5

Grow strong, mutually beneficial partnerships that engage our local, national, and global communities.

A. Sustain and enhance existing partnerships, and establish new ones, with the surrounding public educational entities.

B. Expand and enhance existing as well as new relationships with local, regional professionals, and service organizations that at least partially share missions with the Graduate School and its respective programs.

C. Collaborate with the alumni associations and from graduate students who identify strongly with the Graduate School and the University.

The priorities of the Office of Graduate Recruitment are outlined within the five objectives above, based on priorities exemplified chronologically, and are the responsibility of all staff handling graduate activities and the graduate faculty.

Plan of Action

The Graduate Recruiter will recruit for new graduate students based on the specific programmatic assignment; recruiting in markets that are outlined in the program's Feasibility Study and Marketing Playbook and that have shown the greatest interest in pursuing graduate studies at Bay Path University.

ONGOING

In order to recruit graduate students, The Office of Graduate Recruitment will use web-based technology (Graduate Recruiter) and social media (Facebook, Instagram, and LinkedIn) to engage, inform, strategically recruit, and enroll prospective students regarding graduate programs and activities. This will be conducted on an ongoing basis throughout the academic year.

Recruiters will engage representatives and industry organizations to cultivate international and domestic pipelines for recruitment into graduate programs as appropriate.

They will expand and enhance existing, as well as new, relationships with local, regional professionals and service organizations that at least partially share missions with the Graduate School:

- Meet with representatives,
- Explain the benefit of attending Bay Path University,
- Mail and email Massachusetts Public Schools and surrounding metropolitan area Administrators, and
- Contact teacher and professional associations to market graduate programs.

On an ongoing basis provide training and support for Graduate Program Directors:

- Facilitate Graduate Council Meetings monthly,
- Coordinate speaking engagements and webinars,
- Attend program New Student Orientation, and

Organize fall and spring graduate fair.

WEEKLY

Analyze enrollment data to strategically cultivate enrollment growth by weekly performing graduate prospective analysis. Communicating primary drivers to impact enrollment to influence strategy and resource decisions in order to increase the percentages of completed applications:

- Cultivate prospective applicants on the caseload report.
- Manage a call campaign for applicants.

Quarterly

Establish enrollment targets to develop appropriate recruitment strategies. Review and analyze the National Student Clearinghouse trends data and other sources such as FAFSA data:

- Utilize historical trends and application numbers in order to forecast enrollment numbers, and
- Create an outline to attract, recruit, and enroll the "right fit" students.

Apply graduate assistantships to recruit a diverse population of graduate students when allocating institutional financial support to programs, as appropriate.

Cultivate the relationship with current undergraduate students in order to entice them to attend a graduate program at Bay Path.

In order to cultivate a student-centered atmosphere and recruit the "right fit" student to the university, part of the recruitment process for each new program will include the ideas outlined below:

Graduate students strategic approach	Objective	Timeframe	Resources	Goal
Segmented postcards	To encourage students to complete application	Every 4 weeks from the first post card sent	Graduate Recruitment staff	Convert inquires to applicants and applicants to students.

Telephone campaign	To cultivate new students to encourage them to complete their application	Twice per week	Graduate Recruitment staff	Convert applicants to students.
Online and Campus-Based Open Houses and Webinars	To allow students to visit with programs and apply in person to graduate programs	Fall and Spring semester	Graduate Recruitment staff	Allow applicants to learn about our programs. Encourage students to apply to our programs.
Social media marketing	To engage existing pool of applicants and market programs and events to potential applicants using social media	Ongoing	Graduate Recruitment staff	Engage applicant pool.
GRE/GMAT name purchases	To engage potential students who have already taken the GRE and GMAT	Once the names are purchased	Graduate Recruitment staff	To engage potential students who have already taken the GRE and GMAT.

Systemic Controls and Assessments

The systemic controls that will be put in place for graduate recruitment include processes such as the following:

- Biweekly, perform file reconciliation. By doing this, it ensures that each file has the documents that have been sent versus in miscellaneous bends. This process should increase completion rates and reduce loss paperwork.
- Measure how many applications covert in to enrolled students.
- Gauge graduate fair inquiries that turn in to applications and then become enrolled.
- Perform the call campaign functions, aggressively contacting potential students that apply for programs using the vertical alignment.
- Proactively respond to graduate applications, providing notifications of decisions made.
- Implement survey responses evaluations relative to on campus recruitment events.

Assessment

RESULTS

The results of the five objectives in this recruitment plan will convert prospects into applicants and applicants into students to increase the efficiency and effectiveness of graduate studies at Bay Path University.

Objective	Assessment
Increase efficiency and effectiveness of recruiting activities. Provide effective management of the recruitment, admission, and enrollment of graduate students.	Attend recruiting events within the geographic area where students have historically applied to the university. Scan transmittal forms and supporting documents to Graduate Program Directors for decision purposes; avoid Program Directors copying documents. This should increase the laps of time in Program Directors making decisions which will yield and higher acceptance rate.
Identify current and future trends to forecast graduate school admittance.	Evaluate trends by classification per academic year. Evaluate non-resident population applications from previous semesters. These processes will provide insight regarding the next class enrollment population.
Recruit, retain, and graduate a diverse student body.	Implement predictive assessment to gauge application progress and interest of applicants and likelihood to attend and/or continue studies at the university. This process will increase enrollment and retention for the graduate population.

Support and market the quality of graduate education, and its programs.	Implement end of semester surveys to focus on enrollment management and maintain an active relationship with the graduate population. This process will provide feedback on enrollment management and student perception of courses and the University overall.
Grow strong, mutually beneficial partnerships that engage our local, national, and global communities.	Arrange partnerships with business or agencies to provide education on the relevancy of graduate programs. Quarterly, evaluate the types of relationships built to increase enrollment.

Impact of Strategies and Intervention

The recruitment strategies will target individual students for each program. The recruitment strategies and interventions will directly positively impact the inquiry process, recruitment events, and acceptance process. The strategies and intervention will show the university's efforts at actively recruiting graduate students and increase graduate enrollment by being more persistent and purposeful with interaction with new students.

Accountability

The Graduate recruitment team is responsible for implementation of the graduate recruitment plan to systematically recruit the "right fit" student, cultivate relationships with the applicant pool, and increase graduate enrollment.

CHAPTER 10
ACCREDITATION—WHAT DO I REALLY NEED TO KNOW?

In developing and launching a new program, one of the first, very important things you will want to know is what—if any—accreditation approvals you will need to seek. The answer to this question will vary depending upon the type and level of program you are establishing as well as which accrediting region and state your institution resides in and how you plan to deliver your program among other things. The possibilities for accreditation can range from not needing to do anything—to being required to seek multiple approvals from different entities. Because of the time and cost involved in securing accreditation, it's essential that your feasibility study include a thorough review of accrediting requirements and that you note any possible issues on the front end of your process. For example, if you are launching a program that requires accreditation by an agency that has established specific program staffing ratio guidelines, these need to be built in to your program proforma as well as captured in institutional budget assumptions going forward.

In this chapter, we will review the role and value of accreditation in the United States, accreditation types, process and organization, accreditation expectations and issues, and USDE recognition. This chapter concludes with a key issues and tasks worksheet to use in sorting through the various accreditation issues you may encounter.

MELISSA MORRISS-OLSON

The Role and Value of Accreditation

In the United States the practice of accrediting colleges and universities is a very old practice dating back to the late 1880s and the founding of the very first regional accrediting body, the New England Association of Schools and Colleges in 1885. The federal government had very little interest in the process until the 1950s when federal funding for higher education significantly increased. As originally envisioned with the founding of the first regional accreditors, accreditation is a private, voluntary system of self-examination and peer review. However, the proliferation over the past 100 plus years of multiple types of accrediting organizations, each with its own standards and interests,[175] has created a complex web that is rarely easy for campus administrators to negotiate. The consequence is that an individual campus can occasionally be caught in a power struggle between competing accreditor interests, and new program innovation efforts can be hindered due to an overreliance on standardization.

According to the Council for Higher Education Accreditation (CHEA)—the primary association and advocate for higher education accreditation and quality assurance in the United States--there are five core values that underlie the American accreditation system:[176]

1. Institutions of higher education, not government, should be the primary authority on matters of academics and have primary responsibility for ensuring the quality of their academic programs.

2. An institution's mission is central to judging the quality of its academic program.

3. To maintain and improve academic quality, institutional autonomy is paramount.

4. The American system of higher education has grown and thrived due to the decentralization and diversity of the system.

5. Academic freedom thrives under the academic leadership of institutions of higher education.

The role that accreditation plays in serving as a quality litmus test to prospective students, employers, and other important constituents cannot be overstated. In addition, the system of accreditation is commonly understood to serve a variety of purposes including:[177]

- Verifying to students and the public that an institution meets a set of established standards (e.g., curriculum, faculty, student services, and fiscal stability) and assisting individuals in identifying the institutions that meet the standards.

- Determining eligibility for federal and state funds for higher education.

- Establishing criteria for professional and state certification and licensure.

- Assisting institutions in making determinations in accepting academic credits upon transfer from other institutions.

- Assisting employers in evaluating the academic credentials of prospective employees.

- Providing the public and the private sector with a basis for making determinations about private and public giving.

Providing goals for institutional self-improvement and providing a means for involving faculty and administration in institutional evaluation, planning, and improvement.

Types of Accreditors

Accreditation status is typically denoted on an institutional basis or for specialized departments, programs, schools, or colleges within a college or university that has already been awarded institutional accreditation. Institutional accreditation status is achieved by a college or university that meets the quality standards and fulfills the requirements designated by the accreditation organization. In order to meet the requirements for institutional accreditation status, all aspects of the college or university, including academic quality, administrative effectiveness, and all other related services of the institution, are reviewed by the accreditation organization. Institutional accreditation affirms that the college or university operates with a high level of quality in all its aspects. This type of accreditation is comprehensive and indicates that the institution has achieved quality standards in areas such as faculty, administration, curriculum, student services, and overall financial well-being. Specialized, professional, or programmatic accreditation focuses on particular aspects of the department, program, school, or college's specified academic field of study. For instance, this type of accreditation status recognizes certain aspects of quality in the academic fields of engineering, nursing, law, or education, among others.

Some professions that are regulated by and dependent upon a state or national licensing board may require job applicants to have graduated from specific academic programs that have specialized, professional, or programmatic accreditation status. Specialized, professional, or programmatic accreditation organizations operate all over the United States, reviewing programs and single-service institutions.

There are four broad categories of accrediting organizations. The first three of which accredit the institution; the last—programmatic accreditors—provides specialized, professional, and programmatic accreditation.

- *Regional accreditors.* Organized by region, these entities accredit public and private, mainly nonprofit and degree-granting, two- and four-year institutions. There are seven CHEA-recognized regional accreditation associations.

- *National faith-related accreditors.* Nationally based, these organizations accredit religiously affiliated and doctrinally based institutions, mainly non-profit and degree-granting. There are four associations accrediting over 400 faith-based schools.

- *National career-related accreditors.* Nationally based, these organizations accredit mainly for-profit, career-based, single-purpose institutions, both degree and non-degree. There are two agencies accrediting over 3,500 career-based institutions.

- *Programmatic accreditors.* Also nationally based, these organizations accredit specific programs, professions, and freestanding schools (e.g., law, medicine, engineering, and health professions). There are 61 recognized agencies accrediting nearly 20,000 programs in various fields.

Accrediting Process and Organization

According to CHEA, accrediting organizations derive their legitimacy and "reason for being" from the colleges, universities, and programs that created accreditation, not the government. Whether institutional or programmatic, accreditation takes place on a cycle that can range from every few years to as many as ten years. An important operating principle is the notion that accreditation is an ongoing process; once earned, accreditation must be renewed. Periodic review is a fact of life for accredited institutions and programs.

An institution or program seeking accreditation must go through a number of steps, each of which is stipulated by the accrediting organization. These steps typically involve a combination of several things: preparation of evidence of accomplishment by the institution or program, scrutiny of this evidence and a site visit by faculty and administrative peers, and action by the accrediting organization to determine accreditation status. Key components to the accreditation evaluation process are:[178]

- *Self-Study*. Institutions conduct an in-depth self-study that measures and evaluates their performance based on the standards of their accreditor.

- *Peer-Review*. The review and evaluation of an institution is conducted primarily by a team of faculty and administrative peers. Volunteer institutional peers review the institution's self-study and serve as members of the on-site evaluation team.

- *Site Evaluation.* A team of peer volunteers and members of the public visits the institution to meet with various members of the institutional community to verify in person that the institution meets the standards for accreditation.

- *Judgment by Agency.* Following the review of the self-study and the site visit, the accreditation team makes a recommendation to the accrediting agency. The accrediting agency then makes an accreditation determination. Those judgments may include a variety of determinations: initial accreditation granted, initial accreditation denied, accreditation continued, institution placed on notice or warning, institution placed on probation, or accreditation terminated or denied.

- *Periodic Review and Monitoring.* Following initial granting of accreditation and following granting of reaccreditation, the accrediting agency continually monitors its institutions.

At the core of the accreditation process are the standards. As accreditation is a voluntary, member-driven process, the standards for accreditation are developed and established in collaboration between the accreditors and their member institutions. In becoming accredited, an institution agrees to submit to the standards of its accreditor. Although, standards are established and agreed to by accreditors and their member institutions, the U.S. Department of Education requires its recognized accreditors to assess various elements stipulated by Congress. The required standards are typically focused on an evaluation of the institution's:

- Success with respect to student achievement in relation to the institution' mission, which may include different standards for different institutions or programs, as established by the institution, including, as appropriate, consideration of state licensing examinations, consideration of course completion, and job placement rates.

- Curricula.
- Faculty.
- Facilities, equipment, and supplies.
- Fiscal and administrative capacity as appropriate to the specified scale of operations.
- Student support services.
- Recruiting and admissions practices, academic calendars, catalogs, publications, grading, and advertising.
- Measures of program length and the objectives of the degrees or credentials offered.
- Record of student complaints received by, or available to, the agency or association.
- Record of compliance with program responsibilities under Title IV of the Higher Education Act based on the most recent student loan default rate data provided by the Secretary, the results of financial and compliance audits, program reviews, and any such other information as the Secretary may provide to the agency or association.

Additionally, for institutions offering education-at-a-distance, the Higher Education Act requires that accreditors have standards for institutions to verify that the student who enrolls for a course is the same student who completes and receives credit for the course. [179]

As membership organizations, the activities of accrediting agencies are financed through annual membership dues paid by member institutions as well as through fees assessed on institutions for the cost of the accreditation review. It's important to understand the fee structure and build these costs in to your proforma and institutional budgeting process.

Important Accreditor Expectations and Issues

In order to fully address the full range of standards, there are several issues to keep in mind when planning for new programs or other curricular changes of any kind. Here are the issues that I have found to be most top of mind for accrediting agencies and the reviewers who have evaluated our new program requests:

Alignment with institutional mission and purpose

Every accreditor—institutional and programmatic—is going to want to see evidence that your new program is aligned to a sufficient extent with your stated mission and purpose. This is typically the first standard that needs to be addressed. Alignment with mission becomes especially important when you are proposing to move to a new degree-granting level (such as when a baccalaureate college proposes its first graduate degree), when you are proposing to deliver a program using a new delivery model (e.g., online or competency-based), or when your new program reflects a substantial curricular change for your institution (such as when a liberal arts college proposes to offer a professional program like nursing). Every regional accrediting body has different processes for what they require by way of an approval process. For example, the New England Commission of Higher Education (NECHE) consider changes such as developing new majors or concentrations, changing personnel, and adding and/or dropping courses to fall within the nature and scope of the institution. Other changes, however, are considered by NECHE to be matters that significantly affect the nature of the institution, its mission and objectives, its educational program, and the allocation of its resources, such as: new branch campuses or additional instructional locations, enrolling students in degree programs overseas, offering certificates or degrees where 50% or more can be taken entirely on-line, and moving to the higher or lower degree. In these cases, a substantive change proposal which usually requires a site visit is warranted.

Needs assessment

Particularly for new programs that require professional or specialized accreditation, it's common to be required to conduct a needs assessment as one of the initial steps in the approval process. For example, the Commission on Accreditation in Physical Therapy Education (CAPTE) requires a written needs assessment that "examines the program's/expansion's ability to deliver effective PT/PTA education based on (1) consistency of PT program with institutions' mission (2) available program resources, (3) the demonstrated need for the program/expansion at the local and regional levels, and (4) an institutional structure that assures a commitment to its responsibilities as defined in CAPTE's Standards and Required Elements for Accreditation."[180] These concerns are generally in keeping with what is expected by nearly all professional and specialized accrediting bodies. To whatever extent you can shape your new program's feasibility study (as discussed in Chapter 7) with the information required for the needs assessment, you will be well served.

Enrollment management and marketing plan

These elements have become increasingly important to accreditors as the number of institutions seeking closure or consolidation has increased. You will need to demonstrate that you have done your homework in making the case for your new program by providing evidence of real and ideally deep market interest. This is where market research data come in handy. Accreditors will also want to see that you have thought through how you will recruit students for your new program and that your marketing messages and methods along with your admissions processes and requirements reflect a high level of institutional integrity and transparency.

Financial stability and return on investment

Accreditors want to know that you have taken to time to think through the full set of resources that will be required to launch and sustain your new program. All accreditors will require a multi-year proforma or budget of some kind. They will want to see a realistic accounting of expenses along with a projection of revenue based on assumptions that can be backed up with data. For example, if your budget assumes an enrollment of 25 students in the first year and your tuition rate is set at $750 per credit, you would be well advised to include a competitive program comparison including tuition and enrollment to support your assumptions. Data from sources such as the Gray's Program Evaluation System (PES) can also be valuable evidence for accreditation approval purposes.

Academic resources

Similarly, accreditors want to see evidence that your institution has the capability to deliver this program while ensuring a sufficient level of academic quality and integrity. What this means is that they are going to want to see your faculty staffing plans (including teaching loads and the number of full-time and adjunct faculty assigned to program) and faculty and staff hiring requirements (usually addressed by providing copied of position descriptions). Regarding the latter, accreditors want to know that the learning experience will be delivered by individuals with the appropriate qualifications and experience and that the institution is prepared to support program faculty with the same level of resources and privileges accorded to other faculty in similar roles. While regional accrediting bodies tend to be a bit more flexible in how they define this standard, professional and specialized accrediting bodies tend to be more specific. For example, The Accreditation Review Commission on Education for the Physician Assistant (ARC-PA) stipulates that "the program must have program faculty that include the program director, principal faculty, medical director and instructional faculty, the program director must be assigned to the program on a 12 month full time basis with at least 80% of that time devoted to academic and administrative responsibilities in support of the program, and the program must have at least three FTE principal faculty positions, two of which must be filled by PA faculty who currently are NCCPA-certified."[181]

Governance

The accreditors will want assurance that the institution has a legally constituted and independent governing board that is effectively structured to provide effective oversight of the institution's quality and integrity. Similarly, they will want evidence of an effective internal governance structure and process. For new programs, they will want to see that you followed your established institutional processes for academic program approval and that the faculty had a sufficient voice in determining the content and quality of the proposed program. Especially for new programs that will be delivered off-campus, online, or in collaboration with other partners, it will be critical to demonstrate that the quality and integrity of your new program is in keeping with other programs at the institution. Accreditors will also want to see that off-campus, online and other programs delivered outside of the traditional delivery system are clearly integrated and incorporated into the policy formation, academic oversight, and evaluation system of the institution.

Learning outcomes and assessment

This area has become so important for accreditors that nearly all have a separate standard that speaks specifically to the assessment of student learning outcomes. Not only are institutions expected to define measures of student success and learning achievement, but they must also provide evidence that they have processes in place to ensure regular and systematic collection of information and data. Perhaps most importantly institutions are expected to provide evidence that the information and data are being used to improve learning opportunities and results for students. For new program proposals this means that you need to spell out your assessment plan, including the direct and indirect measures you will use to assess student learning on both a course and program level basis. Institutions are being held to higher standards these days in regard to the types of measures they use; for example, accreditors want to see a good balance of both direct and indirect measures and also that you are tapping external perspectives to gain input on the success of your students' learning (e.g., through such avenues as benchmarks, peer comparisons, employer feedback). For this reason, your new program proposal should include a robust description of your plans for assessing student learning and program outcomes including your timeline and process for periodic program review.

Federal Requirements and State Authorization for Academic Programs

A final piece of the accreditation landscape that is important for academic leaders to understand has to do with something called "the Triad." In brief, the process of regulating and guaranteeing the quality of the U.S. higher ed system involves three separate entities working in tandem according to the regulations that were established under the Higher Education Act (HEA) of 1965. The three entities—the U.S. Department of Education (ED), the states, and the accreditation agencies each play a unique gatekeeping role with the institution and its students positioned squarely in the middle. For students to be eligible to receive Title IV financial aid assistance (e.g., federal grants, loans, and work-study), an institution must be licensed or otherwise legally authorized to operate in the state where it's physically located, accredited, or pre-accredited by an agency recognized for that purpose by the Department of Education (ED) and certified by ED as eligible to participate in Title IV programs. See the following for a description of the role for each:[182]

- *U.S. Department of Education* (ED). ED certifies and ensures compliance with administrative and fiscal rules according to the Higher Education Act (HEA). These rules include meeting financial responsibility standards set by ED, presenting a sufficiently low cohort default rate (CDR)—an accountability mechanism that keeps the lowest-performing schools out of federal aid programs—and meeting other requirements related to compliance with federal student aid laws, regulations, and departmental guidance. Additionally, ED recognizes which accreditors are able to provide recognition for federal student aid purposes.

- *The States.* Institutions of Higher Education must be "authorized" in the state in which they operate.[183] This typically consists of recognition or state licensure that an institution is legally operating within that state. This process can vary by state and can depend on state law or the length of time an institution has been operating. State authorization is important to today's students since it often extends certain consumer protections to them. In recent years, ED has updated guidance that adds more specificity as to what is required of states when they authorize an institution. For example, current regulations require institutions that offer online programs to receive authorization from each state where their students may reside or join a consortium that recognizes authorization reciprocity across multiple states.

- *Accreditation Agencies.* Recognized by ED to accredit institutions of higher education, accreditation agencies apply and enforce statutory standards that pertain to institutional and academic quality—ranging from financial sustainability, student safety and health standards, athletic program integrity, and student outcomes—mainly through reviews which happen every few years. Accreditation agencies also obtain and consider information provided by ED regarding an institution's financial and administrative compliance status as part of an accreditor's overall review.

Recent reauthorizations of the Higher Education Act in combination with regulatory actions taken by the Department of Education have further complicated the maze of requirements that academic leaders must wade through when considering new academic programs. A few things that are important to keep in mind:

- Be sure you have a clear and up-to-date understanding about what your state requires of your institution in terms of authorization for new programs. As noted above, authorization process varies by state and can even vary within a state according to specific institutional characteristics. For example, in the Commonwealth of Massachusetts, independent institutions that meet certain criteria have access to a streamlined process for review and approval of new academic programs that can potentially reduce the time and cost of program approval. Public institutions must follow the standard and more lengthy process. In addition, the Massachusetts Board of Higher Education's authority and procedures apply only to independent institutions of higher education chartered after 1943 and/or institutions that changed their charters after 1943. What this means is that two independent colleges residing side by side in a particular locale may have very different requirements for securing state authorization for new programs. One college, chartered in 1925 would not need to do anything to secure state approval; the other college, on the other hand, chartered in 1944 would need to obtain state approval for its new programs.

- If your students will be taking advantage of any kind of federal financial aid, it's important that you have good processes in place for tracking your student's academic progress. In essence, students will need to meet minimum grade point average requirements, and complete enough classes (e.g., credits, hours, etc.) to keep moving toward successfully completing their degree or certificate in a time period that meets federal guidelines. More details about federal financial aid eligibility can be found on the U.S. Department of Ed website.[184]

- If your program requires professional or specialized accreditation in order for your students to obtain licensure in their chosen field, you will want to make sure that the professional accrediting agency is recognized by a legitimate oversight entity such as The Council for Higher Education Accreditation (CHEA)[185] or The

Association of Specialized and Professional Accreditors (ASPA).[186]

- If you plan to deliver your new program in an online format to students outside of the state where your campus is located, it's critical that you understand and comply with the state authorization regulations where you will recruit students, market your program, and deliver learning. The requirements as to which activities require authorization, the application processes, and the costs to comply vary greatly from state-to-state. To ease the management of state by state institution compliance, a new, voluntary process of state oversight of distance education was created. The State Authorization Reciprocity Agreement (SARA) is a voluntary agreement among its member states and U.S. territories that establishes comparable national standards for interstate offering of postsecondary distance-education courses and programs. It's intended to make it easier for students to take online courses offered by postsecondary institutions based in another state. For everything you need to know about SARA, see the National Council for State Authorization Reciprocity Agreements website[187]

Best Practices for Accreditation Approvals

I want to end this chapter with a brief synopsis of best practices for maneuvering the complex and sometimes frustrating accreditation landscape. Drawn from my personal experience bringing to life many new programs that have required multiple accrediting approvals, these are some of the things I wish I had known when starting out:

Plan well

I cannot overstate the importance of thorough planning. Do your research and make sure you understand up front the full scope of accreditation steps, costs, and the timeline required to bring your program to life. Consider developing a project plan that outlines the requirements for all accrediting entities. I have also found it helpful to appoint someone with strong administrative and organizational skills to be your institution's go-to-expert about all things related to accreditation. At my institution, one of our Vice Provosts has this role which involves staying up to date with all accreditor regulations for the agencies with which our institution is affiliated. For professional and specialized accreditors, it's also helpful to designate a point person within the academic area where the accredited program resides. The point here is that you want someone within the institution to get up every day and have accreditation on their mind. Accreditor relationships need to be carefully managed and nurtured just like the relationships you have with your other key constituencies.

Count the cost

A critical cost of your planning should include getting detailed information about the full range of costs involved in obtaining and maintaining accreditation status. Typically, there is an upfront application fee of some kind in addition to site visit costs (when site visits are required). Additionally, there is usually an annual fee that must be paid to maintain good status. Finally, depending upon the standards, there may be a host of other costs such as minimum number of faculty, required faculty support, academic resources, and so on. Be sure you capture these costs and discuss with your institution's CFO on the front end of your new program approval process so that these costs can be integrated into the institution's budget process going forward.

Build positive relationships with accrediting agency liaisons

I cannot tell you the number of times I have picked up the phone and called our NECHE liaison about any number of issues, some pertaining directly to our accrediting status but not always. I have found her counsel to be extremely valuable for a wide range of academic decisions. Understanding the potential impact that a decision might have on one's accreditation status leads to better decisions and fewer problems down the road. Make sure you attend the professional meetings held by your accrediting bodies, provide feedback when they ask for it, and take the time to have face-to-face conversations with your accreditor liaisons. Be intentional about nurturing these relationships so that you have a good foundation of mutual trust and respect built that you can rely upon when your institution is going through evaluation processes.

Look for shortcuts when possible

Things can get very complicated fast when you are bringing up new programs that have multiple accrediting requirements. For example, when we launched the M.S. in Physician Assistant Studies, we were required to obtain approval from three separate entities—the Massachusetts Board of Higher Education (the state), NECHE (our regional accreditor), and ARC-PA (the professional accrediting body which oversees PA programs)—after obtaining all necessary internal approvals. This is very common with professional programs, particularly those in the healthcare fields. Each of these entities had its own set of standards to address along with distinct evaluation processes, including site visit requirements. Thanks to advice provided by a veteran provost at a neighboring institution, we structured the feasibility study for the internal approval process to include content that would address all the standards for all three accreditors. In addition, we were able to coordinate the timeline and site visit requirements so that we did not need to host three separate site visits. This is where it really helps to have good relationships with your accrediting liaisons. Over the years, I have found these staff to be mostly very helpful in reducing the burden and cost of the accreditation process to whatever extent that they can. At a minimum, be sure you ask about whether it's possible to coordinate your processes in any way. You may be pleasantly surprised by what you learn is possible.

When accreditation is not required, think twice before pursuing

There will be times with specific programs when specialized accreditation is optional. In these situations, you'll want to think carefully before pursuing, as accreditation should never be pursued just for the sake of posting a logo on your website. With some disciplines, you will find a divide among faculty in their allegiance to a particular accrediting agency. Sometimes, this allegiance is derived from a perception that one accreditor has more status or is more elite than another one. However, these perceptions rarely make a difference in the long-term viability of a program, assuming you have done a good job with your feasibility study and program planning. For example, with business programs, there are three accreditors: *AACSB (The Association to Advance Collegiate Schools of Business), ACBSP (The Accreditation Council for Business Schools and Programs),* and *IACBE (The International Assembly for Collegiate Business Education).* Among the three, the AACSB is most widely known and considered to be the gold standard for business program accreditation. However, it's also the most restrictive in terms of its standards and requirements for the institution and the program. Unless you have evidence that the lack of accreditation will limit the program from achieving its enrollment and financial goals, I would caution holding off until you can see how the program performs without these additional restrictions. There are any number of highly successful programs in business and other areas that do not carry these optional accreditations.

Get involved

One of the best ways that I have found to understand the accreditation process and nurture relationships with the accrediting agency is to serve as a peer evaluator for your regional accreditor or professional/specialized accrediting body. Most accrediting bodies are seeking individuals to serve in this role. This is a great way to put the standards into practice in evaluating another institution. Invariably, you will walk away with a deeper understanding about accreditation not to mention important and invaluable intel about how another institution does things.

What's Next

The accreditation landscape is increasingly complex and fluid. There are any number of minefields that an academic leader can easily fall into when trying to negotiate this landscape. Particularly when developing new academic programs, it's critical to understand the history, role, purpose, structure, and process of accreditation. Just as with the other elements covered in this book, a good understanding of context will make all the difference in whether you are successful in bringing your program forward. This chapter provided an introduction to this context, including recommendations, tips, and best practices as gleaned from the field.

In the next and final chapter, we will go deeper still with new program planning by reviewing those institutional infrastructure areas and issues that can impact the success of new program planning. We will consider such areas as staffing, classroom and technological resources, parking, facility planning and integration with existing budgeting, technology and space planning processes, among other things.

> ### KEY STRATEGIC QUESTIONS FOR ACADEMIC LEADERS
>
> These questions are intended for academic leaders to consider the status of their relationships with important accreditor liaisons and what might be done to enhance these relationships. When it comes to successful maneuvering through any accreditation procedures, timelines and good process management are essential. Use these questions to evaluate how your institution is doing in this regard and where you may need improvement.
>
> 1. How would you characterize the relationships you currently have with key accreditor liaisons?
>
> 2. How might you enhance these relationships?
>
> 3. Do you have a mechanism or process in place for good accreditation planning?
>
> 4. Do you have a designated point person on your campus for accreditation-related issues?
>
> 5. What is your institution's track record in obtaining and maintaining accreditation status?
>
> 6. How do you assess your own understanding about the current accreditation landscape?

Appendix A

Appendices A and B outline the full range of issues and tasks that need to be on the academic leader's radar when planning to obtain accreditation to support your new program.

Key Issues and Tasks Checklist for New Program Accreditation

NATIONAL/REGIONAL ACCREDITATION

1. What is the current status of your regional/national accreditation? Is your institution in good standing? Will adding a new program impact your relationship with your accrediting body? Will your accreditor have any concerns that you will need to address?

2. Will your new program require change to your university's mission and vision? Have you revised your mission statement in accordance with these changes with documented input and engagement with the university community, including faculty and board? If not, what is your plan for doing so?

3. Your liaison at the accreditation agency is there to assist and guide you in the accreditation process. Have you sought input and advice from the liaison to your institution from your accreditor about what you need to do to obtain approval for your new program?

The next set of questions will be asked by your national/regional accreditor in the context of your self-study, so prepare ahead of time.

4. Have you worked with your Chief Financial Officer and senior enrollment and marketing staff to create an appropriate Financial and Enrollment Management Plan that will demonstrate adequate enrollment over a three- to five-year period to produce a sufficient return on your investment?

5. Have you included all relevant costs, including marketing, instructional technology, additional faculty, library databases, additional student advisors, additional tutoring, web site changes, and practicum/internship program start-up?

6. The initial idea to create a new program can come from anyone at your institution, but it's vital for faculty to be engaged in its development and own the new program. Besides faculty governance approval, how has the faculty engaged in the process? Have you documented faculty creation of learning outcomes and program structure? Do you have a program director to manage the program and sufficient, appropriately credentialed faculty to teach its students?

7. Every program requires stated, measurable learning outcomes and an assessment plan. It also requires regular program review as part of a larger system and plan of program review for all of your school's programs. Accreditors will also expect to see these plans include improvements based on previous program reviews. Does your new program include strong, measurable student

learning outcomes? Have you created an assessment plan? Does the assessment plan outline how you intend to measure student's learning achievements? Does the plan outline how you will use the feedback from your assessment efforts to improve your program going forward? Does your plan include both direct and indirect measures of assessment? Do you have a program review plan?

8. To ensure adequate numbers of enrollments in your program, you need a good marketing plan including advertising. Who at your institution will take responsibility for this plan? Are faculty and the program director fully involved in decision making about the marketing plan?

9. If you plan well and conduct appropriate market research, you will have no need to be concerned with ending your program prematurely. Accreditors, however, will want to see the teach out plan to ensure students are cared for in the unlikely case that their program ends before they graduate. Have you created such a plan in accordance with the requirements of your accrediting body?

SPECIALIZED PROGRAMS

10. Are you planning to create a program at a new degree level than has been offered previously? Is it a new distance education, online, or limited residency program? Is the program competency-based? If yes to any of these questions, there may be a need to first revise your institution's purpose and mission. It will be important to begin early

with your liaison and/or contact at your regional accreditor to learn if this new program will require a substantive or structural change. These changes often require a specialized self-study, a specialized review, and a site visit.

STATE/FEDERAL APPROVALS

11. Do you know the appropriate state authorization agency in your state? Do you have a designated contact person at your institution to communicate with your state authorization agency to inform them about the new program and to see if there are special requirements in your state?

12. Once you have obtained state approval, you need to inform the U.S. Department of Education. Are you coordinating with designated contact person at your institution to ensure the appropriate Classification of Instructional Programs (CIP) code for your new program is listed with the National Center for Education Statistics (NCES)?

PROGRAMMATIC ACCREDITATION

13. Are you thinking about seeking programmatic accreditation for your new program? Is such accreditation required for students to obtain licensing? If it is optional, have you conducted a cost/benefit analysis to determine whether the cost and resources involved will reap the rewards academically and financially you desire?

14. If your cost/benefit analysis shows it is indeed worth the time and resources to seek programmatic accreditation, you will need to

research the differences in accreditors to choose the most appropriate one. In some cases, there is only one choice for the type of program you are creating; whereas, in others, like business, there is more than one choice. Do you know which accreditor is best for your program? Are you prepared to conduct an additional cost/benefit analysis to choose the best one? Are you prepared to meet the rigorous requirements including a new self-study?

Appendix B

Accreditation Task and Project Plan Worksheet		
Task	**Completed?**	**Comments**
Conduct thorough research to understand regional and state accrediting and authorization requirements, process, timelines, and options.		
Determine whether programmatic and specialized accreditation is required, and if so, what the process, timeline, and costs are.		
If programmatic accreditation is optional, conduct cost/benefit analysis to determine if you will pursue.		

Communicate with accrediting liaison(s) to let them know of your plans and to seek their input.		
Develop project management plan including all accrediting steps, processes, timeline, and costs.		
Identify and engage internal and external stakeholders that need to be included.		
Conduct feasibility study making sure all accrediting standards are addressed.		
Review and align mission statement as needed.		
Develop curriculum and learning outcomes.		
Develop assessment plan.		
Develop enrollment and marketing plan including substantial market research.		
Develop multi-year new program proforma.		
Obtain internal approvals using established governance and decision-making processes		
Obtain accreditor approvals according to your project management plan and outlined process.		

CHAPTER 11
INFRASTRUCTURE AND RESOURCE PLANNING

A book about new academic program planning is not complete without some discussion about the wide range of infrastructure and resource issues that need to be taken into account when considering expansion of your academic program portfolio. In my experience, these are the issues that are addressed after the fact as opposed to being included in a comprehensive campus-wide new program planning process. If you take only one thing away from this book, it should be the following principle: **No new program should ever be developed and launched in a vacuum.**

It is important to remember that your new program will exist within a complex system with many players and many elements. Even while a new program may add important net tuition revenue, it will also place demands on the broader institution. Given that most colleges and universities have strained organizational capacity these days, it's essential that you take the time to understand as fully as possible how your program will tap your institution's capacity. What is organizational capacity? Generally speaking, organizational capacity is a broad term used to describe the various capabilities, resources, and knowledge that are needed for an organization to be viable.

In assessing your program's impact on your institution's organizational capacity, you'll want to consider all of the ways in which your program will potentially tap resources and knowledge, including: staffing levels, instructional and student support resources, space and facility utilization, technology requirements, and parking, among other things. You'll also want to make sure your program's needs are integrated into broader institutional processes, such as budgeting, space, and technology planning. Taking these demands into account on the front end of your planning process helps ensure the institution will be able to accommodate and support the program at a sufficiently adequate level and that your program will be fully integrated into the institution's infrastructure—two things that are important for your program's long-term success.

A comprehensive infrastructure and resource plan for your new program should at minimum address these seven areas:

1. Staffing
2. Instructional and Student Support Resources
3. External Board Support
4. Space and Facility Utilization
5. Technology and Equipment Requirements
6. Parking
7. Integration with Key Institutional Planning Processes

Each of these areas will be discussed in the remainder of this chapter. This chapter concludes with an infrastructure and resource planning checklist.

1. Staffing

Human resource planning to support your new program is a critical first resource element to consider. As discussed in Chapters 6 and 7, you'll want to develop a detailed staffing plan for the first three years of your program, being sure to include both direct and indirect staffing costs. Start by mapping out the curriculum and course flow for at least one full enrollment cycle (e.g., if your program requires two years to complete full-time, you should map out all courses running during that two-year cycle on a session by session basis). You'll want to consider the qualifications, experience, and content knowledge required for each course and ancillary learning experiences along with whether any existing faculty or staff possess these attributes. To whatever extent you can tap into existing resources, even across levels and disciplinary backgrounds, you will save important start-up costs and build program buy-in and support in other corners of the institution.

Here are some critical questions to consider as you complete your new program staffing worksheet:

- Does this program carry external accreditation or licensing? If so, are there staffing ratios or requirements that must be adhered to? If so, what are these ratios tied to (e.g., enrollment) and has your staffing plan captured these going forward?

- What is the minimum and ideal staffing prerequisites for each course or other learning experience in the curriculum? Be sure to distinguish between "truly essential, minimum requirements" and "nice-to-have."

- Are there existing faculty teaching elsewhere in the institution who have the requirements or interest to teach any of the courses?

- If you need to hire new faculty, what will their teaching and workload be?

- How will the program delivery impact staffing requirements? For example, if the program is being delivered entirely at a distance, might the program faculty and staff also work at a distance? If so, is your institution equipped to support faculty and staff who work at a distance?

- How can you maintain flexibility with your staffing configuration as you launch the program? For example, rather than hiring tenure-track faculty, might you utilize a different kind of category, such as a professor of practice (for professional-oriented programs) and faculty in residence (for liberal arts focused programs).

- What level of oversight is required for this program and how might you best staff to achieve this? Do you need a full-time program director or can program oversight be assumed by an existing faculty member of department chair?

- How will the faculty, administrators and students in this program be supported? What level and kind of support if needed? Are there existing staff who can assume oversight for this program, at least during the launch stage?

- What other unique staffing requirements does your program have? For example, is there a clinical or practicum requirement and if so, who will staff these experiences? Is there a laboratory component? If your program is delivered online, who will orient and support your faculty and students in online teaching and learning practices?

A staffing worksheet template is included at the end of this chapter for you to use in mapping out your staffing needs and addressing the above questions.

> **CASE IN POINT**
>
> As noted elsewhere in this book, Bay Path's approach to staffing new programs is both flexible and lean. Except for programs that carry external accreditation and subsequent staffing ratio requirements, our front-end staffing practices typically play out as illustrated in the example here.
>
> When launching the new OTD, a post-professional occupational therapy doctorate, the proforma allowed for one fully dedicated program director and additional full-time faculty to be added in subsequent years as enrollment targets were met. Because the program is fully online, we were able to search nationally for the director and located an accomplished individual who directs the program from her home in the southeast. We have found that allowing this kind of flexibility for program administrators and faculty who direct and teach online programs is an attractive benefit for prospective employees. It also leads to a stronger candidate pool, especially in those areas where candidates may be scarce, such as in some of the healthcare fields.
>
> As a result of accreditation agency processing slowdowns, the OTD program did not launch according to the proforma schedule; hence, the enrollment targets were off a bit from what was originally planned. In terms of staffing, we monitor enrollment on a year-to-year basis and add additional full-time staffing as enrollment warrants.

> **CASE IN POINT**
>
> Given that we did not aggressively staff up at the outset, we did not incur unnecessary financial risk. We have more flexibility to adapt to things such as ACOTE's recent mandate requiring all entry occupational therapy programs to transition to the doctoral level—something that will impact both the design and staffing needs for the post-professional OTD program going forward. Given the dynamic environment in which schools and their programs reside, anything you can do to preserve flexibility in staffing commitments is beneficial.
>
> A second important point with this hire: we hired someone whose background was quite broad and included previous education and experience in education, public health, and health sciences, in addition to her work in occupational therapy. Because of the breadth of her experience, this individual was able to assist the dean with other projects while the OTD was getting off the ground. Additionally, she brought an important interdisciplinary perspective to her leadership role that will serve the institution well as we bring up other health science programs and create interprofessional opportunities for our students across all healthcare fields in the future.

2. Instructional and Student Support Resources

Similarly, it's important to map out the full range of instructional support that the students who enroll in your program will need to be successful. At the end of the day, your students' success will be a key litmus test for the quality of your program. Every program has unique needs in this area; however, most new program developers do not take the time to identify the needs on the front end and often find themselves scrambling after issues arise. For example, if you are bringing up a program that will be delivered at a distance, have you planned how to orient your faculty and staff to online teaching and learning best practices? Have you planned how to support them while they teach in the 24/7 online classroom? If you are developing a program that requires students to meet certain academic requirements in order to sit for a licensing exam, have you built in specific support from the beginning of the program to ensure they can be successful?

Just as you mapped out staffing needs, you want to also map out your program's instructional resources needs on a course-by-course basis. Specifically, identify what library and other instructional resources are required for the delivery of each course. Are these resources already available, and if not, what do you need to do to acquire them? What is the cost? Are there additional ancillary learning experiences that are associated with any of the courses in your curriculum? If so, what resources are needed to deliver these ancillary experiences? Students are increasingly concerned about the additional costs of textbooks and other add-ons beyond tuition and fees. To whatever extent you can tap into open educational resources (OER) in delivering your curriculum, you will save your students' money, and your faculty will be able to create a more personalized and engaging learning experience. *Campus Technology* provides helpful resources for getting started with OER.[188]

Here are some questions to consider as you plan for how you will meet your faculty and students' teaching and learning needs:

- How will your program be delivered, and what support needs will this create?

- If your program is to be delivered entirely online or via a hybrid model, how will your faculty be prepared to teach? How will the instruction be monitored to ensure students are receiving a quality experience? Who, specifically, will orient your faculty and review the syllabi? Who will be available to faculty when they encounter online teaching issues or have questions needing a quick response? Who will check in to the online classroom on a regular basis to ensure best online teaching practices are being followed? At Bay Path, we have adopted the Quality Matters[189] rubrics to use in training, reviewing, and monitoring all online instruction.

- If you program is to be delivered entirely online or via a hybrid model, how will your students be prepared for success? How will they be oriented to the online classroom and best learning practices? Who will be available to provide technology assistance when students encounter log-in and other common issues?

- Does your program culminate in licensing or accreditation? If so, what academic supports do you need to build in to your program from the beginning to ensure your students will be successful?

- Are there unique learning experiences that need support such as writing support for a thesis or dissertation?

- If your program is to be delivered on campus, will your students need housing or other student service support? Can your institution accommodate your students in on-campus housing? If not, what other options might be available? Can your student services staff and programming accommodate the support needs that the students in your program will have?

- What are the specific instructional resources that are needed for delivery of each course and any ancillary experiences? Do you have these resources on hand? If not, how do you acquire them? What is the cost?

- Have you considered OER for any of the courses? Why or why not? With a new program, you have a unique opportunity for piloting new instructional methods and resources such as OER. It is often easier to embed these new and emerging resources on the front end of a program than after it is already established.

An instructional and student support resources worksheet is included at the end of this chapter to help you in working through these questions.

3. External Board Support

External advisory boards are a valuable source of input and intel for new programs, particularly those that are preparing students for direct entry into a profession or career. If thoughtfully structured and populated, such boards can support the program's accountability by providing real-time guidance and feedback, making sure the program's curriculum is relevant for the profession or industry it's preparing students to enter. Students benefit from the presence of an advisory board in many ways. Involvement of advisory board members as guest speakers or mentors provides students with important networking opportunities and the ability to see first-hand how their degree might translate to a wide range of positions. The curriculum will most likely be improved by an active advisory board thus ensuring students receive an education that is responsive to the real needs of the profession. Changes in the profession will most likely be reflected more quickly in the curriculum with ongoing advisory board input and involvement. Given the increased importance of assessing quality of student learning and program outcomes, the presence of an active advisory board ensures a means for ongoing program improvement.

While the benefits are significant, it takes considerable time and resources to structure and manage an advisory board to ensure maximum value. Here are a few questions to consider in determining whether an advisory board provides sufficient benefit for your program and how to structure your board for success:

- If the program carries licensure or accreditation, is there a requirement or expectation for an external advisory board? If so, what do the accreditation standards require in regard to advisory board structure, composition, role, and ongoing management? What resources will it take to fulfill these standards?

- Will your program's success be enhanced by an advisory board? Generally speaking, an advisory board is most effective when:
    - In-depth external expertise is needed;

- Students or faculty need or could benefit from access to professionals in the field or industry;
    - Market insights that are difficult to obtain in other ways are needed;
    - Your program has specific resource needs that require specialized fundraising campaigns and access to professional networks;
    - You are engaging high-profile professionals, who are just getting to know your institution but are reluctant to make a significant time commitment (e.g., they are not able to join your institution's board of trustees) but have interest in a more limited role as a starting point.
- Have you drafted an explicit and relevant mission and vision statement for your advisory board? Is this statement complimentary to your institution's mission and purposes?
- Is there senior-level commitment for your advisory board? Especially with the recruitment of high-profile professionals, you will need the direct support and occasional involvement of your president, and other senior-level administrators.
- Do you have the means and the capacity for disciplined management of the advisory board? This is the factor on which many advisory boards fail to get off the ground. Getting the most out of your advisory board requires discipline and some formality in operating processes—your advisory members need and will appreciate clear guidance

and support to perform their roles. Advisory board members need to be oriented to the board, their role, and the institution, and there should be a means for ongoing feedback about their involvement. Lastly, you will want to establish a clearly articulated framework regarding advisory board size, member terms, meeting frequency, access to information, and so on.

- Just as you carefully structure your institution's Board of Trustees to ensure an appropriate balance of competencies, expertise, and commitment, you want to do the same for your advisory board. Rather than just jumping in and randomly recruiting whomever is available, the best and most effective advisory boards result from a strategic mapping out of the specific competencies, skills, and expertise that your program needs in order to be successful. Many institutions use a composition matrix to identify the most important advisory board member attributes, using the matrix as a guide for recruitment of members. Such a matrix can also be helpful for identifying where your advisory board may have knowledge or expertise gaps, where individual board members are making significant contributions and where there may be a need for education and training.

See below for a sample matrix for an advisory board for a graduate program in cybersecurity.

Graduate Program in Cybersecurity Management **Advisory Board Composition Matrix** **MEMBERS:**							
Industry Knowledge/ Experience	A	B	C	D	E	F	G
Information assurance and security							
Legal and regulatory requirements							
Emergency management							
New and emerging technologies							
Information risk management							
Technical Skills/ Experience	A	B	C	D	E	F	G
Intrusion detection							
Secure software development							

	A	B	C	D	E	F	G
Risk mitigation							
Cloud security							
Network monitoring, access management							
Security analysis							
Data security							
Program Involvement Capacity	A	B	C	D	E	F	G
Guest lectures							
Board leadership							
Access to industry networks							
Provide internships							
Student mentoring							
Fundraising capacity							

4. Space and Facility Utilization

When it comes to space and facility needs, integration with your institution's master planning process is a critical first prerequisite. While it is difficult to predict the future, one thing is a given: with so much of higher education's growth happening online, coupled with the new dynamics of teaching and learning discussed in Chapter 1, planning for the future is a very tricky thing. Institutions that are saddled with significant facility upkeep needs and deferred maintenance have a much more difficult time responding quickly to the changing educational needs of their current and future students. In space and facility planning for new programs, start by considering the institution's net space, current utilization, and what existing space might be repurposed to meet new program needs. Sally Grans-Korsh, Director of Facilities Management and Environmental Policy at the National Association of College and University Business Officers, suggests that the first action step many campuses should take with space planning is to identify and "mothball" 10% of instructional space, yielding a number of operating expense savings. This counsel is premised on her belief that space on most college and university campuses is underutilized, expensive, poorly measured, and many times poorly managed.[190] Michael Haggans, visiting scholar at the University of Minnesota School of Architecture, is even more pointed when he tells campus leaders to adopt the mantra "no net additional square feet" as a strategic objective.[191] This is in contrast to how many colleges and universities plan which is to assume a symbiotic relationship between an expanding program portfolio and an expanding campus footprint. Haggans goes on to offer several additional recommendations for academic leaders to consider when thinking about space planning for the 21st century university:[192]

- *Start with the assumption that you have enough space.* Even when considering supposedly "self-funding" facilities (such as residence halls), Haggans suggests the notion is short-sighted in that every build adds fiscal and operational burden to the institution.

- *Upgrade the best; get rid of the rest.* Good stewardship of campus space requires making hard decisions about what legacy the institution can truly afford to maintain. Many times, decisions to retain old buildings that are no longer viable divert resources from important investments in modernizing "keeper" space.

- *Manage space and time.* Haggans suggests rethinking the campus in terms of patterns and intensity of use rather than area per student, faculty member, library volume, or research dollar. This has particular relevance for new program space planning. Given that the carrying cost of the campus physical environment is 24/7, planners and decision makers need to consider effectiveness and intensive of use in space allocation decisions. Again, this flies in the face of the typical academic decision process, which many times favors privilege and status over true need.

- *Right-size the whole.* Since offices typically make up more than 30% of campus space, think carefully about how you might be able to reimagine faculty and staff offices for greater efficiency and synergy.

The point here is to find those space areas where significant adjustments are justified understanding that it may not be with the classroom space.

- *Rethink capacity.* According to Haggans, most campuses have either too much capacity or too few students. As the learning paradigm continues to shift away from "seat time," he suggests planning to have more capacity (production of degrees per unit of building area).

- *Take sustainable action.* Haggans also suggests making facility decision to reduce the institution's carbon footprint per credit hour delivered (or another educational equivalent). Bottom line, he recommends starting by not building unnecessary facilities and reinvesting in the best of existing assets, getting rid of unnecessary and redundant facilities.

- *Make the campus matter.* Finally, with the shift at even the most traditional institutions from classroom-based learning to digital and asynchronous options, making the case for expansion of the physical campus must be based on something other than enhancing admissions or tradition. The decrease in the "on-campus time per degree" will result in rethinking what and how a campus provides a "sense of place" and to what extent this matters. Using space in new ways to support the progressively important limited face-time interactions will be an increasingly strategic priority.

In considering how student learning needs and paradigms are shifting, the Higher Education Research and Development (HERSDA) offered seven guiding principles for institutions to consider when doing space planning for teaching and learning facilities.[193] Similar to Haggans, these principles reinforce the notion that institutions should aim for "student centered, flexible learning facilities which are less prescribed and function-specific than what has traditionally been the case."

- Design space for multiple uses concurrently and consecutively.
- Design to maximize the inherent flexibility with each space.
- Design to make use of the vertical dimension in facilities.
- Design to integrate previously discrete campus functions.
- Design features and functions to maximize teacher and student control.
- Design to maximize alignment of different curricula activities.
- Design to maximize student access to, and use and ownership of, the learning environment.

The point here is that our understandings about how people learn and what constitutes an effective learning space are undergoing significant change. With this in mind, it's helpful to map out the learning and program space needs giving consideration to these questions:

- How will your program be delivered, and what does this mean for the space your program really needs? How much time will your students and faculty actually be spending on campus? Be brutally honest in your assessment here.

- What existing campus space might be repurposed or reallocated to support your program space needs?

- Ae there off-campus resources where your program might be housed (e.g., local organizations or businesses with available space)?

- What are the demographics of the students who will enroll in your program, and how does this impact classroom and other space and facility needs? What are their learning styles and preferences? What are their expectations for learning space for this program?

- Will the students in this program need access to other campus facilities or services such as recreation, food, etc.?

- How might you get input from your students about learning space?

- What is the pedagogical approach and learning activities to be conducted in each course and across the curriculum? How does this impact your space planning?

- Do any of the courses or learning experiences have unique technology or sound needs that must be accommodated in the learning space?

- What are the long-term plans for the delivery of this program, and how does that impact the decisions you make now? For example, if you are launching this program as campus-based but plan to move it to online or hybrid delivery within three years, you will want to be cautious about upfront capital investments.

- Is there a need for designated study spaces, laboratory, or clinical space?
- If you conclude that you must build out space to support your new program, you will want to start by considering the detailed programmatic requirements for space, such as:
    - Group work or individual study?
    - Noisy or quiet?
    - Formal or informal learning?
    - Can the space be reserved?
    - Will staff require frequent access and/or views into the space?
    - Is the technology fixed or mobile?
    - How long will the average user be in the space?
    - Class size, room size, and shape.
    - Desirability of windows in both interior and exterior walls.
    - Ceiling height.
    - Lighting, HVAC and acoustics.
    - Adjacency and views to/from other spaces.
- How many program faculty and staff must have designated space? Are there available offices that can be repurposed? If not, how can you create flexible office space to serve multiple purposes?

- How will students and faculty interact with each other outside of the formal classroom setting, and how might space be utilized to facilitate this?

- What ethos and culture are you trying to create with this program? How might your program space configurations support this?

See the space and technology planning worksheet at the end of this chapter as a guide for working through these and other questions that are likely to arise.

CASE IN POINT

In 2014, Bay Path University found itself bursting at the seams at its primary Longmeadow campus, due in large part to the burgeoning growth of the graduate programs generally and the master's in occupational therapy specifically. Located in the town of Longmeadow, which has historically had stringent zoning requirements, Bay Path first tried to find a way to expand at its home campus. But given the unique space needs of the occupational therapy program and the University's plan to grow more healthcare programs within the next 5-7 years, the home campus footprint was just not feasible. There wasn't enough room, nor was there available land nearby. "We just couldn't find anything with the space that we needed. Especially for the parking. That was a big thing. We needed to accommodate 350 cars on a daily basis," stated Mike Giampietro, Vice President for Finance and Administration.

After several potential building sites fell through, an 11-acre site at the corner of Denslow and Shaker Road in the neighboring community of East Longmeadow was secured in 2015. Given that Bay Path had not built any new buildings since the early 1960s, this facility had significant importance for the campus.

> **CASE IN POINT**
>
> Most importantly, it needed to serve as both a teaching and learning hub and showcase for the programs in the health sciences, an area where the institution had put a stake in the ground and planned to grow its impact and footprint in the coming years. Collectively, several factors influenced the eventual building design for the Philip H. Ryan Health Science Center.
>
> First, because The Center is about four miles from the university's main campus, the design plan included a mandate that students get the "full campus experience" while at the center. To achieve this, the center includes spacious common areas for both formal group study and informal study, comfortable seating options for short-term breaks between classes or for longer durations, a café serving breakfast and lunch, a self-service kitchen/vending area for those students who choose to "brown bag" it, a library resource room, and a room for wellness activities.
>
> Second, because this Center would house programs that were intended to help boost the institution's reputation and brand as an innovator in the higher ed space, the architect and interior designer created a contemporary, professional academic learning environment well suited for graduate students preparing to enter high-demand professions in the field of health science, including such features as a simulated emergency room where students in the physician assistant program can practice assessing patients and a model apartment where student occupational therapists can practice teaching people living with physical limitations how to perform everyday tasks. Additionally, a stunning lighting design was installed in the Center's first-floor vaulted ceiling which made the building highly visible to all who drive by and created a dramatic visual showcase at a high trafficked intersection.

> **CASE IN POINT**
>
> Third, the building and design project team went to great lengths to get feedback from the students and faculty who would occupy the building to ensure that the space would to accommodate student and faculty collaboration, facilitate a sense of ownership of the space, and be aligned with the program ethos and culture. For example, students were given an opportunity to try out furniture options and provided input on how they liked to study that resulted in the creation of several small-group study spaces that had whiteboard on three walls with the fourth wall glassed so that occupants could see out and vice versa.
>
> Fourth and finally, 10,000 square feet of the total 58,000-foot building design were left unfinished at the outset to accommodate planned academic programs for the future that were yet unnamed. Having this flexibility to build out this space as needed proved invaluable as Bay Path has since added several additional health science programs, each with its own unique culture and space needs that were unknown in 2015. Today, the Philip H. Ryan Health Science Center's 58,000 square feet on two floors is fully occupied and serves as home for nearly 500 graduate students who rotate in and out of the building on varying schedules that are coordinated to achieve maximum utilization.

5. Technology and Equipment Requirements

A fifth very important resource consideration has to do with your new program's technology requirements. Just as with space planning, you will need to map out each course including a detailed analysis of learning activities in order to understand the full range of technology needed to support your program. This is another area where your program will potentially impact your institutional infrastructure, especially if your program has significant technology support needs. For this reason, it's critical that you work closely with your campus technology administrators and make sure that your program's technology-related needs are incorporated in to the institution's technology plan.

As different modes of educational delivery are becoming more common in colleges and universities, and as higher education curricula are becoming more applied and interdisciplinary, the decisions you make about the role and use of technology to support learning have become increasingly complex. Indeed, virtual classrooms, mobile devices, digital readers, on-demand video, online gaming, and cloud-based LMSs are just a few of the innovations that have arrived on the educational technology scene in recent years. According to a recent technology trends report issued by *Training Industry Magazine*,[194] there are at least five important trends that are important for new program developers to consider:

- A key driver for the educational technology innovation is the **adoption rate of new technology** by digital natives and particularly the

Millennial Generation. Their expectations on how to learn and the importance of collaboration will have an impact on how learning is structured and supported going forward. It will be increasingly important to make learning efficient and effective.

- With the influx of mobile devices and the demand for short, object-based content increasing, **learning libraries** have grown rapidly. This rapid growth means that learners have access to virtually any type of learning content they want any time they want it, on virtually any device they choose. Having this abundance of information available can be a positive thing for learners, and savvy institutions will figure out how to leverage this capacity to enhance the learning experience on their own campuses.

- Research suggests that **adaptive learning** has great potential for improving the learning experience of our students. Adaptive learning is about personalizing the learning experience. By using adaptive learning techniques, we can reduce the time it takes learners to become proficient, eliminating the need to cover content they already understand. Traditional approaches to curricular design trended to a one-size-fits-all approach with the learner expected to consume the content. Adaptive learning is about adapting the content to the learner's needs. The future success of adaptive learning is not only in the design of the technology but in the design of content. Content must be shortened and modified into learning objects, so it can be consumed based only on what the learner needs.

- Research related to the science of learning has taught us that one of the most effective techniques for increasing retention and application is to reinforce content over an extended period. Extending the learning experience with multiple touches throughout the learning experience through a **multi-modal learning approach** using mobile apps and e-learning and simulations may be a particularly promising approach for those fields where students must retain large bodies of knowledge for end-of-program licensure exams.

- **Game-based learning** enhances motivation, engagement and knowledge retention. Early imple-mentation of gaming focused on replacing the classroom experience with a game. The next evolutionary step in gaming saw us learning how to embed gaming programs within the learning program. We are now learning that at the heart of every engaging game (e.g., video games) lies an enticing story that pulls players in, appealing to their motivations and emotions. The evolution of gaming theory has found that using the principle of storytelling and engagement is key to appealing to learner emotions while enhancing learner engagement and recall.

Other important trends to have on the radar according to the Society for College and University Planning (SCUP) annual *Trends in Higher Education* report include:[195]

- Overwhelming preference of **Generation Z learners** for use of technology, hands-on learning, and individual attention.

- Use of **virtual reality (VR) and augmented reality (AR)** to expand human intelligence and potential across multiple disciplines, including science, engineering, and medicine.

- Using **data analytics** to improve student performance and success.

- Growing popularity of **learning paths** offered by outside vendors such as Lynda.com and LinkedIn to provide market-ready content to help users learn or update skills in such areas as 3-D animation, music production, small business ownership, graphic design, software development, and IT. Successful students earn certificates of completion or badges.

With these important trends in mind, there are several issues to consider as you map out your new program's technology support needs:

- What are the learning preferences and needs of your students—current and future—and to what extent does your curricular design align with these preferences and needs?

- What are your program's learning outcomes, and how might technology be used to most effectively achieve these outcomes?

- Given your program learning outcomes and student learning preferences and needs, what technology tools, software, and hardware would be advantageous for delivering your program? Have you discussed your program needs with your educational technology staff?

- How will your program be delivered (e.g. campus-based, online, hybrid, etc.) and what technology needs are essential for effective delivery?

- What expectations do you have for student-to-student and faculty-to-student collaboration? What technology is needed to meet your expectations?

- What are the specific technology and equipment needs for each course in the curriculum, as well as the learning activities to be conducted within and outside of the formal curriculum?

- What specific technology and equipment will need to be available within your teaching and learning spaces in order to support the learning experience? (Consider hardware, software, Wi-Fi access, computers, whiteboards, laboratory equipment, and so on.)

- How will your program use your institution's learning management system (LMS), and what resources will you need to support this usage?

- How do your program faculty feel about the use of technology in teaching? Will they need training or support to encourage the adoption of existing or emerging learning technologies?

- What technology will your program faculty and staff need access to (Consider laptops, desktops, mobile devices, etc.)?

Getting program faculty to adopt new technology in their teaching can sometimes be challenging. Having a specific initiative and plan in place to support your faculty, even in small ways, can be a helpful starting point. Giving faculty an opportunity to safely try out and experiment with new learning technologies, providing incentives such as technology grants, and pairing reluctant faculty with seasoned faculty technology users can also be valuable strategies.

6. Parking and Facility Maintenance

If your new program will have a campus presence of any kind, you will need to consider the demands that your program will place on your institution's parking as well as facility maintenance and upkeep. These are fairly straightforward issues to assess beginning with asking the following questions:

- When and for what specific periods of time will your students, faculty, and staff be on campus?

- How will students, faculty, and staff travel to and from campus? Are they likely to have cars, and if so, how many?

- What is the distance between available campus parking and the areas on campus where your students, faculty, and staff are most likely to populate? Is this a reasonable distance?

- If your program is delivered in the evening and on campus, are the parking facilities in a secure, well-lit location?

- Are there alternative off-campus parking resources that would be available to your students, faculty, and staff?

- Have you discussed your program's parking needs with your campus planning and facilities management staff?

- If your campus occupies classroom, office, and other space, what is required for facility cleaning and ongoing maintenance? How often?

- Are there upfront facility cleaning or upgrade costs?

- Does your program's space have particular unique cleaning or maintenance needs (e.g., laboratory or clinical spaces)? If so, what resources are required to address these needs?

7. Integration with Key Institutional Planning Processes

We began this chapter by highlighting the importance of assessing your program's impact on your institution's organizational capacity. Regardless of how and where your program is delivered and by whom, it will tap some institutional resources. Failing to take these resource needs into consideration as part of a broader institutional planning and strategy process could lead to unexpected and potentially adverse surprises down the road.

How do you avoid this? Be sure to collaborate broadly when your program is still on the drawing board. Make sure the appropriate individuals are aware of your plans and have an opportunity for input. This is where a clearly articulated new program approval process can go a long way in ensuring that your program's financial, facility, staffing, and teaching and learning needs are on the radar and are sufficiently integrated into whatever broader planning processes your institution conducts.

Increasingly, academic leaders are conducting their own planning processes as a component of the institution's strategic planning process. The advantages of doing so are many including having a mechanism for monitoring changes in individual program capacity and curricular emphases, new and emerging program needs (including staffing, technology and facilities), student learning preferences, and demographics among other things. By asking individual departments and programs to report out on strengths, challenges, accomplishments, opportunities, and plans for the short-term future, you are able to capture and respond to important variations and trends in a timely manner.

Minnesota University at Mankato has developed an exemplary and robust academic planning process that "serves as a core component of an integrated University strategic planning linking vision, priorities, people, services, resources, and the physical institution in a flexible process of evaluation, decision making, and action."[196] As the introduction to the plan points out, "the process enables them to proactively and intentionally prepare for and shape the future, rather than letting the future happen to them." Other planning process objectives include:

- *Uphold and connect the current strategic plans for the academic colleges—Allied Health and Nursing; Arts and Humanities; Business; Education; Science, Engineering, and Technology; Social and Behavioral Sciences; University Extended Education; Graduate; and the Memorial Library.*

- *Provide coherence in the strategic plans for the divisions of the University—Finance and Administration (i.e., budget, facilities), Information Technology Services, Student Affairs and Enrollment Management, Advancement, and Strategic Partnerships.*

- *Advance the University's Strategic Priorities.*

- *Support the System's Strategic Framework to ensure access to an extraordinary education for all Minnesotans, be the partner of choice to meet Minnesota's workforce and community needs, and deliver to students, employers, communities, and taxpayers the highest value/most affordable option.*

An important process principle is the requirement that academic programs consult with the appropriate designated campus personnel or office in completing particular sections such as technology and facility needs, enrollment, and so on. Once completed, academic plans are reviewed and updated annually to ensure relevance and alignment with the University master plan. (See Minnesota State University at Mankato's academic planning worksheet for degree-granting programs at the end of this chapter.)

What's Next

In this final chapter, we returned to an important principle—namely, that academic program development is a process that exists within an ecosystem. This ecosystem is comprised of all of the elements and people and resources that make up your institution, not to mention the broader community and world in which your institution resides. Nowhere is it more critical to consider your program's impact and the impact it will have than in the area of new program infrastructure and resource planning. No matter how small your program is or how it is structured or delivered, it will make demands on your institution's infrastructure. To whatever extent you can, understand and make these demands transparent. Take steps to ensure that your program's needs can be met and are integrated into your broader institutional planning and resource decision-making processes. Your program's potential for success will be enhanced.

This chapter reviewed the most important infrastructure and resource areas that need to be on your radar as you are bringing your program to life including staffing, external advisory boards, space, technological, as well as equipment resources, parking, facility maintenance, and planning and integration with existing campus budgeting, technology and space planning processes, etc. Considering how student learning needs and instructional paradigms are shifting, flexibility, creativity, and collaboration are critical planning principles to keep in mind and nurture when resource planning for your new program. The traditional assumptions that framed resource planning even five years ago are no longer valid in this context where resources are constrained; the notion of what constitutes "campus space and place" in the 21st century is evolving. While a challenging context for planning new programs, those institutions that are able to harness and leverage the inherent opportunities found in this context will be at great advantage to create unique, responsive, and sustainable programs to meet the needs of the generations to come.

Key Strategic Questions for Academic Leaders

Use these questions when considering resource and infrastructure needs for your new program. These are useful for self-reflection at front end of your planning process as well as in collaboration and discussion with other senior officers at your institution, such as your chief technology, administration, HR, and facility staff.

1. As you consider your program's staffing needs, are you able to utilize existing staff or faculty in other areas of your institution?

2. Have you mapped out your staffing needs for each learning experience—formal and informal—in your program?

3. Do you have a mechanism or planning process in place to ensure that your new program's space, technology, equipment, facility, and staffing resource needs are incorporated into your institution's strategic planning process? If not, how will you ensure your program's needs are on the radar—now and gong forward?

4. To what extent are OER part of your program's instructional resource mix? If not, why not?

5. Have you considered your students' demographics, learning preferences and needs in learning content and delivery, technology, and equipment decisions?

6. To what extent do your program resource decisions allow for flexibility and future change in delivery or student composition?

7. Is your program utilizing existing resources, and if so, where? If not, why not?

Appendix A

Appendix A is useful for making sure you address all of the essential resource and infrastructure planning issues and needs.

Appendices B, C, and D are useful for capturing staffing, instructional and student support and space and technological needs as part of your new program planning process.

Resource and Infrastructure Planning Checklist		
Task	Completed?	Comments
Faculty staffing analysis completed including specialized accreditor review of standards		
Program administration and support staffing analysis completed		
Student support audit completed		
Student support plan developed		
Instructional support analysis completed		
Instructional support plan developed		
Program space need analysis completed		

Program space plan completed in collaboration with facilities staff		
Technology and equipment needs analysis completed		
Technology and equipment plan completed in collaboration with campus technology staff		
Parking needs assessment completed		
Parking and transportation plan completed in collaboration with campus facilities staff		
Space cleaning and maintenance audit completed		
Space cleaning and maintenance needs communicated to physical plant and facilities staff		

Appendix B

NEW ACADEMIC PROGRAM RESOURCE PLANNING WORKSHEET: STAFFING							
Instruction of Formal Coursework							
Course Name/Number	Credits	Delivery Mode	Essential Content Knowledge, Experience, Education	Nice-to-Have Content Knowledge, Experience, Education	Pedagogical or Technology requirements	Other Requirements	Existing Faculty Available to Teach
Instruction of Ancillary and Informal Learning Experiences (e.g. Clinical, Laboratory, Fieldwork)							
Description	Credits	Delivery Mode	Essential Content Knowledge, Experience, Education	Nice-to-Have Content Knowledge, Experience, Education	Pedagogical or Technology requirements	Other Requirements	Existing Staff Available to Teach

Program Administration and Support					
Description of Role/ Duties Needing Oversight	Percentage of Full Time Required	Essential Expertise, Experience, Skills, Education	Location of Role	Technology or Equipment Required?	Existing Staff Available

Does this program carry accreditation, and if so, what are the specific staffing requirements outlined in the accrediting standards? _____ Yes _____ No

If Yes specify:
Faculty:
Administration:
Other:

Appendix C

NEW ACADEMIC PROGRAM RESOURCE PLANNING WORKSHEET: INSTRUCTIONAL AND STUDENT SUPPORT							
Instructional Resources							
Course Name/Number	Library Resources	Textbooks	Other Learning Resources	OER Considered (Y or N)	Course Pedagogical or Technology Support	Syllabus Developed and Reviewed	Cost
Instructional Support							
Course Name/Number	Delivery Mode	Specific Faculty Support Needs	If Online, Specific Faculty Orientation Needs	Course Quality Oversight Support	Instructor Pedagogical or Technology Support	Faculty Support Troubleshooting Support	Other Needs

Student Support			
Description of Specific Support Needs for Students in this Program (e.g., housing, student services, academic support, writing, technology, online course orientation, and troubleshooting)	Plan to Address Each Need	Cost	Other Campus Staff and Offices Consulted

Appendix D

NEW ACADEMIC PROGRAM RESOURCE PLANNING WORKSHEET: SPACE AND TECHNOLOGICAL SUPPORT

Course Space and Facility Resources

Course Name/Number	Delivery Mode	Course Schedule (Session, Week, Day & Time)	Class Location Proximity Requirements	Instructional Needs to Be Accommodated	Student Learner Needs to Be Accommodated	Space Needs Discussed with Appropriate Campus Staff	Long-Term Course Delivery Plan

Course Technology and Equipment Resources

Course Name/Number	Tech Needs	Tech Needs: Fixed or Mobile	Instructional Equipment	Unique Sound or Aesthetics Needs	Availability of Existing Resources	Classroom Hardware or Infrastructure Needs	Cost to Purchase

Other Program Space and Technology Resources

Description of Other Space, Technology, Equipment Needs (e.g., designated study spaces, clinical space, laboratories, faculty and staff offices, file storage, and lockers)	Plan to Address Each Need	Cost	Appropriate Campus Staff and Offices Consulted

Appendix E

PART B: Planning Tool for ACADEMIC AWARD Programs
(Complete for each Academic Award Program)

Department (or Departments, if collaborative) submitting plan:

Program Name and Award	Insert Program Name and Award (Example: Interplanetary Studies, BS)
Existing or New Program	___ Existing ___ Propose New
Program Plan	___ Propose New ___ Grow ___ Sustain ___ Revise ___ Suspend
Rationale for Program Plan	What is your **rationale** to propose new, grow, sustain, revise, or suspend the program? *Note: This may be informed by department plans, college strategic plans, university strategic priorities, MnSCU strategic framework, comprehensive program review, accreditation standards, advisory board recommendations, student employment trends, projected career demand information, etc.*
Collaborative Program	If the program is currently offered or would be **offered in collaboration** with another department or institution, please identify and elaborate below. ___ Program is/would be offered in collaboration/partnership with another institution. Please, identify program partner(s) and discuss the relationship that exists or will be developed: ___ Program is/would be offered in collaboration/partnership with another department at Minnesota State University, Mankato. Please, identify program partner(s) and discuss the relationship that exists or will be developed:

Type of Program Offering (Delivery Mode)	Between Fall 2015 and Spring 2018 we envision that our program will be **offered in the following way(s):**			
	Program Offering: (check applicable boxes)	2015-16	2016-17	2017-18
	Face-to-Face Program (Nearly all or all of instruction is face-to-face)			
	Hybrid Program (Mix of face-to-face and online instruction)			
	Online Program (Nearly all or all of instruction is online)			

Location of Offering* (Mankato, Edina, Normandale, Century, etc.) *This section is not applicable for 100% online programs.	Between Fall 2015 and Spring 2018 we envision that our program will be **offered at the following location(s):**			
	Location(s) where the program is or is planned to be offered in a face-to-face or hybrid format:	2015-16	2016-17	2017-18

Student Enrollment and Success	What are your program strengths, challenges, and opportunities considering **student enrollment, academic achievement, and career success**?

Significant variations from past trends need to be explained.

New Students

	Historical	Historical	Current	Current	Desired	Desired	Desired
	Fall 2011	Fall 2012	Fall 2013	Fall 2014	Fall 2015	Fall 2016	Fall 2017
First-Time	Historical Provided	Historical Provided	Current Provided				
Transfer	Historical Provided	Historical Provided	Current Provided				

Planning Considerations:

Classification of All Enrolled Declared Majors
(not applicable for graduate programs)

	Historical	Historical	Current	Current	Desired	Desired	Desired
	Fall 2011	Fall 2012	Fall 2013	Fall 2014	Fall 2015	Fall 2016	Fall 2017
First-Year (0-29 Credits)	Historical Provided	Historical Provided	Current Provided				
Sophomore (30-59 Credits)	Historical Provided	Historical Provided	Current Provided				
Junior (60-89 Credits)	Historical Provided	Historical Provided	Current Provided				
Senior (90-119 Credits)	Historical Provided	Historical Provided	Current Provided				
Senior + (120 Credits)	Historical Provided	Historical Provided	Current Provided				

Planning Considerations:

Diversity of All Enrolled Declared Majors

	Historical	Historical	Current	Current	Desired	Desired	Desired
	Fall 2011	Fall 2012	Fall 2013	Fall 2014	Fall 2015	Fall 2016	Fall 2017
Ethnic/Racial Minority	Historical Provided	Historical Provided	Current Provided				
International	Historical Provided	Historical Provided	Current Provided				

Planning Considerations:

ACADEMIC ENTREPRENEURSHIP

All Enrolled Declared Majors and Awards

	Historical	Historical	Current	Current	Desired	Desired	Desired
	2011-12	2012-13	2013-14	2014-15	2015-16	2016-17	2017-18
Enrolled Majors	Historical Provided	Historical Provided	Current Provided				
Awards	Historical Provided	Historical Provided	Current Provided				

Planning Considerations:

Student Retention

		Historical	Historical	Current	Current	Desired	Desired	Desired
		Fall Cohort 2010 to 2011	Fall Cohort 2011 to 2012	Fall Cohort 2012 to 2013	Fall Cohort 2013 to 2014	Fall Cohort 2014 to 2015	Fall Cohort 2015 to 2016	Fall Cohort 2016 to 2017
First Fall to Second Fall	Caucasian Students	Historical Provided	Historical Provided	Current Provided				
	Students of Color	Historical Provided	Historical Provided	Current Provided				

Planning Considerations:

Student Completion
(not applicable for graduate programs)

		Historical	Historical	Current	Current	Desired	Desired	Desired
		Fall Cohort 2005	Fall Cohort 2006	Fall Cohort 2007	Fall Cohort 2008	Fall Cohort 2009	Fall Cohort 2010	Fall Cohort 2011
4-Year Rate	Caucasian Students	Historical Provided	Historical Provided	Current Provided				
	Students of Color	Historical Provided	Historical Provided	Current Provided				
6-Year Rate	Caucasian Students	Historical Provided	Historical Provided	Current Provided				
	Students of Color	Historical Provided	Historical Provided	Current Provided				

Planning Considerations:

Student Job Placement/Related Employment/Continuing Education

	Historical	Historical	Current	Current	Desired	Desired	Desired
	2010-11	2011-12	2012-13	2013-14	2014-15	2015-16	2016-17
Employment Rate	Historical Provided	Historical Provided	Current Provided				
Related Employment Rate	Historical Provided	Historical Provided	Current Provided				
Continuing Education	Historical Provided	Historical Provided	Current Provided				

Planning Considerations:

Resources	What are the **resources that you need for program success**?
Identify current and future needs due to program plan	Specialized Technology:
	Instructional Supplies/Laboratory Supplies/Equipment:
	Specialized Facilities/Equipment:
	Library Resources:
	Non-Salary Resources:
	Number of Faculty and Teaching Assistants
			Historical 2011-12	Historical 2012-13	Current 2013-14	Current 2014-15	Desired 2015-16	Desired 2016-17	Desired 2017-18
	Tenured							
	Probationary							
	Fixed-Term							
	Adjunct							
	Graduate (TA)							

Planning Considerations:

Number of Service Faculty, Staff, and Students

	Historical 2011-12	Historical 2012-13	Current 2013-14	Current 2014-15	Desired 2015-16	Desired 2016-17	Desired 2017-18
MSUAASF							
Classified							
Graduate (RA/GA)							
Student Workers							

Planning Considerations:

How might potential anticipated leaves, reassigned time, or **changing faculty personnel impact the future of your program?**

Key Partnerships and Stakeholders	

Program Vision or Considerations: **5, 10, 15 Years, and Beyond**	

Helpful Resources

Here is a short list of resources that I have found helpful for the topics covered in Section III.

Marketing, branding and positioning

www.rhb.com/work/learn-how-RHB-builds-subbrands-for-higher-education-institutions. This series of case studies illustrates how branding can be utilized to enhance an institution's market position and increase enrollment.

Bailey, Richard H. *Coherence: How Telling the Truth Will Advance Your Cause (and Save the World)*. Third Satellite Communications, 2010. This book provides higher education professionals with a broad framework and specific strategies—and lots of good ideas—for successfully engaging constituencies.

Neumeier, Marty. *The Brand Gap: How to Bridge the Distance Between Business Strategy and Design*. New Riders, 2005. There's an excellent series of short and highly entertaining books by long-time marketing guru Marty Neumeier. Visit his website and read the free, quick slideshare version of one of his most popular books, *The Brand Gap*. Marty Neumeier's website: www.martyneumeier.com/the-brand-gap

Godin, Seth. I recommend this fun and inspiring series of books by someone who is on the leading edge of marketing. Seth Godin is a rebellious thinker who tells it like it is. There are too many books to list here but check out his website for lots of free and valuable resources: www.sethgodin.com.

Ries, Al, and Jack Trout. *Positioning: The Battle for Your Mind.* McGraw-Hill Education, 2001. This classic and relevant read will tell you everything you need to know about creating a "position" in a prospective constituent's mind.

Kelley, Tom. *The Art of Innovation: Lessons in Creativity from IDEO, America's Leading Design Firm.* Currency Publishing, 2001. *The Art of Innovation* is a good resource with inspiring thinking about how to come up with better ideas for products, services, and operations.

Yarrow, Kit. *Decoding the New Consumer Mind: How and Why We Shop and Buy.* Jossey-Bass, 2014. This is a practical guide to understanding how and why people make the purchases they do and what this means for them and for our organizations.

The American Marketing Association sponsors an annual Symposium for the Marketing of Higher Education. Their website is a good resource for staying up to date on best practices and new and emerging trends in the world of higher education marketing: www.ama.org.

chiefmartec.com. This blog is helpful for staying up to date on marketing technology and its impact on marketing strategy and management.

Market research and data sources

www.economicmodeling.com. This website provides labor market data, job postings, and other relevant data that can be useful for new program planning, career coaching, economic impact studies, and more.

www.chmuraecon.com. An applied economics and data science consulting firm, Chmura works with clients to help analyze and make sense of data for decision-making purposes.

www.eab.com. EAB is a consulting firm that works with 1,500+ institutions on enrollment and student success strategies among other things. Their website is a good source of research and benchmarking data on specific topics and issues.

cew.georgetown.edu. The Center for Education and the Workforce is an independent, nonprofit research and policy institute that studies the link between education, career qualifications and workforce demand.

www.hanoverresearch.com/education-solutions.
Hanover's Education Solutions is a consulting firm that provides research and data to help institution's address a wide range of issues including assessment of the academic program portfolio. They publish free and helpful research reports.

Social media, digital marketing, website and mobile device optimization

OHO Interactive is a great source for staying up-to-date on website analytics data. Their site is updated annually and paints a broad picture of what is happening nationally across higher education. It provides helpful benchmark data:
www.oho.com/blog/2019-google-analytics-benchmarks-higher-education-websites

Hootsuite.com is a low-cost tool that enables you to manage multiple social networks, connect with constituencies, and grow your brand on social media.

www.moz.com/blog/absolute-beginners-guide-to-google-analytics. Moz provides this quick and easy beginner's guide to understand Google Analytics.

Adult student recruitment practices

RNL (www.ruffalonl.com) is a consulting firm that works with institutions on strategies for optimizing enrollments. They provide free resources and reports on marketing and student recruitment including benchmarking data for recruitment and return on investment.

Learning House (www.learninghouse.com) is a consulting firm that provides wide ranging educational services and online program management. Their website provides free research reports on online learning trends and other cutting-edge topics.

The leading association for professional, continuing, and online education, UPCEA (www.upcea.edu) is a good source of data about administrative practices, marketing and program development.

The only professional organization devoted exclusively to those who work in the graduate enrollment management area, NAGAP (www.nagap.org) is a great source for networking and benchmarking data.

Accreditation

A comprehensive and easily understandable overview of accreditation in the United States can be found at: www.chea.org/userfiles/uploads/AccredRecogUS.pdf

A national advocate and institutional voice for self-regulation of academic quality through accreditation,

CHEA (www.chea.org) is an association of 3,000 degree-granting institutions and recognizes 60 institutional and programmatic accrediting organizations.

www.nasfaa.org/uploads/documents/Accreditation_Reform.pdf. This white paper issued jointly by four government entities reviews recommendations for reforming the higher education accreditation process.

This white paper issued by the Christensen Institute highlights the role that accreditation plays in limiting innovation:
www.christenseninstitute.org/publications/accreditation-innovation-and-transparency-in-higher-education

Infrastructure and resource planning

Learning Spaces. Edited by Diana G. Oblinger. EDUCAUSE, 2006. This book provides dozens of ideas for reimagining the use of campus space to support and improve teaching, learning, and student engagement. The entire book can be downloaded free at: www.educause.edu/research-and-publications/books/learning-spaces

The following free online resources provide case studies illustrating the use of space to enhance learning. The first link provides access to the UK Higher Education Learning Space Toolkit. The second link provides access to case studies that accompany each chapter.

- www.ucisa.ac.uk/learningspace

- www.jisc.ac.uk/full-guide/learning-space-toolkit-case-studies

EDUCAUSE (www.educause.edu) is a nonprofit association whose mission is to advance higher education through the use of information technology. Their site provides a data service for benchmarking along with research reports and publications about higher education technology.

Campus Technology (www.campustechnology.com) is one of higher education's top information sources. They deliver valuable information via a daily site, monthly digital magazine, newsletters, webinars and online tools and provide in-depth coverage on the technologies and implementations influencing colleges and universities across the nation.

College Planning & Management (www.webcpm.com) is a comprehensive online resource center with up-to-date information about facility planning, maintenance and operations, safety and security, technology, business and finance, the learning environment, and more.

The Society for College and University Planning (SCUP) is a membership organization representing higher education and private sector institutions and focusing on institutional planning, academic planning, finance and budgeting. administration, institutional research, IT, and campus and master planning. Good resource for trend data. See www.scup.org.

The EvoLLLution (www.evolllution.com) is an online newspaper that publishes articles and interviews by individuals across the postsecondary space sharing their insights on higher education and their opinions on what the future holds for the industry—all through a uniquely non-traditional lens.

CASE STUDY

CASE STUDY
ACADEMIC PROGRAM INVENTION AS A DRIVER FOR INSTITUTIONAL TRANSFORMATION: BAY PATH UNIVERSITY

Institutional Overview

When Bay Path University first opened its doors to students as a co-ed proprietary institution, typewriters and calculating machines dominated in the classrooms. Today, the University operates in a world driven by iPads, mobile phones, and laptops. Throughout Bay Path's more than 120-year history, it has been true to its core promise of providing innovative, career-focused educational programs that have evolved in response to the economic, cultural, and technological influences of our time.

Founded in 1897 as Bay Path Institute, Bay Path's first location was at the corner of State and Dwight Streets in downtown Springfield, MA. For decades, it enjoyed educational and financial success, becoming one of the largest and most respected business institutes in the region. Known for its accelerated 48-week format and state-of-the-art, relevant courses and certificate programs (Bay Path Business Institute did not grant degrees at this point in time), particularly in business management, accounting, and finance, Bay Path's growth prompted a move in 1920 to a new site at 100 Chestnut Street in Springfield, MA. There, the institution flourished for nearly 20 years, increasing to an enrollment of 1200 students just prior to 1941.

History interceded when World War II profoundly affected Bay Path. All young, able-bodied men enlisted for the effort; meanwhile, young women were working on factory floors and company offices in positions unimaginable before the war. The future would never be the same. Sensing an opportunity to expand the role of women in business, local Springfield businessman, Thomas Carr, purchased Bay Path Institute in 1944 and assumed the role of President. Significant changes ensued including shifting Bay Path to all-women, changing the name to Bay Path Secretarial School for Women, and most importantly, moving the Bay Path physical campus to Longmeadow, MA.

Mindful of the competitive landscape, President Carr set out to create a new and innovative kind of school for women, different from the traditional women's colleges in the region such as Smith and Mount Holyoke but also distinct from the Katharine Gibbs Secretarial School model, which had carved out a niche in educating women with technical and skills-based secretarial training. Carr envisioned a different kind of education for women, one that would prepare them to serve at the right hand of the CEO; by necessity, this would require both the technical training and skills in tandem with a strong liberal arts foundation to ensure graduates had the confidence and educational background to maneuver at the upper echelon of any organization with ease. Such a school did not exist at that time.

In keeping with his vision, President Carr believed it would be important to achieve junior college status, a goal that was realized in 1949 when the school was chartered by the Commonwealth of Massachusetts to award the Associate in Science degree and changed its name to Bay Path Junior College. Approval to award the Associate in Arts degree was granted in 1963. President Carr's nearly 25-year tenure from 1944 – 1968 saw a major expansion of the campus with new buildings, major renovations of existing space, and the acquisition of additional contiguous properties and square footage—thus enlarging the campus footprint.

As the women's movement took hold in the 1960s and women's career aspirations expanded, Bay Path retooled and expanded its academic program portfolio with an eye toward educational options that would meet the workforce and societal needs of the era and in response to the fading or developing of marketable professional training. For example, the early courses that prepared students to become experts in the areas of typing, shorthand, and filing were replaced by courses that introduced students to word processing and other computing skills and the eventual introduction of four-year bachelor's degrees programs in criminal justice, education, and psychology. In 1988, the institution's name was changed to Bay Path College, indicating the Commonwealth's approval to grant bachelor's degrees, the first of which were conferred in 1991.

The early to mid-1980s were an enrollment-challenged time for Bay Path, so much so that the Board of Trustees took the unprecedented step of placing a moratorium on the granting of tenure in 1983. As women's colleges were beginning to go co-ed across the country and as many institutions were shifting from two- to four-year status, Bay Path's status as a women's serving, two-year institution was not at all certain. As Bay Path's enrollments were dropping, the Board took this action in order to preserve flexibility for positioning the institution for what appeared to be an uncertain future. It is important to note that this moratorium has never been lifted; although, Bay Path faculty are now eligible for three-year contracts.

Under President Carol Leary, who arrived in December 1994, a new era of momentous change was ushered in. During her nearly 25-year tenure, the institution has been transformed on every level. With significant enhancements in technology infrastructure and utilization as a foundation, a strategic plan for expanding and shaping the academic program portfolio to more fully leverage Bay Path's mission and impact was put in motion. A center piece of the academic planning process that took place during the early days of Leary's tenure was the emergence of an innovative and forward-looking signature curriculum focused on leadership, communication, and technology. The revised mission strengthened Bay Path's capacity for educating women to become confident and resourceful contributors to an increasingly complex and interdependent world with mastery of a wide range of skills reflecting workforce needs—current and future.

The resulting transformation has three primary markers, which collectively illustrate the power of academic program invention as a tool for institutional renewal and transformation. These markers are: 1) the establishment of the Saturday One-Day Program for Adult Women in 1999; 2) the launch of the first co-ed graduate program in 2001 and subsequent formalization and development of the Graduate School beginning in 2007; and 3) the creation of The American Women's College in 2013. Together, these markers of programmatic expansion reflect Bay Path's historic capacity to change and adapt in response to its evolving marketplace context and to meet the ever-changing needs of society.

1. Commitment to the education of adult women

Beginning in the mid-1990s, Bay Path began the transition from what was essentially a two-year institution to a four-year-plus-graduate institution. By the end of the decade, 93% of the students were enrolled in bachelor degree programs and 7% in associate degree programs. During this same period, the institution reaffirmed its mission of providing quality professional undergraduate education for women grounded in a solid liberal arts and sciences foundation. This reaffirmation of mission and core purpose as a women's college was grounded in a keen and shared understanding about Bay Path's unique role and potential in the broader higher education landscape and served as an essential guiding light for many of the programmatic changes that followed over the next two decades.

When the new president arrived on campus in 1995, she encountered a campus in transition. With the progression from two- to four-year institution well underway, residential campus enrollment fell to an all-time low at about the time of her arrival, accompanied by a corresponding shift in the enrollment composition from full-time to part-time (see Chart 1). Given Bay Path's overwhelming reliance on tuition as the predominant revenue source, the president and her team concluded that enrollment diversification was an immediate priority. The fiscal challenges created by the diminishing traditional aged undergraduate student enrollment prompted them to consider opportunities that might further leverage and expand the institution's unique mission as a women's college.

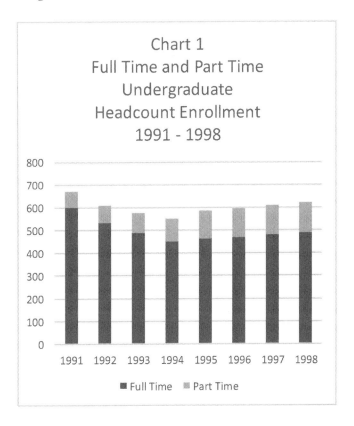

At about this time, a growing body of research documented that adult women were the fastest growing population of students entering higher education with particular growth potential projected for minority women. Given the reaffirmation of the mission and the fact that Bay Path's culture of high touch, holistic support had historically, uniquely translated into a capacity for developing and empowering women for success, the institution initiated an innovative new program—the

Saturday One-Day accelerated degree completion program for adult women. Launched in 1999, this one-of-a-kind program was designed to enable adult women (average age of 38) to complete a college degree in about three years (if they entered with little or no transfer credit) or 18 months (if they entered with the equivalent of an associate's degree) by attending classes only on Saturdays. This accelerated program allowed women to specialize in fields that would prepare them with opportunities for employment or advancement upon graduation, including: business, information technology, and education. Within one year of its launch, the Saturday One-Day program enrolled 240 adult women on Bay Path's Longmeadow campus.

As Chart 2 illustrates, this new program quickly bolstered the struggling traditional aged enrollments and provided Bay Path with an important new tuition revenue stream. As the Saturday One-Day program quickly found its market in the western Massachusetts region, a second campus site for the program was added in central Massachusetts in the Sturbridge area. This teaching location opened in 2003-2004 with 75 students and quickly grew to enroll more than 200 students by 2009. Building on the success at the Longmeadow and Sturbridge locations, a third site was added in eastern Massachusetts in Burlington. Opening in 2006-2007 with 16 students, this location grew to approximately 170 students by 2010.

Thanks to the diversification strategy, Bay Path's undergraduate enrollment grew to an all-time high of nearly 1,600 students by 2010 with more than 60% of the total comprised of adult women who were enrolled in the Saturday One-Day program. Bay Path was clearly an early mover in its region in bringing up accelerated adult women-focused degree completion programs, and this

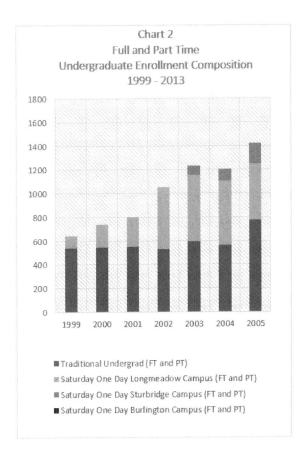

served the institution well for many years. However, as other institutions began to discover this market and respond with their own version of the Saturday One-Day accelerated option—sometimes at a lower cost and using online delivery—the competition began to have an impact. Longmeadow campus Saturday One-Day enrollments peaked in 2010 with an all-time high enrollment of 609 and began a steady slide downward thereafter. Sturbridge and Burlington adult women program enrollments followed suit (as shown in Chart 2). While the traditional undergrad-

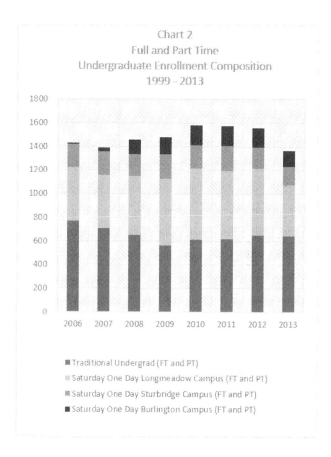

uate enrollments experienced a strong rebound enrolling a record 775 students in 2005-2006, these enrollments have remained remarkably flat across several years.

2. A market-driven, boutique program approach to expanding co-educational graduate education

Bay Path's entrance into co-ed graduate education grew out of the reinvigorated mission and tri-part curricular focus on leadership, communications, and technology, the integration of which was considered quite unique at the time. As the president and her team considered strategies for programmatic diversification, they began to prepare the institution for a move to the master's level. Even amidst the highly strained financial context, the Board of Trustees supported the investment of the necessary resources to ready the institution including expanding library resources, developing the information technology infrastructure, hiring more full-time faculty, and building out the undergraduate curriculum and program to leverage the missional distinctives noted earlier.

This work culminated with the launch of Bay Path's first co-ed, accelerated graduate degree program, the Master of Science in Communications and Information Management (CIM). Enrolling its first class of 35 students in Fall 2001, this program was the first of its kind in New England and one of only a handful of programs in the world at that time that prepared professionals with an integrated mindset and skill set. With its curricular linkage and integration of communications, information systems, business principles, and information management, the program reflected the networked environment that professionals were increasingly encountering in the emerging information age; students were prepared to meet the demands of the current and evolving employment markets in ways that no other program in the region could do. With its eight-week session delivery format, the program could be completed in less than one year, making it one of the first accelerated graduate programs in the region.

The second graduate program, the Master of Occupational Therapy (MOT) enrolled its first cohort of students in 2003. Following the lead of the M.S. in CIM degree, the MOT program built on the undergraduate program and the institution's historic strength in preparing Occupational Therapy Assistants (OTAs) and was designed to be delivered using a distinctive format. One of the first 3/2 programs in the country, Bay Path's program linked the undergraduate and graduate coursework in occupational therapy in such a way that students were able to obtain their bachelor and master's degree in five years.

The third graduate program, the MBA in Entrepreneurial Thinking and Innovative Practices also built on the undergraduate programs—in this case, extending students' core business knowledge at the graduate level while preparing them with the capacity to think in new ways and to problem solve using innovative practices. Designed in part to leverage Bay Path's notable DNA as an innovative and entrepreneurial organization, the MBA was one of the first in the field to integrate the principles of innovative thinking and entrepreneurial practice across the curriculum. As with the M.S. in CIM, the program was delivered using the 8-week accelerated format. Even though competition among MBA programs in the Western Massachusetts region was quite intense, Bay Path exceeded its first-year enrollment goal with an entering class of 43 students.

The financial impact of program diversification on both the undergraduate and graduate level is illustrated by Chart 3. In its inaugural year, the Saturday One-Day program generated gross tuition revenue of $1,090,000 and by FY 2005, this number had grown to $5,905,000. With the expansion of the One-Day program to the Sturbridge location, the gross tuition revenue earned from this additional location added $1,551,000 in FY 2005. By FY2005, the new graduate programs contributed nearly $1 million more in additional gross tuition revenues.

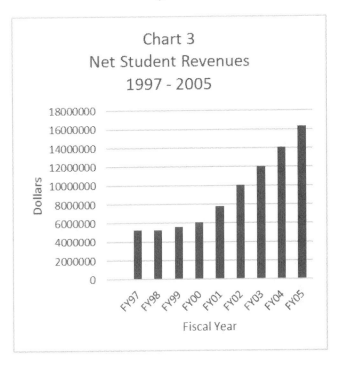

As illustrated in Chart 4, the revenues generated by these new programs resulted in a balance between net student revenues and total operating expenses by FY 2004.

Given the early success with launching mission-extending, boutique, innovative co-ed graduate programs, the institution formalized its commitment to graduate education by establishing the graduate school and appointing a founding dean for graduate education in 2007. Under the leadership of this founding dean who subsequently became provost in 2010, and a team of talented deans who were hired to oversee the rapidly expanding academic portfolio, total institutional enrollment has grown to nearly 3,500 students by Fall 2018 with graduate students comprising 45% of the total. In recognition of the institution's growth, curricular mix, and institutional complexity (particularly at the graduate level), Bay Path received approval on July 1, 2014 to change its name to Bay Path University.

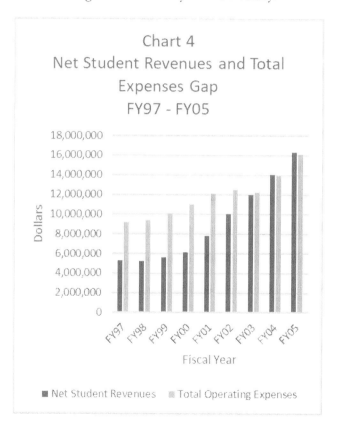

From 2006 to the present, Bay Path has pursued an aggressive, market-responsive strategy of adding at least one new graduate program nearly every year (and more than one in some years) in areas with high occupational demand and/or mission-leveraging potential. With every new program launched, the principles and processes outlined in this book were followed including the development of a comprehensive feasibility study and financial proforma, with particular attention paid to identifying and confirming a compelling and sustainable market niche prior to launch. This niche varies according to each program's marketplace context. For example, with the MFA in Creative Nonfiction Writing, the program was designed to integrate a focus on women's ways of writing, something that did not exist anywhere else at the time. With the recently launched doctoral program in higher education leadership and organizational studies, the curriculum integrates higher education leadership preparation with training in entrepreneurial management and innovative thinking strategies, a unique focus that was not found in other higher education doctoral programs.

As was the case with the first graduate programs, new programs are built on existing undergraduate programs whenever possible, taking advantage of the immediate built-in student pipeline, existing curricula and other natural synergies.

Additionally, a variety of delivery models and calendar formats are utilized (according to the market research obtained through the feasibility study) with a focus on creating flexible options for students, however that may play out in a particular professional and industry area. For some graduate programs that began as campus-based, deans and their faculty have closely monitored student enrollment preferences and have expanded online and other flexible delivery options to accommodate student interest. For example, graduate programs in education and psychology are now offered at locations in Central and Eastern Massachusetts in addition to the Longmeadow campus and online. Courses are structured and technology is utilized so that students can complete courses using all locations within a particular session if desired. For many of the programs, the 8-week accelerated model is used with students having the option to complete their programs either entirely online, on campus or a mix of both depending upon their need for flexibility from session to session.

Chart 5 shows the growth in graduate education at Bay Path beginning with the MS in CIM in 2001and extending to the present. As is illustrated by this trajectory, Bay Path has also added certificates along the way in response to market and workforce needs and opportunities. These certifications, coupled with the flexible design of most of the programs, enable students to customize their programs according to their personal career goals and aspirations. Pathways can easily be created by drawing courses from multiple programs and certification areas—all in the spirit of creating educational opportunities that "bend to the shape of students' lives."

3. Using innovative technology and pedagogy to transform adult women's education

As the adult degree completion market took off nationwide and competitive forces intensified, Bay Path's Saturday One-Day program enrollments were impacted. By 2013, total enrollments across the three campus locations had fallen to 725, a drop of 250 students from

CHART 5
BAY PATH UNIVERSITY
GRADUATE PROGRAM DEVELOPMENT
2001 - 2019

	2001	2002	2003	2004	2005	2006	2007	2008	2009
Communications & Info Management, MS	X	X	X	X	X	X	X	X	X
Occupational Therapy, MOT			X	X	X	X	X	X	X
Entrepreneurial Thinking, MBA					X	X	X	X	X
Nonprofit Management, MS and Cert.						X	X	X	X
Strategic Fundraising, MS and Cert.							X	X	X
Higher Education Administration, MS and Cert.								X	X
Education, MS and Ed.S.								X	X
Forensics, MS									X
Developmental Psychology, MS									X
Physician Assistant Studies, MS									
Clinical Mental Health Counseling, MS									
Cybersecurity Management, MS									
Autism Spectrum Disorders, Cert.									
Enrollment Management, Cert.									
Creative Nonfiction Writing, MFA									
Accounting, MS									
Education in Curriculum and Instruction, MS									
Leadership and Negotiation, MS									
Information Management, MS									
Early Intervention, Cert.									
Language and Literacy, Cert.									
Teaching: Severe Special Needs, Cert.									
Applied Data Science, MS									
Clinical Mental Health Counseling, Ed.S.									
Applied Laboratory Science and Operations*, MS									
Applied Behavior Analysis, MS/Ed.S.									
Communications, MS									
Genetic Counseling, MS									
Occupational Therapy Doctorate (OTD)									
Online Teaching & Program Admin, Cert.									
Teaching; Moderate Special Needs									
Healthcare Management, MS									
Education/Reading, MS									
Nursing, MSN/DNP									
Public Health, MPH									
Planned for 2019:									
Higher Education Leadership & Organizational Studies, Ed.D.									
Health Science, DHS									
HEADCOUNT ENROLLMENT	35	48	72	70	113	158	281	375	553

	CHART 5 BAY PATH UNIVERSITY GRADUATE PROGRAM DEVELOPMENT 2001 - 2019								
	2010	2011	2012	2013	2014	2015	2016	2017	2018
Communications & Info Management, MS	X	X	X	X	X	X	X	X	X
Occupational Therapy, MOT	X	X	X	X	X	X	X	X	X
Entrepreneurial Thinking, MBA	X	X	X	X	X	X	X	X	X
Nonprofit Management, MS and Cert.	X	X	X	X	X	X	X	X	X
Strategic Fundraising, MS and Cert.	X	X	X	X	X	X	X	X	X
Higher Education Administration, MS and Cert.	X	X	X	X	X	X	X	X	X
Education, MS and Ed.S.	X	X	X	X	X	X	X	X	X
Forensics, MS	X	X	X	X	X	X	X		
Developmental Psychology, MS	X	X	X	X	X	X	X	X	X
Physician Assistant Studies, MS			X	X	X	X	X	X	X
Clinical Mental Health Counseling, MS			X	X	X	X	X	X	X
Cybersecurity Management, MS				X	X	X	X	X	X
Autism Spectrum Disorders, Cert.					X	X	X	X	X
Enrollment Management, Cert.					X	X	X	X	X
Creative Nonfiction Writing, MFA					X	X	X	X	X
Accounting, MS					X	X	X	X	X
Education in Curriculum and Instruction, MS					X	X	X	X	X
Leadership and Negotiation, MS					X	X	X	X	X
Information Management, MS						X	X	X	X
Early Intervention, Cert.						X	X	X	X
Language and Literacy, Cert.							X	X	X
Teaching: Severe Special Needs, Cert.							X	X	X
Applied Data Science, MS							X	X	X
Clinical Mental Health Counseling, Ed.S.							X	X	X
Applied Laboratory Science and Operations*, MS							X	X	X
Applied Behavior Analysis, MS/Ed.S.								X	X
Communications, MS								X	X
Genetic Counseling, MS								X	X
Occupational Therapy Doctorate (OTD)								X	X
Online Teaching & Program Admin, Cert.								X	X
Teaching: Moderate Special Needs								X	X
Healthcare Management, MS								X	X
Education/Reading, MS								X	X
Nursing, MSN/DNP									X
Public Health, MPH									X
Planned for 2019:									
Higher Education Leadership & Organizational Studies, Ed.D.									
Health Science, DHS									
HEADCOUNT ENROLLMENT	595	619	812	901	1005	1251	1332	1351	1521

just a few years earlier. Committed to advancing higher education for women, Bay Path recognized that the campus-based program was inadequate for reaching the 76 million women in the country without a baccalaureate degree. The research on this population confirmed that access to educational opportunity was a limiting factor for many of these women. To address this gap while also adapting to the marketplace context, Bay Path made a significant commitment that built upon its long and successful track record in retaining and supporting adult women who were pursuing undergraduate degrees in an accelerated form.

Drawing upon best practices about how adult women learn best, a fully online degree completion program in Leadership and Organizational Studiers for women only was piloted with highly positive results. Students reported exceedingly high levels of achievement and satisfaction; nearly 100% of this first cohort was retained to graduate within two years. Given the success of this pilot, The American Women's College (TAWC), a fully online baccalaureate degree program for adult women, was established in 2013.

Built to scale, it was recognized at the outset that the traditional curricular undergraduate practices and policies would hinder the development of a model that was built to serve hundreds and eventually thousands of online students; hence, the institution took several steps that were important for ensuring the success of this innovative program. First, TAWC was removed from the central academic administrative structure and organized as a separate unit reporting directly to the president. Second, to allow for the creation of a new culture and way of working, TAWC was housed off-site in an office building in downtown Springfield, MA where space was primarily structured as open cubicles. Third, external grant funding was obtained to support the development of a uniquely different and highly innovative learning system that paired pioneering learning analytics with personalized instruction and wrap-around support. Fourth, the staffing structure for TAWC was designed to support this new and very different model by using corporate titles (e.g., chief marketing officer, chief learning officer, etc.) and a mostly adjunct teaching pool. Fifth, a small advisory team comprised of influential board members met often with the president and TAWC's leadership team to monitor metrics and advise on strategy. Lastly, new policies, processes, and practices were developed to support the program's unique model and standardized format (e.g., curricular and course building protocols were instituted to ensure common, high quality learning experiences across all course sections, most of which are taught by adjuncts).

In order to create synergies among the programs focused on serving adult women, the Saturday One-Day program was organizationally joined with TAWC. Programs, course offerings, processes, and procedures were restructured as needed to ensure alignment between the two programs. As TAWC became established and current students learned about the online opportunities, on ground enrollments gradually shifted—so much so that the Eastern Massachusetts teaching site was closed in 2017.

At present, TAWC's distinctive programmatic elements provide options that are designed to accommodate the lives of busy adult women and support their educational achievement, including:

- Twenty plus degrees that can be completed entirely online—or through hybrid on campus Saturday classes at the Longmeadow or Central Massachusetts locations.

- Program options in highly marketable industries where women are in demand (e.g., cybersecurity, food science and safety, health sciences, nursing, etc.).

- An accelerated pace that enables quick degree completion—in 1-31/2 years depending upon transfer credits (e.g. courses run in six-week sessions).

- Six different sessions and start dates each year enabling students to jump in when they are ready and according to their schedule.

- The option to transfer in up to 90 credits toward the 120-credit bachelor's degree including credits earned years ago, thus eliminating the potential for repeating coursework and duplicating unnecessary credits.

- Low cost tuition and fee structure: TAWC programs are offered at a competitive flat tuition rate of $400 per credit with no added-on administrative fees, making the degree a great value. In addition, most of the learning resources are built right into the course in most cases, meaning that students do not pay extra for textbooks or other learning resources.

- Credit for prior learning earned through work, volunteer, or military service is also an option.

- Wrap around support systems provide each woman with her own personal educator coach, someone who stays in close contact and is available to guide students through their program.

- The award-winning SOUL (Social Online Universal Learning) system that uses adaptive learning pedagogy and cutting-edge learning analytics in tandem with personalized instruction and support enabling instructors and educator coaches to anticipate and response to each woman's unique academic needs quickly, increase- ing her overall likelihood of college success.

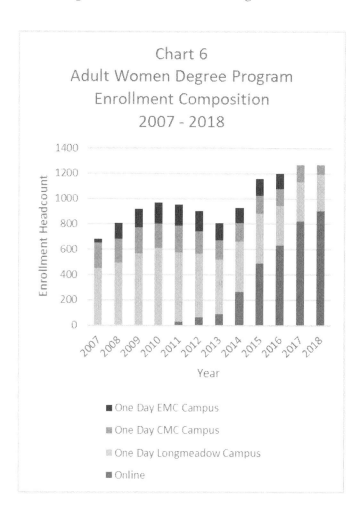

As shown in Chart 6, TAWC total headcount enrollment (including the One-Day campus enrollments) hit an all-time high of 1,270 in Fall 2017; since then, the headcount appears to be leveling off. While the introduction of TAWC has certainly served to stem the bleeding with the Saturday One-Day campus enrollments and provided a compelling and accessible option for women in the region and worldwide, the market competition grows ever fiercer by the day. Plans are currently underway to roll-out new program options in high demand fields, as well as to create partnerships and eco-systems, both of which are important strategies for future growth and diversification.

Lessons Learned

Bay Path University is one of the great success stories in American higher education. Its capacity to reinvent itself in response to the marketplace context while leveraging its mission in new and compelling ways has served the institution exceedingly well over the course of its 120+ year history. How did Bay Path achieve all of this? The answer can be found in the DNA of this unique institution. The crises that tested the very existence of the institution at various points in its trajectory forged an ethos of resilience, optimism and forward-looking momentum that are true of the Bay Path culture to this very day. Indeed, the Bay Path motto, "Carpe Diem" (or "Seize the Day") has been operationalized in deep and enduring ways.

Bay Path stands as a tribute to the power of great leadership–by trustees, administrators, faculty and staff, students, alumni, and long-serving presidents and senior staff. Especially in the most recent era, the institution has been well served by having senior leaders including the president, provost, CFO, and other senior leaders, including many academic deans. The momentum that Bay has experienced, especially in the past decade is undoubtedly due in part to the fact that the institution now runs like a well-oiled machine; senior leaders have a keen and deep understanding about the institutional context, its challenges and opportunities, and what it takes to leverage opportunities and find synergies in this particular milieu. This kind of understanding can take years to develop. With the increased pace of turnover among college presidents and provosts of late, the learning that is typically lost during transition as new leaders get up to speed can substantially slow down the entrepreneurial work and energy on any given campus.

A second important success factor to note is Bay Path's ability to at once honor and refresh its core mission and purpose. For example, while Bay Path has engaged in vigorous discussion over the years about remaining women-focused at the undergraduate level, the school's leaders recommitted on several occasions to the position that was staked out by Thomas Carr in the mid-1940s. Even as increasing numbers of women's colleges were going co-ed, Bay Path's Board and senior leadership opted to courageously follow a unique pathway and reinvent itself with the women's mission at the core. For example, when the undergraduate curriculum was last revised, a new one-of-a-kind signature program called WELL—Women as Empowered Learners and Leaders—was instituted and embedded within the core curriculum. Designed to operationalize the women's serving mission in concrete and impactful ways, WELL is a four-course series which includes co-curricular service learning and ensures that every undergraduate student's education is enhanced by a journey of self-discovery. In brief, WELL is structured to help students discern and articulate their goals in life and to give them the confidence, skills, and knowledge to achieve those goals successfully. As discussed earlier, the ability to fully leverage one's core purpose has been identified by some of the most influential thinkers of our time as an essential key ingredient for a high-performing organization. Bay Path's core purpose serves as a glue that has held the institution together and provided a sense of clarity, authenticity, and alignment as the institution has grown, expanded, and diversified.

Several other important lessons emerge from this case study, many of which echo principles considered throughout the book. Here are 10 take-a-ways that are important for academic leaders who want to grow and strengthen their institutions to keep in mind.

1. Program and revenue diversification are paramount

From its earliest days, Bay Path has executed a diversification strategy but always in alignment with the institution's mission and core educational purpose. From the shift from a co-ed business institute to a secretarial school for women, a junior college, a four-year college, and then a university, the institutional leaders have focused on identifying and exploiting opportunities to expand and strengthen program offerings in service to the mission. Whether co-ed or single gender, undergraduate or graduate, a common theme throughout the 120+ year history is the focus on delivering unique professional programs in a liberal arts context using state-of-the-art pedagogy and technology to prepare students for a constantly changing world. The importance of the diversification strategy in strengthening the institution's financial position in recent times is evident by the data shown in Chart 7.

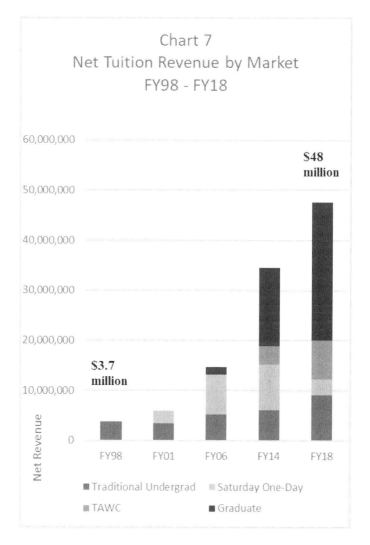

Without the expansion of the undergraduate program to create a niche with adult women or the expansion of the undergraduate program to educate women and men at the graduate level, Bay Path's story would undoubtedly have a very different ending.

2. Even when times are tough, do not stop investing for the future

Throughout Bay Path's history, we see example after example of bold, courageous, and forward-looking leadership. When the institution struggled and lost enrollment during the Great Depression, the school invested in new technologies; a school newspaper article from October 1929 described new inventive coursework in "stenotypy" —utilizing "the latest and best method of recording speech, a handsome little machine weighing about four pounds." Flash forward a few years to the purchase of a new campus in Longmeadow and the shift in mission and program focus. When President Leary arrived in the mid-1990s, she found a campus infrastructure in dire need of upgrading. Even while the budget was significantly challenged, the Board of Trustees invested in Bay Path and its new president, creating the conditions for success that have since played out in remarkable ways. In these current times, there is a tendency to turn to short-sighted strategies (such as cost-cutting, program elimination and staffing reductions) as the primary and immediate means for addressing financial challenges. While these strategies are sometimes warranted, they are never sufficient in and of themselves. Even in the direst of times, there are opportunities to be found for those who can above the trenches and consider the full range of assets available to any institution. Sometimes these assets are found in partnership with other institutions and organizations in your area. The point is to look outward and consider your resource base in the broadest terms possible.

3. Avoid the temptation to rest on success; in this current environment, it's almost always short-lived

There have been many places in Bay Path's history where the leaders were undoubtedly tempted to sit back and rest on their success. Yet, as discussed earlier in Chapter 4, it's precisely when things are going well that one needs to position the institution for what is still to come. This is perhaps one of the most difficult challenges of academic entrepreneurship. Continual reinvention is exhausting and can take a toll on any campus, its faculty, and staff. Had Bay Path passed on any of its many adaptations over the years, it would have quickly fallen behind. In a highly fluid context, continual adaptation and reinvention is the new normal. However, leaders must work very hard in such a context to communicate as transparently as possible, to connect the entrepreneurial strategy to the mission and viability of the institution, and to invest in hiring and supporting a workforce that can deliver what is needed.

4. Find that market gap that you are uniquely equipped to meet and leverage it to your maximum capacity

When President Carr reinvented the institution in the 1940s as women-focused, he had no idea how this mission would play out over the next 80 years. However, he saw a market gap and an opportunity that he believed his retooled school could meet, and he assembled the necessary resources to fulfill his vision. As the traditional undergraduate enrollment declined in the early 1990s, President Leary and her team anchored their bold strategy in a plan to fully leverage Bay Path's core competency in educating and supporting women—but with a unique twist and focus on adult women. Likewise, every graduate program has been developed in response to a compelling market gap that the institution believed it could meet, a strategy that has helped to ensure the success of nearly every program launched in the past several years. It takes considerable courage to carve out a distinctive pathway and stay the course, especially when the headwinds are blowing in the opposite direction. For Bay Path, the decision to moor its future with the women's serving mission at the core albeit with continual reinvention of how the mission was leveraged proved momentous on many levels.

5. Don't be afraid to copy others, but find a way to do it better

Marie Antoinette is believed to have once said, "There is nothing new except what has been forgotten." When it comes to generating ideas for new programs, this is certainly the case. Many of Bay Path's new graduate programs originated in ideas seen elsewhere. Through the feasibility study and the supporting market research, the end goal is to find a gap in the competitive context that the Bay Path program can uniquely deliver on, thus giving the program its reason for existence in what is often a crowded marketplace. Sometimes the gap and ensuing niche can be as simple as a different delivery method, unique calendar, or curricular emphasis. This is where the art side comes into play as finding that sweet spot for a new program often requires standing back and connecting the dots when considering competitor programs. Taking the time to do the market research and identify that niche is always worth it. Once the program is launched, it's important to keep your eye on that niche and refresh it as needed. Nearly every program you launch will exist in a fluid market context. As new programs enter that context or as market and industry factors shift, your niche can be easily impacted.

6. When balancing operating efficiencies and market responsiveness, always err on the side of market responsiveness

One of the ongoing tensions in any entrepreneurial organization is the need to achieve operating efficiencies and reduce complexity while operating in a flexible and highly adaptive manner. Not easy at all. This a tension that is certainly alive and well at Bay Path. Given the wide range of delivery models, calendars, pricing schemes, and curricular arrangements, there's always someone who believes the balance has tipped too far in one direction or the other. Yet, it is Bay Path's ability to respond "on a dime" to market opportunities by structuring programs in a flexible and adaptive way that provides the institution with an advantage that most of its competitors do not possess. Ironically, one needs to also be aware of the potential for new innovations to lose their flexibility once they are enveloped into the institution's structure. This leads to the next point.

7. Commit to the practice and discipline of academic entrepreneurship

The Bay Path entrepreneurial culture looks almost effortless from a distance. Still, the institution has worked hard over the years at new program ideation, creation, and execution. The institution's leaders are relentless in pursuing new opportunities and in monitoring and adjusting the strategy when the market does not respond as anticipated. With every new program roll-out, there is a discipline around ongoing program performance measurement with metrics that are closely watched. At most institutions, once a new program is launched it's off the radar and enveloped in the academic bureaucracy. At Bay Path, systems and triggers have been put in place to catch and intervene with underperforming programs before it's too late.

8. Don't be afraid to rewrite the rule book

With the establishment of The American Women's College (TAWC) and many of the new graduate programs, Bay Path created out-of-the box ways of working and educating students. In creating new academic initiatives, the institution typically starts by asking, "What will it take for this program or initiative to be successful?" For example, with TAWC, institutional leaders knew that the very different, state-of-the-art learning approach needed a different kind of operating environment to be successful; hence, the decision was made to unbundle TAWC from the academic bureaucracy and physically relocate it to a space that would facilitate creativity, collaboration, and innovative thinking. The TAWC model was built to scale; therefore, standardization and automation were critically important operating principles that needed to be embedded at a deep level. This resulted in a distinctly different set of priorities than what was in place for the traditional undergraduate and graduate programs.

9. Exploit synergies—they are everywhere

Much of Bay Path's success with new program invention originates in the institution's facility in leveraging synergies that are right in sight. For example, the first graduate programs and many thereafter were built on top of existing undergraduate programs, providing a built-in student pipeline from the outset. Many of the graduate programs were designed so that students can customize their programs with coursework and certificates from other areas, leading many to stay on and complete additional degrees. Plus, the multiple delivery models enable students to complete their degrees "their way," something that has given the institution an important competitive advantage. As noted earlier, every institution has unspent assets that can be leveraged to create new opportunities; rather than looking for that next big "shiny thing" try, shift your focus to what already exists and see what low hanging fruit you might be able to find.

10. Always maintain the long view

One of my favorite Kaizen management principles has to do with maintaining the long view in all things. Clearly, Bay Path's trajectory reinforces the importance of maintaining an outward looking perspective while disciplining yourself to always think two or three steps ahead of where you are at any moment. When Bay Path's Saturday One-Day program was at its high point, institutional leadership was already looking ahead to consider how the program might be strengthened as increasing numbers of competitors were going online. When the baccalaureate occupational therapy program enrollments fell in the early part of the 2000s due to external regulatory issues, the president and her team decided to stay the course and not eliminate the program, a strategy many other institutions were doing at the time. Maintaining the long view in this case meant that, as the regulatory issues worked themselves through, Bay Path's program was able to quickly adapt and accommodate the burgeoning student demand. Occupational therapy is now Bay Path's largest graduate program. Given the pace of change and experimentation within the higher education world these days, academic entrepreneurs must maintain that forward looking eye and be ready to adapt quickly—but in such a way that the changes leverage the institution's core mission and purpose, its strengths, and its potential.

FINAL THOUGHTS AND NEXT STEPS

I began this book by talking about the challenges facing higher education. Indeed, the challenges of this current era are more complex and difficult than perhaps at any previous time in the history of higher education in our country. History is always a wonderful leveler for angst about change and disruption. For example, I find it helpful to remind myself that the current structure and traditions of higher education as we have come to know them are not really all that old—many of them originated in the upheaval that took place following the Civil War, an era marked by profound disruption and transformation. At some point in the not-so-distant future, our successors will similarly look back to these current times as a marker for the systems and traditions they have inherited—and perhaps wonder, "What were they thinking?!"

In these challenging times, I am quite hopeful about the future of higher education. Over the course of my long tenure working in institutions that were not resource abundant, I have seen firsthand what the power of academic entrepreneurship—when fully leveraged—can accomplish. I personally believe that it's precisely when times are tough that the most creative and transformative strategies are likely to emerge. This starts with a willingness and discipline to honestly consider your institution's context—it's bona fide marketplace position and potential—and then to find the courage and foresight to carve out a path that your institution is uniquely equipped to travel.

In this current era, I believe that academic leaders—provosts, deans, department chairs, and program directors

—have the toughest job in the academy. Especially in the more traditional institutional setting, you are called on to mediate the divergent cultures on a daily basis and to translate back and forth while also moving forward an academic agenda that will contribute positively to your institution's bottom line. I am also keenly aware that our jobs and the expectations placed on us by others, our campus colleagues or those outside the institution, are not well understood. I was reminded of this on a recent flight where I was seated next to a first-year student traveling back to her campus following the winter break. Her question "What do you do?" led to a flight long conversation about what a provost does and why it is that she and her fellow students had little understanding about the role of the provost on her campus. Yet, when I explained how and in want ways her provost was ultimately responsible for just about every aspect of her experience, she was stunned. She also told me that she planned to make an appointment to meet her provost, which made me very happy.

As academic leaders, we play an immensely important role within our institutions in determining the future and impacting the overall financial condition. As you are the primary audience for this book, I hope you will find it to be a useful resource for honing your entrepreneurial mindset and toolbox. Throughout the course of my career, I have been inspired by many academic leader colleagues who have lived out the notion of academic entrepreneurship in quiet yet profoundly impactful ways on their campuses. Especially in my early days as provost, I was the beneficiary of much kindness and wisdom shared by these sage leaders who took the time to enlighten, encourage and inspire me.

So, I end with this. None of us work in isolation. Not on our campuses, nor in the academy more globally. We need each other today more than ever before. The challenges we face on our individual campuses can be overwhelming, and we need the perspective that comes in community with others. Long gone are the days where our campuses existed in silos. The notion of an ecosystem is the new metaphor that will shape how our institutions operate going forward. I encourage you to consider your role as an ecosystem builder and mentor. Be proactive in reaching out to the other academic leaders in your region and in considering what you might learn from each other, how you might work together, and how you can be an encourager to each other. Academic leaders today need to think and act differently than our predecessors did just a few years ago; this starts with an understanding of your role and work in the context of the broader academic community. Seek out diverse experiences to build your capacity for academic entrepreneurship. It is only through the practice of the skills and principles outlined in this book that one gains competence and confidence. Commit to your own professional development and find organizations that will nurture your entrepreneurial drive and skill set. Consider how you might begin now to share your wisdom and experience with others.

Thank you for taking the time to read this book. There are many wonderful resources out there that can help you strengthen your capacity for academic entrepreneurship; many of these are noted in the resource pages following Sections I, II, and III. Let me conclude with two in-depth training resources that are especially noteworthy.

Make sure to check out the conferences, webcasts, workshops, and articles on all things academic at Academic Impressions: www.academicimpressions.com.

Bay Path University has recently launched a new doctoral program in higher education leadership and organizational studies which features a core set of courses designed to develop students' capacity for entrepreneurial thinking and innovative practice in the higher ed context. For those who already have the doctorate, be aware that the five-part core course series can be taken as a stand-alone program:

www.baypath.edu/academics/graduate-programs/higher-education-leadership-organizational-studies-doctorate-edd/

ACADEMIC ENTREPRENEURSHIP

ACKNOWLEDGMENTS

One of the unexpected surprises of writing this book is the important reminder of how much I have learned and been inspired by so many people over the course of my life. Indeed, without their influences—big and small—my professional trajectory would look very different.

So much of the content of this book and my thinking about academic entrepreneurship has been shaped by the senior leaders with whom I have been privileged to work. In David Horner, who currently serves as president at The American College of Greece, I was first exposed to academic entrepreneurship as a management approach. The transformation of North Park College to North Park University during the 1990s and early 2000s is due in no small measure to his ability to adeptly leverage both the art and science of institutional management. From Carol Leary with whom I have served for nearly 15 years at Bay Path, I have learned much about the power of always looking forward, having the courage to ask the hard questions, and staying steadfast to the vision within.

The Bay Path story and my role in it would not be possible without the talented team of executive staff, deans and directors with whom I have been privileged to work on a daily basis. Representing a wide range of backgrounds, personalities and experiences, these individuals inspire me and challenge me to learn and grow. We have navigated challenges and successes together and I am immensely grateful for the role that each one has played in my professional life.

Finally, my accomplishments are made possible only through the unwavering support and belief of my family.

My parents, Joe and Helen Morriss, did not have the benefit of higher education. But they sacrificed to ensure that my brothers and I would have a college education. From my earliest days they instilled within each of us a belief in the power of education to transform one's life. For their confidence in my potential, I will be forever grateful.

And to my husband Glenn and my daughters, Madeleine and Grace, you have—individually and collectively—truly been the wind beneath my wings. You have supported my professional pursuits—even when it has taken me away from you—and you have believed in and encouraged me. For your presence in my life, I am truly blessed and grateful.

ABOUT THE AUTHOR

MELISSA MORRISS-OLSON, Ph.D, currently serves as provost and founding director of the doctoral program in higher education leadership and organizational studies (HELOS) at Bay Path University, a 3,500 student women-focused institution located in Longmeadow, Massachusetts. As provost, she serves as the institution's chief academic officer, overseeing all academic departments and programs, serving as chief assessment officer and providing leadership for Hatch Learning Commons, undergraduate and graduate admissions, enrollment marketing and analytics, student life, and the campus wide diversity and inclusion initiative.

Throughout her career, Dr. Morriss-Olson has gained a reputation as a creative academic entrepreneur. As Bay Path University Provost, she has led the re-engineering of the learning community including the development of the *Thumbprint*—Bay Path's distinguishing educational aspirations—as well as the *Women Empowered as Learners and Leaders (WELL)* program. Under her leadership, a new academic structure consisting of schools and colleges was established and faculty resources were diversified and strengthened. Dr. Morriss-Olson has led the development and launch of more than thirty new graduate degree and certification programs, resulting in significant gains in both student headcount enrollment and revenue (under her leadership, graduate enrollment headcount has increased by nearly 1,700 and net incremental tuition revenue has exceeded $300 million).

Dr. Morriss-Olson worked previously at North Park University in Chicago where, as Vice President of Enrollment Management she overhauled the enrollment management program, resulting in a 300% increase in total enrollment. Under her leadership as Senior Vice President for University Relations, the University successfully completed its first-ever comprehensive capital campaign, raising $40 million in capital and endowment funds and increasing annual gift income from $5 million to $9 million. Dr. Morriss-Olson also founded and directed North Park's nationally recognized Axelson Center for Nonprofit Management, one of the first academic centers of its kind in the country and held the first Axelson endowed professorship in nonprofit management.

A first-generation college student, Dr. Morriss-Olson obtained the PhD in Educational Leadership and Policy Studies from Loyola University of Chicago. Her doctoral dissertation, which focused on successful small college management, received the prestigious faculty designation "completed with distinction."

Dr. Morriss-Olson is a nationally recognized higher education thought leader, speaking and writing often on topics such as higher education innovation, disruption and leadership. Her blog, *The Accidental Provost*, can be found at accidentalprovost.com, or you can follow her on Twitter @BayPathProvost.

ACADEMIC ENTREPRENEURSHIP

ENDNOTES

[1] Lederman, Doug. "Clay Christensen, Doubling Down." *Inside Higher Ed.* 28 April 2017. www.insidehighered.com/digital-learning/article/2017/04/28/clay-christensen-sticks-predictions-massive-college-closures.

[2] "Digital Transformation: An executive look at the challenges and opportunities for the newspaper industry." MECLABS Institute. meclabs.com/research/discovery/newspaper-transformation-business-leader-flint-mcglaughlin

[3] See WICHE, *Knocking at the College Door*, https://www.wiche.edu/pub/knocking-9th.

[4] Blumenstyk, Goldie. "Meet the New Mega-University." *The Chronicle of Higher Education.* 11 November 2018. www.chronicle.com/article/Meet-the-New-Mega-University/245049

[5] Lederman, Doug. "Leading in Turbulent Times: A Survey of Presidents." *Inside Higher Ed.* 9 March 2018. www.insidehighered.com/news/survey/survey-college-presidents-finds-worry-about-public-attitudes-confidence-finances

[6] Busta, Hallie. "How many colleges and universities have closed since 2016." *Education Dive.* Industry Dive. 29 March 2019. www.educationdive.com/news/how-many-colleges-and-universities-have-closed-since-2016/539379/

[7] Schroeder, Dan. "Why the Cost of College Has Tripled." *Dan's Diary.* Blogspot. 30 August 2015. dvschroeder.blogspot.com/2015/08/why-cost-of-college-has-tripled.html

[8] Pettit, Emma. "A Fifth of Private Colleges Report First-Year Discount Rate of 60 Percent, Moody's Says." *The Chronicle of Higher Education*. 14 November 2018. www.chronicle.com/article/A-Fifth-of-Private-Colleges/245092

[9] "10 Universities with the Biggest Endowments." *U.S. News and World Report*. Edited by Farran Powell. 16 October 2018. www.usnews.com/education/best-colleges/the-short-list-college/articles/10-universities-with-the-biggest-endowments

[10] "Strength in Numbers: Strategies for collaborating in a new era for higher education." *Parthenon-EY Education* Practice. Ernst & Young, LLP. cdn.ey.com/parthenon/pdf/perspectives/P-EY_Strength-in-Numbers-Collaboration-Strategies_Paper_Final_082016.pdf

[11] Prensky, Marc. "Digital Natives, Digital Immigrants." *On the Horizon*. MCB University Press, Vol. 9 No. 5. October 2001. www.marcprensky.com/writing/Prensky%20-%20Digital%20Natives,%20Digital%20Immigrants%20-%20Part1.pdf

[12] *College Scorecard*. U.S. Department of Education. collegescorecard.ed.gov/

[13] "Unveiling SNHU's 2018-2023 Strategic Plan." *President's Corner: A President's Reflections*. Southern New Hampshire University. 16 October 2018. blogging.snhu.edu/leblanc/2018/10/unveiling-snhus-2018-2023-strategic-plan/

[14] *The State of American Jobs*. Pew Research Center. 6 October 2016. www.pewsocialtrends.org/2016/10/06/the-state-of-american-jobs/

[15] Tapscott, Don, and Alex Tapscott. "The Blockchain Revolution and Higher Education." *EDUCAUSE Review*. EDUCAUSE. 31 March 2017.

er.educause.edu/articles/2017/3/the-blockchain-revolution-and-higher-education

[16] Hill, Phil. "Online Educational Delivery Models: A Descriptive View." *EDUCAUSE Review*. EDUCAUSE. 1 November 2012. er.educause.edu/articles/2012/11/online-educational-delivery-models--a-descriptive-view

[17] Biemiller, Lawrence. "Small Colleges Find New Revenue Streams Close to Home." *The Chronicle of Higher Education*. 8 January 2017. www.chronicle.com/article/Small-Colleges-Find-New/238830

[18] Neumeier, Marty. "The Onlyness Test." *Marty Neumeier website*. www.martyneumeier.com/the-onlyness-test/

[19] *Needed: A New Style of Leader for the New Era*. AGB. agb.org/trusteeship-article/needed-a-new-style-of-leader-for-the-new-era

[20] *Charts and Data*. The Council of Independent Colleges. www.cic.edu/resources-research/charts-data?search=&CDCategory=Reports

[21] *Leadership Traits and Success in Higher Education: A Witt/Kieffer Study*. Contributors: Witt/Kieffer and Hogan. American Association of State Colleges and Universities. 2013. www.aascu.org/corporatepartnership/WittKieffer/Leadership.pdf

[22] Connolly, Matt. "America's Ten Most Innovative College Presidents." *Washington Monthly*. Sept/Oct 2015. washingtonmonthly.com/magazine/septoct-2015/americas-ten-most-innovative-college-presidents/

[23] Kim, K.H. *Persistence: The Key to Creativity and Innovation*. Idea to Value. 26 May 2017.

www.ideatovalue.com/crea/khkim/2017/05/persistence-key-creativity-innovation/

[24] Parry, Marc. "Helping Colleges Move Beyond the Credit Hour." *The Chronicle of Higher Education*. 29 April 2013. www.chronicle.com/article/Helping-Colleges-Move-Beyond/138805

[25] Brown, Paul B. "Entrepreneurs Are 'Calculated' Risk Takers -- The Word That Can Be The Difference Between Failure And Success." *Forbes*. 6 November 2013. www.forbes.com/sites/actiontrumpseverything/2013/11/06/entrepreneurs-are-not-risk-takers-they-are-calculated-risk-takers-that-one-additional-word-can-be-the-difference-between-failure-and-success/#743b3cd03e14

[26] Castleman, Benjamin L., and Lindsay C. Page. *Summer Melt: Supporting Low-Income Students through the Transition to College*. Harvard Education Press. 2014.

[27] Selingo, Jeffrey J. "Networked U's: This Is What Will Save Higher Ed." *The Chronicle of Higher Education*. 8 November 2017. www.chronicle.com/article/Networked-U-s-This-Is-What/241724

[28] Furr, Nathan, et al. "If Your Innovation Effort Isn't Working, Look at Who's on the Team." *Harvard Business Review*. 9 November 2018. hbr.org/2018/11/if-your-innovation-effort-isnt-working-look-at-whos-on-the-team

[29] Butler, Timothy. "Hiring an Entrepreneurial Leader." *Harvard Business Review*. March/April 2017. hbr.org/2017/03/hiring-an-entrepreneurial-leader

[30] "Kaospilot." InnoveEdu. Creative Commons. innoveedu.org/en/kaospilot

[31] Edelman, Gilad. "The Sixteen Most Innovative People in

Higher Education." *Washington Monthly*. September/October 2016. washingtonmonthly.com/magazine/septemberoctober-2016/the-sixteen-most-innovative-people-in-higher-education/

[32] dos Santos, Ricardo. "Effectuation – The Best Theory Of Entrepreneurship You Actually Follow, Whether You've Heard Of It Or Not." *Necrophone*. 20 January 2014. necrophone.com/2014/01/20/effectuation-the-best-theory-of-entrepreneurship-you-actually-follow-whether-youve-heard-of-it-or-not/

[33] Adapted from "Quiz: How Entrepreneurial Are You?" *Every Woman*. www.everywoman.com/my-development/learning-areas/articles/quiz-how-entrepreneurial-are-you

[34] Unglesbee, Ben. "Higher ed consolidation could pick up in 2019, Fitch says." *Education Dive*. Industry Dive. 7 December 2018. www.educationdive.com/news/higher-ed-consolidation-could-pick-up-in-2019-fitch-says/543798/

[35] Couros, George. "The Principal of Change." *The Innovator's Mindset*. George Couros Blog. 2015. georgecouros.ca/blog/the-innovators-mindset-book

[36] Drucker, Peter F. "The Discipline of Innovation." *Harvard Business Review*. August 2002. hbr.org/2002/08/the-discipline-of-innovation

[37] Allen, Meredith. "Can You Learn Creativity? The Answer Might Surprise You." *General Assembly Blog*. General Assembly. generalassemb.ly/blog/can-you-learn-creativity/

[38] *Center for Innovation in the Liberal Arts*. St. Olaf College. wp.stolaf.edu/cila/

[39] Johnson, Steven. *Where Good Ideas Come From: The Natural History of Innovation*. Riverhead Books. Reprint edition: 2011.

www.amazon.com/Where-Good-Ideas-Come-Innovation/dp/1594485380

[40] *The American Women's College.* Bay Path University. www.baypath.edu/academics/undergraduate-programs/the-american-womens-college-online/

[41] *Center for Innovation & Impact.* Oberlin College & Conservatory. 2019. www.oberlin.edu/innovation-and-impact

[42] Lindegaard, Stefan. "Why Networking is Important for Innovation." *LinkedIn*. LinkedIn Corporation. 30 October 2014. www.linkedin.com/pulse/20141031042003-46249-why-networking-is-important-for-innovation

[43] Seltzer, Rick. "Farewell to Departments." *Inside Higher Education.* 21 June 2016. www.insidehighered.com/news/2016/06/21/plymouth-state-announces-layoffs-restructuring-around-interdisciplinary-clusters

[44] Ashton, Kevin. *How to Fly a Horse: The Secret History of Creation, Invention, and Discovery.* Anchor. Reprint edition: 2015. www.amazon.com/How-Fly-Horse-Invention-Discovery/dp/0804170061

[45] Khan Academy. www.khanacademy.org

[46] Deschamps, Jean-Philippe. "The Eight Attributes of Bottom-Up Innovation Leaders." *Innovation Management.* 28 February 2017. www.innovationmanagement.se/2017/02/28/the-eight-attributes-of-bottom-up-innovation-leaders/

[47] DesMarais, Christina. "25 Ways to Be More Creative." *Inc.* 5 September 2013. www.inc.com/christina-desmarais/25-ways-to-be-more-creative.html

[48] Rock, David. "A Hunger for Certainty." *Psychology Today*. 25 October 2009. www.psychologytoday.com/us/blog/your-brain-work/200910/hunger-certainty

[49] Mishra, Shanu, and M.B. Mishra. "Tobacco: Its historical, cultural, oral, and periodontal health association." *Journal of International Society of Preventative & Community Denistry*. U.S. National Library of Medicine. January-June 2013. doi: 10.4103/2231-0762.115708
www.ncbi.nlm.nih.gov/pmc/articles/PMC3894096/

[50] "Motor vehicle fatality rate in U.S. by year." *Wikipedia*. Updated: 5 May 2019.
en.wikipedia.org/wiki/Motor_vehicle_fatality_rate_in_U.S._by_year

[51] Porter, Jane. "How to Cultivate a Creative Thinking Habit." *Fast Company*. Mansueto Ventures, LLC. 25 February 2014. www.fastcompany.com/3026816/how-to-cultivate-a-creative-thinking-habit

[52] Michalko, Michael. "Thomas Edison's Creative Thinking Habits. *LinkedIn*. LinkedIn Corporation. 7 November 2015. www.linkedin.com/pulse/thomas-edisons-creative-thinking-habits-michael-michalko

[53] Grazer, Brian, and Charles Fishman. *A Curious Mind: The Secret to a Bigger Life*. Simon & Schuster Paperbacks, 2016.

[54] Wolf, G., et al. "Steve Jobs: The Next Insanely Great Thing." *WIRED*. 2018. www.wired.com/1996/02/jobs-2/ Accessed 7 December 2018.

[55] "Albert Einstein and bicycles." *Cycling is Good for You*. Blogger. 2018. cyclingisgoodforyou.blogspot.com/2009/05/albert-einstein-and-bicycles.html. Accessed 7 December 2018.

[56] Steinberg, Hannah, et al. (2018). "Exercise enhances creativity

independently of mood." *PubMed Central (PMC)*. Provided by BMJ Publishing Group. U.S. National Library of Medicine. September 1997. www.ncbi.nlm.nih.gov/pmc/articles/PMC1332529/ Accessed 7 December 2018.

[57] "The Neuroscience of Imagination." *Psychology Today*. 2018. www.psychologytoday.com/us/blog/the-athletes-way/201202/the-neuroscience-imagination. Accessed 7 December 2018.

[58] "Text of J.K. Rowling's speech." *Harvard Gazette*. 2018. news.harvard.edu/gazette/story/2008/06/text-of-j-k-rowling-speech/ Accessed 7 December 2018.

[59] Gilbert, Elizabeth. *Big Magic, Creative Living Beyond Fear.* Riverhead Books. 2016.

[60] Rousmaniere, Dana. "No One Is Too Busy to Be Creative." *Harvard Business Review*. 2 December 2015. hbr.org/2015/12/no-one-is-too-busy-to-be-creative

[61] *deBono Thinking Systems*. www.debonothinkingsystems.com/about/Edward.htm

[62] Linke, Rebecca. "Design thinking, explained." *MIT Sloan School of Management*. Massachusetts Institute of Technology. 14 September 2017. mitsloan.mit.edu/ideas-made-to-matter/design-thinking-explained

[63] "Shunryu Suzuki." *Zen-Buddhism.Net*. www.zen-buddhism.net/famous-zen-masters/shunryu-suzuki.html

[64] Wolf, Gary. "Steve Jobs: The Next Insanely Great Thing." *WIRED*. 1 February 1996. www.wired.com/1996/02/jobs-2/

[65] Science Writer. "Why Traveling Abroad Makes Us More Creative." *Big Think*. 18 May 2012. bigthink.com/insights-of-genius/why-traveling-abroad-makes-us-more-creative

[66] Davidson, Cathy. "Mix it Up! How Equity Can Enhance Innovation--and How #FuturesEd Works Toward Those Goals." *HASTAC*. 14 January 2015. www.hastac.org/blogs/cathy-davidson/2015/01/14/mix-it-how-equity-can-enhance-innovation-and-how-futuresed-works

[67] Pierce, Susan Resneck. "Producing Academic Leaders." *Inside Higher Ed*. 26 January 2011. www.insidehighered.com/advice/2011/01/26/producing-academic-leaders

[68] Bacow, Lawrence S. and William G. Bowen. "Double Trouble." *ITHAKA S+R*. 21 September 2015. sr.ithaka.org/publications/double-trouble/ DOI: https://doi.org/10.18665/sr.273603

[69] Flaherty, Colleen. "Years of Work, Tabled." *Inside Higher Ed*. 26 April 2017. www.insidehighered.com/news/2017/04/26/duke-undergraduate-curricular-reform-vote-tabled-indefinitely-after-years-work

[70] *Standards for Accreditation*. New England Commission of Higher Education. 1 July 2016. cihe.neasc.org/standards-policies/standards-accreditation/standards-effective-july-1-2016

[71] Horn, Michael. "Accreditation's Insidious Impact on Higher Education Innovation." *Forbes*. 10 July 2018. www.forbes.com/sites/michaelhorn/2018/07/10/accreditations-insidious-impact-on-higher-education-innovation/#4c55f4a0147a

[72] Simplicio, Joseph. "The University Culture," 2012.

[73] Svrluga, Susan. "Alumnae vowed to save Sweet Briar from closing last year. And they did." *The Washington Post*. 3 March 2016. www.washingtonpost.com/news/grade-point/wp/2016/03/03/alumnae-vowed-to-save-sweet-briar-

from-closing-last-year-and-they-did/?noredirect=on&utm_term=.181ebad55334

[74] *Peter Russian*. Management Innovation eXchange. https://www.managementexchange.com/users/peter-russian

[75] Flaherty, Colleen. "The New, New Education." *Inside Higher Ed*. 24 August 2017. www.insidehighered.com/news/2017/08/24/cathy-davidson%E2%80%99s-new-book-manifesto-teaching-students-and-institutions-how-survive

[76] Baumgartner, Jeffrey. "Why Diversity is the Mother of Creativity." InnovationManagement.24 November 2010. www.innovationmanagement.se/imtool-articles/why-diversity-is-the-mother-of-creativity/

[77] Garcia Mathewson, Tara. "Council of Independent Colleges panel lists tenure as 'negotiatble.'" *Education Dive*. Industry Dive. 7 January 2016. www.educationdive.com/news/council-of-independent-colleges-panel-lists-tenure-as-negotiable/411695/

[78] Busta, Hallie. "How many colleges and universities have closed since 2016." *Education Dive*. Industry Dive. 29 March 2019. www.educationdive.com/news/how-many-colleges-and-universities-have-closed-since-2016/539379/

[79] *Stephen Remedios*.Management Innovation Exchange. https://www.managementexchange.com/users/stephen-remedios

[80] Puccio, G.J., et al. *Creative Leadership: Skills That Drive Change*. 2nd edition. Sage. 2011.

[81] *Unlocking Talent and Opportunity: 2018-2023 SNHU Strategic Plan*. Southern New Hampshire University. snhu-externalaffairs.app.box.com/s/7k526w442reszti50fdtceyrre2f1il8

[82] "President's Innovation Network." Westminster College. www.westminstercollege.edu/about/office-of-the-president/president's-innovation-network

[83] "Work + Learn Futures Lab." Institute for the Future. www.iftf.org/learningfutures/

[84] "Center for Innovation & Impact." Oberlin College & Conservatory. www.oberlin.edu/innovation-and-impact

[85] Thomas, Sarah, and Ben Jonash. "In Pursuit of Innovation: A CEO Checklist." *Deloitte*. Deloitte Touche Tohmatsu Limited. 2019. www2.deloitte.com/us/en/pages/life-sciences-and-health-care/articles/center-for-health-solutions-ceo-checklist.html?id=us:el:rs:chsblog:awa:chs:020315deloittehealth

[86] Adapted from: Glor, Eleanor. "An Innovative Manager's Checklist." *The Innovation Journal: The Public Sector Innovation Journal*. Vol. 6 No. 2. Article 3. 2001. www.innovation.cc/discussion-papers/2001_6_2_3_glor_innovate-mgmt-checklist.htm

[87] "Reimagine Education Awards 2018/19: Winners." *Reimagine Education*. Wharton University of Pennsylvania. 2019. www.reimagine-education.com/reimagine-education-award-winners-2019/

[88] Morse, Robert, et al. "Most Innovative Schools Methodology." *U.S. News & World Report*. 9 September 2018. www.usnews.com/education/best-colleges/articles/most-innovative-schools-methodology

[89] "History and use of brainstorming." *Brainstorming.Co.Uk*. Infinite Innovations, Ltd. www.brainstorming.co.uk/tutorials/historyofbrainstorming.html

90 Wolfe, Alexandria. "Brian Grazer's Curious Connections." *The Wall Street Journal*. 10 April 2015. www.wsj.com/articles/brian-grazers-curious-connections-1428682859

91 *The Student Clearing House*. studentclearinghouse.org/

92 *Ansoff Matrix*. www.ansoffmatrix.com/

93 Collins, Jim, and Morten T. Hansen. "Great by Choice." *Jim Collins*. October 2011. www.jimcollins.com/books/great-by-choice.html

94 "Social Online Universal Learning (SOUL)." *Bay Bath University*. The Women's College at Bay Path University. www.baypath.edu/academics/undergraduate-programs/the-american-womens-college-online/student-services/online-tools-resources-soul/

95 A "professor of practice" is an appointment that is made on an annual or multi-year contractual basis, does not carry tenure and is typically focused primarily on teaching with exemption from the other faculty duties such as committee service and research.

96 "Definitions of Marketing." *American Marketing Association*. October 2004. www.ama.org/AboutAMA/Pages/Definition-of-Marketing.aspx

97 Students are pegged as stealth applicants if the first recorded time that they reached out to a school is when they apply.

98 Brinker, Scott. *5 Disruptions Reshaping Marketing as We Know It*. Marketing Tech Media, LLC. 2017. cdn.chiefmartec.com/wp-content/uploads/2017/03/martech_5_disruptions_ebook.pdf

99 See Drucker, Peter F. *The Essential Drucker*. HarperBusiness. Reissue edition. 2008.

[100] See Lynn, Michael. "Segmenting and Targeting Your Market: Strategies and Limitations." *School of Hotel Administration*. Cornell University. scholarship.sha.cornell.edu/articles/243

[101] Primary source data includes information obtained directly from a source, such as a survey conducted with prospective students or employers. Secondary source data consists of information that has been gathered and sometimes interpreted by other researchers or organizations and recorded in books, reports, or online.

[102] "Marketing Theories – The Marketing Mix – From 4 PS to 7 PS." *Professional Academy*. www.professionalacademy.com/blogs-and-advice/marketing-theories---the-marketing-mix---from-4-p-s-to-7-p-s

[103] Fusch, Daniel. "Recruiting and Admitting Adult Students." *Academic Impressions*. 1 October 2011. www.academicimpressions.com/blog/recruiting-and-admitting-adult-students/

[104] "SWOT Analyses – Definition, Advantages and Limitations." *MSG Presentations*. Management Study Guide. www.managementstudyguide.com/swot-analysis.htm

[105] Created by Christine Mauro, Director of Enrollment Marketing, Bay Path University.

[106] "Choose your learning track." HubSpot. 2019. www.hubspot.com/acp/learning-tracks

[107] Chen, Jenn. "15 Facebook stats every marketer should know for 2019." *Sprout Social*. Sprout Social Inc. 2019. sproutsocial.com/insights/facebook-stats-for-marketers/

[108] "Branding Principles." *TheSumOf*. 2019. thesumof.com.au/branding-principles/

[109] Bryant, Julie. "What influences nontraditional student enrollment." *Education Insights Blog*. RNL. 29 August 2012. blogem.ruffalonl.com/influences-nontraditional-student-enrollment/

[110] Black, Jim. "The Branding of Higher Education." *SEMWorks*. January 2008. www.semworks.net/white-papers-books/the-branding-of-higher-education.php

[111] "Strategic positioning in higher education." The Free Library. 2014. www.thefreelibrary.com/Strategic+positioning+in+higher+education.-a0208747719. Accessed 1 February 2019.

[112] "How to Write a Brand Positioning Statement." *Brandwatch*. 29 September 2016. www.brandwatch.com/blog/write-brand-positioning-statement/

[113] Black, Jim. "The Branding of Higher Education." *SEMWorks*. January 2008. www.semworks.net/white-papers-books/the-branding-of-higher-education.php

[114] "Best Practices in Higher Education Marketing Strategy." *Hanover Research*. 15 November 2018. www.hanoverresearch.com/reports-and-briefs/higher-education-marketing-strategy/

[115] "Marketers Will Focus on Mobile More Than Ever Before in 2014." *Oncampus Advertising*. 10 July 2014. oncampusadvertising.com/marketers-will-focus-on-mobile-more-than-ever-before-in-2014/

[116] "Social Media for Higher Education." ExactTarget. www.exacttarget.com/sites/exacttarget/files/social-media-for-higher-education.pdf

[117] Engel, Craig. "Ten enrollment roadblocks for graduate and professional programs: Part one." *Education Insights Blog*. RNL. 25

October 2011. blogem.ruffalonl.com/ten-enrollment-roadblocks-graduate-professional-programs-part/

[118] "Preferred Recruitment Strategies of U.S. Graduate Schools." http://monitor.icef.com/2012/08/preferred-recruitment-strategies-of-us-graduate-schools/

[119] Hootsuite's main site is hootsuite.com.

[120] Marr, Bernard. "The 10 best cities to find a big data job." *Data Science Central*. 6 August 2015. www.datasciencecentral.com/profiles/blogs/the-10-best-cities-to-find-a-big-data-job

[121] "Online Master's Degree in Data Science." Merrimack College. onlinedsa.merrimack.edu/lp-data-science-2/?utm_medium=SEM&utm_source=Google&utm_campaign=Branded-Exact&utm_content=LPB

[122] "Masters in Analytics." *McCallum Graduate School of Business*. Bentley University. admissions.bentley.edu/graduate/masters-in-analytics

[123] "Masters of Science in Computer Information Systems concentration in Data Analytics." Boston University. www.bu.edu/met/programs/graduate/computer-information-systems/data-analytics/

[124] "MS in Data Science." *Khoury College of Computer Science*. Northeastern University. www.ccis.northeastern.edu/program/data-science-ms/

[125] "Data Science Certificate." *Harvard Extension School*. Harvard University. www.extension.harvard.edu/academics/professional-graduate-certificates/data-science-certificate

[126] "Master of Science in Data Science." *John A. Paulson School of Engineering and Applied Sciences*. Harvard.

www.seas.harvard.edu/programs/graduate/applied-computation/master-of-science-in-data-science

[127] Burtch, Linda. "Students Flocking to Analytics & Data Science – A Good Thing?" *Burtch Works*. 30 November 2015. www.burtchworks.com/2015/11/30/students-flocking-to-analytics-data-science-a-good-thing/

[128] "Boston Apache Spark User Group." *Meetup*. www.meetup.com/Boston-Apache-Spark-User-Group/

[129] "Boston Machine Learning." *Meetup*. www.meetup.com/bostonml/

[130] "New England Artificial Intelligence." *Meetup*. www.meetup.com/intelligence/

[131] "Cognitive Computing Boston." *Meetup*. www.meetup.com/Cognitive-Computing/

[132] "Bio-Entrepreneurs Forum." *Meetup*. www.meetup.com/Bio-Entrepreneurs-Forum/

[133] "Big Data Developers in Boston." *Meetup*. www.meetup.com/Big-Data-Developers-in-Boston/

[134] "Boston Data-Mining." *Meetup*. www.meetup.com/Boston-Data-Mining/

[135] "The Data Scientist." *Meetup*. www.meetup.com/The-Data-Scientist/

[136] "Boston Predictive Analytics." *Meetup*. www.meetup.com/Boston-Predictive-Analytics/

[137] "Western Mass Statistics and Data Science." *Meetup*. www.meetup.com/Pioneer-Valley-and-Five-College-R-Statistical-Meetup/

[138] "Strata Data Conference." O'Reilly Media, Inc. 2019. conferences.oreilly.com/strata/strata-ca

[139] "IEEE Conferences." IEEE. www.ieee.org/conferences_events/index.html

[140] "KDD Conferences." *KDD*. Association for Computing Machinery. 2018. www.kdd.org/conferences

[141] "Joint Statistical Meetings." American Statistical Association. www.amstat.org/ASA/Meetings/Joint-Statistical-Meetings.aspx

[142] PAPIs. www.papis.io/

[143] "Meetings / Conferences on AI, Analytics, Big Data, Data Mining, Data Science, & Machine Learning." KDnuggets. 2019. www.kdnuggets.com/meetings/

[144] "Calendar." *Innovation Enterprise Summits*. The Innovation Enterprise, Ltd. theinnovationenterprise.com/summits/calendar/

[145] "Boston Data Festival 2016." ODSC. 2016. bostondatafest.com/

[146] http://h41382.www4.hpe.com/hpe_bdc/

[147] "Sports Analytics Conference." *MIT Sloan*. ESPN. 1-2 March 2019. www.sloansportsconference.com/

[148] "ODSC East: Boston 2019." Open Data Science Conference. www.odsc.com/boston

[149] McCann, Adam. "Best & Worst Metro Areas for STEM Professionals." *Wallet Hub*. 8 January 2019. wallethub.com/edu/best-worst-metro-areas-for-stem-professionals/9200/

[150] "Innovation that Matters 2016." 1776. www.1776.vc/reports/innovation-that-matters-2016/

[151] "The State of Data Science." *Stitch*. Stitch, Inc. 2019. www.stitchdata.com/resources/reports/the-state-of-data-science

[152] "Massachusetts." *Research! America*. 2019. www.researchamerica.org/advocacy-action/research/research-funding-and-economic-impact-funding-states/massachusetts

[153] "NewHaven.IO." *Meetup*. www.meetup.com/newhavenio/

[154] "Connecticut R Users Group." *Meetup*. www.meetup.com/Conneticut-R-Users-Group/

[155] "Connecticut Big Data." *Meetup*. www.meetup.com/Connecticut-Big-Data/

[156] "CT Predictive Analytics." *Meetup*. www.meetup.com/CT-Predictive-Analytics/

[157] "Data Science in Stamford." *Meetup*. www.meetup.com/Data-Science-in-Stamford/

[158] "Hartford Artificial Intelligence & Deep Learning." *Meetup*. www.meetup.com/Hartford-Artificial-Intelligence-Deep-Learning/

[159] "Hartford Tech Meetup." *Meetup*. www.meetup.com/Hartford-Tech-Meetup/

[160] "New Haven Data Science Meetup." *Meetup*. www.meetup.com/New-Haven-Data-Science-Meetup/

[161] "Strata Data Conference." O'Reilly Media, Inc. 2019. conferences.oreilly.com/strata/strata-ca

[162] "Predictive Analytics World." Prediction Impact, Inc. & Rising Media, Inc. 2019. www.predictiveanalyticsworld.com/

[163] "IEEE Conferences." IEEE. www.ieee.org/conferences_events/index.html

[164] "KDD Conferences." *KDD*. Association for Computing Machinery. 2018. www.kdd.org/conferences

[165] "Hartford Regional Tech Summit." hartfordsummit.org/

[166] The Connecticut Technology Council. ct.org

[167] "Events Calendar." University of Connecticut. calendar.uconn.edu//

[168] "Conferences and Events." *Center for Customer Insights. School of Management.* Yale. som.yale.edu/faculty-research/centers-initiatives/center-for-customer-insights/center-events

[169] "Yale Day of Data." Yale. elischolar.library.yale.edu/dayofdata/

[170] Yale. https://www.city.yale.edu/

[171] "Main Menu." *Office of Corporate Research.* Yale. ocr.yale.edu/

[172] "Main Menu." *Office of Corporate Research.* Yale. ocr.yale.edu/ "Grow." *Office of Corporate Research.* Yale. ocr.yale.edu/grow

[173] The Connecticut Technology Council. ct.org

[174] "Resources." *Innovation Destination: Hartford.* 2019. resources.innovationhartford.com/Startups

[175] As of 2013, there were 85 recognized institutional and programmatic accrediting organizations operating in the United States according to the *CHEA Almanac of External Quality Review.*

[176] "Overview of U.S. Accreditation." *Council for higher Education Accreditation*. CHEA International Quality Group. www.chea.org/overview-us-accreditation

[177] "Higher Education Accreditation." *Post Secondary National Policy Institute*. New America. 1 March 2013. www.newamerica.org/post-secondary-national-policy-institute/our-blog/higher-education-accreditation/

[178] Retrieved verbatim from Eaton, Judith S.. *An Overview of U.S. Accreditation*. CHEA. 2015. www.chea.org/sites/default/files/other-content/Overview%20of%20US%20Accreditation%202015.pdf

[179] Section 496(a)(4) of the Higher Education Act.

[180] "CAPTE Accreditation Handbook." *Commission on Accreditation in Physical Therapy Education*. American Physical Therapy Association. 5 April 2019. www.capteonline.org/AccreditationHandbook/

[181] *ARC-PA Accreditation Manual*. Fourth Edition. Accreditation Review Commission on Education for the Physician Assistant, Inc. May 2018. http://www.arc-pa.org/wp-content/uploads/2018/05/AccredManual-4th-edition.rev5_.18.pdf

[182] These descriptions are retrieved verbatim from "101: Higher Ed and the Triad." *Higher Learning Advocates*.1 February 2018. higherlearningadvocates.org/2018/02/01/101-higher-ed-triad/

[183] A directory of each state's authorizing agency can be found here: http://dpinnell.com/ApprovalandLicensureAgencies.htm

[184] "Staying Eligible." *Federal Student Aid*. U.S. Department of Education. studentaid.ed.gov/sa/eligibility/staying-eligible

[185] "CHEA- & USDE-Recognized Accrediting Organizations." *Council for higher Education Accreditation*. CHEA International Quality Group. www.chea.org/chea-usde-recognized-accrediting-organizations

[186] Association of Specialized and Professional Accreditors. www.aspa-usa.org/

[187] National Council for State Authorization Reciprocity Agreements. www.nc-sara.org/

[188] "16 OER Sites Every Educator Should Know." *Campus Technology*. 2 July 2014. campustechnology.com/articles/2014/07/02/16-oer-sites-every-educator-should-know.aspx

[189] Quality Matters. www.qualitymatters.org/

[190] "Make Space! Curbing Campus Growth and Using Space Wisely." *Better Buildings*. U.S. Department of Energy. 10 May 2016. betterbuildingssolutioncenter.energy.gov/sites/default/files/2016-Make-Space-Curbing-Campus-Growth-and-Using-Space-Wisely-Commercial-TUES.pdf

[191] "To Build, or Not to Build." *Campus Maters*. WordPress. 2 June 2013. campusmatters.net/to-build-or-not-to-build/

[192] "To Build, or Not to Build." *Campus Maters*. WordPress. 2 June 2013. campusmatters.net/to-build-or-not-to-build/

[193] HERDSA: Higher Education Research and Development Society of Australasia. www.herdsa.org.au/

[194] www.nxtbook.com

[195] "Trends for Higher Education: The Future of Learning." *Society for College and University Planning*. College of Coastal

Georgia. Fall 2016.
www.ccga.edu/uploaded/Institutional_Effectiveness/TrendsFor
HigherEd_Fall2016.pdf

[196] "Academic Planning: An Overview." Academic Plan.
Minnesota State University, Mankato.
www.mnsu.edu/academicplan/overview.html